THE COUNCIL FOR MUTUAL ECONOMIC ASSISTANCE

The Thorny Path from Political to Economic Integration

ADAM ZWASS

M. E. SHARPE, INC.
Armonk, New York
London, England

Available in the United Kingdom and Europe from M. E. Sharpe,
Publishers, 3 Henrietta Street, London WC2E 8LU.

Library of Congress Cataloging-in-Publication Data

Zwass, Adam.
      The Council for Mutual Economic Assistance : the thorny path from
political to economic integration / by Adam Zwass.
            p.   cm.
      Bibliography: p.
      Includes index.
      ISBN 0-87332-496-X
      1. Council for Mutual Economic Assistance—History. 2. Europe,
Eastern—Economic integration—History. 3. Europe, Eastern—
Economic policy. 4. Europe, Eastern—Economic conditions. I. Title.
HC243.5.Z83   1989
337.1'1717—dc19   89-4198
                                                                        CIP

Printed in the United States of America

*To my son Vladimir,
daughter-in-law Alicia,
and grandson Joshua,
with love*

Contents

List of Tables

Preface and Acknowledgments

The first incentive to undertake this study was provided by the most recent measures undertaken under Gorbachev's leadership to accelerate economic integration in the Eastern countries and to improve their economic steering mechanisms, whose inability to function had condemned to failure the integration efforts of his predecessors. The second incentive was the changing situation in the trade relations between East and West, which had developed dynamically in the 1970s but for some years now have stagnated. Yet another important consideration is the CMEA's negotiations with the European Economic Community, which have been largely fruitless owing to differences in steering mechanisms and in the respective authorities and powers of the two communities. The agreement between them in June 1988 brought mutual recognition but cannot lead to far-reaching economic cooperation.

We shall show how difficult it is for the planned economies to develop multilateral trade relations and accomplish economic integration, given their autarkically oriented trade mechanisms.

The main theme of this book is the chronic conflict between the CMEA's ambitious integration goals and the meager mechanisms available for implementing them. This conflict is examined over the most decisive phases of development of the Eastern community, down to the present. We begin with Khrushchev's efforts to create an economic community of sovereign states, initially through an authoritative CMEA executive; and then, when this project foundered on the resistance of some member countries, through economic mechanisms—which also failed, owing to their limited functionality. Next came Brezhnev's integration efforts, which led to the far-ranging Comprehensive Program of 1971, but which left the steering mechanisms at the underdeveloped level of the earlier phase of development and, instead of deepening the integration of the community, merely intensified the division of labor with the industrial states of the West.

We then turn to the most recent phase of development, since the coming to power of Mikhail Gorbachev, the aim of which has been to drive forward integration of the Eastern community at whatever cost. Numerous measures to achieve this goal have already been undertaken. I shall show how Gorbachev has attempted to correct the initial error that he, like his precedessors, made: namely, first postulating integration as a goal, and only then looking for mechanisms to realize it. The path so far has led from the CMEA Comprehensive Program adopted nine months after Gorbachev took office, to the 43rd special session of the CMEA on October 15, 1987, where an intra-CMEA division of labor, and the economic mechanisms necessary for this, were outlined. The *perestroika* law, adopted by the Supreme Soviet on June 30, 1987, and elaborated by the 19th Party Conference of the CPSU on July 2, 1988, as well as reform processes in the other CMEA countries, are examined.

The conclusion is evident: the reforms will introduce more market mechanisms, but leave unchanged many of the command mechanisms of a planned economy. They will therefore be unable to overcome the dichotomy residing in sacrosanct "democratic centralism" and transform it into a functioning synthesis. The changes contemplated in these systems and the steadily growing self-awareness of the smaller countries are more likely to lead to a differentiation in the economic systems and to a deepening, rather than a convergence, of interests. The search for adequate working mechanisms continues, but the hope is still slight that the convertible currencies necessary for a developed foreign trade and for intensification of economic integration, or exchange rates and prices that fit into the world system, will become a reality in the foreseeable future. The two largest economic communities of Europe will continue to face off against each other with different steering mechanisms and unequal powers for a long time to come. While the EEC regulates the trade relations of its member countries, the CMEA has the authority to negotiate only on a very limited number of questions.

Gorbachev's report to the 19th Party Conference gives hope that if his new approach were to succeed, it could have a decisive influence on the relations between the Soviet superpower and its partners in the CMEA. If the Soviet system were eventually to institutionalize genuinely democratic methods of rule, it might be possible to restructure the CMEA into a genuine commonwealth with equal rights and obligations. With democratic executive bodies and correspondingly new economic mechanisms, the insoluble problem of realizing ambitious integration goals might finally be overcome. If this were to come about, the Western European Common Market envisaged for the year 1992 might confront a revitalized and competitive Eastern market.

* * *

I would like to express my gratitude to the Board of Directors of the Austrian National Bank and especially its late President, Professor Dr. Stephan Koren; to Dr. Rudolf Schneider, of the Creditanstalt Board of Directors and to its consultant, Dr. Philipp Reger, for their financial support of this project; and to Dr. Robert Schediwy of the Austrian Chamber of the Economy for his careful perusal of the text. I thank Miss Romana Illetschko for transcribing the manuscript, my wife Friderike for her abundant assistance, and Michel Vale for translating this book, our fifth such collaboration.

New York
August 1988

THE COUNCIL FOR MUTUAL ECONOMIC ASSISTANCE

Genesis

The theory of the community of the planned economies is sometimes portrayed as a version of integration theory. Bela Balassa, Jozef van Brabant, and Paul Marer in the United States, Marie Lavigne in France, Jozsef Bognar in Hungary, Oleg Bogomolov in the Soviet Union, Pawel Bozyk and Jerzy Kleer in Poland and a number of others have helped to clarify the similarities and the differences. Of course the world's interstate communities could be said to have a lot in common, but the community of the planned economies is a unique phenomenon. Its differences from all other such communities prevail over its similarities, especially because the national planned economies have not evolved together into a community, but have been forged together into a bloc for political reasons. Its unique composition—namely, one economic and political superpower and a number of small countries at diverse stages of development—is still today the determining factor for its activities as well as for its advantages and disadvantages.

Usually, economic integration of a group of nations takes place when the respective countries have reached a certain degree of industrialization, since economic integration means first and foremost an organic interlinking of national industrial plants in the machinery construction sector. Even before World War I, Western Europe, already economically (and today also politically) integrated, was the greatest industrial power in the world. Most of the countries of Eastern Europe were still agrarian economies before World War II. In 1913 Western Europe had 49.2% of industrial output and 76.2% of exports of industrial goods, while Eastern Europe accounted for only 7% of industrial output and 5.5% of exports of industrial goods.[1] The figures for the United States were 38.1% of industrial output, and 10.6% of exports.[2] The damage done to Europe by World War II shifted economic capacities in favor of the United States: in 1950 Western Europe's share in world industrial output had shrunk to 24.4%, while its share of world exports had fallen to 33.4%. The shares of North American industrial output and world exports, on the other hand, increased to 47.2% and 21.5% respectively, while the shares of the CMEA countries were 6.6% and 6.8%, and Eastern Europe without the USSR only 4.9% and 4%.[3]

The prerequisite for an economic integration in which all the participants have equal status is cooperation without subordination and domination, and without the predominance of a superpower. These conditions, however, existed more in Western than in Eastern Europe. The greatest economic and political power in the Western world restricted itself to economic aid without making any demands for direct participation in shaping these countries or in their common activities. The Marshall Plan, which was also offered to the countries of Eastern Europe, but was rejected by them for political reasons, helped Western Europe to recover from the devastation caused by World War II and transform itself from a recipient of aid to an economic partner of equal status. By 1963 Western Europe's share in world trade had increased to 41.3%.

The Eastern economic community had its origins not in the natural evolution of economic relations from an escalating exchange of goods to industrial cooperation, as in Western Europe, but in the consequences of World War II and the Yalta and Potsdam agreements. These agreements placed the countries of Eastern and South-eastern Europe in the sphere of influence of a superpower which later, in accordance with the medieval principle of *cuius regio eius religio*, took the momentous decision of imposing its social system, which had been shaped by its own cultural and political conditions, upon these countries, all of which had developed and were structured differently.

What use are proclamations of equality and sovereignty of all member nations, when one of them produces 70% of the total community national product, and moreover supplies all the other members with raw materials and fuels? The effect of the unequal capacities of the community members is all the stronger if one takes into account that the small countries have only a very slight margin of free play in choosing their internal system of government, and that the decisive factor in shaping CMEA mechanisms is the conventional steering system of the superpower and not the somewhat modernized steering models of the small countries.

Ideology and economic system transplanted to a foreign body

Semi-feudal South-eastern and Eastern Europe and Tsarist Russia were no more prepared for a post-capitalist economy in 1917 than they were for Marxist-Leninist ideology. Their reorganization into a "sphere of influence" could only be justified in terms of superpower interests and opportunities for defense, but the same can certainly not be said for the transplantation of an alien ideology and social system which was unknown to broad layers of the population. We must be clear, however, that what was transplanted was not the utopian Communism of Marx, but the real state socialism of Stalin. The countries of Eastern and South-eastern Europe had no economic links with one another, and even fewer with the Soviet Union. Politically and socially they were far removed from the Western democracies, and even more so from the Soviet social system: Albania, Bulgaria, and Romania were kingdoms, Poland and Hungary were ruled by a military or semi-feudal authoritarian leadership, East Germany had not the least rudiments of an independent state, and only Czechoslovakia had been able to develop a Western pluralist democracy in the period between the wars. The party landscape was dominated by social-Christian, liberal, social democratic, and fascistoid movements. The Communist parties, which usually led an illegal existence, had never played an essential role in the political life of Eastern Europe, and had acquired no notable sympathy among the population. Poland's illegal Communist Party had no more than 7,421 members in 1935, according to the estimates of the Polish historian Jozef Kowalski (this did not include the eastern regions of the country, the western Ukraine and western Belorussia).[4] The Communist Party of Romania never had more than 2,000 members. The Communist Party of Bulgaria was more influential, and in the parliamentary elections of 1919 it won a fifth of the delegates. As long as it was able to operate legally it was one of the two most influential parties in the country.[5] But even after it had become illegal, and functioned under the pseudonym "Independent Workers' Party," it won 31 mandates out of a total of 274 in the parliamentary elections of 1931. At the time the "Fatherland Front," which it dominated, seized power in September 1945, it nonetheless had no more than 25,000 members. The Communist Party of Czechoslovakia had been able to acquire some influence in a few periods between the wars. Bohumil Smeral, who split the Social Democratic Party in May 1921, brought half, i.e., 300,000 members, into the newly founded Communist Party, and in 1925 won 13.2% of the votes in the parliamentary elections. However, the Communist Party of Czechoslovakia saw its influence wane under the dogmatic Stalinist Klement Gottwald, and its membership decreased to 25,000. If the Communist parties of Eastern Europe were able to chalk up a barely perceptible influx of members just after World War II, this was due not to the attractiveness of the imported social system, but to the ability of a governing Party to find accomplices in the exercise of power (Table 1).

The rapid growth of the Communist Party in all the countries of Eastern and South-eastern Europe was no sign of the realization of proletarian international-ism in politics or in economic relations. The unified economic system did not create the preconditions for international cooperation of economies which a few years previously had been embedded in a quite different structure of the interna-tional division of labor. Economic egoism is therefore stronger here than else-where simply because no country is inclined to renounce even the least bit of its national product, created with such difficulty, for the benefit of another, and because the experience of the first postwar years was quite negative for all of them, because the planned economies are more introverted as a consequence of state property and the autonomous economic mechanisms.

Neither before nor immediately after World War II were there any precondi-tions for a closer economic interrelation between the countries of Eastern and South-eastern Europe or between these and the Soviet Union. The proportion of Eastern Europe (excluding the GDR) in the total trade of the Soviet Union was

Table 1

Number of Communist Party Members in 1945 and 1946

	1945		1946	
Bulgaria	254,000	(Mar.)	500,000	(Mar.)
GDR	—		511,000	(Feb.)
Poland	235,000	(Dec.)	555,866	(Dec.)
Romania	217,000	(Sept.)	710,000	(June 1947)
Czechoslovakia	712,766	(Aug.)	1,081,554	(Mar.)
Hungary	150,000	(May)	653,000	(Sept.)

Source: Zbigniew Brzezinski, *The Soviet Bloc: Unity and Conflict*, 1971, p. 86

insignificant before the war and declined steadily. In 1929 it was 3.4%, but in 1938 only 1.5%; Czechoslovakia's exports decreased from 6.6 million rubles to 3.3 million rubles, Poland's exports from 10.4 million to 0.3 million rubles during the same period. The foreign trade turnover of Bulgaria and Romania with the Soviet Union was 0.2 and 0.1 million rubles in 1939, while Hungary's was only 0.8 million in 1929 and 0 in 1939.[6] Of course political motives played some role. The autarkic economic policy of the Soviet Union and the cumbersome monopoly of foreign trade and currency, adopted by the countries of Eastern and South-eastern Europe after World War II, was a crucial factor in the decline in foreign trade. Foreign trade of the Soviet Union decreased from 10,090 million in 1913 to 1,207 million rubles in 1939, but then rose to 2,157 million in 1940 as a result of the expansion of trade relations with Germany.[7] The economic structures of the Eastern countries were more competitive than complementary. They exported mainly foodstuffs and raw materials which made up 90% of Poland's exports in 1938, 70% of Hungary's, 96% of Romania's, and as much as 99% of Bulgaria's exports in the same years. In contrast these countries imported mainly finished industrial goods and raw materials. The share of these items in total imports in 1938 was 91% for Poland, 94% for Hungary, 96% for Romania, and 98% for Bulgaria.[8]

The level of development of the Eastern European economies was low, and their participation in world trade was even lower. The East German and Czech economies were relatively highly developed: their share of world industrial output in 1938 was 2.8% and 1.28% respectively, while that of Poland was only 0.82%, Hungary 0.36%, Romania 0.33%, and Bulgaria 0.11%.[9] The respective shares of these countries in world exports in 1938 were 2.4% for East Germany, 1.6% for Czechoslovakia, 0.9% for Poland, 0.7% for Hungary and Romania each, and 0.3% for Bulgaria. The Soviet Union's share in world industrial output was about 10% in 1941, but its share in world exports in 1938 was no more than 1.3%.[10]

Table 2

Per capita national product (1938) relative to Romania

	National product per capita in US$	Ratio to Romania in %
Romania	*38*	*100*
Bulgaria	43	113
Poland	63	166
East Germany	189	497
Czechoslovakia	103	271
Hungary	63	166

The per capita income reflected most clearly the differing levels of development. There was a substantial difference between Romania, which was the most underdeveloped, and the other countries of Eastern Europe (Table 2).[11]

Before World War II, the economic level of industrially developed East Germany was five times higher than the most underdeveloped country, and almost three times that of Czechoslovakia. Poland and Hungary were at equal levels: their superiority compared to Romania was about 60%. The discrepancy between Bulgaria and Romania, however, was only 13%.

The economic structure also tells us something about the level of development. The countries of Eastern and South-eastern Europe rank as either agrarian and raw materials countries or agrarian-industrial countries. Bulgaria and Romania belong to the first group, each with a 79% rural population. Agriculture accounted for 66% and 60% of the total product in Bulgaria and Romania respectively. Poland and Hungary fell into the second group with a 65% and 67% rural population respectively, with agriculture accounting for 56% of the total product in each case. Czechoslovakia, which had a 47% rural population, with agricultural production accounting for 42% of total output,[12] could have been ranked among the industrial countries by prewar standards.

Before World War II the countries of Eastern Europe had never cultivated an extensive foreign trade with one another, and certainly not industrial cooperation. Industrialization was just beginning in most of the Eastern European countries. Immediately following World War II, they very rapidly switched over to trade with above all the Soviet Union, since there were no customs barriers to break down, and the choice of trading partners was extremely limited. None of the requisite conditions for closer economic cooperation existed despite the rapid reconstruction. The mixed corporations set up by the Soviet Union in some Eastern countries had nothing to do with industrial cooperation, but was rather a kind of reparation. In most of the countries industrial plants were totally or partially destroyed. Forty percent of the national product of Poland and Hungary was lost during the War. Romania's principal economic sector, petroleum production, was at a standstill. Industrial output in East Germany also suffered considerable damage. Many plants which had not been destroyed were dismantled and carried off. The war damage was less in Bulgaria and Czechoslovakia. The Soviet Union's share in world industrial output decreased from 8.23% in 1938 to 7.38% in 1946; Eastern Europe's share, however, decreased from 5.7% to 3%, while Eastern Europe's share in world exports decreased from 6.7% to 1.9%.

Economic integration is hampered by the dominant concept of development

The level of development from the outset was extremely low, but the will to restore the destroyed economies as rapidly as possible was great. The nationalized industrial plants and banks gave the state broad possibilities to concentrate on what was most important. There was no lack of labor and the will to work at that time. The countries of Eastern and South-eastern Europe not only adopted the Soviet Union's economic system, they also adopted its blueprint for development, which meant industrialization with emphasis on heavy industry. A vast complex made of iron and steel was to be erected. The Soviet Union was prepared to provide them at any time with gigantic reserves of fuels and raw materials in exchange for urgently needed machinery and other manufactured goods. However, the unified concept of development oriented toward a unified economic structure furthered neither the international division of labor nor the economic integration of the socialist world system. The industrial model, aimed at creating a universal composite economy, created competing rather than complementary economic structures. A long-term structure of trade emerged centered on the exchange of Soviet fuels and raw materials for manufactured goods from the smaller countries, resulting in the dependency which still exists today. The unified foreign trade and currency monopoly influenced the unified model of foreign trade, in that priority was given to imports to supply the economy with its needs, while exports were relegated to a secondary role of a source of financing.

The first postwar years were more favorable for the economic growth of the Soviet Union than for the smaller countries since many of them had been forced to pay reparations to the Soviet Union. Economic growth was considerable: the annual growth rate was an average of 23.5% between 1947 and 1950, while exports increased by 35.2% yearly. The Eastern economies showed more vigorous growth than the world economy which had an annual growth rate of 10.3% between 1947 and 1950. The share of the Eastern bloc in world industrial output increased from 10.4% in 1946 to 16.6% in 1950. The vigorous growth in the share in world output was due first and foremost to the economic expansion of the Soviet Union, which reached the unprecedented level of 25.3% per year between 1947 and 1950.[13] Its share in world industrial output had risen to 11.7% in 1950 and was not only much greater than in 1946 (7.3%) but even greater than in 1938 (8.24%).[14] While the share of the smaller countries in world output rose by one percentage point, it was still 0.8 percentage points lower in 1950 than in 1938. Its share in world exports was also lower: 7% in 1950 compared to 8% in 1938. The more vigorous growth of the Soviet Union compared with the smaller countries had not only to do with the abundance of readily accessible production resources, but also to the soaring enthusiasm engendered by the great victory in the Second World War. The smaller countries, on the other hand, had to go about their own reconstruction in the midst of social and political upheavals as well as a perceptible loss of managerial cadres. The painful recovery of East Germany was an important factor of influence on the relatively slower progress of the small countries. East Germany's share in world output decreased from 2.8% in 1938 to 0.96% and then rose again to 1.6% in 1950 to a level that was 37% lower than before World War II.[15] But its exports, especially to the Soviet Union, showed an above average high growth rate of 92.2%. The reconversion of the other Eastern countries to totally different economic relations (before World War II they did almost 90% of their foreign trade with the West) had no positive effect on their economic development; indeed, for economic efficiency it was if anything detrimental. A peculiar form of integration was achieved, but mainly owing to their redirecting their imports and exports to the Soviet Union from which they received raw materials and fuels in return for manufactured goods. But this market was more oriented to quantity than to quality from the very outset. Foreign trade was mainly a source of supply—it had ceased performing an efficiency-promoting function. There were no adequate instruments for precise cost-benefit analysis and, owing to the chronic shortage in foreign exchange, the rate of potential trade partners was limited. The sellers' market usual in the planned economies acquired an international dimension. A peculiar barter type of trade developed which was oriented toward a bilateral balance of trade turnover, the latter being limited to the potential of the weaker partner, but also toward an exchange of hard goods for hard goods and soft goods for soft goods. The "hardest" goods were and are still today exchanged for hard currency in intra-bloc trade. The Export Central Act of 1949, based mainly on political considerations, reduced East-West trade to a minimum in the first postwar phase, and the Eastern countries have found it very difficult since then to find a niche for their manufactured goods on the demanding Western markets. It has become even more difficult since 1984 when the CMEA summit of June 1984 obligated the small countries to deliver top quality goods meeting world standards to the Soviet Union for its "hard" fuels and raw materials.

It would be impossible for the same social system to create favorable conditions for an economic integration that was of advantage to all when the political, cultural and economic conditions of the participants were so unequal. The reshuffling that began in the postwar period created a sensitivity to any kind of economic discrimination. As time passed, that sensitivity to economic discrimination

Table 3

Share of industrial employees in total employment (1950)

	%
Bulgaria	13.0
Czechoslovakia	30.0
East Germany	41.2 (1952)
Poland	17.8
Romania	12.1 (1951)
Hungary	19.7
Soviet Union	23.5

Table 4

Per capita industrial output in 1950 compared to the Soviet Union (%)

Soviet Union	*100*
Bulgaria	43
Czechoslovakia	143
GDR	136
Poland	70
Romania	31
Hungary	78

grew more acute than sensitivity to any other factor. It was much easier to establish a common foreign policy than a common economic policy. The economically underdeveloped countries such as Bulgaria and Romania, and later Mongolia, Cuba, and Vietnam, were interested in achieving economic equality with the other member countries, as proclaimed in CMEA documents, especially in machinery construction. The GDR and Czechoslovakia, on the other hand, which were developed industrially, strove to maintain the structural status quo, which ensured them the favorable position of being the main suppliers of machinery and equipment. The economic policy of the Soviet Union, which wanted to keep pace in the armaments race despite having half the gross national product of the United States, was compelled to pursue a different policy. It was unable to show the generosity the smaller countries expected. Its share in the financing of the arms spending of the Warsaw Pact is oppressively high. Price negotiations, especially for oil, were more difficult and their outcome more disadvantageous for the smaller countries than they had hoped.

The transformation of a political community of nations showing a wide diversity in development and structure into an economic community was more difficult than was initially imagined. Given the underdevelopment of the economic mechanisms, the only possibility for advantageous economic cooperation was a unified steering system and a unified economic policy, but this in turn was only possible under Stalin's rule. The different levels of development required different economic policies, which could be effected only with a steering system adapted to national conditions. Each country posed for itself the same objective, namely, to industrialize as rapidly as possible. But the starting positions were different in each case (Table 3).[16]

We see that industry was everywhere still underdeveloped at the time of the founding of the CMEA, with the exception of the GDR and Czechoslovakia, where 250% to 300% more people were so employed than in Bulgaria or Romania. The difference becomes even clearer in a comparison of per capita industrial output (Table 4).[17]

Thus at the time the CMEA was founded, Soviet industry was much more highly developed than that of Bulgaria or Romania, also more developed than in Poland and Hungary, but less so than in the GDR and Czechoslovakia. These differences have evened out considerably during the course of time. In 1970, the GDR had become the most industrialized country of the Eastern bloc, 54% ahead of the Soviet Union, while the advantage of Czechoslovakia in this respect had declined to 10%, but Bulgaria's and Romania's lag had reduced to 18% and 37% respectively.[18]

The planned economies have achieved their quantitative targets within a historically short period. They have developed from agrarian to industrial societies and created the industrial proletariat whose dictatorship they have proclaimed but never realized. However, they were and still are unable to bring the quality of their manufactured goods up to world standards since the precondition for this, i.e., establishing an economic and political system suited to a modern industrial society, was never created. This was possible at neither the national nor the international level.

Economic policy in the five-year period before the creation of the CMEA

As the data in Table 5 show,[19] economic interrelations had reached a considerable scale by the time the CMEA was created. Bulgaria and Romania had switched 90% to intra-bloc trade, and all the other Eastern countries with the exception of Czechoslovakia and Poland were doing 60% of their trade within the bloc. As mentioned earlier, the choice of partners was extremely limited at that time. The exchange of Soviet raw materials and fuels for manufactured products from the smaller countries boomed, although there was certainly no trade integration in the true sense. Trade was exclusively bilateral, or with third countries. But it should

---

Table 5

Share of CMEA in total exports in 1950 (%)

Total	61.4
Bulgaria	91.8
Czechoslovakia	54.1
GDR	68.0
Poland	55.9
Romania	89.2
Hungary	66.4
Soviet Union	58.1

---

be borne in mind that in the late '40s and early '50s bilaterialism was not specific to the Eastern countries, but was a rule for the whole of Europe. Western Europe was first able to restore currency convertibility and multilateral intensive commerce only with the aid of the Marshall Plan and the European Payments Union. Later it became evident that bilateralism was not a transitory phenomenon of the crisis years in the East, but a constitutive component of the system, a consequence of the system-related non-convertibility of the national currencies and exchange rates that had no basis in economic realities. In this respect nothing has changed. At that time there was no such thing as true industrial cooperation as there were as yet no large industrial complexes that would have been able to cooperate. Many years later, when the industrial basis for this had been created, there was no adequate infrastructure for cooperation, i.e., valid prices, exchange rates, and conditions for a basic cost-benefit analysis. In one respect, the conditions for cooperation at that time differed from those existing at present: the steering system was still the same everywhere, and a centrally administered economy had become a component part of Eastern Europe's economic and political system. But in the course of time this virtue was to become the greatest disadvantage. The pious dreams of the politicians chosen in Stalin's grace to lead their countries to establish general frameworks modified in accordance with the specific conditions of their countries were never fulfilled. All, or almost all, CP leaders in Eastern Europe had expressed dreams of this sort. In September 1946 Georgi Dimitrov said: "Bulgaria will not become a Soviet republic but a people's republic, in which the functions of the government will be exercised by the vast majority of the people: the workers, peasants, craftsmen, and the native intelligentsia."[20] Neither this wish of the former Comintern leader and later head of government, nor his dream of a federation of countries which would include not only the Balkan countries but also Poland and Czechoslovakia, and Greece should the Communists win it, were ever fulfilled. Dimitrov, who showed unparalleled courage in defying Hermann Goering at the Leipzig trial, dared offer no resistance to Stalin. He died in 1949 at the age of 67 and his successors faithfully introduced the Soviet system in Bulgaria. It is interesting that one of the most farsighted Communist leaders of Eastern Europe, Rezso Nyers, member of Hungary's Politburo at the time as well as many years later, was of the opinion that a community could be more successful without the superpower, which upped the stakes in all, than with it. Dimitrov was not the only Communist leader who wanted to establish a social system that fitted the conditions of his country. On June 11, 1945, the Moscow-loyal Communist Party of Germany declared that their program would be a minimal one of radical democratic demands and not a maximum one of full socialist demands, and that the establishment of a one-party Communist regime was out of the question.[21] The Kosic program of April 5, 1945, inspired by the Communist Party of Czechoslovakia, called only for the nationalization of heavy industry, and not total nationalization of all the means of production, as in fact was to take place three to four years later. A radical agrarian reform was envisioned, but not total collectivization of agriculture; there was to be friendship with the Soviet Union but no subordination or domination. No one had depicted so clearly the direct, organic connection between total nationalization of the means of production and the resultant totalitarian political power than Hubert Ripka, at that time Czech Minister of Foreign Trade: "Total nationalization of the economy leads ineluctably to totalitarian politics which can only be effective through the dictatorship of a single party."[22] But the Czech leader Klement Gottwald declared even before the last free elections of 1946 which gave the Czech Communist Party 38% of all the votes: "The working class, the employed, will find adequate means, weapons, and ways to adjust the simple and mechanical election results which had been influenced by saboteurs and reactionary elements." And he found these ways and means to correct the will of the people in the great Unor (February) in 1948. He took over total power on the back of a workers' uprising prepared long in advance. The legally elected prewar and postwar president of the country, Edward Benes, resigned. As in the other Eastern countries, if somewhat more consistently and much more dogmatically, Czechoslovakia swung abruptly into line, and embarked upon the path toward a one-party regime. At the time of the great purges, there were 124 concentration camps operating. Fifty of the 97 Central Committee members and six of the seven Central Committee secretaries, along with Rudolf Slansky, General Secretary, were victims of the purges. The Unity Party was born on June 27, 1948, and the once influential Social Democratic Party merged with the Czech Communist Party. The same happened in all the other East European countries. A unified economic and political system was adopted in an astonishingly short time in the whole of Eastern Europe. Postwar conditions were at least favorable: liberation from the Nazi reign of terror and from its native sympathizers created considerable sympathy for the Soviet Union and aroused the hope that the social system, defined as socialist, would be juster and more prosperous than the not so especially loved regime of the prewar years. It had also done quite a bit to hasten the reconstruction of the destroyed economies. The Soviet Union supplied the needed raw materials and fuels, but also demanded a good price, sometimes all too high.

Realization of the medieval principle of *cuius regio eius religio* in the establishment of a unified social system had created favorable conditions for the political cohesiveness of the sphere of influence, which was formed in Stalin's likeness. The methods of rule were suited to guarantee a frictionless cohesiveness. But they were unsuited to economic integration in the usual sense of the term. The precondition for cooperation on an equal footing was ruled out beforehand by the unconventional composition of the community. But Stalin did not create the CMEA for the purpose of permitting it to prevail as a supranational economic authority in the Soviet Union as well as in the whole of Eastern and South-eastern Europe. He was not inclined to share his power with any authority, especially not one which might lay claim to supranational authority.

Mutual economic assistance rather than economic integration

The final communiqué of Albania, Bulgaria, Czechoslovakia, Poland, Romania, Hungary, and the USSR on January 8, 1949 on the establishment of the Council for Mutual Economic Assistance did not envisage economic integration. The purpose of the newly founded international organization was as follows: "The conference has deemed it necessary to create the Council for Mutual Economic Assistance to bring about a closer economic cooperation between the people's democracies and the Soviet Union; the Council shall be made up of representatives endowed with equal rights of the countries participating in these deliberations with the task of exchanging economic experience and providing mutual technical assistance as well as assistance in raw materials, foods, machinery, and equipment."[23] Let it be noted that the name given to the newly created organization, namely, the Council for Mutual Economic Assistance, explicitly stresses its auxiliary character. The political motives for the new organization are clearly formulated: to contribute to the expansion of economic cooperation in order to create an independence of the discriminatory tendencies in the capitalist countries. Poland's CMEA expert L. Ciamaga interprets the emphasis on economic assistance by pointing out that many endeavored to blind themselves to the way things were going, namely, the inevitable transition from cooperation to integration, because they, as he said, "disregarded the laws of economic development, lacked imagination, and had a primitive perception of the problem in that they regarded economic integration as an invention of bourgeois economists."[24] In retrospect, it would seem clear that if the transition from cooperation to integration was not easy, it was not because of a lack of imagination. What was lacking was the preconditions for such a transition. The primary obstacle was, and still is, state ownership of the means of production, which finds it much more difficult than private property to cross borders and merge with the property in other countries. The transfer mechanisms in the form of a functioning credit and capital market are underdeveloped. The planned economies have still not found a substitute for the traditional mechanisms, and will not be able to find one as long as the economic mechanisms of the member nations have no functions on the world market because of currency inconvertibility and the economically unrealistic exchange rates, and hence are unable to function in intra-bloc relations as well.

For Stalin the CMEA was not an economic executive for regulating or reorganizing economic relations. For him, economic and political integration was an accomplished fact by virtue of the unified social system. Borders were for him not the least obstacle to exercising his authoritarian power everywhere throughout Eastern Europe. His power was the only unifying factor of consequence. No other power, especially not an international executive, would have been able at that time to contest or contravene his orders. He had devised an important role for the CMEA in line with his own purposes. It was to be an alternative to the International Foreign Trade and Currency Institute which had been established at the same time, and above all an alternative to the Marshall Plan. Although the Soviet economy and the economies of Eastern Europe were on the verge of ruin, Stalin was prepared neither to accept economic aid from the West for the Soviet Union, nor to permit such aid within his sphere of influence. Western politicians showed more trust in the goodwill of the Soviet leader than he did in the policies of the West. Harry White, Under-Secretary of State of the United States and author of the Bretton Woods Project, which, it should be noted, was also accepted by the Soviet Union, was prepared to steer as much as five billion US dollars in economic aid the way of the Soviet Union to enable it to implement the basic principles of the International Monetary Fund. In a statement on November 30, 1945, White declared his intentions as follows: "The major task that confronts American diplomacy and the only one of any real value in the major problems that confront us is to devise means whereby continued peace and friendly relations can be assured between the United States and Russia."[25] White's proposal, which he justified with a statement that "In the face of this task, everything in international diplomacy recedes into the background,"[26] found a powerful ally in Henry Morgenthau, Secretary of Commerce, who wanted to double the proposed aid package. In his letter accompanying White's memorandum to the President of the United States he expressed his hope that the realization of an American reconstruction program for Russia would clear up many problems in American-Soviet relations. Influential US politicians had come to the same conclusion as Lloyd George, who in 1920 proclaimed the following on the occasion of the signing of the first British trade agreement with the Soviet Union after the total embargo and the failed military intervention: "We have not succeeded in building up Russia with force, I hope we can save it with trade."[27] But Stalin's resolve to impose the 'real-socialist' system that he had fashioned upon the countries of Eastern Europe could not be broken. He had opposed the efforts of Poland, Czechoslovakia, and Hungary to participate in the Marshall Plan. The countries of Eastern and South-eastern Europe found themselves compelled to undertake the reconstruction of the destroyed industrial plant with their own forces, and some of them had also to pay considerable reparations to the Soviet Union—and not only East Germany and Hitler's former allies, but also some of his victims after they had already adopted the Soviet social system. Nor was there any great difference between the magnitude of Marshall Plan aid and the size of the reparations: between April 4, 1948 and June 30, 1952 the Marshall Plan granted total economic aid of 16.4 billion US dollars to sixteen European countries, while the reparations of East Germany and other Eastern European countries were, according to the data of the American expert Jan Wszelaki, about 20 billion US dollars. The greatest amount was paid by the GDR: 15 billion US dollars (four times as much as the Federal Republic had received from the Marshall Plan: US 3907 million dollars).[28] Romania and Poland paid two billion US dollars and Hungary one billion US dollars, according to the same source.[29] And the results of the activities of the joint share companies are not included: two hundred of these Soviet-controlled mixed corporations were operating in the GDR (SAG), there were 16 in Romania (Sovrom) and a few in Bulgaria and Hungary as well. These firms, in which the Soviet Union participated with confiscated German capital, supplied machinery and foods and other goods to the Soviet Union. They functioned until Stalin's death, and were dissolved by Khrushchev. It is noteworthy that the CMEA, founded in 1949, played no role in them.

It should be stressed that the Soviet Union spared no effort in making known its determination to participate in all economic regulatory institutions that had been prepared during the War and were to begin their activities immediately after its end. Its intention to build barriers around itself and the sphere of influence of these institutions did not become fully mature until after the social transformations in Eastern Europe had been completed and the CMEA was founded. Of the two subjects discussed in 1943 for the new monetary system, namely, John Maynard Keynes's Clearing Union and Harry White's International Monetary Fund, the Soviet Union accepted only the latter. It even put through a number of proposals which were designed to make the projected IMF more functional and more acceptable to those countries which had incurred heavy debts during the War. It was thanks to a Soviet proposal that the member countries who had suffered considerable devastation during the War were granted a 75% reduction in the gold quota and that a formal compromise was achieved according to which a member country would pay its foreign exchange quota at a rate equivalent either to 25% of the total quota or 10% of its foreign exchange reserves, whichever was greater. The Soviet Union was one of the 44 participants in the Bretton Woods Conference convened between July 1 and July 22, 1944 to set out the statutes of the IMF. The Soviet Union's participation (1.2 billion dollars) was the third largest after that of the United States (2.75 billion dollars) and Great Britain (1.3 billion dollars). The total was set at 8.8 billion dollars.[30] But the Soviet Union never ratified the Bretton Woods agreement and India took over its permanent place in the Board of Directors. A few years after the founding of the IMF, on March 13, 1950, Poland withdrew from membership on the basis of Article VI of the statutes, while Czechoslovakia's membership was suspended in 1953 for its refusal to pay its established quota of 625,000 dollars. On December 31, 1954 the country was expelled from the IMF and the World Bank. Cuba also withdrew from the Bretton Woods Institutes. On the other hand reunited Vietnam remained a member of the IMF and the World Bank on the basis of South Vietnam's membership. Isolation from these international monetary institutions had permanent consequences: not only were these countries deprived of sources of credit which could have been very important for them, they were also forced to adopt different clearing and foreign trade models in intra-bloc trade and in trade with third countries. This had important implications when it came to choosing trading partners, as well as for liquidity considering that balances in intra-bloc trade could not be used in trade with third countries. When Hungary and Romania became members of the IMF and World Bank in 1971 and 1982, respectively, it was on the basis not of Article VIII of the Statutes, but on the basis of Article XIV, which was designed for developing countries which were unable to establish currency convertibility because of their underdeveloped economies. However, in their cases inconvertibility was a condition of the system and not of the economic situation. The industrially developed countries of the CMEA were also forced to mold their economic relations with other countries as developing countries owing to the exigencies of their foreign trade and foreign exchange monopolies.

The absence of conditions for multilateral relations was the main cause of slow progress in the CMEA

The CMEA was unable to develop any special activity in the first ten years. Its statutes were not ratified until ten years after it was founded, i.e., in December 1959. The most important economic decisions of that time were made outside the CMEA. The decision to adapt the five-year plans for 1951 through 1955 to existing conditions and especially to the needs of the Korean War was taken not by the CMEA authorities but in the Hungarian Holohasa (1954), where the governments of East and South-eastern Europe were called upon to adjust their economic structures more toward heavy industry and the armaments industry. This marks the beginning of the iron and steel model of growth. The most important CMEA meeting during the first period of its activity, namely the second meeting in August 1949 in Sofia, regulated foreign trade relations for the next five years; they were to be settled bilaterally without any squaring of clearing balances in gold or foreign exchange. The momentous decision to provide the results of research, licences, etc., free of cost was also taken in Sofia. Only technical costs of preparing and copying the relevant documents were to be covered. During the period the Sofia decision was in force, between 1949 and 1965, the Soviet Union passed on 21,000 scientific and technical documents to its

CMEA partners free of charge and received 11,000 from them. During this same period, 36,000 experts from the smaller countries studied in the Soviet Union, and 18,000 Soviet experts perfected their professional competence in Eastern Europe on an exchange basis.[31] Only three CMEA conferences were held during Stalin's lifetime: two in 1949 and one in 1950. The fifth Council Conference took place the year after his death on March 26 and 27, 1954. The CMEA had to make do with a very modest administration consisting of a small office with representatives of all member countries and a Soviet secretary.

A comparison of the first stage of CMEA operations with that of the European Economic Community shows that differences in performance, measured in terms of the extent of economic interlinking, derived not only from the different situations at the start (the ratio between the economic capacity of the most advanced and the most underdeveloped member was 1:2 for the EEC and 1:3 for the CMEA), but rather first and foremost in different levels of development of the economic infrastructure. An economic community is in the first instance a common market in which conditions exist for the free transfer of values, i.e., conditions for multilateral economic and monetary relations. The EEC did not begin its activities until the preconditions for establishing currency convertibility, ergo for a multilateral, developed trade, had been created. The economic community of the Eastern countries began its activity without these preconditions, nor was it thereafter ever able to create them. The conditions which would make possible a transition from bilateral to multilateral trade are still lacking. It may be plausibly argued that where there is no convertibility there is no common market and therefore no authentic effective economic community. As long as conditions permitting convertibility are not created, organized and administered integration will have more a bilateral than multilateral character. In contrast to the initial stage, bilateral trade relations are no longer regarded as a virtue of the planned economies, as was often heard at that time, but rather as a systemic evil which apparently no amount of effort is able to surmount.

Of course the transition to convertible currencies was no easy task in the West either. But there, at least, inconvertibility was at variance with the system, whereas in the East it seemed to fit the system. Whereas in the West the condition for eliminating inconvertibility was an alleviation of economic problems, in the East the task was to adapt the cumbersome foreign trade and foreign exchange monopoly to the requirements of modern trade, something which so far no planned economy has been successful in doing. Neither the IMF (until convertibility of the main currencies was achieved), nor the IBEC (even today) was able to develop an effective credit market. In the period of the greatest payments difficulties, between 1947 and 1949, the IMF was able to release no more than 777.3 million US dollars, and in the next years between 1950 and 1955 only 439 million dollars for loans.[32]

It was easier to overcome inconvertibility caused by economic problems than it was to create the conditions for convertibility in the East. The attitude of the superpowers was decisive here. Whereas the United States, always solicitous of preserving the classical market economy, had done a lot to restore conditions for convertibility in Western Europe, of course in its own interests, the Soviet Union applied its efforts to maintaining the anti-convertibility economic system it had fashioned within its sphere of influence. The Marshall Plan had done a lot to enable the Western European economies to regain the level of efficiency required to restore currency convertibility. But the United States had also made vast loans available in the postwar period to accelerate currency convertibility and thereby to help the IMF to commence credit operations. The 4400 million dollar loan it granted on December 6, 1945 enabled Great Britain to introduce the transferable pound with which 40% of West European foreign trade was then cleared.

The Eastern countries had undertaken measures similar to those in Western Europe to break out of the straitjacket of bilateralism, and initially Western Europe was by no means more successful. The endeavor of the Benelux countries in 1947 failed. The second attempt on November 11, 1947 to introduced multilateral clearing, initiated by Belgium, Luxemburg, Holland, France, and Italy (which the English and American zones in West Germany later joined, followed by the other OECD countries) was unable to overcome bilateralism. Multilateral clearing accounted for only 516 million US dollars between December 1947 and September 1948, while between October 1948 and June 1950 the figure was only 160 million US dollars. The agreement on ''intra-European payments and settlements,'' concluded on October 16, which was supposed to cover outstanding balances with drawing rights, was no great success. During the period this agreement was in force, which was only nine months, only 5.8% of total turnover was settled multilaterally, while 37.6% was cleared with the drawing right limit; for the remainder (56.6%) other means had to be found, namely, bilateral agreements.[33] The European Payments Union, founded on September 19, 1950 by fifteen countries of Western Europe, and endowed by the United States with a capital of 350 million US dollars, was finally able to pave the way to currency convertibility and multilateral trade.[34] For the West the path to convertibility was a return to the traditional currency and foreign trade relations without which a normally functioning market economy is unthinkable. For the planned economies, on the other hand, convertibility was a concept of the alien capitalist market which resulted in chaotic conditions at variance with the plan. The chairman of the Standing Committee on Currency and Finances of the CMEA, the Soviet Finance Minister Vasili Garbuzov, was totally closed to the idea, and if he had approved of a few multilateral arrangements, it was always at the behest of Poland or Hungary. He was never able to muster an understanding for multilateral trade and settlements. For him the function of foreign trade had nothing to do with comparative cost advantages. Insofar as foreign trade served as one of the channels of supply to the planned economies, the exchange of physical units, which was only possible through bilateral relations, was decisive. Functionaries in the Soviet Ministry of Foreign Trade as well as Soviet experts in the currency and foreign trade departments of the CMEA were of similar opinions. Nor did Soviet economics professors think too much of multilateral foreign trade and defended bilateral clearing as the best possible means of settlement. The currency expert Professor L. Frei wrote: "The Soviet Union and other socialist countries make use of this form of settlement, created by bourgeois countries under the pressure of economic crisis, but give it a new content."[35] Professor I. Slobin took the same tack: "This form of settlement," he wrote, "was taken from capitalism, but socialism has altered its character and adapted it to its own needs. . . . The clearing system expresses the new production relations of the socialist world system."[36] Professor A. Smirnov was even clearer with regard to the promotion of clearing to the status of a mode of settlement in the CMEA: "Clearing in international trade, which uses neither gold nor foreign exchange for settlement purposes, is the most rational and most progressive form of settlement of those countries which develop their economies according to a plan, and which have introduced a monopoly over foreign trade. . . . This form of settlement, created by capitalist practice, is used as an instrument of planned organization of mutual trade in order to expand that trade; it therefore creates favorable conditions for building socialism and Communism."[37]

The statements quoted above were of course tailored to presenting the unavoidable system-related evil as a virtue of the planned economies. It should be recalled that it first raised its head in the '60s when, after failed attempts to clear multilateral balances bilaterally by means of ad hoc agreements, the greatest venture of the Khrushchev era, namely, the founding of the first international CMEA bank, was embarked upon. Soviet theoreticians and businessmen were agreed that multilateral economic relations had no future in the CMEA. Ad hoc multilateral settlement agreements for the Soviet Union were never a means through which, at some point, the transition from bilateral to multilateral economic relations would be initiated; it was rather only to make a few limited transactions possible. Thus on January 26, 1948 the Soviet Union concluded an agreement to transfer the outstanding balances of bilateral settlements to third countries, with the consent of both partners. On June 9, 1949, the Soviet Union, Czechoslovakia, and Finland concluded a trilateral agreement; in return for Finnish housing components, timber, and ships to the amount of 100 million rubles delivered to the Soviet Union, Poland was to receive coal (80 million rubles) and Czechoslovakia farm machinery and consumer goods (20 million rubles) in exchange for Soviet foods, delivered in appropriate qualities by the Soviet Union to Poland and Czechoslovakia. After many amendments, the Soviet Union signed the agreement concluded at the 7th Conference of the CMEA on June 26, 1958 on multilateral settlements between Albania, Bulgaria, Czechoslovakia, Poland, Romania, Hungary, and the Soviet Union. With the consent of the interested countries, outstanding balances on bilateral clearing were to be settled. However, bilateral clearing was to remain intact and continue to serve as a basic form of trade and settlements in intra-bloc trade. However, the settlement chamber established for this purpose in the Soviet State Bank (Gosbank) handled no more than 1.5% of total turnover.[38]

The signatories of this agreement, who had come into possession of positive clearing balances as a consequence of the nonfulfillment of delivery plans by the other contracting parties, wanted to receive the goods they had ordered, which were needed in production, and not the unplanned settlement of their accounts through third countries. The International Bank for Economic Cooperation, founded in 1964, was also unable to alter the clearing character of foreign trade in the planned economies. It has multilaterized settlement, but not foreign trade. As long as currencies are inconvertible, no effective credit and capital market can develop, and without money that functions as money, no effective international bank can be formed. The transferable ruble, which was conceived as the collective monetary unit of the CMEA, was never able to develop into an effective unit of payment, and hence has never had real buying power. Its limited functionability showed up even more clearly in 1971 when the International Investment Bank was founded. The extremely limited credit market proved to be an insuperable obstacle for developing the CMEA as an institution providing economic assistance, and it was much more difficult to promote the economic integration of the member countries. Credit relations have never reached any significant volume. In the period between 1947 and 1957, only Bulgaria was able to obtain a relatively large loan from the Soviet Union which financed 27% of its capital investments. In the years between 1947 and 1959 Soviet loans financed only 4% of Hungary's, 6% of Romania's, and only 2% of Poland's capital investments.[39]

The CMEA has done quite a bit for economic development in the forty years of its existence. But it was and still is unable to develop the properties of a common market through currency convertibility and the free transfer of goods and capital.

Khrushchev—the main architect of the CMEA

Stalin needed no economic executive body to keep the East bloc together. He was the sole judge and the sole law from Vladivostok to the Elbe. Stalin's death and Khrushchev's revelations of his reign of terror at the 20th Party Congress undermined the autocratic power in Eastern Europe as well. His successors very quickly realized that the now weakened political cohesiveness of the huge empire could only be guaranteed through deeper and irreversible economic interrelations. For Khrushchev, the CMEA, founded in 1949, and the Warsaw Pact, created in 1955, were the two crucial links that could cement the economic, political, and military integration of the East bloc. Khrushchev's successors also regarded these two international institutions as the principal instruments of the alliance between the Soviet Union and its sphere of influence in Eastern Europe. But the transition from Stalin to his epigons marked a change in power relations not only in the Soviet Union, but also relations between the Soviet Union and its allies. Stalin needed no institution based on community to cement his autocratic power. Khrushchev was the architect of both the Warsaw Pact and the CMEA. Anyone who had been able to observe the development of the CMEA as an insider, like the author of these lines, can say with confidence that Khrushchev had the best intentions with regard to transforming the relations of subordination and dominance in the partnership. He stopped the reparations in one way or another; he disbanded the joint share companies in the GDR, Romania, Hungary, and Bulgaria, and stopped deliveries at prices which were not always able to cover the costs of transport (between 1945 and 1954 Poland delivered 50 million tons of coal at a price of 1.28 US dollars per ton, which was only one-tenth of the price it could have had on the world market). Khrushchev was willing to write off a portion of the credits granted from the books as repayment for the damage caused, including 3.2 billion zlotys and 22.3 million US dollars of Poland's debt. According to Wszelaki's data the total sum of cancelled Soviet loans at this time was 1.8 billion US dollars.[40]

Khrushchev's activities in the CMEA, and his efforts to eliminate unequal and unfair relations, were directly tied into the policy of detente he introduced between East and West. It was his genuine objective to improve living conditions in the Soviet Union and in Eastern Europe, and this he could only achieve by a perceptible reduction in arms spending. He urgently needed resources for the restructuring of industry, and for capital investments in agriculture. This had been totally neglected (harvest yields in 1953 were no higher than forty years previously) and he wanted to relieve it of the unbearable burden of paying for the costs of accelerated industrialization through low prices for farm products. In the very first phase he turned his attention to calming the tensions between Eastern and Western Europe; it was this which served as the rationale for accepting a neutral status for Austria and his efforts to achieve an agreement of neutrality for reunified Germany.

The available sources indicate that Khrushchev was willing to forgo direct influence on East Germany in order to achieve neutrality for the whole of Germany. In a premonition of labor unrest, measures were undertaken that could have brought about a crucial political turn in the whole of Germany. The *Tägliche Rundschau*, the official newspaper of the Soviet occupation forces, wrote of these measures on May 13, 1953, stressing that they involved "fundamental changes in the policy of the SED and the GDR government," and that their effects would be far broader than merely economic. According to the *Tägliche Rundschau*, these decisions would be of "major international importance" and were directed toward the "objective of a reunification of the German people into a united national German state." Two weeks before the workers' uprising on June 17, 1953, Vladimir Semenov, later Vice-Foreign Minister and Soviet Ambassador to the FRG, came to East Berlin to hand over an important "memorandum on the normalization of the situation in Germany" to the GDR government.[41] Soviet initiatives to reunify Germany with a neutral status are confirmed in the notes sent to the Federal Republic and the four powers in 1953 and 1954: the note of

August 15, 1953 states verbatim: "The fundamental aims of the Potsdam Agreement to promote the creation of a peaceloving and democratic Germany continue to express the interests of all European peoples, the German people included, and must be guaranteed through the conclusion of a peace treaty with Germany."[42] Konrad Adenauer saw in this note an improvement on the resolutions of the Potsdam Conference and the Soviet note of March 10, 1952 addressed to the governments of the USA, Great Britain and France. According to the Potsdam Agreement, the "peace treaty with Germany was to be agreed upon among the victors and them submitted to the Germans."[43] Adenauer pointed out that the Soviet government had now abandoned this standpoint, but was standing firm on the basic principle, i.e., "Germany is forbidden to enter into any treaty or alliance with any other state in which it had formally been at war. It shall receive a limited national army. These are the two crucial points and they shall remain." In other words, as Adenauer summed up, the aim was the "neutralization of Germany, as provided for in the Potsdam Agreement." The same principles were reiterated by a declaration on February 1, 1954 by Molotov, then Soviet Foreign Minister, at the Berlin Conference. The main political points were: "Germany will be restored as a unified state, and all armed forces of the occupying powers must be withdrawn from Germany at the latest one year after the peace treaty shall come into force. At the same time, all military bases on German territory will be liquidated."[44] But the Federal government no longer believed the good intentions of the Soviet leadership after what had taken place in Eastern Europe. It submitted the following statement to journalists at a press conference on February 2, 1954: "We do not want neutralization. You must please clarify this again and again to the public. Even a reunified Germany that had been neutralized would become a satellite state within a relatively short time, since we will neither receive nor will be able to create the armed forces necessary to defend our neutrality with any prospects of success."[45]

Curiously, Khrushchev later disavowed the policy of German reunification that he had initiated in the early '50s. Ten years later he complained that Beria, who had been overthrown on July 14, 1953 and executed in December 1953, and Malenkov, former Prime Minister who had been dismissed in 1955, had proposed "liquidating the Soviet zone as a socialist state and stopping the construction of socialism."[46] This charge against the two most prominent Soviet politicians fully accords with Walter Ulbricht's declaration to the Plenary Session of the Central Committee of the SED on July 24–26, 1953,[47] in which he directly linked the overthrown Soviet secret police chief and the SED opposition. It must be remembered that the head of the GDR secret police Wilhelm Zaisser and editor-in-chief of *Neues Deutschland*, Rudolf Herrnstadt, were removed from their posts only four days after Beria's fall from power. It is noteworthy that Adenauer considered his opposition to neutralization of a reunified Germany to be in harmony with the situation in Austria at the time: "Although Austria has made it clear that she is willing to declare herself neutral after all," he said in an information briefing on

February 19, 1954, "the Austrian question has moved no further."[48] But Austria had persistently pursued its policy to attain the status of neutrality in the conviction that only such a policy could free the country from the occupation forces. Leopold Figl declared on February 16, 1954 in Berlin, in response to Soviet proposals on an Austrian state treaty: "This government would do everything to keep itself free of foreign military influences, and it follows that we will not concede military bases to foreign powers." Konrad Adenauer was also supported in his policies by the German Social Democratic Party. The SPD head, Kurt Schumacher, who died on August 28, 1952, commented as follows, according to the Social Democratic Press Service, on February 14, 1951 on the question of German neutralization: "The usual discussion of German neutralization is in practical terms a not unimportant component of the political and psychological tactics of Soviet Russia to weaken democratic forces in West Germany." And further: "The neutralization of the German Federal Republic was, and is, no problem for the Social Democratic Party; it has been, and will always be, rejected unequivocally." Austrian socialists had supported the coalition government at the time in its efforts to negotiate an honorable state treaty, and Austria has remained a country dedicated to democratic ideals. It is, as generally assumed, an economically and politically useful revolving stage between East and West. Soviet ministrations at the time pursued not so much the intention of abandoning East Germany, as that of acquiring some influence on the whole of Germany. It should be remembered that East Germany, which had been destroyed by the War and totally pumped dry by reparations, gave no signs of rapid recovery. The gross national product per capita in 1950 (US $553) was 135 US dollars lower than that of Czechoslovakia and only 122 US dollars higher than the CMEA average.[49] West Germany, on the other hand, made rapid progress in restoring its gravely damaged economy thanks to the Marshall Plan and the Western allies' renunciation of reparations. Although the Eastern countries showed a dynamic economic growth—average annual growth rate was 23.5% between 1947 and 1950—this was due to a steadily growing share of capital investments in the national product at the expense of consumption, which was already low. The socially costly economic policy was the cause of the June 1953 uprising in East Germany and the displeasure of the Polish population who were beginning to feel more and more the effects of the growing share of capital investments in the manufactured national product (38.2%[50] in 1953). After devaluing the Polish zloty by 100:1, and raising wages and prices by 100:3 on October 28, 1950, the Polish government soon found itself forced once more to initiate new drastic deflationary measures in early 1953, raising prices by 40% but wages by only 30%. A similar economic policy in all the other Eastern countries had acted as a brake upon the reconstruction plan that had prevailed in the first postwar years and caused unrest. The embargo of March 1, 1948 had caused considerable damage. It had totally reversed the now perceptible restoration of prewar relations (the Western share in Poland's total trade increased from

Table 6

Share of Eastern trade in total trade in 1948 and 1953 (%)

	1948	1953
Bulgaria	83	86
Poland	46	70
Romania	71	84
Czechoslovakia	33	78
Hungary	34	76

30% to 51% in 1947, in Czechoslovakia from 78% to 86%, and in Hungary from 30% to 53% in that same year).[51] See Table 6.[52]

However, growing intra-bloc ties gave no cause for rejoicing since Eastern Europe and the Soviet Union found themselves suddenly cut off from important sources of supply. The Germany policy introduced by the Soviet Union was without a doubt aimed at alleviating the economic pressure caused by the embargo. The differences between the United States and Western Europe were hardly to be disregarded. But Western Europe found itself compelled to go along with the policy, especially under the pressure of Article 117 (d) of the Marshall Plan which gave the United States the possibility of stopping deliveries of any goods to Western Europe which were on the embargo list if there were any likelihood that they would be passed on to third countries. The embargo list, jointly compiled, and in effect since January 1, 1950, made the policy of containment into a common cause of the West. But whereas the United States reduced its exports to the East in 1949 and 1950 to 36% and 16% respectively of the 1948 volume, and in 1951 ceased exports entirely, Western exports to Eastern Europe increased by 28% in 1951, 36% in 1953, and 67% in 1954 compared with the base year of 1948; the ratio between Marshall Plan aid and European exports to Eastern Europe was 6:1 in 1949, but by 1953 showed a decline to 1.5:1.[53] By all evidence it seemed that the Soviet government was attempting to weaken the Western alliance with its initiatives in the Germany question, and wanted to use Western Europe, and especially a unified Germany, as an economic support for the Eastern bloc, as at Rapallo in 1922. A few weeks before the Berlin Conference of Foreign Ministers in February 1954, the major European and American newspapers reported on Soviet intentions to place the resumption of trade relations between East and West at the center of the agenda of this Conference as an essential factor in detente in world politics, and pointed out that Moscow was responding to a certain readiness in French and British economic circles to engage more actively in business with the East and so to become somewhat more independent of the United States.[54] On February 17, 1954 Molotov put forth the proposal to create a general German committee to coordinate internal German trade, culture, and athletic relations, indicating that the Soviet Union was in a hurry to unify the German economy and make Germany an important trading partner of the East. However, the Western powers rejected this proposal, saying that the correct means to improve relations was to create a government on the basis of elections for the whole of Germany and instructed the Supreme Commissars to pursue day-to-day relations with the Soviet High Commissar through the normal channels.[55] The Berlin talks of February 1954 made certain the further course of events in central Europe: the GDR became the important economic member of the Eastern bloc in Eastern Europe, and the FRG assumed the same role in Western Europe.

The first uncertain steps
toward activating the CMEA

The economic embargo imposed in 1948 forced the CMEA countries to reduce their foreign trade to internal relations among themselves. The consequence was a trade integration forced by the political situation at the time, i.e., East-West confrontation, but certainly not by an economically justified escalation of mutual ties. Khrushchev recognized this circumstance better than any other Eastern politician, and after the negotiations to achieve a radical change in the power structure in central Europe failed, spared no efforts to activate the CMEA, which had been founded in 1949, but was dormant. But he too, who was without a doubt oriented more toward partnership than to domination, had no clear idea how to establish a community consisting of countries with different structures and at different levels of development, and how equitable relations could be molded between a superpower which produced 70% of the common product and the other smaller countries. However, he had the unbendable will to make the CMEA into the mainstay of Eastern Europe's political cohesiveness by proliferating mutual economic ties. There was no model and no conception for a steering system for a community of autonomous planned economies because the domestic steering systems were based on an administrative and not an economic arrangement. An economic steering system with convertible currencies, exchange rates, etc., could be internationalized, but administrative systems could not, except on the condition of renouncing at least a part of state sovereignty and making it accountable to an international authority which would have to make allowances for the existing unequal composition of the member countries. Khrushchev's intention of steering the interplay between the domestic planned economies as an organically integrated economic unit, i.e., through a CMEA economic plan that was to be husbanded to fulfillment by a supranational executive, very quickly proved to be a pure illusion. The small countries, now liberated from Stalin's autocratic rule, suddenly discovered that they had their own domestic economic priorities which were not easy to reduce to one single international denominator. The laborious and costly recovery period, borne on the backs of working people and the relations of domination and submission shaped by Stalin's methods of rule, and under which the national self-determination had been reduced to an intolerable level, aroused a national consciousness not only among the population but also in the ruling apparatus. This consciousness had to be defended in order to maintain the existing power structures. It was suddenly discovered that the international emphasis in the CMEA reduced national interests of the smaller countries to a denominator that corresponded to their relative potential, and, it was concluded, following Jozsef Bognar, a Hungarian economist: "A national economy is an organic economic framework of history and tradition, of property and distribution conditions, determined by the given system of interests, a framework within which the available economic potentials can at a given time best be mobilized."[56]

It was discovered that defense of national economic interests under the given geopolitical conditions, and a planning system to steer the economy, must encounter much greater difficulties than under the ruthless and anonymous conditions of the world market. However, the advocates of a superplan for the economic and political mega-region also discovered very rapidly that the ground was gradually being drawn out from under them. Indeed, it was becoming increasingly difficult under the new conditions which emphasized the priorities of the national economy to realize the precondition for a unified economic plan carried to fulfillment by an international or supranational executive, namely, a common economic policy and a standardized steering system. The differentiation of the steering system which had originally been based on a unified model began a few years after Stalin's death and could no longer be restrained, despite all the unavoidable setbacks. In Marxist terms, the relations of production had come into contradiction with the forces of production which had been extensively built up after the War. The progressive differentiation of economic policies oriented toward national priorities and the methods used to fulfill these priorities gradually undermined the possibility of creating an international CMEA steering system as well as a synthesis of the various domestic steering systems. The steering systems within the CMEA had been formed as a compromise between the real-socialist, highly centralized steering system of the Soviet Union and the extremely limited economic mechanisms which some of the small countries had used from time to time to loosen somewhat the throttling grip of the economic bureaucracy. Some of the smaller countries which had attached greater importance to economic mechanisms in the domestic sphere, then attempted to use them within the CMEA as well.

But these attempts failed inasmuch as they had always been forced to yield to the predominant influence of the centrally steered national economies. However, with the growing national consciousness and emancipatory aspirations of the small countries, traditional administistative methods could not hope to be effective in steering international relations. Only nine months after Stalin's death, some of the small countries began to show wills of their own as independent subjects in the international arena. To mention only a few examples, on January 30, 1954

Otto Grottewohl, Head of Government of the GDR, sent a memorandum to the Conference of Foreign Ministers of the four Allied powers in Berlin proposing a solution to the Germany question[57] and Poland and the GDR made their wish known through diplomatic channels to send observers to the Berlin Foreign Ministers Conference in February 1954.[58] Although it can't be ruled out that these shows of independence had been coordinated with the Soviet Union before-hand, they do mark a turning point in the foreign policies of the small countries which reached a peak with Albania's dissent in 1960 and Romania's declaration of its independent course on April 26, 1964.

With these progressive steps toward emancipation on the part of the partner countries, Khrushchev began his initiatives to revive the CMEA. One year after Stalin's death the first CMEA meeting of the post-Stalin era, and the fourth after the founding of the community, was convened on March 26, 1954. The objectives spelled out at that time found expression seventeen years later in the Comprehen-sive Program of June 1971 and thirty years later in the decisions of the June summit of 1984, although there was no question of introducing qualitatively new steering methods. The fourth Council meeting committed the member countries to adopt progressive modes of cooperation from an indirect division of labor (through the exchange of goods in foreign trade) to interlinkings in production in the form of industrial cooperation and specialization. The final communiqué also reported on the exchange of opinions of the CMEA meeting on economic plans for the years 1956 through 1970, without however any reference to the coordina-tion of these plans. But when Khrushchev declared his programmatic intentions about the main lines of his policy with regard to the small countries this was not within the context of the CMEA but in his declaration of reconciliation in Yugoslavia on June 2, 1955. This was eight years after the dramatic Cominform resolution of June 1948 which threatened to exterminate the "Tito-Rankovic group of spies." The declaration agreed upon with Tito declared solemnly: "Mutual respect, nonintervention in internal affairs, for any reasons, whether economic, political, or ideological, because questions of internal order, differ-ences in the social system, and differences in the concrete forms of development of socialism are exclusively the affair of the peoples of the countries con-cerned."[59] Nonetheless, even with this very conciliatory declaration of inten-tions, Khrushchev did not succeed in returning Yugoslavia to the Soviet fold. It was not until ten years later, on September 17, 1964, that the CMEA signed an agreement of partial association with Yugoslavia. Yugoslavia pursues an inde-pendent foreign policy and remains a nonaligned nation. But Belgrade's declara-tion was received with great relief by all the Eastern countries as a tiding of independence, in their regard as well.

Khrushchev's resuscitation efforts in the CMEA took place during a serious struggle for power both within the Soviet Union and in a number of countries of Eastern Europe. His dramatic struggle against Stalin's personality cult, which was basically against Stalin's cohorts in the Soviet leadership, began in full force only a half year after the Belgrade Declaration: at the 20th Party Congress of the CPSU on February 25, 1956. His report on Stalin's reign of terror, read with passionate intensity only to the Soviet comrades, shook the whole world. It was supposed to have been kept secret, but could be obtained for a month's wages at the Warsaw "Rushizki-Bazar." Khrushchev needed a year and a half to get rid of his opponents. In the smaller countries, most notably Poland and Hungary, the well-known but now officially admitted (if in secret) methods of terror had triggered unsuspected reactions. Boleslaw Bierut, Poland's most likable leader during the Stalin era, did not survive the shock of the revelations. Informed circles said that he had killed himself. He returned home from the 20th Party Congress in a coffin. Klement Gottwald, Stalin's favorite, died one week later. Bierut was replaced by the true believer Edward Ochab, but only for half a year. The rage of the Polish people grew unrestrained, portending nothing good. In Czechoslovakia, Antonin Novotny, a tried and true Stalinist, assumed power for a brief transitional period and retained it until February 1968. Stalin's monument, which elsewhere had long since been torn down, remained enthroned on the Moldau. The reaction of the Czech people was all the more violent in the brief Prague Spring. The Polish people were not to be placated, and the workers' uprising in Posen in June 1956 shook the established structures of power at their foundations. For the first time in postwar history, Poland's Communists put a person in the leadership of the Party hierarchy without first obtaining Moscow's blessing. Wladyslaw Gomulka, martyred and imprisoned during Stalin's regime, was elected General Secretary of the Polish United Workers' Party. Khrushchev, together with his three closest Politburo colleagues Mikoyan, Molotov, and Kaganovich (the latter two were removed ten months later in a bloodless power struggle), arrived in Poland in that fateful October of 1956 to undertake measures on the spot to induce Poland's Communist leaders to change their minds. The rebellious comrades refused the Kremlin boss's participation in the historic 8th Congress of the Central Committee. He learned about the dismissal of the Soviet Marshall Konstantin Rokossovskii, who had been Poland's Minister of Defense and member of the Politburo since 1950, and the election of a new Party leadership headed by Wladyslaw Gomulka (with whom he refused even to shake hands on his arrival in Warsaw before the doors of the Party building). His patience later paid off. Within a few years, Gomulka became one of his closest comrades-in-arms in the CMEA reform. The new Party boss who had celebrated his triumphal come-back with the entire Polish people stopped the unsuccessful collectivization of agriculture, dissolved the lifeless collective farms plagued with losses, introduced a half-hearted economic reform, achieved a reconciliation with the Church, and submitted a fat bill to the Soviet Union for underpaid deliveries of coal and meat and for the unjustified plant disassemblies; but he awakened no prospects of severing the umbilical cord with the Soviet empire. A few years after assuming power, after having silenced the liberal wing of the Party, annulled the economic reform, transformed the new elected co-participa-

tory factory councils into a collection of obedient trade-union and Party functionaries, and thus having definitively lost the sympathies of the people which he had
gained in the Polish October, Wladyslaw Gomulka advanced to the position of
Khrushchev's most intimate advisor and adjutant in the new order in the CMEA.

The situation in Hungary developed much more dramatically. Popular rage
could not be placated with minor concessions. Here the Stalin era had been much
more severe and had had many more victims than in Poland. It was this country's
destiny to show in that fateful October of 1956 how far the limits of tolerance of
the geopolitical factor went. After the Prime Minister Andras Hegedüs and the
Party Secretary Ernö Gerö had invited Soviet troops, Imre Nagy assumed power
and persuaded the Soviet comrades to withdraw. Two days later, on October 30,
1956, he proclaimed Hungary's withdrawal from the Warsaw Pact, the country's
neutrality, and in addition, the establishment of a parliamentary regime on the
Western model. But with this the limits of the Soviet leadership had been exceeded.[60] He shared the fates of the rebels. He was retrieved from the Yugoslav
Embassy whence he had fled for safety, and executed shortly thereafter. And so
the tolerance threshold lay where the inviolability of the political alliance and the
ruling Party's monopoly on power are publicly called into question. The oft-
proclaimed pluralism must not exceed the limited margin of freedom permitted
by the existing geopolitical unity. Within a few months after the dramatic inci-
dents in Poland and Hungary, Khrushchev revised his June 1955 Belgrade interpretation of the notion of plurality. On July 11, 1957, he announced: "We
recognize different paths, comrades. But among these different paths, there is
one common path, you know, like one great river with its tributaries."[61]

The dramatic events in Poland and Hungary in 1956 certainly hindered progress in the resuscitation of the CMEA initiated with the 4th Council meeting of
March 26, 1955, but their effects were further compounded by the bitter struggle
for the power in the Soviet Union itself after Stalin's death. It was not until 1957
that Khrushchev was able to remove his closest rivals Malenkov, Molotov, Bulga-
nin, Kaganovich, and Georgii Zhukov (whom he himself appointed Minister of
Defense after Stalin's death) from the Party leadership and consign them to
political oblivion. The first major economic reform since the NEP in 1922 was
then initiated. Many had a hope that once he was free of the dogmatic Stalinist
politicians Khrushchev would carry out a thorough reform that would free the
economy of its oppressive bureaucratic shackles and begin a process of decentralization and liberalization throughout the whole of Eastern Europe. It seemed that
Khrushchev had recognized the limits of effectiveness of a centrally administered
economy as clearly as Oskar Lange, Chairman of the Economic Committee of
Poland's Council of Ministers and world-famous economist, who described the
following difference between the dynamics of the growth factors of the first
postwar decade and the passivity of the present in a much publicized lecture in
Rome: "The economies of the socialist countries developed for historical reasons
in a manner that I would describe as extensive. There were considerable reserves

of labor, an abundance of as yet untapped natural resources, etc. It was a situation that is characteristic of underdeveloped economic structures. The only thing that this situation required was capital investments to employ workers and to tap the natural resources. The historical problems of planning at that time were uncomplicated, and the planning methods were primitive. Now the situation is different. Now there is always the choice that must be made between several capital investment projects, and technical progress continually imposes new criteria for such choice." Lange's terse conclusion was: "In the jet age, steering methods must be different from those used in the period of the Wright Brothers airplane."[62] A quarter century has passed since Lange voiced this opinion. During this time the economy of both the Soviet Union and its Eastern and South-eastern European partners has continued to grow dynamically. The Soviet Union was the first country in space and has been able to bring its armaments industry up to world standards. However, the quality of goods and productivity have remained far behind world standards. The description which Oskar Lange gave at that time has hardly changed. Robert H. Hormats, the knowledgeable economic adviser of the US government, said in June 1985: "It is highly industrialized and capable of impressive technical achievements, but its economy overall has failed to innovate and fallen seriously behind. It is an unattractive model for the rest of the world and generates little domestic enthusiasm."[63] Thus was the description of the Western economist, and so too did the General Secretary of the CPSU describe the economy of his country in the same month of June 1985: "We must not only bring economic development up to a qualitatively new level, and drive forward at an accelerated pace in strategically important industrial sectors, we must also restructure industrial production, move from extensive labor to intensive labor, and confront more thoroughly the country's social problems."[64]

The tenacity of the defects in a planned economy is stressed to show the ineffectiveness of ways and means used to combat them. The oft-repeated reproach that planned economies are averse to reform is simply not true. No market economy has initiated so many reforms in the last thirty years as the planned economies of the Eastern bloc. Khrushchev understood the most clearly that the conditions for a thriving international collaboration would not exist until adequate steering mechanisms were instituted in the domestic economies. After eliminating dogmatic politicians from his Politburo he initiated one of the greatest reforms in Soviet history. He smashed the central economic apparatus, the powerful economic ministries, and the super-powerful state planning board and shifted economic powers to the new "Sovnarkhozy" (regional economic administrations). However, he retained the basic principles of a planned economy. The local patriotism generated by the regional administrations did more damage to the economy than did the self-centered tendencies of the economic ministries, now dissolved. Khrushchev himself recognized this in the course of time and attempted to combat the centrifugal tendencies of the Sovnarkhozy by creating innumerable new central economic committees. Brezhnev and Kosygin, the executors of the revenge of the smashed centralized economic and political apparatus, restored the old centrally organized structures. In Poland and in a number of the other smaller countries as well, the attempt was made to transfer economic powers and responsibilities to the industrial enterprises, but these halfhearted decentralization measures were just as unsuccessful as in the Soviet Union. It became clear that within the political framework set by a one-party regime, a thorough decentralization of economic decisionmaking powers was impossible because the central apparatus cannot or will not give up its influence. Far-reaching reforms aiming beyond the given political framework, as twice in the mid-'50s and in the early '80s in Poland, the mid-'50s in Hungary and in 1968 in Czechoslovakia, were ruthlessly swept away by the ruling apparatus or by forces outside it.

Khrushchev put through his great CMEA reform under circumstances which never allowed him to introduce an adequate steering system which could have functioned as the mainstay of the reformed CMEA mechanisms. However, these mechanisms had become so differentiated that the administrative methods in the CMEA could no longer be reduced to a common denominator. The steering system of an international community can function no better than the internal steering systems of the member countries. It is necessarily more cumbersome than the mechanism of the market economies insofar as it is obstructed by the inertia of state property and its inability to intermesh with the property of the other planned economies and even less with those of the market economies. The renowned Soviet economist Dr. Anatoli Botov, when asked in Vienna on December 18, 1985 about the prospects of joint ventures, made precisely this point: "The possibilities are very limited, since state ownership of the means of production is set down in the constitutions."[65] And this property is isolated from the other economies by autonomously functioning economic mechanisms limited to the domestic economy. Romania's declaration of independence on April 11, 1964 is even more precise: "The planned steering of the economy is one of the fundamental, essential, and inalienable attributes of the sovereignty of the socialist state because the state plan is the principal instrument for achieving its political and economic and social goals" and further, in direct connection with the internal reorganization of the CMEA: "If such a lever passes into the sphere of authority of bodies above or independent of the state, sovereignty would become a vacuous term. The state plan is one and indivisible."[66] The other members were more restrained in their statements, but basically shared the same opinion. They wanted neither supranational nor international executive authorities because they knew quite well that with the present CMEA membership, the existing proportionalities would inevitably prevail in determining economic policies, despite all the solemn declarations. As Khrushchev said on April 17, 1964, in a conversation with his friend Gomulka: "There can be no great and no small in the socialist family, no infallible teachers and no obedient pupils. . . ." They were quite aware that under the existing conditions their influence would be only that of "tributaries" of a "great river," roughly as Khrushchev had formulated it in somewhat different terms seven years previously. Khrushchev attempted to replace the lacking economic mechanisms with innumerable CMEA agencies, his ingenuity in inventing new organizational forms was astonishing. Council meetings were sometimes held twice a year. The First Party Secretaries met three times in the Khrushchev era to decide on the fate of the CMEA. Khrushchev's closest comrade-in-arms was Poland's Party chief Gomulka; Romania's Party leader Gheorghiu-Dej was not his only opponent, but the only one in the last two years of his and Khrushchev's rule who voiced his opposition loudly.

The three Council meetings, the 6th in December 1955, the 7th in May 1956, and the 9th in April 1958 (the 8th Council meeting on June 18–22, 1957 was concerned wholly with the grave economic consequences of the October uprising in Hungary and raw material and fuel provisions to the other countries) established the main lines of economic cooperation among the CMEA countries. Each country was to specialize in production in those economic sectors and with those products for which it had the most favorable conditions. The national economic plans of the member countries were to be coordinated with one another for both the short term and the long term. The final communiqué of the 7th Council meeting on May 18–25, 1956 states: "The coordination of the economic plans of the CMEA countries is a unique task in their histories."[67] This meeting also took decisions on important specialization measures in machinery construction, chemistry, and ferrous and nonferrous metallurgy for the period 1956–1960. A joint electricity network was taken up, and details were set down at the 8th Council meeting in June 1957. At Poland's request, the development of a number of Polish coal deposits with the aid of other interested countries was put on the agenda. It should be noted in passing that this proposal of the Polish Party leader (the 8th Council meeting took place in Warsaw) was realized neither then, nor later during his time in office down to the end of 1970. The final communiqué of the 8th Council meeting of June 1985 once again stressed the participation of interested countries in the development of Polish coal deposits, which in the interim had become quite depleted, as a CMEA affair.

Khrushchev, as Gorbachev today, attempted to bring the First Party Secretaries of the member countries into the renovation process in the CMEA. The three summit meetings in May 1958, June 1962, and July 1963, ratified three fundamental resolutions: the CMEA Statutes and the "Basic Principles of the International Socialist Division of Labor" were approved and the multilateralization of foreign trade relations was put on the agenda. The June 1962 summit, convened on the initiative of the Polish Party leader, placed the coordination of economic plans at the focal point of CMEA activities. The final communiqué of this meeting stated: "In connection with the entry of the socialist world system into a new phase of development, the coordination of current and long-term economic plans should be the principal method of CMEA activity"; and further "These working procedures will accelerate economic development of each country, perfect the utilization of existing production resources, and help to level out differences in the levels of development of the individual member countries.'' Specific reference was made to the necessity of introducing specialization and cooperation measures, especially in the production of types of machinery in short supply as well as in other industrial branches which could contribute to a crucial extent to the technical progress of the member country. It was recommended that the most important capital investment projects in the processing industries and in mining be coordinated with one another and if necessary that joint ventures, research project centers, and construction centers, be built. The June 1962 summit did not recommend isolation from the world outside, but rather attached great value to the development of the economic relations with all countries of the world. The convening of an international foreign trade conference with the participation of all interested countries, and the expansion of foreign trade relations with third countries, were proposed to bring peace to the nations of the world.

Khrushchev created the organizational structure of the CMEA

Under Stalin, the Eastern economic community was sufficiently served with a few dozen functionaries of the member countries. A small office in the former Chamber of Commerce from Tsarist days, at Petrovka Street no. 34, took care of the unimportant administrative activities. Khrushchev had built a powerful organizational structure in the Moscow center, as well as in the member countries without, however, being able to transform the latter into an executive supranational agency of the planned economies. The emanicipatory aspirations of the small countries had already come too far.

The CMEA statutes, ratified on December 14, 1959 at the 12th Council meeting in Sofia and later amended by decisions of the 16th, 17th, and 18th meetings, marked the organizational structure of the CMEA and set down the basic tendencies of its activities. Their principal bodies are the Council meeting, the Executive Committee, the CMEA International Organization Committees, the Standing Sectoral Committees, and the CMEA Secretariat with its headquarters in Moscow. The Council meeting is the highest CMEA authority and is empowered ''to take counsel on all questions coming under the Council's authority, and to adopt recommendations and decisions in accordance with this statute.'' The Council meeting is made up of delegations appointed by the governments of the member nations and headed by the Prime Minister or his deputy. Regular Council meetings are held at least once a year alternately in the capital cities of the member countries of the Council; they are chaired by the leader of the delegation of that country in which the Congress is taking place. The principal executive body of the Council is the Executive Committee, which was formed in June 1962, with one representative from each member country enjoying the status of Deputy of the Head of Government. In accordance with the decisions of the

Council meeting, the Executive Committee administers all activities and monitors the fulfillment by the CMEA member countries of their commitments, directs work on coordinating plans for the development of the domestic economies and on specialization and cooperation, directs the activities of the Committee, the Standing Committees, and the Secretariat, as well as the activities of other Council bodies. The Executive Committee usually convenes its meetings once every quarter.

The Executive Committees were created by the Council to guarantee comprehensive treatment on a multilateral basis of important problems of cooperation in the area of economics, science, and technology. Three committees—for cooperation in planning, in the technical aspects of material supplies, and for scientific and technical cooperation—are authorized to form working groups to prepare particular problems in their area of competence for treatment, and to organize scientific and technical conferences and other consultative arrangements.

The Standing Committees were created to contribute to the further development of economic relations between the Council members and to organize multilateral economic, scientific and technical cooperation in particular areas of the economy. There are at present 23 Standing Committees further subdivided by branches and particular problems. Their seat is in the country with a particular interest in their activities; for example, the Committee for Machinery Construction has its seat in Prague, that for the chemical industry is seated in East Berlin, the Geology Committee is in Ulan-Bator, the Coalmining Committee is seated in Katowice, while the Standing Committees for foreign trade, currency and finance problems, and statistics and planning, are in Moscow. Each Standing Committee has its own department in the CMEA Secretariat the task of which is to prepare analyses, outlines, and multilateral agreements in the area of economic and scientific and technical cooperation.

The CMEA Secretariat organizes the preparation and oversees the convening of the meetings of the Council bodies, prepares documents, compiles economic surveys, records the fulfillment of the recommendations and resolutions of the Council bodies, and performs other activities stipulated in the Council statutes. The Secretariat consists of the Council Secretary (so far two Secretaries have held office, both Soviet Russians, Nikolai Fadeev, and since 1982 Viacheslav Sychev), his deputies from the smaller countries of the CMEA, and the staff necessary for performing the Secretariat's functions. The staff consists of citizens of the member countries in numbers proportional to each country's share in the Secretariat's costs. The Secretariat consists of departments, usually paralleling the Standing Committees. There are between ten and twenty assistants, experts, and advisors, depending on the area of activity.

Specialized international institutions occupy an important place in the multifaceted organizational structure of the CMEA. These are subdivided into research, production, and trade organizations. The scientific and technical institutions are either engaged in research themselves, or coordinate research activities of the member countries. One of the first multilateral institutions was the Institute for Nuclear Research in Dubna, USSR, established in March 1956. Its members included, in addition to the CMEA countries, China and North Korea as well; however, China withdrew from the Dubna Institute in 1965 at the peak of its political conflict with the Soviet Union. Other scientific organizations were founded somewhat later, as for example the Institution for Standardization in June 1962, the International Center for Scientific and Technical Information founded in February 1969, and the Institute for Economic Problems of the Socialist World System and for Problems of Industrial Management, founded in late 1970. Cooperation in research moved a step further with the Comprehensive Program for scientific and technical cooperation over the next fifteen to twenty years, approved on December 18, 1985.

The production and trade enterprises of the CMEA are not multinationals in the usual sense of this term, and indeed are not directly engaged in production. Their task is to coordinate production and trade in areas of production important to the participants. One of the first international production and trade organizations was the Ball Bearing Coordination Center, with its seat in Warsaw, founded in 1964 by Bulgaria, Czechoslovakia, the GDR, Poland, and Hungary. The Soviet Union joined in 1965, and Romania in 1971. A few months later, Intermetall, with its seat in Budapest, was founded to coordinate production in the metal industries. The founders were Poland, Czechoslovakia, and Hungary; the Soviet Union, the GDR and Bulgaria joined somewhat later. In 1969, Interchim was established with its seat in Halle-Salle (GDR). Romania joined in 1971, so that now all the European CMEA countries are participants. The energy grid network, which transmits electricity surpluses of some member countries to others suffering shortages, founded in 1962 with the participation of all the European CMEA countries, exercises a regulatory and redistributive function. The international CMEA enterprises draw up balance sheets for existing production capacities and needs and recommend measures to eliminate shortages in order to reduce imports from the West. Their task is to maximize the output of production enterprises to make it possible to use the latest scientific and technical achievements. The recommendations of the multinational organizations play a major role in defining cooperation and specialization measures of the CMEA in the various areas of production.

International organizations in the transport sector exercise an important coordination function along with the coordination organization for railroads, founded in June 1956 on the basis of an agreement among twelve socialist countries (the People's Republic of China, North Korea, and North Vietnam participated in addition to the CMEA members). Its principal task is to devise proposals for national communications networks and for regulating transport fees. The Conference of Ministers of the participating countries heads this organization and has an administrative committee under it. In December 1963, a joint "railroad car depot" was created by the European member countries to facilitate the rational deployment of rolling stock of the CMEA countries and to prevent unused capacity. Each participating country furnishes an agreed-upon quota of railroad cars to the joint organization, although they remain the property of the participating country. However, each of them is also authorized to use the cars in its domestic and international transport within the limits of its quota. If the quota is exceeded, a penalty is provided for. The participants bear the costs of the car depot equally. The Coordination Center in Post and Telegraph Communications, founded in December 1957, exercises a similarly useful function. Its task is to coordinate communication in this area on an international level, as well as radio and television transmissions. This activity is also directed by the Council of Ministers of the participating countries.

The international banking system has had an important role in economic cooperation with the CMEA countries. The first CMEA banking institution, the International Bank for Economic Cooperation, was founded on the basis of an agreement on October 22, 1963. The built-in multilateral settlement system was expected to create the preconditions for a functional credit system on the basis of the collective CMEA currency, the transferable ruble, and to facilitate the transition from bilateral to multilateral foreign trade. The agreement of July 1970 established the second international credit institution of the CMEA, the International Investment Bank, the purpose of which was to provide capital investment credits for production projects of common interest.

The efficiency of the international CMEA organization is not everywhere equal. Some of them, such as the Energy Union or the Collective Rolling Stock Depot, achieve considerable savings of electricity and rolling stock. The contribution of the production and trade enterprises, which have no deciding influence on the production or trade activities of the member countries, is much smaller. A number of difficulties have emerged over the course of time in the coordination of their activities with other CMEA bodies, e.g., with that of the Standing Committees. They have still found no adequate platform for cooperation with the national economic authorities of the member countries. The hopes which the initiators, especially Poland, attached to the foundation of the international CMEA banks have not been fulfilled. It became quite clear that a functioning bank cannot be created without a functioning money. Neither at the time they were founded, nor today, have they been able to multilateralize foreign trade or to promote capital investment activity. The half-hearted, limited credit activity shows more clearly even than the activities of other CMEA bodies that the planned economies, which have reduced the function of economic steering mechanisms to a minimum domestically, have not been able to create the adequate international communications instruments necessary for an international community to be able to function as such.

The Magna Carta of the Council for
Mutual Economic Assistance

In June 1962, the second summit meeting of First Party Secretaries was to have effected the great breakthrough. After the 20th Party Congress of the CPSU, which shook the power structure of the socialist world system, and after the change of power in Poland and the October uprising in Hungary, the situation in the Eastern countries stabilized for a short time. But East-West confrontation became sharper. Khrushchev allowed the summit conference of the four super-powers, already announced, to founder on account of a trivial case of espionage, the shooting down of Gary Powers. After the spectacular gesture of detente on the occasion of the Khrushchev-Kennedy summit in 1961, in Vienna, it was time for the Bay of Pigs. The Kremlin leader was forced to withdraw the missiles from Cuba but tensions remained. The de-Stalinization process in Eastern Europe suffered its first setback in Poland. Wladyslaw Gomulka, in whose stormy come-back both the right and the left had placed great hopes, broke definitively with the liberal wing and effected a renaissance of the centrally administered economy, with grave consequences for economic growth. More than five years after the historic 20th Party Congress of the CPSU, Antonin Novotny declared on Novem-ber 15, 1961: "Each of us ought to pay tribute to the cult of personality," and had no thoughts of initiating de-Stalinization in Czechoslovakia. Walter Ulbricht denounced Romania's opposition policy in the CMEA—Romania's spectacular dissent, already looming, would not actually break out into the open until 1964. Hungary's 133 experts who would later initiate the most successful economic reform in the history of the Eastern bloc were just beginning their work. Khru-shchev had just ratified the third Party Program at the 22nd Party Congress in 1961, in which he promised the transition from developed socialism to the highest phase of civilization, Communism, during the lifetime of this generation. In 1980, the per capita income of a Soviet citizen was to be higher than that of the Americans and everyone would be paid according to need rather than according to performance. Khrushchev wanted to bind the entire Eastern bloc to this ambitious program and to this end convened the second meeting, which ended its deliberation on June 17, 1962. It was this meeting which passed the Magna Carta of the CMEA countries, the "Basic Principles of the International Socialist Division of Labor,"[68] which was wholly in the spirit of the Party program ratified the preceding year.

The overarching theme was the "creation of a material basis for a more or less simultaneous transition to Communism within a historical epoch." The member countries are sovereign and free: "All are progressing to socialism and Commu-nism united by their common interests and goals, and by the indissoluble ties of international socialist solidarity," it was stated with due clarity. "All socialist countries shall be rigorously guided by the principles of total equality, mutual respect, independence and sovereignty, fraternal mutual assistance, and mutual advantage'' and "in the socialist camp, no one has, nor can have, any special rights and privileges.'' Of course each member country had an equal voting right, as in any other community. But no other economic community anywhere in the world has a superpower whose national product accounts for 70% of the total community product while the other nine countries account for only 30%. This fact remains despite any solemn declaration of equality and sovereignty. Goodwill notwithstanding, international relations are shaped in accordance with the real relations of economic strength. While the difference between the highly developed and less highly developed member countries has diminished in the course of time, the economic potential of Cuba, Mongolia, and Vietnam are still underdeveloped compared with Romania or Bulgaria, and the economic strength of these countries, in turn, along with the GDR, Czechoslovakia, and all the other small countries together, cannot measure up to the economic strength of the Soviet Union.

The "basic principles" see the principal instrument of the international division of labor to lie in the coordination of the economic plans of the member countries, and this method is presented much more clearly than in the other CMEA documents of the time. It is stated that "the coordination of economic plans is the voluntary, common, and planned activity of socialist countries which is oriented toward the maximum utilization of the political and economic advantages of the world socialist system in the interests of ensuring as rapid as possible victory of socialism and Communism.'' But the coordination of economic plans is seen only as a means to the actual end of CMEA cooperation, namely, that of "promoting the international specialization of production and the comprehensive (multilateral) development of the economies of the individual socialist countries in the interests of the fullest and most expedient utilization of the natural and economic resources of production, including the workforce.''

The "basic principles" misunderstand the era in which the Eastern countries exist and the objectives they should strive for in the next historical stage. "Subjectivist and voluntarist miscalculations'' (Khrushchev's policies were described thus in the official documents) are also discernible in the CMEA Magna Carta. The premises for the higher stage of civilization staked out in the 1961 Party Program and in the "Basic Principles of the International Socialist Division of Labor'' in 1962, still do not exist today, a quarter of a century later. Brezhnev, the new Party leader, declared at the 23rd Party Congress of the CPSU, the first of Brezhnev's era (March 29 through April 8, 1966): "Our plans for the future must contain no unrealistic positions.'' Konstantin Chernenko, who was the first to correctly introduce the amendment to the Third Party Program, justified his decision with the argument: "Certain points must be brought into better line with reality.'' According to Chernenko, the Soviet Union was at the beginning of a long period which he, and later his successor Mikhail Gorbachev, called the epoch of "developed socialism,'' and this assessment was adopted in the new version of the Party Program ratified by the 27th Party Congress on February 25,

1986. The goal of leading socialist countries to Communism "within a historical epoch" is just as unrealistic as the goal of creating a transition to Communism in more or less the same time. It should be remembered that at the same time as the "basic principles" were ratified, namely in 1962, Mongolia became a full member of the CMEA, followed a few years later by Cuba and Vietnam. Even if the prerequisites for transition to Communism are an "excess of material and cultural goods" and a condition in which "each one shall receive what is necessary in accordance with his needs," it is hardly conceivable that this prerequisite could be created within a historical epoch "more or less" simultaneously for the GDR and the Soviet Union as well as Vietnam or Mongolia. In 1980, which was when Khrushchev's Party Program promised that the American standard of living would be overtaken, the national income of the Soviet Union was at least 50% lower than that in the USA; the supplies to the population in Poland and Romania for the next five-year planning period were quite frankly terrible.

The level of economic, scientific and technical cooperation alluded to in the "basic principles" has not yet been achieved since the "unity of methodological principles, the development of plan targets, and the statistical determination of these parameters and on this basis the insurance of comparability" proclaimed in this document are remote from reality. The economic reforms adopted in the interim with an extremely widely varying degree of decentralization if anything made it more difficult to reduce the necessary to a common denominator. The postulate contained in the "basic principles" that the balance of payments must be squared, also proved to be unrealizable. After the dramatic price rises for fuels in early 1975, a year before the expiration of the agreed-upon term, the Soviet Union had become a creditor of all CMEA countries with the exception of Romania, with a claim of more than 10 billion US dollars, half of which had gone to Poland.

However, Khrushchev's actual goal was not to coordinate economic plans, but to achieve a unified economic plan for the entire CMEA territory. This intention was only vaguely alluded to in the "basic principles." With reference to Lenin it is stated: "The consolidation and expansion of economic relations of the socialist countries will favor the development of the objective tendency demonstrated by Lenin toward the future creation of a Communist world economy that would be regulated by the victorious workers in accordance with a unified plan." Khrushchev openly stated his fundamental project of steering the Eastern countries in accordance with a unified common economic plan only a few months after the solemn passage of the "founding principles." He wrote: "A harmonious unified economic complex is being gradually created in which everyone will be assigned his place and his tasks, and in which every country and every nation will receive continuous support in dealing with its national tasks of building socialism." A few lines later Khrushchev is even clearer: "With regard to the task of employing capital goods as effectively as possible, the transfer of such goods from country to country is taken into account, of course with the approval of the countries concerned," and then explicitly: "The possibilities exist of not only bringing several indices of industrial output together, but also to determine economic proportionalities that correspond to our common interest." Finally the Kremlin leader expresses his own wish: "A kind of overall balance should be considered which would assume the function of a selective development plan for each CMEA country." Khrushchev envisions the development of unified production plans for the most important branches of industry, the aim of which would be to satisfy not only the domestic needs of each country, but also the needs of the community as a whole.[69]

Khrushchev's integration projects were unequivocally supported by the Party leaders of Poland, Czechoslovakia, and the GDR: "To win the competitive race with capitalism," wrote Poland's Party leader in the Party's central organ, "cooperation in the form and extent which they have had up to now is no longer sufficient."[70] The idea of a unified economic plan for the whole of the CMEA as well as the idea of supranational executive bodies, was also unequivocally supported by the 12th Party Congress of Czechoslovakia in late 1962, while the GDR Party leadership also expressed itself positively with regard to Khrushchev's projects. However, existing conditions prevented not only the development of a unified economic plan, but also an all-round coordination of economic and capital investment plans. Quite apart from the fact that not all the CMEA countries were willing to agree to this undertaking, the necessary mechanisms for establishing economic ties were lacking. Autonomously formed prices and exchange rates could not serve as such instruments. At the same time as Khrushchev, Gomulka, Novotny, and Ulbricht were expressing their desires in various national and international contexts to step up economic cooperation, institutions and working committees at both national and international CMEA levels worked to develop economic mechanisms capable of realizing the envisioned intensification of the international division of labor.

Protracted but futile attempts to introduce economic mechanisms

The reproach is justified that the CMEA has up to now not succeeded in creating a price basis rooted in internal cost relations, nor has it succeeded in multilateralizing foreign trade relations on the basis of an at least partial currency convertibility. But the author of these lines, who transferred to the CMEA headquarters in October 1963 as Poland's CMEA advisor for currency and finance problems, can say with confidence, as an insider who was confronted directly with these problems, that perhaps in no other economic community was so much effort expended in so many discussions, international conferences, deliberations, etc., as in these CMEA bodies. If no essential progress has yet been achieved in these areas even today, the responsibility does not lie with the people who were or are encharged with dealing with these problems, but with the steering system, on which they had never had influence.

In the early '60s Poland was the principal proponent of measures to multilateralize settlements in intra-bloc trade as a prerequisite for overcoming bilateralism in mutual trade. Poland's representatives in the CMEA, later supported by their Czech and Hungarian colleagues, understood that an international economic community cannot be steered by the commands of international authorities, and what is more, that a centrally administered economy for the entire CMEA territory would have grave consequences for domestic economic interests of the member countries, and that without economic mechanisms that function on an international basis neither multilateralization of foreign trade nor still less the passage from integrated trade to integrated production would be possible. But the Soviet CMEA experts never showed any enthusiasm for mature monetary relations. They were quite well aware of the difficulties attendant on bilateralism, but considered them the lesser evil compared with multilateral trade free of quotas. Their centrally administered economy with its inherent monopoly on foreign trade and foreign exchange had after all been in operation for a quarter of a century more than in the other Eastern countries. Most of them did not believe in any viable alternative to the existing centrally administered system. A state economy is easier to steer without anonymous economic mechanisms than with them. Most Soviet economists still share this conviction today. A quota-based foreign trade, in which specific goods are exchanged in physical units, suited them much better than foreign trade volumes expressed in monetary values. Foreign trade had never played a decisive role in the Soviet economy, with its self-sufficient overall structures, and has certainly not served as an incentive to efficiency. Comparative cost advantage as a consideration in foreign trade was rejected as bourgeois theory, nor indeed did it correspond to foreign trade practice. The Soviet Union had from the very outset been interested in importing high-grade technology and, since Khrushchev's time, in grain imports as well.

They usually have paid for these goods with raw materials and fuels, and paid outstanding balances with gold. The share of foreign trade in total economic output was never very large, and it was simply not worth the effort to call into question the basic principles of a centrally administered economy merely out of concern for improving the effectiveness of foreign trade. The Soviet experts have never stood in the way of research to improve currency relations and the price system. But their position on the basic questions of economic mechanisms was made known to the CMEA Secretariat later than the positions of the other CMEA countries, and in most cases they supported the minimum proposal. The division of responsibilities within the CMEA also caused certain difficulties in dealing with this problem. Problems that were organically interrelated were studied by different departments: currency problems in the standing committee and the Secretariat division for financial and currency affairs; and prices in intra-bloc trade in the economic committee and department. Although there was some cooperation between these different bodies, the divided responsibility had a negative influence on the fruits of research.

The path chosen to establish economic mechanisms in a technical fashion using an international average of values which were formed autonomously, shielded from the international price system and world currency system, and hence extremely diverse as a function of the specific economic policies of each member country, proved to be unviable. Moreover, this occurred at a time when it proved impossible even to reduce the community's economic policy to a common denominator. But one thing was absolutely clear: the times when the evil of market economies, namely, bilateral clearing, could be redefined as the virtue of a planned economy, as the Soviet currency experts Professors Frei, Slobin, or Smirnov were wont to do, were consigned to oblivion. With them went the theory of prices freed of cyclical and speculative factors of the capitalist market as the most suitable price basis for intra-bloc trade. Intra-bloc trade increased by eightfold between 1960 and 1970. But while the industrial countries of the West had succeeded in finding their way back to a developed, i.e., multilateral trade, the planned economies remained captives of antiquated barter—not because it could be managed more rationally in a planned economy, but because, despite innumerable studies, discussions, and proposals, no viable alternative to the traditional mechanisms of the world market could be found, nor could these mechanisms be assimilated in a suitable manner by the heterogeneous system of the planned economies.

Over the course of time considerable modifications were made in the price system and settlement system. Initially the current world market prices were used in intra-bloc trade, somewhat later stop prices were introduced, then the stable prices in one five-year period were used in the following five-year period, and since 1975 the average prices of a five-year period have been used over a one-year period of validity. The principle, however, remained intact: in the intra-bloc trade of the planned economies the price basis is not the international price system based on national cost relations, but appropriately adjusted prices of the world market. Major changes were also made in the settlement system, especially with the multilateral settlement system built into the International Bank for Economic Cooperation. However, foreign trade continues to be settled bilaterally. Multibilateralism remains the hallmark of intra-CMEA economic relations, and to overcome it multilateral steering mechanisms would be required which, however, under the given conditions, have no chances of being realized. The CMEA was and is unable to introduce the free transfer of money and goods from country to country on the basis of economically sound prices and exchange rates without establishing the necessary conditions for this in the domestic economies of the participating countries. A regional solution could be implemented only by integrating domestic values into the world system. But this has never even been envisioned. Nor has an interim solution ever been conceived as a step toward a final solution that had been planned beforehand. Stability has been preferred over sound economic reasoning.

The foreign price basis of intra-bloc trade

Until 1950 world market prices were used as the price basis in intra-bloc trade. But after the drastic price rises in the aftermath of the Korean War, stop prices were introduced so as not to endanger the stability of the factors of planning activity. Stop prices were used between 1954 and 1957 with certain adjustments agreed upon in bilateral negotiations. However, different prices were used for identical goods in every bilateral foreign trade relation. The 9th Council meeting of June 1958 made the first major attempt to find a multilateral solution for the unsolved problem of prices. An interim solution for the next period and a final solution for the long term were proposed: world market prices were to be used as a basis for intra-bloc trade until a price basis rooted in internal cost relations could be developed. But the interim solution was to be based not on current world market prices, nor on the stop prices for a single year, but on ''those prices which have taken shape in trade between the socialist countries over a period of years on the basis of world market prices, adjusted, however, to eliminate cyclical influences of the capitalist market.''[71] In contrast to earlier practice, intra-bloc trade was to be based on ''identical prices for identical goods'' as well as stable prices for the duration of a trade agreement concluded for a period of several years.

But it was not so easy to translate the resolution of the 9th Council session into practice. The somewhat modified average prices of 1957 came into use in intra-bloc trade roughly eight years after this resolution. Three years were spent in negotiations during which the working group established for this purpose made a thorough investigation of the prices of 35.6% of all machinery, 69% of raw materials, and 41.3% of farm products sold in CMEA trade. Agreement was finally reached in 1965 to use the average world market prices between 1960 and 1964 as the price basis for intra-bloc trade for the five-year period from 1965 to 1970; then the average prices for the preceding period were to be used in the next five-year period from 1970 to 1975. But this agreement was annulled in early 1975, a year before it was to expire, on pressure from the Soviet Union. A sliding price basis was introduced in 1975 on the basis of the decision of the 80th meeting of the Executive Committee. The principles set by the 9th Council meeting in 1958 to use a five-year average as a price basis for intra-bloc trade had retained its validity. This average was not only extremely laborious to determine, it was also fairly questionable as an economic instrument for the foreign trade of a community of ten countries since, while world market prices can be established for raw materials, grains, etc., they certainly cannot be determined for diverse machinery and equipment. The Polish experts called these prices historical prices and instead advocated the current prices on the world market. Hungary's experts also shared this opinion, especially after the introduction of the basic principles of the new economic mechanism which endeavored to realize the postulate that domestic prices should be brought to the level of world market prices.

However great the inclination was to present this emergency solution as a virtue of price formation on an international scale in the planned economies (with the argument, inter alia, that a several-year average for a set of prices was in consonance with the Marxist theory of value according to which the value of a commodity is determined by the average socially necessary cost of its production), the pragmatic content and the associated disadvantages could not be concealed. Neither the distorting effect of international firms and cartels on price formation nor the effect of the relation between supply and demand could be excluded. These two phenomena of the world market were projected into the totally alien relations of the market of the planned economies which basically are little affected by such developments. The attempt to objectify this state of affairs by using a several-year average was unable to eliminate negative effects; indeed, the contrary was the case. More important than all the other pros and cons was the circumstance that internal costs of price relations of the overall CMEA market had no influence on prices in intra-bloc trade. The former Hungarian CMEA Secretary Imre Vincze describes this extraordinary practice of price formation as follows: ''The CMEA foreign trade prices are derived from the world market and as such they are independent of the producer prices and production conditions of the individual CMEA countries. At the same time the fact that the foreign trade prices are derived from the world market means that the actual supply and demand relations of CMEA markets are not expressed in them. Because of this, an exaggerated demand arises for certain items, the satisfaction of which the other member countries do not undertake.''[72] The well-known CMEA expert Pawel Bozyk had a similar well-reasoned critique of the existing methods of price formation: ''The world market stop prices not only provided no incentive for accelerating technical and qualitative progress, they even impeded it. Such progress presumes a rise in the cost of production. However, the stable prices of a five-year period ruled out any rise in prices in the foreign trade among the CMEA countries. Thus differences arose between the industrially developed countries and the CMEA countries; as a consequence, interest in the imports of industrial goods from the CMEA countries diminished, and interest in importing from industrially highly developed countries outside the CMEA grew.''[73] Other experts of the CMEA countries think along similar lines with these leading Polish CMEA experts.

The change introduced in early 1975 according to which the average prices of the preceding five-year period would not be in force for five years but only for one year (a sliding price base) was meant as no fundamental change in the existing practices of price formation, but rather pursued a simple pragmatic aim: namely, to allow the previously agreed-upon price basis to expire a year earlier so as to introduce the October 1973 dramatic price rises for crude oil in 1975 instead of waiting until 1976. The negative consequences of this rather curious practice were not ruled out: until 1985 the Soviet Union granted a steadily decreasing price subsidy for the small countries in the CMEA, and after that year there was a small-nation subsidy for the Soviet Union. The machinations of the world cartels were even more difficult to obstruct, although the average over many years, in accordance with the decisions of the 9th Council of 1958, was supposed to neutralize their effects. The Comprehensive Program of June 1971 also retained world market prices as the basis for price formation in intra-bloc trade. Its provisions state: "In the unspecified but upcoming future, the CMEA member countries will continue to apply the existing principles of price formation. The harmful influence of cyclical factors of the capitalist market should, however, be eliminated." At the same time, the member countries were committed to carrying out a comprehensive investigation to be completed by the end of 1972 in order to be able to perfect the existing practice of price formation. However, as of 1986 only one single change was made—in early 1975, when the period of validity of the pegged prices was reduced from five years to one.

Both the method, i.e., the average price for the preceding five-year period, and the basis of reference, namely, world market prices, remained unchanged. A transition from world prices to price and cost relations of the CMEA countries would mark a fundamental turn in price formation techniques, but the conditions necessary for such a transition are lacking.

Why the domestic prices of the CMEA member countries are not used as a basis for intra-bloc trade

For thirty years, no one proposed using the prices of the largest trading partner in the CMEA as the basis for intra-bloc trade in discussions on improving the existing practices. But the Soviet share in total trade is greater than the share of trade with the West for almost every CMEA country (Table 7).

The Soviet share of trade was somewhat lower than the share of the West in 1981 only in Poland and Romania. However, these proportions changed considerably over the next five years, with the Soviet share growing: in 1985 the Soviet share in Poland's total trade increased to 37%, and by 1990 it is projected to reach 43%. Domestic prices were not used as a basis for valuing goods traded in intra-bloc trade for two reasons: both the prices and the exchange rates are formed autonomously and are not integrated into the international price system, and price policies vary from country to country. The components of price formation are also different. Not all CMEA countries levy interest on basic capital and circulating capital as an incentive to a thrifty utilization of production capital. Where interest is levied, the basis for calculating interest is different: in some countries interest is levied on gross capital, in others on net capital; in some countries interest is levied on profits (Bulgaria, GDR, Poland, Soviet Union), and in others on the costs of manufacture (Hungary and Czechoslovakia). Profit is calculated in different ways: as a ratio to basic capital and circulating capital as in the Soviet Union or Hungary; or as a relation to the costs of production (total value minus the value of the materials used and the services purchased). The main difference

Table 7

**Share of Soviet Union and the West in total exports of
CMEA countries in 1981 (%)**

	Share of the Western countries	Share of the Soviet Union
Bulgaria	11.5	48.3
Czechoslovakia	19.6	37.6
GDR	26.5	36.5
Poland	29.5	34.2
Romania	29.8	20.8
Hungary	30.2	41.8
CMEA (6)	29.5	35.9

Source: *Rat für Gegenseitige Wirtschaftshilfe*, Ostkolleg der Bundeszentrale für politische Bildung, Cologne, 1985, pp. 160, 162.

consists in the fact that some countries such as the Soviet Union or the GDR finance the prices, especially prices for consumer goods, to a large degree with budget money; others, especially Hungary, prefer cost-covering prices. The Soviet Union, whose prices could be used as a basis for determining intra-bloc prices, since it is after all the largest trading partner of each of the CMEA countries, is disqualified as a country of reference because price subsidies play a greater role there than elsewhere: in early September 1985, in a speech in Tselinograd, Gorbachev complained that meat alone was subsidized with 20 billion rubles.[74] State subsidies for farm products increased from 17 billion rubles in 1970 to 37 billion rubles in 1980, and amounted to more than a half of the national product.[75]

In the discussion that has been going on for several years on an adequate price basis for intra-bloc trade, the autonomously formed prices of individual countries or the prices of the Soviet Union, as the largest trading partner, were not taken into consideration, with preference going to an average of appropriately adjusted prices of the member countries. CMEA experts as well as all the other participants in the discussion seemed to be of the same opinion, namely, that the obstacles to using domestic prices of the member countries in mutual trade are likewise a decisive obstacle to the use of an average, however carefully it is adjusted. Prices are economic categories which cannot be managed in technical ways. They are a category of an authentic market that is an integral part of the overall system. A suitable solution to the price problem is therefore dependent on the transformation of the market in the planned economies into an authentic part of the world market.

The unrealizable concept of an "intrinsic price basis" for intra-bloc trade

The demand for an "intrinsic price basis" was first voiced when ways and means to multi-lateralize CMEA foreign trade began to be sought toward the end of the '50s. The 9th Council meeting in 1958 began the search for an "intrinsic price basis" which would be based on member countries' internal conditions of production and sales. The concept of an intrinsic price basis was oriented to efforts to promote economic integration, but it was also intended to contribute to a solution of one of the most important components of foreign trade relations. The lack of a unified price basis rooted in internal production and trade conditions is the main obstacle to an effective transferability of the collective CMEA currency and for fashioning it into a unified standard of value. The discussion is still going on but it has subsided considerably after no compromise between the alternative proposals (a CMEA average for existing national sales prices or appropriately adjusted costs of production with a jointly agreed-upon uniform profit supplement) could be found. The differences in opinion were clearest at the Budapest conference of CMEA experts (April 1967). Only the Soviet and Bulgarian delegations continued to advocate establishing and introducing an "intrinsic price basis." The Soviet Union wanted the latter to be able to obtain higher cost-covering prices for its raw materials and fuels, the tapping of which in Siberia and the Far East required more and more capital investment and higher and higher costs of production. Boris Ladygin, the Soviet representative at the Budapest conference, voiced the opinion that the supplier had every right to demand a price which corresponded to his standard of efficiency.[76] The Bulgarians, on the other hand, wanted to reap a 40% price increase for its farm products through the use of an intrinsic price basis. Meanwhile the Soviet Union has obtained prices for its raw materials and fuels which are much higher than the cost expenditures, not owing to the introduction of an "intrinsic price basis" but to the rise in world market prices. It therefore had no longer any reason to advocate this solution. The Bulgarians, Romanians and Hungarians, who are still voicing their demand for cost-covering prices for their farm products, do not have enough influence to put through their demand. Those member countries which import both raw materials and farm products had no reason to support the notion of an "intrinsic price basis" that promised them only poor terms of trade in intra-bloc trade. From the very outset they advocated world market prices as the only correct basis for forming prices in CMEA trade. Romania's representative at the Budapest conference provided a trenchant argument for this practice: "Autarkic tendencies in the two world systems are just as absurd as autarkic tendencies within the country," he said.[77] The GDR representatives gave similar arguments. But neither the Romanian nor the Hungarian representatives concealed the fact that world market prices must be used for a heterogeneous criterion for setting value because no other instrument of valuation was available. The other experts wanted to use world market prices, but as a category of an authentic CMEA market. This opinion was most emphatically voiced by the Czech and Hungarian experts. The Czech expert Petrivalsky said: "What is meant is not the use of world market prices in intra-CMEA trade, but the shaping of world market prices on the market of the CMEA countries."[78] Hungary's economic expert G. Csikos-Nagy was even clearer: "The immediate goal is not to create a common price basis, but to create a common market, and the prerequisite for this is a solution to the currency problem and to currency convertibility."[79] The Budapest conference in April 1967 swept the notion of an intrinsic price basis rooted in internal cost ratios, for intra-bloc trade, off the agenda of CMEA research. The difficult problem of prices for intra-bloc trade remains unresolved and no new initiatives have been undertaken since the introduction of the "sliding price base" in 1975. The opinion that the CMEA price system could only be dealt with as an organic component of the economic steering mechanisms is being heard with increasing frequency.

The dream of a money-free society has come to an end

For the utopian and scientific authors of Communism, gold and money had always been the creator and bearer of evil. They were unable to even imagine a healthy Communist future with money. On Thomas More's Island of Utopia, gold was used only for dinner plates. According to Marx, "Money debases all gods of mankind and transforms them into a commodity. Money is the alienated essence of man's labor and his existence and this alien being dominates him, and he worships it." In his utopian vision of a Communist society, money would be replaced by assignations, i.e., paper coupons on the basis of which the producer of goods could receive a quantity of consumer goods from the social stocks of goods, in proportion to his labor time. "These coupons," said Marx, "are not money since they do not circulate."[80] These words are more than a hundred and twenty years old, but just a few months before the Great October Revolution in 1917, Lenin had the same notion of the society he was striving for, in which no money would be used. In his monumental work *State and Revolution*, written in August and September 1917, he had the following to say about the first phase of the Communist society: "All citizens are transformed into paid employees of the state formed by the armed workers. All citizens will become employees and workers of a state syndicate embracing the entire people. The only issue of importance is that they all work in equal measure, that they correctly observe the standard of work, and that they all receive equivalent wages."[81] Production relations were to be uncomplicated and no complex money relations were to be permitted. Lenin went on to say: "Capitalist society created large-scale production, factories, railroads, the post, and telephone, and most of the functions of the old state power have been united on this basis and can be reduced to such simple operations as registration, making entries, and supervision, so simple that all persons who are able to read and write would be able to exercise these functions." Lenin, the great intellectual, adjured his compatriots: "*We* (my emphasis—A.Z.) workers *ourselves* (Lenin's emphasis) organize large-scale production, assuming that what capitalism has already created will be maintained by the state power of the armed workers, based on other work experience, and with the aid of the strictest internal discipline; we will make state officials into simple executors of our errands, to be responsible, replaceable, modestly paid supervisors and book-keepers." Later it would be even better, since large-scale production should lead of itself to the "dying out of any official bureaucracy."[82] Of course a society so simply managed needed no money and just after the Revolution it seemed that money, after functioning several thousand years, as well as the bureaucracy and the state, was doomed to extinction by the victorious proletarian revolution: the Party Program approved by the 8th Party Congress in 1919 took the historical decision to "take measures to abolish money."[83]

But money abolished itself by totally losing its value. Like the great French Revolution and the American Revolution before it, the October Revolution was accompanied by a tremendous inflation, described by John Kenneth Galbraith in his well-known book *Money, Whence It Came and Where It Went* (1975) as follows: "A wagonload of money would scarcely purchase a wagonload of provision" (p. 72). The real value of the huge 1921 issue of 16 trillion rubles was only 140 million rubles.[84] The natural consequence of this galloping devaluation of the money was reversion of economic relations to barter in kind: in early 1919 the proportion of money in a worker's household was 42%, but by the end of 1920 this figure was only 13%. The Second Congress of the Supreme Council of the Economy, in January 1920, required economic units to introduce a permanent instrument for calculations of a kind in which the basis was to be one unit of labor (*tred-trudovaia edinitsa*) and since it seemed that the exalted promises of the classics of Communism were in the process of being fulfilled, all credit activity was stopped, and the credit system, nationalized immediately after the October Revolution, was incorporated into the Commissariat for Finances. War Communism of the period 1918 to 1921 had the appearance of anything but the ideal society that had been the goal of the Revolution. It was a state of emergency in which hunger and destitution were the rule of daily life. The productivity of labor in factories administered by their workforce decreased to 85% of the 1913 level in 1917, 44% in 1918, 22% in 1919, and 26% in 1920.[85] Hunger, but also equal wages were the causes of the expanding economic misery. Lenin had been wise enough to understand that socialism could not be built through primitive War Communism, which offered equality of hunger and destitution for the proletariat now freed of capitalist oppression. He sounded the retreat: in March 1921 the

10th Party Congress took the decision to introduce the New Economic Policy (NEP), no more nationalizations were to be undertaken, and industry and a large number of commercial enterprises were to be reprivatized. Military relations were given a broad margin in NEP. The All-Union Executive Committee took the decision in its 4th Congress of October 12, 1921 to restore the banking system, which had already been pronounced dead, and the 11th Party Congress (February 27-April 2, 1922) took the historical decision to return to a money based on gold. The decisions of the Party Congress stated: "Our economic and financial policies are resolutely oriented toward a return to the gold standard for money; gold remains the world money and this role of money on the world market is also expressed in the relations of a country in which a part of the economy is managed as planned on the basis of nationalization of the principal branches of the economy and the transport system.[86] The first banknotes (*chervonets*), with a gold content of 7.74234 grams, were put into circulation on the basis of the government decree of October 11, 1922. A stable exchange rate was set and the money policy was improved so much that the market deviation from the official course was reduced to 2.5% in 1924. This gold-based money could also be used to a limited extent outside the country. The Soviet Union participated actively in the reorganization of international monetary relations at the world conference held in Genoa in 1922, which had as its only result the fateful Rapallo agreement, concluded in a suburb of Genoa with a defeated Germany.

From authentic money to the "money" of a centrally planned economy

Lenin's NEP, with gold functioning as in a market economy, did not last long. To exist, Lenin's mixed economy needed a genuine, authentic and traditional money with all its economic functions, for the reorganized and partially reprivatized economy was to be managed by economic mechanisms and not administered by central state authorities. The 11th Party Congress in 1922 recorded the following: "The state shall grant individual firms the freedom necessary for their economic activities and not attempt to replace this freedom by administrative measures."[87] Lenin's successor had set his sights on an omnipotent state to which the totally nationalized economy was also to be subordinated. The NEP fell victim to his will for power—but not because the NEP had failed; on the contrary, it was successful: between 1922 and 1925 production in key branches of industry had increased from 2.6 billion to 7.7 billion rubles.[88] In the view of its founder, the state-administered economy was suited for fulfilling the historical tasks of making up for centuries of backwardness in the shortest possible time. The destiny of the NEP was sealed by the 14th Party Congress in 1925, which passed a resolution for a plan for "general industrialization," and by the decision of the 15th Party Conference of November 1926 concerning the sources through which industrialization was to be financed.

There was no more talk of a money-free economy. The traditional monetary system, with money, credits, interest rates, exchange rates, etc., had been retained. But this system had lost its pure economic content and its immanent steering functions. The money that resulted was a castrated money. It could no longer be used as a true parameter and allocation factor. The centrally administered economy needed and therefore created a form of money to be used for accounting purposes without any functions in foreign trade. This economic system, with its functionless monetary system, was adopted in the small countries of Eastern and South-eastern Europe as a part of the overall social system.

An Obstacle to the Internationalization of CMEA Economic Relations

Systemic inconvertibility

The opinion represented in the early stages of the Eastern economic community that bilateral clearing, practiced during the years of crises by the market economies, was the best possible form of trade for the planned economies as well, proved very quickly to be an emergency solution made into a virtue. Bilateral clearing was just as unsuited for mature foreign trade of planned economies as for trade among the market economies. It became clear that here too a developed modern monetary system was an absolute prerequisite for a developed, many-faceted foreign trade. The intensification of CMEA activity in the second half of the '50s therefore also placed the problem of internationalization of the monetary relations of the member countries on the order of the day. Toward the end of the '50s, the establishment of an international CMEA currency was already being considered. But no national currency, not even the Soviet ruble, was capable of assuming the role of a key currency. None of these currencies was capable of becoming an international measure of value and therefore could serve neither as a universal purchasing power nor even less as a means of payment or a means of accumulation of wealth because domestic prices were formed autonomously, shielded from the international methods of price formation, and the exchange rates were dictated not by international conditions but by the needs of domestic economic accounting. The US expert Franklyn D. Holzman described the imperfections in the monetary relations in the planned economies as follows: "The various Eastern currencies are all inconvertible into each other because, in the first instance, exchange rates can have no meaning when they equate irrational price systems."[89] Though it must have been clear at the time the IBEC was founded that the conditions which made it possible for transferable national currencies to function also made international monetary relations within the bloc impossible, it must be emphasized in defense of this undertaking that no one in the CMEA had contemplated a functional bank at the very beginning of its activity.

There were differences in opinion at the time: some, such as the representatives of the Soviet Union, Romania, and the GDR, had not seriously considered authentic bank activity, not even in the far-off future; others, on the other hand, especially Polish representatives, wanted to do everything possible to include provisions in the prepared agreement on multilateral settlements and in bank statutes which would make it possible for the CMEA bank, which initially functioned as a clearing house, to develop into an authentic international banking institution. The developments of the last two decades, however, have borne out those who wished no general banking activity in the CMEA. As is evident, they had estimated the possibilities of developing the premises necessary for this more realistically than those who made a vision rather than reality the basis of their far-ranging banking postulates.

Neither the IBEC, functioning since 1964, nor the IIB, which has been operating since 1971, have been able to develop into authentic international credit institutions. This is not because the CMEA countries or the CMEA authorities showed little interest in it. Quite the contrary; the CMEA banks and credit relations were in the focal point of international cooperation and proposals on how to improve their functioning were respectably represented in the most important CMEA decisions, such as in the Comprehensive Program of July 1971 or the final communiqué of the July summit in 1984. They received a general approval, but also mild criticism. For example the January 1985 meeting of the Executive Committee commented as follows in the discussion of the report: ''The credit and settlements mechanisms contributed to the development and deepening of scientific and technical cooperation in the spirit of the decisions of the summit meeting of June 1984; they have made possible a smoothly functioning settlement system, the expansion of foreign trade, and the narrowing of the developmental gap between non-European and European member countries. . . .''[90] This stereotypical evaluation of the settlement and credit system, which was repeated in all other CMEA documents, would not have even been worth mentioning were it not for the remarkable additional comment that this mechanism had ''shielded national economies from the negative influence of the capitalist economy and created and currency and credit policy independent of imperialism.''[91]

Considering that the leader of the authoritative CMEA section, Professor Konstantinov, was aware that this mechanism had established a viable settlement system but no functional credit system, he therefore qualified the above estimation somewhat by stating that no mechanism, however perfect it may be, could remain unchanged. The last part of the January 1985 resolution of the Executive Committee sounds somewhat grotesque in the light of developments over the past fifteen years. Indeed, at no time in postwar history was the influence of Western economic and capital markets and economic events in Eastern Europe so great as in the '70s. The indebtedness of the CMEA countries to the West increased from five billion US dollars in the early '70s to about 80 billion US dollars in the early '80s, and moreover not only individual CMEA countries, but also both CMEA banks took out loans. The CMEA countries were dependent on the interest rates, exchange rates, and prices on Western markets. Western credits were basically a means to an end, that of making modern technology of the industrial countries of the West a vehicle for scientific progress. The "shielding hypothesis" becomes more understandable if one recalls that it was during the times of vigorous activity of the CMEA banks that Romania, in 1972, and Hungary and Poland ten years later, attempted to surmount their payments debacle by becoming members of the Bretton Woods institutions.

Soviet CMEA functionaries, who tended to view the newly founded international bank merely as a multilateral settling house, had good reason to give a positive rating to its activity—settlements in intra-CMEA trade functioned flawlessly. But CMEA countries such as Poland, which hoped that the community's banking institutions would develop real bank-lending activities and would be able to help in the financing of their ambitious capital investment projects, were forced to turn to Western markets and in the process lost their credit-worthiness. The proponents of modest practicable solutions were quite justified in pointing out that at the very outset they had called attention to difficulties that stood in the way of building a modern developed monetary and credit system into the system of a planned economy. Moreover, Poland's representatives, as well as those of a few other CMEA countries, wanted to reform the inefficient steering system and would not be deterred. They had the example of the European Payments Union in mind which, in only eight years, had restored currency convertibility in Western Europe on December 27, 1958, and freed foreign trade from the shackles of bilateralism and quotas: a few months before the founding of the EPU only 30% of Western European foreign trade was quota-free, but by early 1957 this figure was already 90%.[92] Polish proponents of a functional monetary and credit system in the CMEA had, however, not only miscalculated developments in their own country (the economic and political reforms begun with the change of regime in October 1956 were abandoned in the early '60s), they had also overestimated the reform potential in the other CMEA countries, and particularly in the Soviet Union, whose steering system had of necessity a decisive influence on CMEA activity. Although they had been able to get all clauses that were necessary for a functional modern bank into the agreement and the IBEC statutes, they were unable to see that they were also fulfilled. A few modifications have been made in the course of the years the IBEC and the IIB have been functioning. However, the basic problem of effective transferability and at least partial convertibility of the transferable ruble, which was a precondition for going beyond bilateralism in intra-CMEA trade and establishing effective credit activities to fuel the economy, has not yet been solved.

A comparison of the thinking of that time with the conditions existing today will give an idea of how little the provisions that are crucial for developed international monetary relations have changed. At the time of the agreement on multilateral settlements and the founding of the IBEC, on October 22, 1963, the author of these lines was in Moscow, together with two experts, as an adviser to the newly established CMEA division for currency and financial questions. The hope that the Standing Committee for Currency and Financial Affairs and the IBEC, established on the basis of the decision of the 7th Council session (December 17–20, 1962), would have its seat in Warsaw and that Poland would provide the bank president, had not been fulfilled. In an article written before the departure for Moscow[93] I wrote the following: "The IBEC intends to introduce settlements and credits in transferable rubles in a monetary unit which could serve as the basis for multilateral settlements in the socialist market. But there can be no doubt that the necessary economic conditions must exist beforehand to establish even a limited transferability of the monetary unit." Even more explicitly: "The renaming of the clearing ruble as a transferable ruble will change nothing in the present state of affairs as long as the newly created monetary unit has a different value in each of the member countries." And further: "If the economic conditions are not created, most trade will continue to be based on mandatory quotas and on bilateral squaring of annual turnovers. Transfer of outstanding balances to third countries will be an exception and a reduction of foreign trade turnovers to the level of the economically weaker partner will be the rule." The disadvantages of maintaining different foreign trade and settlement conditions on the CMEA market from those existing on the Western markets were emphasized with all due clarity: "The problem of creating a functional unit of the collective CMEA currency is especially acute in light of the existence of two markets mutually shielded from one another; hence the proposal that all measures taken in the currency domain must take into account the consequences of both East and West trade, as well as their mutual influence." The solution was sought in the convertibility of the collective CMEA currency, which was supposed to eliminate currency-related biases in choosing foreign trade markets.

On January 1, 1964 the first International CMEA Bank began operations. Its chairman was the former Section Head of the Soviet State Bank, Konstantin I. Nazarkin. The settlement procedure introduced may be regarded as a success from the technical perspective compared with bilateral clearing, insofar as the unsettled balances of a member country are pooled in a single cumulative balance with all other trading partners. This settlement procedure is also more streamlined with regard to the practice stipulated in Article 5 of the agreement, of encashment with a later bill on exchange from the receiver of the goods, as this accelerates the settlement proceeding by several days. The fear expressed before the bank was established that some of the members would become chronic debtors, and others chronic creditors, as was the case in the European Payments Union, proved to be unfounded. The credits granted in the first year of the bank's activity amounted to no more than 14% of the payments turnover, and two-thirds of the credits granted in the first nine months were paid back. The amount of credits taken out was 40% lower than in the preceding year when CMEA foreign trade was settled in a bilateral clearing procedure. But this clear improvement in settlement procedures had no influence on CMEA trade. It continued to be cleared bilaterally and that is still the case today. The IBEC differentiated its types of credit and interest, but was unable to develop a mature credit system to stimulate economic activity and trade. One year after the agreements on the founding of the IBEC was signed, I wrote the following from the CMEA headquarters: "The unsolved currency problems are having a disintegrating effect on the foreign trade of the member countries. The limited transferability of the collective CMEA currency and the divergent trade conditions create preferences and have a negative influence not only on the differentiation of flows of goods but also on intra-CMEA trade." It was postulated that the instruments of exchange would be integrated through the effective transferability of the CMEA currency within and outside the socialist market, and that this would bring about the establishment of an IBEC capital in freely exchangeable foreign exchange.[94] The solution proposed in this article was to make the transferable ruble convertible, since that would require less time for preparation, and to aim at a switchover to convertible national currencies. However, in the light of later knowledge this appears somewhat unrealistic. For without the necessary conditions in the individual countries, especially in the Soviet Union, the convertibility of the collective currency would be a vacuous concept and unusable. But that time marked only the beginning of the fruitless discussion that is still going on today. The agreement to found the IBEC left open every option, i.e., both maintaining the bank as a clearing house of intra-CMEA trade as well as developing it into an authentic bank. Article 1 was certainly written with this maximalist option in mind: "settlements from multilateral and bilateral agreements and individual contracts on mutual deliveries of goods, as well as agreement on other payments between the parties to an agreement, should take place in transferable rubles after January 1, 1964. Every party to an agreement who has a positive balance in accounts in transferable rubles may freely dispose over these monies. In concluding trade agreements, every party to an agreement will be guaranteed that incoming and outgoing payments will be balanced together with all other parties to agreements in transferable rubles within the calendar year." The settlement procedure introduced by the IBEC was unequivocally meant to serve the multilateralization of intra-CMEA trade. Incoming and outgoing payments were henceforth to be balanced no longer bilaterally, but together with all other trading partners, and every party to an agreement was permitted to dispose freely over transferable ruble deposits to settle with other trading partners. Measures were introduced by the Standing Foreign Trade Committee to make the fulfillment of this clause of the agreement possible. There were to be two stages in the negotiations: bilateral agreements were to be followed by multilateral negotiations to make possible the clearing of balances not settled bilaterally in trade with the other CMEA partners. The second multilateral stage of the negotiations has, however, only rarely led to positive results. The volume of deliveries it made possible never reached more than 1-2% of total turnover. Despite innumerable decisions intended to ease quota requirements, foreign trade turnovers are balanced bilaterally. Although Article 1 of the Agreement on Multilateral Settlements in Transferable Rubles was a maximalist clause, it is implemented in accordance with conservative trade and settlement methods, and still is so today.

The maximalists also hoped to transform the first CMEA bank into an international banking institution with credit activities, and succeeded in getting the relevant Article 2 of the agreement formulated in accordance with their proposals. This article states: "The IBEC is commissioned by the interested countries to finance and provide credits for the construction, reconstruction, and exploitation of joint industrial ventures and other projects with the funds provided by interested nations for these purposes." However, this desire of the maximalists suffered the same ultimate fate. The IBEC was never able to perform this function. The International Investment Bank founded in 1971 was no more successful. During the first decade of its activity, down to the end of 1981, it had granted credits amounting to 2734.5 billion transferable rubles (about 3.8 billion US dollars) to the member countries,[95] i.e., only a fraction of what the CMEA countries were able to raise on the world market, and a very small amount compared to what an ordinary bank in an ordinary Western country manages and a negligible quantity compared with what actually was needed. The necessary conclusion was that centrally administered economies with their built-in currency inconvertibility are unable to create a functioning international monetary and credit system.

The transferable ruble performs all the functions of money, but not the function of an international currency

The former advisor to the Federal Reserve Bank in New York, George Garvy, coined the term "moneyness." The national currency unit and the collective CMEA currency perform all the functions of money, but are unable to administer the economic intensity of these functions. Garvy described money in a planned economy as follows: "The monetary system of the Communist countries represents a classic case of fiat money, the internal value of which is maintained by administrative controls over its supply."[96] This description gets right to the core of the problem. Allocation orders of state authorities play a greater role than the possession of money in commerce between firms. Money alone is not enough to begin economic activities or to purchase the requisite means of production. If economic activity is necessary, the financing or bank authorities will provide the money necessary. This relationship between business and money is described by the IMF expert Mark Allen as follows: "If an enterprise obtains a good this is not because it has spent money from its bank account, but because it has been allocated that good by the plan. The plan is the motive force, and the money flows are merely a response to what has already been decided."[97] The money flows in the principal sectors of the economy are shielded from one another and are regulated by different state plans. The money flow maintaining the consumer market is steered by the "balance sheet for money incomings and outgoings of the population" and by the cash plan. The money circulation in commerce between firms is regulated by the "credit plan." The moneyness of money is more pronounced on the consumer market than in intra-firm commerce. The state plans regulating money flows are organically related with one another by the identical balances of the moneys put into circulation and taken out of circulation. But in international commerce the situation is different: there the currency units of the planned economies have no function whatsoever. The state's monopoly over foreign trade and currency isolates importing and exporting firms from the foreign market. Hungary and Poland have, in recent years, made certain adjustments in this classical foreign trade system, but the Soviet Union had not until 1986.[98] In the Soviet Union foreign trade is in the hands of foreign trade enterprises. Manufacturing firms have no contact with foreign markets. They are paid for the goods they export or import in domestic currency at domestic prices. Foreign trade as such, the choice of market, and its terms of trade, have no effect on the financial results. The foreign trade enterprise settles foreign trade balances in the form of price differences with the state budget. The payments balance sheet computed by the state plan has no direct connection with other state plans that regulate the country's money flows. But the payments balance sheet itself is no consistent and unified state plan. The trade markets of the CMEA countries are totally separate from one another; trade and settlement conditions and the currency used for settlement vary. The payments balance sheet is divided into two parts: the first part covers trade relations with CMEA countries, the second part deals with the market economies. There is no organic connection between the foreign exchange flows since foreign trade with the industrial countries of the West are usually settled in the freely exchangeable currencies of the country concerned which, as George Garvy states, are, "according to their textbooks, inherently unstable, but from a practical point of view are irreplaceable."[99] Intra-CMEA trade is settled in non-convertible transferable rubles.

As Poland's currency expert Professor Stanislaw Raczkowski writes: "The transferable ruble is the 'international money of the CMEA countries but is not perfect money, since it has no universal buying power that could be used in any country at any time.'"[100] The transferable ruble exercises its function in the CMEA country as imperfectly as the national currency units in domestic commerce. It functions as a standard of value, but does not express the cost and price ratios of the member countries, nor even a CMEA average; its content is solely the appropriately adjusted prices on the world market. In this case the transferable ruble functions as a conversion factor but not as a bearer of value on the CMEA market, which is one of the most important functions of a traditional currency unit. The transferable ruble functions as buying power on the CMEA market, but this function is restricted to the CMEA since, as Raczkowski writes: "It permits the procurement of goods only within the limits of the quantity or value quotas which are established every year in bilateral agreements and are unusable outside the CMEA.''[101] The transferable ruble is money insofar as deposits are made in transferable rubles in the IBEC and loans are granted in the transferable rubles. But no one will want to build up reserves in this defective money for which he can purchase nothing outside the established quotas. Deposits and credits are functions imposed by the existing settlement system. Deposits usually are formed when deliveries are not made in time, while deliveries generate a loan to suppliers who have not received payment. The transferable ruble is also not a means of payment, for the final payment in intra-CMEA trade takes place not in clearing money, with its limited functions, but in goods deliveries which should be compensated, but for some reason cannot be.

It is impossible to raise bank capital in clearing money; the impossible made possible

Of course it was realized that a unit of settlement is not money in which functioning capital can be created in an international bank. The International Investment Bank was well aware of the experience of the IBEC, founded seven years earlier, which after the in-payment of 20% of the declared capital had to stop further in-payments for two reasons: the capital-forming procedure was extremely difficult and the capital raised could not be used in the settlement house. But how can an international bank exist as a real bank without bank capital?—that was after all what was expected from the bank both within the community and in outside dealings. Therefore a bank capital with limited application was created in two institutions. On the basis of Article 3 of the agreement on the founding of the IBEC, it was set at 300 million transferable rubles (and increased to 305 million transferable rubles after Cuba and Vietnam became members), while the shares of the individual countries was made dependent on their share in intra-CMEA exports. See Table 8.

The decision to have only 20% of the subscribed capital paid in in the first year of banking operations was in accordance with international banking practice. But the in-payment practice was not, hence the money necessary for paying in the capital could be neither raised outside the IBEC (the transferable ruble originates in the IBEC, and has no use outside of it) nor could it be created in internal trade. The transferable ruble was created in settlement procedures, and may be used for this purpose; the settlement procedure puts no capital into circulation and needs no other money since it is only a unit of settlement. This impossibility of using settlement money to form capital became evident with the first attempt to fulfill Article 3 of the Agreement. A basic capital of 60 million transferable rubles was formed, but mainly through the granting of settlement credits. But the capital created in this way has not made the bank more efficient. Settlements, even multilateral ones, do not need capital, and the basic capital formed through settlement money was of no use for capital allocation. What does a capital of 60

Table 8

Share in IBEC capital

	In millions of transferable rubles	In %
Soviet Union	116	39
GDR	55	18
Czechoslovakia	45	15
Poland	27	9
Hungary	21	7
Bulgaria	17	6
Romania	16	5
Mongolia	3	1

million transferable rubles mean compared with an annual turnover of 195.7 billion transferable rubles (1984) and an annual volume of credits granted of 13.6 billion transferable rubles (1984)?[102] The first in-payment provided no incentive for the next; none of the member countries made use of Article 3 of the Agreement to raise its share of the basic capital in freely convertible currencies or in gold. The 7th Session of the Standing Currency and Finance Commission (October 1965) took the decision on the urging of Poland and Hungary to form 10% of the basic capital (amounting to 30 million transferable rubles) in freely convertible currencies. The other countries would not accept the suggestion to set the amount of capital in foreign exchange at 100 million transferable rubles and to consider the agreed-upon 30 million transferable rubles only as the first payment; this modest capital of 30 million transferable rubles was to be used for short-term credits and foreign exchange on somewhat more favorable conditions than it was possible to obtain on the world market. But the effect of these conditions was that every member country drew on its foreign exchange credits to an amount equal to its capital share without allowing a collective credit fund to be created. The foreign exchange share is the only effective segment of the basic capital of the IBEC and in 1971 a decision was made to double it. The foreign exchange capital, it should be noted, was used not in intra-CMEA trade, but in East-West economic relations, which are not included in IBEC settlements. The IBEC capital paid in transferable rubles neither helped nor harmed banking activities. However, the situation of the International Investment Bank, founded in 1971, was fundamentally different. A settlement procedure can get along without a basic capital, but for an investment bank of the planned economies, which has no access to deposits in the national currencies of its participants, the basic capital was presumably the only possible source of credits. However, in both CMEA banks the transferable ruble is the currency in which settlements are made and credits are granted. Functionability was the same in both banks. Merely creating an investment bank

Table 9

**Share of member countries in IIB basic capital
(in millions of transferable rubles)**

Bulgaria	85.9
Czechoslovakia	129.9
GDR	176.1
Cuba	15.7
Mongolia	4.5
Poland	121.4
Romania	52.6
Hungary	83.7
Soviet Union	399.3
Vietnam	3.0

and wanting to grant capital investment credits was not enough to give the transferable ruble the properties of capital. The same difficulties as experienced in the IBEC arose again when the endeavor was made to fulfill the provisions of the IIB statutes with bank resources. According to Article 8 of the Statutes, these resources were to be created by members' payments into the basic capital, a special fund of the interested member countries, their deposits, monetary resources raised on the international money market, the use of the part of the profits for reserves, and through a special bank fund. Article 3 of the Agreement establishing the IIB set the basic capital at one billion transferable rubles; Romania's admission later in 1972 raised the capital by 52 million transferable rubles, and the admission of Cuba and Vietnam raised this sum by another 18.7 million transferable rubles. The first payment of 175 million transferable rubles was to be paid in immediately; the second, of the same amount, was to be paid during the second year and the rest "depending on the development of the bank's business and its need for funds, in accordance with the regulations and terms set by the Bank Council." In contrast to the IBEC, the share of the member countries was set on the basis of their share in the CMEA national product and not on the basis of their share in intra-CMEA trade. See Table 9.

The difficult experiences with payments resulted in no more payments in the IIB as well; fifteen years after the bank was founded, the amount of capital had remained at the level of the first payment. After the agreement was signed, L. Siemiatkowski, the President of the Polish National Bank, explained: "I can say with full responsibility that the creation of a real basis for the in-payment of capital—since the bank will only be able to fulfill the function specified in the statutes under this condition—is the principal concern of the participants."[103] A half year later, his deputy, Professor Z. Fedorowicz, brought some clarity to the picture with regard to the accumulating difficulties: "Since the transferable ruble is only a unit of settlement, and no unit of currency, subscription of capital shares entails the commitment to supply agreed-upon capital investment goods or other goods to credit recipients determined by the investment bank and moreover independently of the quotas agreed upon in the trade agreement. . . ."[104] The 30% share in foreign exchange was raised without difficulty, and also readily transformed into credits. But it was difficult to raise the capital, and it was also difficult to use it. In 1984 Imre Vincze, Hungary's former CMEA Secretary, said: "The member countries who founded the bank created the possibility for the IIB to receive transferable rubles (through their subscription to the registered capital) without any definite obligation for the supply of goods"; and further, even clearer: ". . . this problem is also closely connected to the fact that the common currency of the CMEA can only be used in a planned system and is restricted by bilateral relations."[105] The same fate was reserved for the decision to establish a special fund to support developing countries; this fund was set at 1 billion transferable rubles, but only 29 million transferable rubles was paid in.

A credit system conceived for a mature banking system but suited only to a settlement procedure

An imperfect collective unit of currency in which no basic capital capable of functioning as such can be raised cannot develop a modern credit system capable of promoting economic growth. Although its function met the demands of the maximalists, neither its content nor its scope was able to fulfill Article 6 of the Agreement. This article provided for a complete normal banking credit system for the newly established IBEC. Six types of credit were to be available according to the needs of the member countries:

(a) To settle trade in goods when payment commitments exceed payments received for a short period (settlement credit). The size of this credit is determined by the Bank Council, but is granted automatically in accordance with the course of trade.

(b) To finance uncovered amounts between payment commitments and payments received owing to seasonal and other causes related to production or sales. The term is determined by the Bank Council with the provision that the loan must be paid back during the course of the calendar year.

(c) To finance the temporary unplanned payment surplus as a result of delays in deliveries. These credits are provided at high interest rates with the obligation to pay them back before the end of the year.

(d) To increase foreign trade turnover beyond the contractually agreed quotas against a commitment of the borrower to pay back the credit before the end of the next year.

(e) To square the balance of payments in the case of temporary difficulties in goods turnover; in rare cases this credit can be granted on the basis of a decision of the Bank Council, but its term is limited to the end of the next calendar year.

(f) For joint capital investment projects, the construction and modernization of industrial enterprises, and other projects; the funds required are to be made available by the interested parties.

Thus we see that the type of credits prescribed in the agreement establishing the IBEC were conceived for an authentic international bank. But the IBEC, reduced to a clearing house, diluted the content of the credits to a bridging instrument for transitory foreign trade deficits without being able to contribute to economic growth or increased exports. The volume of credits granted by the IBEC between 1970 and 1984 was about 100 billion transferable rubles,[106] i.e., not much more than the CMEA countries had raised on the world market. However, the economic content of these credits is quite different. Whereas the non-convertible transferable ruble credits were only able to facilitate settlements, the credits raised in convertible currencies helped to develop the economy and made possible the purchase of up-to-date technology, grain, licences, etc. The volume of IBEC credits increased from 1.5 billion transferable rubles in 1964 to 13.6 billion transferable rubles in 1984.[107] Three-quarters of these were clearing credits, however, to bridge over temporary trade deficits[108] which were paid back within a year, as may be seen from Table 10, which shows credits granted during the course of a year and not paid back by the end of the year.

It should be noted that clearing credits are formally, if not actually, designed to fulfill another purpose than that of keeping the settlement process functioning smoothly. Former IBEC President Konstantin Nazarkin pointed this out in 1970, and since then nothing has changed in the content of IBEC credits. In his opinion the inordinate differentiation of types of credit according to purpose is meaningless. He observed:[109] "If a credit is granted to pay for an import which exceeds the proceeds from exported goods, there is no way to distinguish why the bank of the member country which takes out the credit needed it, because of seasonal fluctuations in production and exports, or because of a delay in fulfilling export commitments, or because of a short-term difference between incomings and payments which is usually bridged over by a clearing credit." The credits granted by the IBEC differ from technical credits in bilateral clearing, since they are not the result of standing balances in trade between only two trading partners. The IBEC is the collective creditor and debtor of all the participating countries which have commitments only to the bank and not to one another. However, the bank-like form is built into a settlement structure which is unable to fulfill it with appropriate economic content.

The credit system, which was devised for developed economic and trade relations, had to fit into the existing underdeveloped cooperation model. IBEC credits no longer resemble technical credits of bilateral clearing; they are in fact no more than technical credits of multilateral clearings. The bank was forced also to take into account established practice. At its meeting in July 1970 the IBEC Council simplified the extensive credit structure on the basis of the decision of the

Table 10

IBEC credits in the period from 1964 to 1981
(in millions of transferable rubles)

	Credits granted	Status at end of the year
1964	1,511	126
1965	1,799	204
1970	1,975	466
1975	4,097	955
1979	8,306	1,244
1980	9,703	2,117
1981	11,739	3,319

Source: Imre Vincze, *The International Payments and Monetary System in the Integration of the Socialist Countries*, Budapest, 1984, p. 12.

24th CMEA meeting. The six credits provided in the founding agreement were reduced to two types: (a) settlement credits to finance the need of authorized banks for funds when payments out rarely exceed payments received. This type of credit is a revolving credit and is automatically granted without a term of repayment being established; (b) term credits to finance the need of the authorized banks for funds over longer periods. This type of credit is used for specialization and industrial cooperation, expanding goods turnover, squaring the balance of payments, and seasonal needs, and is granted on the application of the member banks for a period of up to one year, or in some cases two to three years on the decision of the Bank Council.[110] However, this simplified classification altered nothing of the economic content of the credits. By its very nature, any credit granted in the settlement procedures of a bank which has no functioning convertible money is only a settlement credit, regardless of its form.

Freely disposable money deposits cannot be created
in a settlement currency

According to Article 1 of the Agreement, the authorized banks may have deposits in transferable rubles and dispose over them freely. But these deposits differ fundamentally from technical negative balances of bilateral clearing in that they represent the country's cumulative balance vis-à-vis all other IBEC members. But the objective of stimulating exports by making them a form of banking and levying interest on them has not been achieved. Deposits differ fundamentally from traditional bank money in the IBEC settlement system in which foreign trade quotas are determined in the plan and are cleared bilaterally. These deposits impart a monetary expression to goods that are not delivered in time, i.e., they register in monetary form the value of all goods of all CMEA trading partners that have not been delivered in time. However, no one would deliberately use an export excess to create money reserves, since nothing could be achieved with such reserves within the CMEA except for the established quotas, to say nothing of outside the CMEA. Transferable ruble deposits do not represent an independent universal buying power and can only be transformed into concrete, agreed-upon quotas of goods. The possibility provided by Article 11 of the Bank's Statutes of disposing freely over transferable ruble deposits is illusory in practice since no money transfers are permitted without the delivery of goods. The transferable rubles have no way of entering into the domestic markets of the IBEC members and the deposit holder cannot transform the deposits into the money of other countries from which it has imported. Although two types of transferable ruble deposits, namely, sight deposits and time deposits, are distinguished, they are in fact no more than sight deposits; their transformation into time deposits is brought about by a lingering delay in goods deliveries. Transferable ruble deposits are extremely rarely the result of an ahead-of-time delivery or exceeding the planned export quota.

However, the IBEC was successful in foreign exchange transactions with Western banks, although these activities are carried out separately from the main activity, i.e., the settlement of intra-CMEA trade. There is no organic connection between these two areas of activity because of the inconvertibility of the transferable ruble. The overall IBEC balance is calculated in transferable rubles on the basis of the official transferable ruble exchange rate, although this is only a calculation factor and not a conversion factor.

Article 24 of the IBEC Statutes stipulates that: "the bank carries out settlement, credit, deposit, arbitrage, guarantee, and other transactions in freely convertible and other currencies as well as in gold, insofar as it has the funds available." Settlements with Western countries are effected outside the IBEC, although deposit transactions in free convertible currencies have developed. Poland was the first member country to make a deposit in convertible currency, in mid–1964. The IBEC makes sight and time deposits mostly with Western banks and only negligibly with member banks, making them available to the member countries, and to some extent to a few Western banks as well. These are short-term deposits, predominantly 3–6 months. The total volume of foreign exchange transactions increased from 900 million transferable rubles in 1964 to 27.2 billion transferable rubles in 1972.[111] The volume doubled over the next decade, and in 1980 reached the equivalent level of 56.6 billion transferable rubles. In 1965, 25% of these deposits had been made by the member countries of the IBEC, the rest by Western countries; but 87% of the foreign currency on deposit was made available to the member countries.[112] There has been little change over the years in the proportions of money supplied and in its distribution. The IBEC entered the Euromarket in the '70s to borrow middle-term credits which were then passed on to IBEC members: twice in November 1971, when it borrowed 20 million dollars and 11 million dollars for the period of five years from Credit

Lyonnais, Commerz Bank, Banco di Roma, and Société Générale; three times in 1979 when it borrowed 60 million dollars for five years in foreign currency from Credit Lyonnais, another 60 million dollars from a British bank consortium also for five years, and 20 million dollars from a French-Belgian finance group, 150 million dollars in April for seven years from the Credit Lyonnais, and 60 million dollars in December for five years from the same bank.[113] IBEC credit operations on the Euromarket have been mainly done on the order of the member countries. This mediating role was discontinued in the mid-'70s. But transactions in foreign currencies in the form of short-term deposits were continued undiminished.

The International Investment Bank of the CMEA has no credit resources capable of functioning as capital

It was realized beforehand that the Investment Bank would experience major difficulties in raising the resources necessary for granting credits. However, just as in the case of the IBEC, the advocates of credit activities wanted to create a structure which could then be filled with the desired content later when the moneyness of the collective CMEA currency was strengthened. It should be recalled that the IIB was created on the basis of the decision of the 23rd Council session in April 1969 which also took a decision to prepare the Comprehensive Program, approved in July 1971, on deepening economic integration of the CMEA countries. The Investment Bank was supposed to help finance the joint investment program provided in the Comprehensive Program. But the function-ability of the collective currency had not increased in the period between the founding of the IBEC in 1964 and the establishment of the IIB in 1971. The proposals of Poland and Hungary to make the transferable ruble at least partially convertible were rejected. Yet this unit of settlement was supposed to be the currency in which the IIB was to grant capital investment credits. As with the agreement on the establishment of the IBEC before it, the agreement to establish the IIB was also a compromise between the countries that wanted to intensify economic integration through developed commodity and money relations, and those who had no intention of making major changes in the domestic and CMEA steering systems. Just after the programmatic 23th CMEA meeting, the Deputy Prime Minister and Standing Representative of the Soviet Union in the CMEA, Mikhail Leshechko, said the following: ''Intensification of commodity and mon-ey relations means a reconsideration of market relations which are not compati-ble with the planned economies of the fraternal countries.''[114] But in a centrally steered planned economy, there were no conditions for developing the functions of the national unity of currencies of the member countries and even fewer conditions for developing the moneyness of the transferable ruble. The IIB was founded without anyone knowing how the stipulated basic capital was to be raised and how credit activity was to evolve. Of course capital investment credits were granted within the CMEA even before the IIB was founded. In the period from 1957 to 1962, sixteen credit contracts were concluded to build five industrial plants in Poland and four in the Soviet Union. Czechoslovakia provided 60% and the GDR 20% of these credits.[115] J. van Brabant, whose research covers the period from 1955 to 1971, sets the total volume of the most important capital investment credits at 1658.5 million transferable rubles. Czechoslovakia was the main creditor, supplying 74.1% of the total volume, followed by the GDR with 20.7%. The Soviet Union heads the list of borrowers with 54.6%, followed by Poland with 30% and Romania with 12.3%.[116] These credits were provided in the form of machinery, semi-finished materials, and raw materials, and usually paid back with finished products manufactured by the plants built with their help. The hope that the International Investment Bank would be reliant on bilateral transactions and the commodity form of investment credits, and introduce a collective credit fund in the expectation that the difficulties would be confined to the first stage and later overcome have not been realized. The Vice-President of the Czech National Bank, L. Rusmich, had the following to say after the IIB was opened: "The bank will have to use unconventional methods in the first stage of its activities to be able to provide borrowers the funds to obtain the capital goods necessary to ensure a high technical level of the planned projects; its work will by no means be easy."[117] The condition which Rusmich set for the full development of the bank's own activities, namely, "the achievement of universal validity of its financial resources," has not yet been realized, since for IIB resources to become universal in this sense the unit of currency used in the IIB would have to become fully transferable, and foreign trade would have to be freed of bilateral quotas. But the transferable ruble continues to function as a unit of settlement and there are no signs that the conditions for developing its functionality will exist in the foreseeable future.

The IIB has indeed financed a considerable number of capital investment projects of the member countries—a total of 83—between 1971 and 1983. The total value of the credits granted for the community, which produces a third of the total world industrial product, was only 2.9 billion transferable rubles, i.e., about 4 billion US dollars, including 77 million transferable rubles in 1982 and 108 million in 1983,[118] a sum which would have to be deemed modest even for a provincial bank somewhere in Austria. And this modest sum was not financed from the bank's own funds or those of the member countries. The agreement establishing the IIB states in Article 6: "The bank may mobilize funds in the collective currency (transferable ruble), in the national currencies of the countries concerned, and in freely convertible currencies, by obtaining financial and bank credits, loans, and by accepting middle-term and long-term deposits, and in other ways. The Bank Council can take decisions to issue interest-bearing bonds to be invested on international capital markets." Of course the IIB was unable to attract deposits in the national currencies of the member countries or place interest-bearing bonds on the international capital market, but it has obtained foreign exchange credits on Western markets since 1973. The first Eurocredit amounting to 50 million US dollars in March 1973 was followed by a credit of 70 million dollars in February 1975, and another one of 350 million dollars in October 1975 to finance the Orenburg pipeline. These in turn were followed by a credit of 600 million dollars from the Dresdner Bank in February 1976; further credits for the Orenburg pipeline in June 1977 and December 1977 amounting to 500 million dollars and 600 million dollars; and a credit of 500 million dollars in July 1978 from the Dresdner Bank for capital goods and large piping, also for the Orenburg pipeline.[119] These data indicate that the Orenburg pipeline was one of the most important and costly of the capital investment projects financed by the IIB. Funds were provided by the large Western banks. Basically the IIB was only an intermediary. Since this project was financed with the participation of the small countries of the CMEA, the credits were passed on to them and not the Soviet Union. This rather complicated credit mechanism is described in the Soviet *Ekonomicheskaia gazeta* as follows[120]: "The IIB grants a credit in foreign currency to the countries participating in the Orenburg pipeline; they then use this money to purchase machinery, equipment, and piping in the West; other expenditures such as wages and salaries are financed by the participating countries with their own funds."[121] It is usual in world banking practice for banks, even large banks, to raise financial resources on the outside to beat the existing demand for credits. But it is also usual for such banks to function as creditors abroad. It is not usual for an international bank to raise foreign funds as resources, which it itself does not have because its currency is not functional, without also being able to enter the world market as a member. In the case of the IIB, Western credits became the principal means of financing the credits which it granted to the CMEA countries: indeed their share in the bank's resources was about 75% on January 1, 1984.[122]

Cheap interest rates for "soft" money

The officials of CMEA banks as well as CMEA authorities correctly point out that the interest rates of the two international banks are much lower than in the West; the average interest rate of the IBEC in recent years has never been higher than 3.4%. "However, the CMEA countries must pay three to five times that figure for credits they obtain in the West," stated the head of the CMEA Division for Currency and Financial Affairs, Iurii Konstantinov.[123] However, it should also be pointed out that these credits were cheap because they were granted in inconvertible settlement currency, which was limited in its function; the world market interest rate is paid for convertible money raised abroad both in the IBEC and in the IIB. The IBEC interest rate policy took shape in a hard-fought debate between Poland, Hungary, and the Soviet Union on the one hand, who regarded interest-rate policy as an important instrument in trade discipline, and Bulgaria, Romania, and Mongolia, which did not want the multilateral settlement system to impair the terms of interest payments compared with the bilateral clearing system. It should be pointed out that the volume of technical credits in bilateral clearing fluctuated between 1.4% and 6.5%.[124]

Article 6 of the Agreement establishing the IBEC concedes to the demands of proponents of a low interest rate. It stipulates the following: "In accordance with the decision of the IBEC Council, a clearing credit can also be granted interest-free. Seasonal credits can also be granted interest-free taking into consideration the special features of the commerce of the individual countries, with the reservation that the total sum of the interest-free credits shall not exceed 3% of the annual foreign trade turnover of the member country." The second IBEC Council meeting set the interest rates at 1.5% for seasonal credits and interest-free credits at 2.5% of the annual turnover of each country with all the other IBEC countries. Under these conditions, the average interest rate for 1964 was no more than 0.8% (between 0.44% and 1.13%) and in 1965 it even declined to 0.64%. The average interest on deposits, however, increased from 0.55% in 1964 to 0.64% in 1965, reaching the level used for credits. To avoid losses, the 12th IBEC Council meeting in July 1986 passed the decision to permit half of the credits granted to remain interest free, on the condition, however, that they not exceed 2.5% of the total turnover of the member country. Under the pressure of those countries that advocated an active credit policy the interest rates for credits as well as for deposits were differentiated according to the term of the credit, i.e., 2% for credits of 3 months, 2.5% for up to 6 months, 2.75% up to 9 months for clearing and seasonal credits, and 2% to 2.5% (for one to two years) for credits to expand goods turnover and 4% for overdue and unplanned credits. Thus the average interest rate was increased from 0.64% in 1965 to 1.16% in 1968. But the interest rate for time deposits was also increased from 0.5% to 1.5% for one-month deposits and from 1.5% to 3.5% for deposits over six months. Another adjustment was made in IBEC interest rates on the basis of the decision of the 24th CMEA meeting in July 1970. The interest rate for the first half of the limit set for clearing credits was set at 2%, while that for the second half was set at 3%. Interest rates for term credits were differentiated according to the payment periods: up to 6 months 3.25%, up to one year 3.5%, up to two years 4%, and up to three years 5%.[125] Interest rates for deposits were also differentiated: from 1.5% for one-month deposits to 4% for deposits over 12 months.[126] Credits for developing countries of the CMEA were given reduced interest rates: 0.5% to 1% for Mongolia and Vietnam, and 0.5% to 2% for Cuba.[127]

The interest rates of the International Investment Bank are much lower than the market rates and are also differentiated according to the term of payment: 3% for five-year credits, 5% for credits from 14 to 15 years.

Of course the IIB had also to take into account the credit practices that prevailed before its establishment, when capital investment credits were granted for interest rates of only 2% on the basis of bilateral agreements. Credits obtained on Western markets, however, bore world market interest rates as in the IBEC.

There are certain reductions for developing countries in the Investment Bank as well. For example, Mongolia pays only 1.5% for credits in transferable rubles, and the interest rate on credits for exploration of the Orenburg gas deposits as well as for building the pipeline section between Orenburg and the western Ukraine was only 2%.[128] Interest in the CMEA banks is not the price of money; it has no more economic content than credits and money deposits. In the IBEC interest both fulfills the function of a penalty for delayed goods deliveries when credits are obtained, and serves as compensation for goods not delivered in time in the case of bank deposits. The interest on capital investment credits granted in transferable rubles is also not the price of money; it is lower than the world market price and therefore is as little functional as a credit granted in nonconvertible currency.

The exchange rate reduced to a conversion factor

More than any other economic steering mechanism, the extremely limited function of the exchange rate of the currency of the planned economies confirms von Mises's hypothesis: "If some of the categories of the capitalist market retain their validity in the planned economies, their scope is different from that of authentic market mechanisms."[129] The exchange rate is in fact this currency instrument, which cannot fulfill its traditional function of an integration factor for the domestic market into the world market if it does not have an external effect. But the monopoly on foreign trade and currency introduced in the Soviet Union on April 22, 1918, and later into the steering systems of Eastern Europe, has hermetically sealed off the units of currency in the Eastern economy from the world market. This has remained the case to the present, even in Romania or Hungary which have been members of the International Monetary Fund since 1972 and 1982 respectively. However, their membership was based not on Article 8 of the IMF Statutes, which was designed for industrially developed countries, but on the basis of Article 14, for developing countries. None of the national currencies, nor the transferable ruble, are quoted on the world market. The national currency units have a price on the grey market in the Western countries, but it is much lower and in the case of the Polish zloty is several times lower than the officially set exchange rate. The precondition for incorporating the currencies of the planned economies into the international monetary system, namely, integration of the domestic price system into international cost and price relations, is at the same time the condition for transforming the exchange rate from a conversion factor into a transaction factor. But the planned economies have an autonomous price policy that is independent of world price relations. It prevents prices in intra-CMEA trade from being based on internal prices of the member countries; and the prices in CMEA trade that are based on world market prices have no economic relationship with the autonomously set prices of the member countries. The exchange rate is unable to fulfill the function of an economic connecting link between the domestic market and the world market at either the national or international levels in the CMEA.

The sealing off of the price system and exchange rate system from international values did not take place in the planned economies as a consequence of an economic crisis or major payments difficulties, as is the case in market economies; rather, it is a condition inherent to the system. No unit of currency of a planned economy was incorporated into the world system at any time during the postwar period and the collective CMEA monetary unit, the transferable ruble, was never convertible into national monetary units of the IBEC member countries, and certainly not into the currencies of third countries. Of course, under the conditions of the classical foreign trade and currency monopoly, a currency that was integrated into the international monetary system on the basis of an economically grounded exchange rate would have no meaning since exporting and importing industrial enterprises are shielded from the world market. Relations between them and the world market are mediated by the foreign trade associations. Industrial enterprises active in foreign trade are not responsible for foreign trade transactions, so an economically meaningful exchange rate would be no more informative than a world market price. It serves neither as a parameter nor as a transaction factor. Results of foreign trade are accounted for at the macro-level between foreign trade enterprises. Although Hungary and, to a certain extent, Poland have eased the rules of the classical foreign trade monopoly somewhat, they nevertheless have not gone so far in their foreign trade reforms as to be able to integrate their system for setting prices and exchange rates into the world system. Although foreign trade results are now incorporated at the micro-level, this is done on the basis of conversion factors and not an exchange rate serving as a transaction factor.

The exchange rates in the planned economies are still based on an archaic gold content

The exchange rate of the planned economies, which is extraneous to the world economy and does not react directly to it, is even today based on the gold content that was assigned to the monetary unit in the first postwar years, and which lost its function as a factor determining the exchange rate when the dollar was taken off the gold standard in the early '70s. Since 1961, the refined gold content of the Soviet ruble (0.987412 grams) has remained unchanged. With this gold parity and the gold content of the US dollar (0.73662 grams in 1971) one ruble was equal to 1.11 dollars until the first dollar devaluation in 1971, then 1.21 US dollars until the second devaluation in 1973, and is currently 1.39 dollars. For a long time the official exchange rates of the planned economies remained unchanged, but lost every relation to reality and served mostly as statistical indicators for converting foreign exchange volumes into domestic values. For example, in Poland, the official rate has fluctuated between 3 and 4 zlotys for 1 US dollar

Table 11

Ratio of US dollar to zloty according to economic sector (in 1968 exports)

	US$ = Zlotys
Average	*48.0*
Machinery and equipment	36.0
Raw materials and fuels	44.8
Agrarian products and foods	83.2
Industrial consumer goods	51.2

for almost a quarter century after World War II, but in relations between foreign trade enterprises, the State Bank, and the state budget, a dollar-zloty ratio of 1:24 is used. The buying power parity calculated on the basis of dollar prices and zloty prices was completely different, as shown in Table 11.

These data show the differentiation in buying power parity of the Polish currency in a few sectors of foreign trade, but it also shows the considerable difference between the official and the effectively obtained rate compared with the buying power parity. Proceeds differed depending on economic region: in intra-CMEA exports 1 dollar was equal to 40 zlotys; in exports to the developing countries 1 dollar was equal to 52 zlotys; and exports to the industrial countries of the West, 60 zlotys. Of course these differences have a great deal to do with differences in commodity structure and quality; but also with differences in terms of trade resulting from the divergent functionality of the currency used in foreign trade. Poland established an exchange rate with a realistic relation to purchasing power parity in the middle '70s, for the two major trade regions: 54 zlotys for 1 dollar and 44.44 zlotys for 1 transferable ruble. Similar discrepancies existed in Hungary. The official forint-dollar course was 11.6:1 during the period from the monetary reform in 1950 to the international regulation. After the economic reform on January 1, 1961, a conversion factor of 60 forints for 1 dollar was introduced. After the international adjustment in 1971 the official exchange rate was reduced to 55.26 forints for 1 US dollar, and to 50 forints per dollar after the dollar devaluation in 1973. On October 1, 1981, a unified exchange rate (for both commercial and non-commercial payments) of 35 forints to the dollar was established. Over the following years the exchange rates in both Poland and Hungary adapted to developments on the world market. In Poland, the first major adjustment was undertaken in early 1982 when the zloty exchange rates were set at 80 zlotys to the dollar and 68 zlotys to the transferable ruble. The zloty was devalued a number of times thereafter to keep pace with inflation. On February 1, 1986, it was adjusted from 147 to 169 zlotys per dollar and from 88 to 91 zlotys for a transferable ruble. In 1982 it was devalued twice relative to Western currencies, the last time on June 1, 1985, by over 16%.[130] The same occurred with the

Hungarian forint: on June 28, 1985 the forint-dollar ratio (average rate) was 50.69:1 and the forint-transferable ruble ratio was 26:1.[131] Hungary and Poland pursue an active exchange rate policy to fit with the reformed foreign trade system in which major industrial enterprises enter into direct contact with the world market, and in order to give them adequate parameters for foreign trade. The Polish and Hungarian trade rates are not transaction factors since neither Poland's zloty or Hungary's forint are exchangeable for foreign currencies.

The exchange rate, reduced to a conversion factor, is determined on the basis of the buying power parity of the national unit of currency. However, this leaves the function of the equilibrium factor which a viable exchange rate must perform out of account. This factor cannot be determined purely arithmetically; it is created by the interplay between the internal and external markets. However, a planned economy does not have an authentic market and therefore has no authentic economic mechanisms. The domestic market in a planned economy is also not integrated into the world market through effective economic mechanisms. The conditio sine qua non for this would be a convertible currency that was incorporated into the international monetary system through economically realistic exchange rates. However, this condition cannot be fulfilled under the given conditions of the system. But some considerable progress has been made in administering the regulations of the classical foreign trade and currency monopoly. The times when imports were only elements in supply and exports were their sources of financing, while comparative cost advantages as a motivation for trade was considered as an evil invention of bourgeois economic theory, have definitely gone. The terms of trade and the price of goods sold on foreign markets and obtained from abroad are playing an ever-growing role in the criteria of selection both in intra-CMEA trade and trade with the West. Industrial firms, once shielded from the world market, now have a direct or indirect hand in foreign transactions, not only in Poland in Hungary, but also in a number of other planned economies. In the Soviet Union, Article 73 of the October 1977 Constitution confirms that the classical foreign trade monopoly is fully in force: "Foreign trade and other external economic activities in the Soviet Union are the responsibilities of the supreme bodies of power and their state administration on the basis of the state monopoly." The roughly fifty foreign trade enterprises which administer this monopoly the representatives of industrial enterprises, their associations and branch ministers have a hand in decisions concerning foreign trade transactions in accordance with the government decision of May 1978. In 1987 the Soviet government permitted 70 large enterprises and 20 economic ministries to enter into direct contacts with foreign firms.

Businessmen were unable to work with the archaic "exchange rates" which had lost every connection with reality; informative transaction parameters had to be made available. The historical exchange rates were adapted to the current market developments and conversion factors were determined on the basis of their buying power parity. The criteria for defining a functional exchange rate or

Table 12

Exchange rates of Eastern European currencies in the years 1970 and 1983 (in West German marks)

	1970	1983
Bulgaria (1 leva =)	0.90	0.60
GDR (100 marks =)	22.50	18.50
Poland (100 zloty =)	2.00	0.15
Romania (100 lei =)	7.75	3.75
Czechoslovakia (100 kr. =)	8.50	7.00
USSR (1 ruble =)	0.48	0.54
Hungary (100 forints =)	7.00	4.25

conversion factor are still disputed, however. The debate between those who advocate an average value and a marginal exchange rate which would make an average effectiveness or an effectiveness that was economical for every enterprise participating in foreign trade is still going on. Polish foreign trade expert P. Gotz Kozierkiewicz commented on how difficult it was for Poland to determine a course[132]: "The zloty costs of a dollar in exports of the processing industrial sectors were used as a basis for the exchange rate of 1 dollar = 80 zlotys established in early 1982. Raw materials, export goods, and import components were excluded from the calculations. Farm products, whose profitability is much lower than that of other export goods, were also left out of account. Exchange ratios of 1980 were taken as the point of departure along with internal and external price developments and changes in the export structure that had taken place between 1980 and 1982." However, there was an awareness from the very outset that the new ratio between the Polish zloty and the US dollar and the transferable ruble could not serve as an effective exchange parameter, not only because raw materials, farm products, and foods were eliminated from the calculations, but also because no appropriate variants between an average and a marginal ratio have been found. A compromise was reached, which made it possible to make about 85% of exports to Western industrial countries profitable. However, it is laborious to determine a market category, i.e., the product of multi-leveled economic relations domestically and abroad, by pure calculations. The official exchange rates have developed more realistically over the course of time than was the case in the early '70s, as is evident in Table 12.[132]

The exchange rates of Poland and Hungary, but also Bulgaria and Romania, were more realistic in 1983 than in 1970. It seems quite certain that the exchange rate adjustments undertaken during the economic reforms will be continued. There can still be no talk of a unified exchange rate since in most countries there are different exchange rates or conversion factors in addition to the official exchange rate for intra-CMEA trade as well as special exchange rates for non-commercial payments in dealings with the socialist countries as well as special rates for Western tourists.

A limited convertibility in non-commercial payments

Measures had to be taken in the sphere of non-commercial payments where foreigners come into direct contact with the market of the planned economies earlier than was the case in commercial transactions; these measures, moreover, had to be taken by all countries to establish a realistic exchange rate independent of the official exchange rate. There were three stages in this process each marked by different clearing methods: the postwar stage up to 1956, the stage between 1956 and 1963, and from 1963 down to today. Until 1956, non-commercial payments were wholly dealt with in bilateral clearing, but evaluated differently. Some of them, i.e., services involving the exchange of goods such as sea transport and port services, goods insurances, post and telegraph, etc., which usually could be assessed in accordance with internationally valid rates, were dealt with in convertible currencies and converted into the clearing unit on the basis of the existing exchange rate. A second group of payments, especially from tourism, were assessed in the national currencies and also converted into clearing units. Clearing in the domain of services settled in national currencies gave rise to considerable discrepancies as a result of divergent price and exchange rate policies. Countries which pursued a stable price policy through massive budget subsidies also subsidized foreign tourists to some extent. The lack of equivalence has been especially perceptible since the mid-'50s when tourism revived and many other non-commercial payments such as fees, licences, etc., began to undergo a greater development than previously. Since the mid-'50s, therefore, bilateral agreements have been concluded to guarantee a maximum equivalence on the basis of conversion factors calculated especially for non-commercial payments. Most CMEA countries introduced exchange rates with a special supplement only for non-commercial transactions. However, clearing continued to be bilateral in relations between two countries.

In autumn 1959, multilateral negotiations were begun among between twelve socialist countries to arrive at a unified agreement on non-commercial trade. The outcome was the signing of the Prague Agreement of February 8, 1963. The CMEA members at that time were joined by China, North Vietnam, and North Korea, in an agreement on a new unified mode of clearing. Unlike tourist trade with the West, in which usually only a unilateral exchange of foreign currencies into the currencies of the planned economies is possible, a mutual convertibility of national units of currency was made possible by the twelve signatories of the Prague Agreement in non-commercial transactions on the basis of exchange rates kept exclusively for this sphere. These special rates were calculated on the basis

Table 13

Exchange rates of Polish zloty in noncommercial trade

	June 1,1963	1982	In force since
100 Albanian leks	18.28	516.00	4/10/1982
100 Bulgarian levs	1961.54	4909.09	1/7/1982
100 Czech crowns	158.55	432.00	1/7/1982
100 North Korean won	1062.50	1250.00	8/2/1982
100 GDR marks	473.13	1350.00	1/6/1982
100 Mongolian tugruks	366.03	1033.49	3/1/1983
100 Romanian leus	184.34	520.48	1/12/1982
100 Hungarian forints	116.70	292.88	8/6/1982
100 Vietnamese dongs	796.88	376.46	8/2/1982
100 USSR rubles	1530.00	4320.00	
100 Cuban pesos	1738.74	3243.24	1/6/1982

Source: J. Wesolowski, "Kursy niehandlowe—preszlość czy przyszlość," *Handel Zagraniczny* (Warsaw), 1983, No. 5.

of buying power parity in a basket of goods, including 33 foods and luxury articles, 22 industrial consumer goods, and 14 services. This basket, adapted to the consumption of a diplomatic family of four persons, proved over the course of time to be unsuited to guarantee an equivalent exchange as tourism and other non-commercial payments grew. In mid–1969, therefore, negotiations were begun prefatory to an agreement on an expanded basket of goods consisting of 76 items including 35 foods, 24 industrial consumer goods, and 17 services which served as a basis for determining adjusted exchange rates in non-commercial transactions. However, price policy remained unchanged. In the Soviet Union, the GDR, and Czechoslovakia prices were kept stable by budget subsidies. In other countries, such as Poland and Hungary, they are continuously adapted to costs. So on January 1, 1980, the signatories of the Prague Agreement came to a new agreement that permitted revaluations and devaluations of the national currencies if they diverged more than 20% from the multilaterally set exchange rate.

The development of the exchange rate system for non-commercial payments may be illustrated on the example of Poland (see Table 13). The data show a clear devaluation of the Polish zloty which, however, is not immediately cancelled out in the CMEA average since price developments had also taken place in a number of the other CMEA countries. The significance of the Prague Agreement in 1963 was that it was able to set a unified conversion factor which made it possible to convert non-commercial transactions carried out in the national currencies into the collective CMEA currencies. The balances of non-commercial transactions of the CMEA countries were henceforth, usually at the end of the year, converted into Soviet rubles and the ruble value, converted into transferable rubles, was channeled into the flow of IBEC settlements. However, the conversion factor of 1 transferable ruble = 3.4 Soviet rubles, agreed upon in 1963, did not reflect the correct ratio between foreign prices and domestic prices and was detrimental especially to the tourist countries of the CMEA which always had a positive clearing balance. Czechoslovakia resisted vigorously since in bilateral negotiations it had been able to bring about a reduction of the conversion factor from 3.4 to 2.0. On July 28, 1971, an adjustment was made that had already been agreed upon at a multilateral level; henceforth the outstanding balances of non-commercial transactions were to be converted into transferable rubles on the basis of a 2.3 conversion factor. It was reduced to 1.9 on January 1, 1978, and to 1.7 on January 1, 1981.[133]

The exchange rates used in non-commercial transactions together with the agreed-upon conversion factors into transferable rubles made possible a kind of de facto convertibility of the national currencies, and the latter into the collective CMEA currency, within a limited domain of tourism and other services. However, they are unable to give due consideration to the peculiarities of each participating country since the autonomous price system differs from country to country, and non-commercial services cannot always be distinguished from commercial services. Exchange quotas are regulated. Still, this solution represents considerable progress over the clearing methods used before the Prague Agreement.

The exchange rate of the transferable ruble functions as a conversion factor

The transferable ruble is not a convertible currency and hence no currency for business transactions. Its exchange rate is meaningful for intra-CMEA trade and the transferable ruble is not involved at all in East-West trade. However, it is indispensable for purposes of conversion. The world market prices are used as a price basis for intra-CMEA trade, which, however, is cleared in the IBEC in transferable rubles. World market prices must therefore be converted into transferable rubles. As mentioned, the IBEC not only clears intra-CMEA trade, it is also increasingly involved in foreign exchange transactions in currencies of its Western correspondents. However, the IBEC balance is in transferable rubles, and a conversion rate is also necessary for this.

The conversion rate of the transferable ruble was set at the level of the Soviet ruble, on the basis of a more symbolic than effective gold content which is statutorily identical, i.e., 0.9874. The ratio to the US dollar was set at 0.9 transferable rubles on the basis of this gold content, and this ratio remained in force until 1973, after which the exchange rate of the transferable ruble as well as that of the Soviet ruble have been regularly adjusted to the exchange rates of freely convertible currencies. The US dollar-transferable ruble ratio is currently 100:72. The inconvertible transferable ruble has not so far been effectively exchanged into convertible currencies. The partial conversion of transferable ruble clearing balances introduced on an experimental basis by a number of CMEA countries on January 1, 1973, was stillborn and has been abandoned. However, payments in convertible currencies for unplanned delivery of "hard" goods for which the other Party in the transaction was unable to come up with a qualitative counter-value, have grown somewhat. The share of settlements in foreign exchange in total intra-CMEA trade is estimated at around 10%.

The transferable ruble does not come into any contact with the national currencies of the member countries in intra-CMEA trade. Until the mid-'70s there were also no official exchange rates between the national unit of currency and the collective CMEA currency. However, intra-CMEA trade had to be integrated into overall economic calculations. The conversion usually took place on the basis of official exchange rates of the national currencies and of the transferable rubles to the convertible currencies of the Western industrial countries. The economic reform that was carried out in some countries, and above all the involvement of major enterprises in foreign trade transactions, made it necessary to adjust the existing exchange rate system. More realistic exchange rates or conversion factors, differentiated for transactions in foreign exchange and in rubles, were introduced.

The Polish and Hungarian practice of using different exchange rates for the two different major economic regions shows clearly how far removed the purchasing power of parity achieved in trade is from the official exchange rate. According to the official exchange rate the transferable ruble is about 40% more expensive than the US dollar. However, the ratio of the Polish zloty and the Hungarian forint to the transferable ruble and the US dollar, calculated on the basis of buying power parity, shows the opposite: 1 US dollar is equivalent to 196 zlotys (February 1, 1986) and 50.7 forints (June 28, 1985), but 1 transferable ruble is equivalent to only 91 zlotys and only 26 forints.

The inadequate exchange rate brought neither losses nor advantages. After all the transferable ruble is only a clearing currency, not a business currency. Yet it creates difficulties, as Polish currency expert Kazimierz Zabielski put it, "in comparing turnovers in East and West as well as in the analysis of the terms of trade."[134]

But the lack of an economically realistic exchange rate between the national units of currency and the transferable ruble became increasingly more perceptible in the '70s, as joint ventures, international CMEA enterprises, etc., grew. Studies therefore were begun between 1971 and 1974 to establish such an exchange rate. However, substantial differences in the price-setting practices of the member countries—the determination of an internal price basis resting on internal price relations—created obstacles to the broader use of the rates determined in 1975.[135]

Monetary relations, limited in their functions, as well as the limited functions of other economic mechanisms, became the principal obstacle to the further development of economic cooperation in a cohesive integrated community. This problem emerged into the open in the third major stage of development under Brezhnev.

The CMEA in the 1970s

The Comprehensive Program of July 1971— the most important CMEA document of the Brezhnev era

The economic cooperation among the member countries of the CMEA that was begun within the framework of the expanded CMEA organizational structure created by Khrushchev, and on the basis of Khrushchev's cooperation model, was continued after his resignation on October 15, 1964. Intra-bloc trade was coordinated and smoothly cleared in the IBEC. The IBEC stepped up its foreign exchange transactions and thus made an important contribution to financing trade with the West. A number of important joint ventures were realized and specialization, especially in machinery construction, was continued. But the underdeveloped economic mechanisms and the limited powers of the CMEA executive body prevented the further development of the CMEA into a functioning integrated community. CMEA activities took place within the traditional framework and there was nothing to indicate any breakthrough with regard to the extent, content, or methods of cooperation.

The Prague Spring and its bitter end, as well as the escalating economic and political crisis at the end of the '70s in Poland, had, just as the tragic events in Spring 1956 in Hungary before it, placed an intensification of economic integration on the order of the day as a precondition for the political cohesiveness of the Eastern bloc. A few months after the Prague Spring was crushed, the 23rd Special Meeting of the CMEA (April 23–26, 1969) made the decision to introduce a long-term integration program: seven working committees—the national groups were headed by a minister or a deputy prime minister—were to present proposals for their area of competence. The preparations lasted more than two years and were completed in mid–1971. The "Comprehensive Program for the Further Deepening and Improvement of Socialist Economic Integration of the CMEA Member Countries" was approved on July 27 by the 25th Council meeting in Bucharest, and the ends and means of the CMEA were set out for the next 15–20 years. A comprehensive document, in four parts with 17 sections, was published, which was comparable in terms of its content and its significance with the "Basic Principles of International Socialist Cooperation" ratified in 1962.

The first part summed up the achievements of the community and outlined further development: "The superiority of the CMEA member countries compared with the developed capitalist countries with regard to the economic growth rate continues to strengthen their positions in the world economy," it is stated in the first point of the Comprehensive Program. The most important objective is the "deepening and improvement of economic and scientific and technical cooperation of the CMEA member countries and the development of socialist economic integration," as a precondition for "an all-round acceleration of technical progress, improving the efficiency of social production, and increasing the prosperity of the population and, of course, taking into account the demands of the class struggle against imperialism."

But this document, written after the crushing of the Prague Spring, also contained the obligatory references to truly fraternal relations. Point 1 of the first section therefore states: "The further deepening and improvement of cooperation and development of socialist economic integration of the CMEA member countries will be continued in accordance with the principles of socialist internationalism on the basis of respect for state sovereignty, independence, and national interests, non-intervention in the internal affairs of sovereign countries, and full equal status in mutual advantage and comradely mutual assistance."

The really existing power relations, and not the rather limited executive powers of the community authorities set down in the Comprehensive Program, were to guide CMEA activities over the long term in which the Comprehensive Program was in force, i.e., from 15 to 20 years. Point 1 of the first section states: "Socialist economic integration takes place on a fully voluntary basis and does not involve the creation of supranational bodies; it does not affect questions of internal planning and financial activity, based on economic accounting, of organizations." The CMEA powers are more restricted than those given to the European Community, whose founding agreement of 1957, Article 113, invested it with the authority to conclude trade agreements. This difference in the respective powers of the two economic communities of Eastern and Western Europe has made negotiations on cooperation more difficult, even after Brezhnev recognized the EEC as the economic organization of Western Europe in his speech to the 15th Congress of the Soviet Trade Unions on March 20, 1972. Negotiations on cooperation between the two communities have shown only slight progress, even after the meeting between Gorbachev and Craxi in May 1985 after a long interruption. An agreement between the two countries was concluded in June 1988. The limited powers of the CMEA authorities have no special influence on the overall activities of the community, since it is the real power relations and not the paragraph in the community statutes which carry the decisive weight.

The Comprehensive Program, like previous CMEA documents, contains another recurrent ideological aspect, namely, the postulate of the "creation of a modern highly effective commodity structure, the gradual convergence of the member countries in their level of economic development." This objective was to be realized through, for instance, lower interest rates for the developing countries of the CMEA, Cuba, Mongolia, and Vietnam, for IBEC credits, and by giving greater consideration to specialization projects. Of course the period in which the Comprehensive Program was to be in force, namely 15–20 years, was too short to overcome the centuries of backwardness of these countries. The gap between their level of development and the CMEA average has scarcely diminished over time. This ideological aspect is, however, an object of permanent controversy between economically less-developed Bulgaria or Romania and the developed industrial nations of Eastern Europe (the GDR and Czechoslovakia), which is reflected in the debate in negotiations on the assignment of specialization in the progressive industrial sectors.

The second part of the Comprehensive Program outlines the principal ways and means of achieving the deepening of cooperation and the "development of socialist economic integration." The following forms and methods of cooperation are proposed: "Mutual multilateral and bilateral consultations on basic questions of economic policy; deepening of multilateral and bilateral cooperation in planning, including cooperation in forecasting, coordinating five-year plans, and coordinating plans for a longer term in important economic branches and areas of production; expansion of joint planning of some coordinated branches of industry and particular production processes by the countries involved as well as an exchange of experience on improving the system, the planning, and the management of the economy; planned expansion of international specialization and cooperation in production, science and technology; and unification of efforts of the interested countries through prospecting for and developing deposits of natural resources, in building industrial plants, and in research work." In addition to these principal forms of cooperation, stress is also placed on "expanding the efficiency of mutual trade," "expanding direct relations between branch ministries, economic organizations, and research institutes, creating new international economic organizations," and on "improving the legal foundations of cooperation."

But progress in coordinating economic plans, so long desired, and closer cooperation in those industrial branches that were crucial for the continued development of the overall economy, have not been achieved. The principal precondition for this, namely, direct relations of cooperation between the branches of production, could not be created under the given conditions. Differences in the steering system still constitute an obstacle. The authority of the production unit in Hungary or Poland is much greater than in the Soviet Union. This is why very few direct contacts have been established between production units or their associations, in accordance with the wishes and the formulation of the reform-inclined countries even in the later CMEA documents of 1984 and

1985, although this also accords with the actual possibilities afforded by the conservative steering system.

Focal points of the Comprehensive Program

The most important branches of industry of the member countries were to cooperate more closely with one another. Perfecting of the forms of cooperation was to lead to an efficient utilization of natural resources and contribute to technical progress. Pious priority was placed on prospecting for raw materials and fuel deposits, especially in Mongolia, for the purpose of meeting the needs of the member countries with internal resources. A balance sheet for supply and demand in the energy sphere was to be set up for the entire CMEA region and the most thrifty methods of utilization were to be established. There was to be closer cooperation in the steel foundries, in the production of cast iron, copper, nickel, tungsten, etc., through, for instance, joint ventures. Specialization was to continue with a view to the resources, experiences, and production capacities of the member countries. However, main attention was given to achieving the highest possible quality in machinery construction and in products of short supply in the CMEA, such as equipment for nuclear power plants, for mining, plant for steel foundries, the chemical industry, paper and paper pulp factories, etc. Highest priority was placed on radio technology and electronics, as well as on automatic control systems. Joint capital investment projects, especially in the chemical and paper pulp industries on Soviet territory, i.e., where suitably abundant deposits were located in Karatan and Kingissep, were to begin. Great value was attached to deepening joint research, by specialization and through the creation of joint research institutes. But the development of agriculture and improving agricultural productivity, as well as the intensification of cooperation in the production of foods, were also emphasized. The food industry was to occupy a leading place among the industrial branches within the CMEA.

A wide-ranging program of integration for the industries of the member countries was ratified. It was to modernize the national economies and orient them toward higher quality and productivity. Specialization of production, taking into account the best utilization of existing resources, experience, and qualifications, was to adapt the economic structures within the CMEA to the needs of the times in order to satisfy the needs of the population better than hitherto. Attention was also given to bringing the level of development of the economically backward members of the CMEA to the level of the industrially developed countries of Eastern Europe. The composition of the community is indeed strange: Cuba, Mongolia and Vietnam alongside the industrially developed Czechoslovakia and GDR; the second biggest economic power in the world alongside little Bulgaria; and the Soviet Union accounting for 70% of the total product of the CMEA. This composition was therefore to have a decisive influence on the location of major projects "of joint interest." In effect, it petrifies existing structures instead of being able to alter them essentially: nine-tenths of the joint capital investment projects outlined in the Comprehensive Program are located on Soviet territory, and are to be built with the financial assistance of the smaller countries, in particular, giant pipelines, which are to be financed by the investment bank founded in 1971. However, the effective lenders are Western bank consortia, the borrowers are the small countries of Eastern Europe, and the effective beneficiary is the Soviet Union. Poland's coal deposits in the Lublin basin, as well as the huge deposits of brown coal in the Belchatow region, are relatively disregarded. Poland's petition to have these mines recognized as projects of joint CMEA interest and to develop them with the help of the other CMEA countries was not granted until the CMEA summit meeting in June 1984, and then only partially.

The highest integration stage set out in the Comprehensive Program, to be achieved by joint investment projects and the international CMEA enterprises, has but slight chances of success under the given conditions of the system. There are many obstacles: the limited scope of economic mechanisms, which are designed for internal consumption; the autonomous price-setting practices; the nonconvertible currencies; exchange rates reduced to conversion factors; bilateral trade with its strict quotas; and also the very narrow interpretation of how the planned economies were to link up with the world economy. Romania gave this interpretation a rather flagrant expression in its famous "declaration of independence" of April 22, 1964. Planned management of a national economy is seen as a "fundamental attribute of the sovereignty of a socialist state," and further, even more clearly, "if such an instrument should pass under the authority of supranational or extra-national bodies, that would render the notion of sovereignty vacuous." The practice of blocking off state-owned enterprises from the outside world is the same everywhere, as is the fear of the smaller countries to be drawn into international activities through unequal power relations or by supranational bodies which would cross their national economic plans; effective joint ventures are easier to establish with private Western firms than with the cumbersome and relatively impotent state enterprises of the CMEA partner countries. The immobilism of property in the East stands in crass contrast to the growing mobility of private capital, which is passed from country to country through the power of the large banks and the industrial multinationals, past national boundaries with inimitable facility, yet at the same time furthers technical progress.

Many international enterprises, research institutions, and joint ventures were started after the establishment of the Comprehensive Program. However, their purpose is to coordinate manufacture and sales, and promote scientific and technical cooperation, but not to introduce a joint production activity through the merger of property. During the 37 years of the CMEA activity only two industrial enterprises based on joint property have been created, namely, the Hungarian-Polish "Halbex" with its seat in Katowice in Poland, which processes Polish coal tailings in the Silesian coal deposits into useful coal; and the Polish-East German textile combinate in Zawiercie in Poland. The planned economies are more introverted than the other economic formations in this world, more nationalistic than internationalist, and a considerable obstacle to scientific and technical progress, which has in fact become especially notable during the course of the third scientific and technical revolution.

Foreign trade should take advantage of progress in international specialization in industrial activity, and promote the international division of labor in the CMEA; the exchange of the products of the machinery construction industry should become the most important component of intra-CMEA trade; greater importance than heretofore should be attached to the technical servicing of exported machinery, the manufacture of spare parts, and to repair centers. Intra-CMEA exchange of raw materials and fuels should be one of the manifestations of the closer cooperation in prospecting for and developing new deposits, as specified in the Comprehensive Program. The Soviet Union is to concentrated on delivery of iron ore and semi-finished products, copper, nickel, and crude oil; Poland on the delivery of hard coal, coke, zinc, and sulphur; and more importance is to be attached to the exchange of farm products and foods, which are still under-represented in trade, as stressed in the Comprehensive Program.

Intra-bloc trade grew vigorously in the first ten years of the Comprehensive Program. The relative share of intra-bloc trade in the total trade of the individual members varied considerably in 1981: Mongolia headed the list with 97.1%, followed by Cuba with 71.5%, Bulgaria 70.8%, Czechoslovakia with 67.1%, the GDR with 62.7%, Poland with 59.5%, and Hungary with 51.3%, followed in last place by the Soviet Union with 47.6% and Romania with 38.7%.[136] The relatively small share of intra-bloc trade in the Soviet Union's total trade was a result of oil exports to the West, which increased in value, owing to the considerable price rises. The low share of CMEA trade in the total trade of Romania was due to the relatively low share of oil imports from the Soviet Union. The Comprehensive Program has had no special influence on the development of the commodity structure. The Soviet Union continues to be the main supplier of raw materials and fuels, the GDR and Czechoslovakia the main suppliers of machinery and equipment, while the most up-to-date technology as well as grain are imported by all CMEA countries from the West.

Nothing has changed in how trade is conducted. The Comprehensive Program states: "Trade relations between the CMEA member countries will continue to develop on the basis of state monopoly over foreign trade as the principle of planning is further strengthened and perfected." Of course the program also yielded somewhat to the wish of Poland and Hungary to permit "non-quotaed trade" which, as it is stated, "does not necessarily have to be cleared bilaterally." Trade without quotas, however, remains a marginal phenomenon; agreed-upon commodity quotas continue to be cleared bilaterally. Nor could it be otherwise since nothing has changed in the basic principles of the steering systems of the most important CMEA countries. No preconditions for enhancing the economic content of intra-CMEA communication mechanisms were created, even though these mechanisms ought to have been modified appreciably under the pressure of the reform-oriented member countries. The section of the Comprehensive Program which deals with improving currency and financial relations devotes considerable attention to the ''collective CMEA currency.'' The transferable ruble was to have all the basic functions of money, especially the function of a measurement of value of payments and accumulation funds; however, it was above all to facilitate the establishment of economic ties among the member countries, and make economically sound decisions possible. The transferable ruble was to have played an important role in the multilateralization of intra-CMEA trade. In the period between 1971 and 1973, the CMEA countries were to take measures to expand multilateral trade with the aid of the transferable ruble, which was to play an important role in the exchange of non-quotaed goods and in clearing with third countries. The development of the monetary functions of the transferable ruble was premised on its convertibility with the national currencies of the member countries. Economically sound exchange rates were to have been agreed upon and connections established between domestic prices and foreign prices. The Comprehensive Program found no adequate solution for the paradoxical price-setting practices in the CMEA. It states that ''the member countries will continue to base their mutual trade on the price-setting principles now in force during the upcoming period.''

Recommendations of the Comprehensive Program in capital investment projects begun even earlier on Soviet territory were fulfilled. The giant pipelines were built within a short time with the assistance of the smaller countries and put into operation. They have made possible considerable oil and gas exports to Eastern and Western Europe. But the most important instrument of integration was still lacking for implementing the ambitious integration program: namely, an executive body capable of giving recommendations. The steering system and above all the economic policies of the small countries have become even more differentiated in the '70s and made it more difficult for CMEA authorities to make use of their powers, which are already limited, especially the economic steering mechanisms. Two dates were set for perfecting the instruments provided for in the Comprehensive Program: the CMEA countries were to find ways to establish realistic exchange rates and gold parities before the end of 1975, and measures were to be introduced within the same period to enhance the functionability of the transferable ruble and thereby promote the multilateralization of intra-CMEA trade. In 1973 the member countries were to discuss conditions necessary to make possible the convertibility of the transferable ruble into the national currencies as well as the mutual convertibility of the national monetary units. In 1974, economically sound exchange rates between the national currencies and the transferable ruble as well as exchange rates and conversion factors between them were to be established. Another step in this direction was to be made between 1976 and 1979: namely, the conditions were to be created for a unified exchange rate of the national currency units and the decision to introduce a unified exchange rate system that could be used in all payments transactions was scheduled for 1980.

The perfecting of monetary relations undertaken in 1971 on the basis of the approved Comprehensive Program was not realized for well-known reasons. The exchange rate calculated in 1973 for the national currencies, as well as the partial convertibility of ruble balances in the IBEC, agreed upon by some of the CMEA countries, were of no use. In the early '70s, however, the expansion of CMEA monetary relations contemplated was taken very seriously, and indeed more in the West than in the East. Franz Pick, the editor of the *Pick Currency Yearbook*, commented in 1973: "In the not too distant future, the Soviet unit could become more convertible than the mini-dollar." This was an allusion to the dollar devaluation in 1973 and a praise for the stability of the CMEA currency. But in the East bloc itself, currency stability was no special occasion for rejoicing, given the chronic shortages. Although it continued to be praised in the CMEA documents as a great achievement of the planned economies, no progress was made in perfecting the function of money. The postulates in the Comprehensive Program for expanding currency relations were referred to less and less, and even less was done. CMEA documents continued to speak of consolidating CMEA monetary relations, but there was no longer any mention of currency convertibility. In the '70s, economic integration was avoided in conversation, and the Comprehensive Program fell into oblivion. Impulses and material values for accelerating technical progress were sought in other quarters.

Expansion of economic relations with the West as a vehicle of modernization

The Comprehensive Program generated impulses that extended far into the future, even though they were minimal and their effect on the present was of brief duration. Detente between East and West, which evolved throughout the '70s, induced the CMEA countries to restructure their foreign trade relations differently from the direction which the Comprehensive Program, approved by the 25th Council session, had intended. It was recognized that the existing steering system created no possibilities either nationally or internationally for the CMEA to link up with the worldwide third scientific and technical revolution that was progressing with undiminished strength. Half-hearted economic reforms were unsuccessful. The radical, far-sighted economic reform in Czechoslovakia was not permitted to achieve a requisite maturity. Efforts therefore turned in other directions to achieve the modernization that had become absolutely necessary, but which could not be achieved by the CMEA countries on their own forces: namely, the attempt was made to use Western technology financed with Western credits. East-West trade developed at an unprecedented pace in the '70s: exports to the OECD increased from 6.6 billion dollars in 1971 to 42.3 billion dollars in 1980. Imports from the OECD increased from 7.0 billion dollars to 42.8 billion dollars,[137] while the Western share in total exports increased from 21.6% in 1970 to 29.7% in 1980, and the Western share in imports increased from 25.6% to 34.2% during the same period.

The restructuring of foreign trade with the major economic regions is especially evident in the case of the Soviet Union: the Western share in Soviet exports increased from 18.7% in 1970 to 32.0% in 1980, while imports increased from 24.1% to 35.4%. The figures for Eastern Europe were 23.7% for 1970 and 27.6% for 1980 for exports and 26.7% to 30.1% in 1980 respectively for imports.[138] The difference between the Soviet Union and the small countries is attributable to the extremely favorable terms of trade for the Soviet Union and much less to a change in the commodity structure. Between 1970 and 1980 Soviet exports to the West reached a value of 7.75 billion US dollars at constant prices, and 66.8 billion dollars at current prices. This gigantic difference was one of the consequences of the dramatic price rises for crude oil and natural gas. The value of oil exports to the OECD countries increased from 1.176 billion rubles in 1973 to 12.085 billion rubles in 1982, i.e., by more than ten-fold. The quantity, on the other hand, increased from 46.4 million tons to 66.3 million tons, i.e., by only 43%. A similar development was chalked up by total exports: the value of exports increased from 22 million rubles to 2.739 billion rubles, while the total volume increased only from 2.0 million cubic meters to 25.1 million cubic meters.[139] The favorable terms of trade for fuels increased the share of fuels in total exports of the Soviet Union to the OECD countries from 30.5% in 1970 to 80% in 1982.[140]

Even though the share of the OECD countries in CMEA imports was only 25.8% in 1983, and the CMEA share of OECD imports was only 3.3%, East-West trade is important for both sides. The opening up of the huge Eastern market creates new jobs in the industrial countries of the West. For the Eastern countries, on the other hand, the world market is an important source of supply of modern machinery and equipment produced in very small quantities in the CMEA if at all. The commodity structure of East-West trade is also extremely varied. OECD imports from the CMEA countries consist mainly of mineral fuels, agricultural raw materials (wood, cork, skins, furs), etc. However, imports of machinery and other finished products are insignificant. Only 10% of total imports from the Eastern countries were accounted for by machinery in 1970 and 1982. The share of the six small countries of the CMEA in OECD machinery imports increased from 0.5% to 0.7% between 1970 and 1982. For commercial finished products, this figure remained stable at a relatively low level of 1.5% in glaring contrast to the threshold countries (Brazil, Hong Kong, Yugoslavia, Mexico, Singapore, South Korea, and Taiwan), which increased their share in OECD imports of finished products from 3.3% in 1970 to 8.5% in 1982.

The CMEA countries, on the other hand, import mainly machinery, equipment, iron and steel, foods, and luxury articles from the West. Differences in the commodity structure of the OECD-CMEA foreign trade may be seen in the OECD balances in trade with the East, broken down by commodity group (Table 14).

Table 14

OECD surpluses and shortfalls in trade with the East between 1972 and 1982 (in billions of US dollars)

	Soviet Union	Small CMEA countries
Total	+ 3.2	+ 26.5
including:		
Mineral fuels	− 98.9	− 23.3
Agricultural raw materials	− 15.5	0
Textiles and clothing	+ 4.4	− 1.9
Finished products	+ 18.8	− 3.4
Machinery and transport vehicles	+ 44.3	+ 32.5
Foods and luxuries	+ 31.6	+ 2.0
Iron and steel	+ 27.8	+ 4.8
Chemical products	+ 7.1	+ 15.3

Source: *Wochenbericht des DIW*, 1984, no. 45–46, p. 556.

It is clear from the data that the Soviet Union financed its considerable shortages of machinery and means of transportation, foods and luxuries, iron and steel, and other finished products with a gigantic surplus of mineral fuels and agricultural raw materials of 114.4 billion US dollars. But the surpluses in mineral fuels, accompanied by a very small range of finished products, in the small CMEA countries, were insufficient to offset shortfalls in machinery and means of transportation (32.5 billion dollars) and chemical products (15.3 billion dollars). The cumulative shortage of these items in OECD trade in the period from 1971 to 1980 was 43.9 billion dollars; the cumulative shortfall for the Soviet Union, however, was only 7.8 billion dollars.[141] The situation in agriculture, which is chronically grave, has had an extremely negative influence on the balance of trade with the Western countries and has forced the Soviet Union and the smaller CMEA countries to import massive quantities of farm products and foods. The share of this commodity group in total imports from the West increased during 1970 to 1980 from 8.1% to 23.2% in the Soviet Union, from 11.7% to 23.2% for the small CMEA countries, from 14.1% to 24.8% in Poland, and from 15.3% to 29.5% for the GDR, and from 5% to 15.3% for Romania. Only Hungary was able notably to reduce the proportion of farm products in its total imports from the West from 12.4% in 1970 to 7.4% in 1975 and 4.8% in 1980.[142]

The hope for a revolutionary effect from Western technology was not fulfilled

The massive imports of technology from the West contributed considerably to the modernization of numerous plants and even industrial branches. But only deception would have awaited those who expected foreign technology to be able to modernize an entire economy which had fallen behind because of an inadequate steering system. But it could not have been otherwise. Foreign technology, however much is imported, was unable to replace lacking internal influences. Imported modern technology created an oasis of progress which, however, contributed little toward modernizing the economy as a whole. It had been transplanted into a social system which impeded progress and was hence not able to infuse it with its own dynamic. The delayed economic reforms which it was hoped the foreign technology and foreign money would replace were not continued in the relatively favorable '70s and there was nothing to put in the place of the foreign technology and foreign money. Because no means had been found to link up with worldwide scientific and technical progress, it proved impossible to expand the range of exportable goods which could have closed the accumulated payments gap. The state monopoly on foreign trade and currencies, which had been established in 1918 in the Soviet Union when that country was shut off from the external world and was later passed on to Eastern Europe, was totally unable to create impulses for a modern, dynamic foreign trade in the '70s compared with the modern if crisis-prone Western trade and currency system. Compensation transactions and a reversion to bilateral clearing of commodity flows grew especially toward the end of the '70s, but there was no commensurate growth in free exchange of goods and services. The Eastern countries were able to make use of the Western money markets to finance their payments deficits, but the Western countries were unable to freely sell their goods on Eastern markets or make use of Eastern credit facilities. Even the industrially developed countries of Eastern Europe acted as simple developing countries in foreign trade with the West, due to their backward foreign trade and monetary systems.

The structure of exports of CMEA countries was no larger in the late '70s than in the early '70s. It exceeded even that which cautious Eastern experts had predicted: a tremendous mountain of debt of about 80 billion US dollars accumulated. Poland, which had oriented its foreign trade to Western imports more than the other CMEA countries, but had less to offer than the other countries, covered no more than 61.5% of its imports from the West in the first half, and no more than 69% in the second half of the '70s,[143] and accordingly plunged into a severe economic crisis. It suspended servicing its debt, which toward the end of the decade was 2.5 billion dollars, but had reached 29.5 billion dollars toward the end of 1985 and around 39 billion dollars in 1988. Romania had to suspend its payments a short time later. The GDR and Hungary also fell into a liquidity crisis. The Western countries waited in vain for the Soviet Union to open its protective umbrella over the insolvent smaller countries as some respected experts had promised. It refused further credits even to those CMEA countries whose creditworthiness was not in question.

Neither the Soviet Union nor the smaller countries had been able to effect a link-up with the worldwide scientific and technical revolution, even though the financial situation of the Soviet economic power was different from that of the smaller CMEA partners. The Soviet Union was the major beneficiary of the oil price increases which it also supported and of the manifold rise in the price of gold. These two principal components of Soviet exports brought it at least 70 billion dollars more earnings in the '70s. It was unable to force the world prices for oil and petroleum products on its partner countries, but was able to annul the price basis for mutual trade agreed upon for the period 1971 to 1975 one year before its scheduled expiration, and obtained 32.6% improvement in its terms of trade with the other CMEA countries in 1975. Despite this unexpected windfall, the '70s were more a period of decline than one of boom for the Soviet Union, as Mikhail Gorbachev emphasized in his dramatic speech on June 17, 1985: "Since the early '70s the country has neglected to adapt the forms and methods of economic management, the real psychology of economic activity, to the needs of the time."[144] He and his colleagues Ligachev and Ryzhkov stressed the country's backwardness even more clearly at the 27th Party Congress. The unexpected flow of money resulting from the unexpected price explosion was insufficient to guarantee the planned upswing. Forms and methods of economic management corresponding to the times, and the real psychology of economic activity, cannot be imported.

The smaller countries of Eastern Europe were even less able to effect a link-up with worldwide scientific and technical progress. Not only did they have a growing deficit in trade with the West, their trade with the Soviet Union was negative as well. In 1972 and 1973 they were still able to chalk up a positive balance of 960.3 million transferable rubles and 712 million transferable rubles, respectively, in trade with the Soviet Union, but in the following years the deficit increased rapidly. (See Table 15.)

Poland was of course the principal borrower with a deficit of 809.8 million and 1.7105 billion transferable rubles in 1980 and 1981. Czechoslovakia also recorded a considerable deficit in trade with the Soviet Union for the period from 1975 to 1981, amounting cumulatively to 918.6 million transferable rubles. For the same period, the cumulative deficit was 723.9 million for Hungary, 1563 million for Bulgaria, and 2859.2 million transferable rubles for the GDR.[145]

In the face of the refusal of further loans from Western banks, the Eastern countries found themselves constrained to throttle their imports from the West drastically, which had a devastating effect on their economies. In the first three years of the '80s, East European imports from the West decreased by 9.8%, 19%, and 3%, including 33.1%, 29.5% and 3.1% for Poland, 11%, 45.2%, and 25.1% for Romania, 12.1%, 10.1%, and 6.4% for Czechoslovakia, and 1.9%, 12.4%, and 8.9% for Hungary.[146]

The upswing in East-West trade that began in the '70s was unable to help the Eastern economies to modernize their backward technology nor to accelerate their growth. Quite the contrary, for the first time in the postwar period, the Soviet Union and the smaller countries of Eastern Europe experienced an eco-

Table 15

Positive balance of Soviet trade with Eastern Europe (in millions of transferable rubles)

1974	105.2
1975	554.6
1976	880.4
1977	1,414.3
1978	169.6
1979	1,057.5
1980	1,824.2
1981	3,149.4

Source: *Vneshniaia Torgovlia SSSR* for these years.

nomic recession punctuated by an acute shortage of supplies and a growth rate approaching zero. The average growth rates of the six European countries decreased from an annual average of 4.9% for the period 1970–1975 to 2.0% in the next five-year period, and 1.2% for the period between 1980 and 1984; Poland's recession of 3.2% and 6.8% in 1980 and 1982 was a major factor in the decline in growth in Eastern Europe, but Bulgaria had lower or even negative growth rates: 2.8% in 1980, and after plus rates of 3.0% and 3.1% in the next two years, a negative growth rate of 1.7% in 1983; the figures for Czechoslovakia were 1.7% in 1980, –0.5% in 1981, 1.4% in 1982, and 1.0% for 1983. For the GDR the figures were 2.4%, 2.0%, 0.0% and 1.6% respectively. Hungary's figures were 0.5%, –0.1%, 1.5% and –1.2% and finally Romania's growth rates were –1.7%, 0.5%, 2.3%, and 0.3% respectively for the years 1980 through 1983.[147]

The economic situation in the early '80s was no better in the Soviet Union which, unlike the smaller CMEA countries, who had to shoulder considerable losses as a result of the dramatic price rises, was able to chalk up tremendous profits. Gorbachev described the unfavorable economic situation most clearly as follows in his speech to the 27th Party Congress: "A discrepancy has arisen between the requirements of society and the achieved level of production, between solvent demand and the quantity of goods available to cover it." Boris Yeltsin, the former Moscow Party leader appointed by Gorbachev, did not shy from using the ominous word "stagnation," hitherto reserved only for capitalist society: "Why do we discuss the same problems from one Party Congress to another?" he asked the 4,993 delegates to the Party Congress, and continued with even greater acerbity: "Why do we see reason to include a new term, 'stagnation,' previously alien to it, in our Party vocabulary?"

Growth rates were more favorable over the next few years than in the early '80s. However, nothing indicated that it would reach its former levels in the foreseeable future. Yeltsin himself said why nothing else could be expected: "Because we were unable to eradicate the bureaucracy, eliminate injustice and the abuse of power, because the call for radical reforms came to nothing in the inert lobby of opportunist functionaries with Party cards. . . ." Of course, other causes than these could be adduced for the economic malaise. But the measures taken to eliminate them are more important.

The conclusion drawn from the unfavorable developments in the late '70s and early '80s was, as in the second half of the '50s and the end of the '60s after the dramatic developments in Hungary, Poland, and Czechoslovakia, a renewed recourse to factors stimulating cooperation in the CMEA.

No comprehensive option for implementing the 1971 Comprehensive Program

No other period in the thirty-seven years of existence of the CMEA provoked so much controversy in its assessment as the '70s. There are still extreme differences of opinion in evaluating the terms of trade after the price explosion in October 1973. This is certainly no easy task if one considers that the price-setting practices in intra-CMEA trade, which were always complicated, had become more complicated. Mark-ups and mark-downs, negotiated bilaterally on the basis of world market prices, in the expanding range of goods exchange in CMEA trade became more frequent, political considerations began to play a greater role than previously, and supply dominated over profitability as a motive in trade. Cost-benefit analysis of foreign trade increased in importance, but only among economists, not among businessmen. However, only wrong conclusions would result from assessing price developments independently of one other important event of the '70s, namely, the decision taken in 1975 for the smaller countries of the CMEA to participate in the tapping of raw materials and fuels as a necessary condition for meeting their growing consumption needs. The advantages and disadvantages of mutual trade derived therefore not directly from price developments, but from the costs of participation of the smaller countries in large Soviet projects.

If the CMEA countries are able to set and manage their prices for raw materials and fuels in intra-CMEA trade more easily and analysts find it easier to compare these prices with world prices, nonetheless in the light of other developments, and especially the decisions of the 29th Council meeting of 1975, a unilateral assessment of the advantages and disadvantages of trade in raw materials and fuels is unsuited for evaluating the overall trade results, to say nothing of evaluating economic relations between the Soviet Union and the smaller CMEA countries, which are determined by many non-economic factors.

The active observer and participant in CMEA developments in the '60s could say the following: "There is no conscious practice of exploitation in the CMEA. No one here wants to demand sacrifices of another country or sacrifice anything for altruistic reasons—neither the very large member country nor the smaller countries. There are unequal power relations which must be taken into account; but the smaller countries have learned to defend their economic interests ever more effectively.''

Many interesting studies have been published on CMEA developments in the '70s. The study by Marrese and Vanous[149] was especially interesting with its sensational estimates of Soviet price subsidies for the smaller countries, amounting to 5.3 billion or 5.9 billion dollars annually in the years from 1974 to 1978. The discussion became even more remarkable after the Hungarian Laszlo Csaba,[150] the Austrian Raimund Dietz,[151] the Sorbonne Professor Marie Lavigne,[152] and their critic Jozef M. van Brabant[153] published their articles.

Lavigne's view that the Soviet Union had not made complete use of the opportunity available to make profits in foreign trade with the smaller countries, but had initiated a ''policy of imposing its scheme for a 'production' integration linking together the capacities of the Comecon member states as opposed to the 'market' integration advocated by some of its partners and most strongly by the Hungarians,'' was not palatable to J. van Brabant. He writes: ''Marie Lavigne is mistaken if she links these events with a deliberately granted subsidy which the Soviet Union then later used to bring pressure to bear on its partners to accept its notion of integration.'' There was certainly some connection between the price developments and the integration measures initiated in 1975, but not in the sense formulated by Lavigne. The insider, Hungary's CMEA expert Laszlo Csaba, was astonished over some statements by Western observers. He wrote: ''The discrepancy between nominal CMEA prices and world market prices for raw materials and especially fuels has misled economists and economic policymakers into drawing perfunctory and over-hasty conclusions.'' Csaba's use of the term ''nominal'' to describe intra-CMEA prices is certainly not accidental: every insider knows quite well what he means, namely, that multilaterally established CMEA prices have no universal and unequivocal use, and that the advantages and disadvantages for a particular item and for a particular commodity group, quite apart from a total turnover, cannot and may not be determined at the same time for every bilateral foreign trade relation, and that arithmetic can be used as an auxiliary in making estimates but not as a definitive instrument of evaluation.

The CMEA entered the '70s with the most important document in its history, namely, the Comprehensive Program of July 1971, which marked the first time that the Eastern economic community pinned itself down with the term ''integration.'' It has a content which is suitable enough for a community striving for integration, if it coinvolves every economic area of the participant countries into international cooperation. It also sets the institutional framework and economic communication mechanisms for the contemplated integration measures that were then later prepared and introduced step by step in the '70s.

As with any programmatic CMEA document, the Comprehensive Program was also a compromise between the reform-inclined countries whose vision extended into the nebulous future and those countries which would brook no departure from the principles of central administration to make available the requisite economic communication mechanisms for the contemplated integration measures. Therefore, the realization of this farsighted document was bound to suffer the same fate as other programmatic documents in the past. Although the wishes of all the member countries were taken into consideration, only those projects were realized which could be within the systemic framework of the other member countries. The requisite institutions and complex economic mechanisms for carrying out this complex integration program were lacking. The complex projects were reduced to partial measures that were realizable within the existing system.

Reforms in the system had long been an indispensable condition for linking up to the scientific and technical revolution; but they could not be substituted by imports of modern technology from the pioneer countries of the West, and still less be realized by an integration program which could only be effected through a modern international communication system. Oleg Bogomolov, a Soviet member of the Academy of Sciences, lamented the contradiction between the high level of the forces of production and the backward relations of production,[154] but this contradiction could not be surmounted by the collective forces of all the member countries which were suffering under the same contradiction. It should be recalled that the far-sighted integration program was not begun with the wave of reforms attendant on the Prague Spring, but immediately after the armed violence of the Warsaw Pact had put an abrupt end to them.

One point must be clear: contrary to Lavigne's thesis, the Soviet Union did not impose an integration of production as an alternative to the "market integration" proposed by the other CMEA countries, and especially Hungary. Integration of production, i.e., a kind of harmonizing of the national economic policies of the member countries, is considered a higher stage of integration in the CMEA as well in comparison with an "integration of trade."[155] But a market integration could hardly be an adequate model for the planned economies with their different steering mechanisms. Even in Hungary, where the term "market socialism" was coined and where broad decentralization measures had been implemented, there are very few people who could imagine that a market integration in the CMEA would have any prospects of success under the given conditions of the system, or who entertained any illusions that little Hungary could impose its "market ideas" on the CMEA giants. The differences of opinion with regard to the development of cooperation were not alternative options of integration of production versus market integration, but rather regarded differences in respect of steering methods between the advocates of direct links between production units of the member countries on the basis of economic mechanisms and those who regarded internationally agreed-upon specialization and trade agreements as more feasible given the centralized national steering systems. The reform-inclined countries, or rather their reform-inclined representatives in CMEA bodies, are to be thanked that the Comprehensive Program contains such instruments for integrating production as direct ties between production units of the member countries or expansion of non-quotaed and multilateral foreign trade and above all the stages plan for developing currency and credit relations which was to have led to partial convertibility of the national units of currency and the collective CMEA currency via economically realistic exchange rates. The countries who have remained true to the conservative central administration system, above all the Soviet Union, wished, on the other hand, to advance the integration of production stipulated in the Comprehensive Program by means of organizational and institutional measures. They saw to it that the Comprehensive Program stipulates explicitly such international steering methods as consultations on planned socioeconomic developments and scientific and technical measures which exceed the capacities of the individual countries and must be carried through with the assistance of others, as well as consultations on long-term economic developments, on economic policy, and on planning and administration methods of the broadly conceived coordination of the five-year plans and the longer-term plans. These measures were to comprise the most important economic sectors. In science and technology, a joint planning was to have been introduced and measures, jointly agreed upon, were to receive a legally binding form in international agreements. One important institutional and organization measure was the expansion of international enterprises which, however, continued to be regarded as coordination centers rather than as production units with a mixed international ownership.

Economic development had, however, come so far that even perfected administration and planning methods were no longer sufficient to provide a place to the progressive worldwide scientific and technical revolution. Institutional and organizational measures proved to be less useful for introducing a broad cooperation in international CMEA relations than in the domestic sphere. What was lacking was an executive body with executive functions which would have been able to give jointly reached decisions the binding status of a directive. The countries bound to centrally administrated methods prevented the development of the economic mechanisms contemplated in the Comprehensive Program. The institutional and organization measures, on the other hand, proved to be inadequate for establishing total economic integration. After the period of disintegration between 1970 and 1974, the Comprehensive Program was reduced to a feasible partial program in 1979 in direct connection with the adjustments made in price-forming practices in the same year. The victims were the big modernization projects which could not be realized within the given narrow international communications framework.

A progressive disintegration instead of comprehensive integration

All the CMEA countries very quickly recognized the small chances of any impulses coming from the Comprehensive Program, forged with such great

Table 16

CMEA share in total exports and imports, 1970 and 1974 (%)

	1970		1974	
	Exports	Imports	Exports	Imports
Bulgaria	75.8	73.0	72.9	68.0
Czechoslovakia	64.7	63.8	62.0	60.1
GDR	68.6	66.1	64.8	57.6
Poland	60.5	65.8	53.0	42.3
Romania	50.3	48.3	36.5	32.9
Hungary	61.8	62.3	63.4	54.9
USSR	54.3	57.0	47.8	50.1

Source: Statisticheskii ezhegodnik stran-chlenov SEV, Moscow, 1975.

effort and so many mutual concessions, for stimulating scientific and technical progress. The international division of labor received a stimulus in relations with the industrial states of the West, and not within the CMEA. The CMEA share in total exports of the member countries decreased from 61.3% to 54% between 1970 and 1974. But there were considerable differences among the individual countries, as may be seen from Table 16.

Hungary was the only country which increased the CMEA share in total exports, although its share in total imports had decreased by 7.4%. The discrepancies between the CMEA share in Soviet exports (47.8%) and imports (50.1%) reflected the difference in oil prices in Eastern and Western trade in 1974. Poland and Romania had more radically redirected their commodity flows toward trade with the West than the other CMEA countries, and imports more than exports. The CMEA share in Poland's imports and exports decreased by 23.5% and 7.5%, respectively, between 1970 and 1974. Therefore Poland and Romania experienced greater payment difficulties than the other countries and in the early '80s were forced to suspend their debt service.

1975: an interlude in relations between the Soviet Union and its CMEA partners

There was already talk in the smaller countries of the CMEA of a progressive disintegration, but then the unexpected oil crisis occurred which brought about a radical turn in relations between the Soviet Union and its allies. What the Soviet Union had been unable to achieve in long years of negotiations, namely, a higher price for petroleum products sufficient to cover costs, became possible as a result of the price shock of October 1973 on the basis of developments on the world market and not on the basis of a special regulation. It must be taken into account that the price formula approved by the 9th Council meeting in 1958 had regarded the "average world market price, freed of cyclical and other extra-economic influence," as an interim solution which was to be applied until an "intrinsic" price basis, one resting on internal costs and price relations, could be determined. From the very beginning, the Soviet Union had been as dissatisfied with the relatively low prices for raw materials and fuels determined on the basis of existing world market ratios as Bulgaria and Romania were with their relatively low prices for farm products. These CMEA countries were in fact the most zealous advocates of an "intrinsic" price basis in intra-CMEA trade. Discussions went on for ten years on how to determine this price basis, but finally stopped. The price policy in the individual member countries, which was shaped autonomously, totally shielded from the outside world, was unable to establish an appropriate basis for price formation, especially the heavily subsidized prices of the Soviet Union. Although the 1971 Comprehensive Program had encouraged further research, it did specify that the member countries should for the time being apply the currently valid principles of price formation. The Bucharest price formula of 1958 served therefore as a basis for intra-CMEA prices for the five-year period between 1965 and 1970 (the average world market prices for the period from 1960 to 1964 were used as the basis for determination) and for the five-year period from 1971 to 1975 (the world market prices for 1965 to 1969 were used as the basis for price determination).

The price increases brought about by the oil-producing countries and supported by the Soviet Union enabled it to charge higher prices for oil in intra-CMEA trade compared with the price which it could obtain if it had its own "intrinsic" cost-covering price basis. In October 1973, however, the jointly agreed-upon price basis was still in force and would not expire until the end of 1975. Since the Soviet Union was able immediately to take advantage of the outstanding possibility of raising its oil prices in world trade, a tremendous gap arose between the oil price charged in trade with the West and the actual price of oil in trade with the East. Pressure on the smaller countries grew steadily. But they were able to defend themselves: the legally agreed-upon CMEA prices retained their validity until the end of the five-year period but the point was made that the Bucharest price formula of 1958 had excluded just such price-forming circumstances that had led to a fourfold increase in the oil price in October 1973, namely, the speculative influence of the world monopoly, i.e., the influence which the oil cartel had brought to bear in October 1973 to raise the low price of oil by an unprecedented amount.

There was no doubt that the international multinationals had depressed the price of oil to an intolerably low level before 1973, and that this price was extremely ill-designed to please the Soviet Union which, because oil deposits were moving further and further into the remote areas of the country, was unable to cover the growing costs of capital investment and extraction. Nor is there any doubt that the multiplication in the price of oil in October 1973 was forced upon the world market by extra-economic factors, i.e., factors which the Bucharest price formula of 1958 wanted to eliminate as a component of price formation.

It should be remembered that in a similar situation, when prices, especially for raw materials, rose rapidly in 1950–1953 as a consequence of the Korean War, the 1950 stop price was used in intra-bloc trade. At that time Josef Stalin was still in power.

The negotiations between the Soviet Union and its allies to find a new price formula lasted a whole year; a compromise was first reached in January 1975. The price basis in force from 1971 to 1975 was taken out of effect one year earlier than had been agreed. The basis itself, a five-year average of world prices, was maintained, but 1975 was made an exception: the basis was to be three years (1972 to 1974) instead of five years as would otherwise be the case. This concession of the smaller countries enabled the Soviet Union to increase its terms of trade with the East by 32.6% in 1975. They were scheduled to increase annually by 8% between 1976 and 1980.[156] The new sliding price formation practice enabled the Soviet Union to bring its oil prices in intra-CMEA trade up to the world level in 1979 (about 65 transferable rubles per ton). But the scissors gap between world market prices and intra-CMEA prices opened again as a result of the renewed price rise. Between 1979 and 1985, the difference had almost completely disappeared again. The price of Soviet oil increased by 249.2% in Poland between 1979 and 1985, but the world market price increased only 150%.[157] The Soviet Union renounced not even a fraction of the world price. When oil prices again began to show a downward trend in 1975, the price formula remained unchanged. Only the period used as a basis of determination was changed, from five to three years, as in 1975.[158] The oil price in intra-bloc trade in 1986 was still 26 US dollars a barrel, while the world price fluctuated between 15 dollars and 10 dollars, and nothing indicated that the resultant losses would be less than the price subsidies of the past ten years.

Soviet price subsidies for the smaller countries and the participation of smaller countries in large Soviet projects

The January 1975 decision of the CMEA Executive Committee enabled the Soviet Union to impose a monopoly price which could be justified by more than mere reasons of profitability upon its CMEA partners, step by step if not immediately. The new price formula agreed upon in early 1975 enabled it also to gradually gain back the price subsidies it had granted in the interim, when the price of oil again began to decrease in the mid-'80s. This gave rise to the question of whether these had been price subsidies in the strict sense. The question was answered affirmatively only by those observers who had regarded the development of the price of oil separately from other important events, apart from, above all, the adjustment made also in 1975 in customary forms of cooperation. The insider Laszlo Csaba evaluated the situation differently: ''At this stage it became evident that this form of cooperation (investment contribution, A. Z.) is in fact a substitute for the market clearing function of the price mechanism."[159] The insider Csaba is averse to see price developments apart from the newly introduced forms of cooperation, and justifiably as well, since 1975 marked a turning point in relations between the Soviet Union and other countries of Eastern Europe, not only because of the price adjustment, but also because of the decision taken at the 29th Council session in Budapest on "The multilateral community plan of integration measures in the CMEA." The relationship between the adjustments in price and cooperation made in this same year of 1975 gives a somewhat different picture of the advantages and disadvantages of economic relations between the Soviet Union and its allies from that which emerges when these two determining cooperation factors of the '70s are viewed in isolation.

The discussion on the terms of trade between the Soviet Union and its CMEA partners has a relatively long history. It grew in importance at the end of the '50s and early '60s when Horst Menderhausen[160] and Franklyn Holzman[161] made public their opinions on the advantages and disadvantages. The trade conditions of the first Stalinist period were thoroughly analyzed in the first part of this book. Khrushchev had made an essential adjustment in the terms of trade which had been unthinkable for the smaller countries. Between 1955 and 1975, intra-CMEA foreign trade prices were formed under the influence of the low world market prices for raw materials and fuels. The terms of trade were therefore unfavorable for the Soviet Union. Edward A. Hewett calculated that between 1955 and 1974 the Soviet Union had to accept a deterioration of 20% in the terms of trade. Hewett asserts that the reasons for this were that the Soviet Union was willing to pay higher prices for machinery and raw materials to accelerate specialization in machinery construction. However, this argument is not very convincing. Soviet terms of trade with the East really did deteriorate, but above all owing to the low prices for raw materials and fuels on the world market, and shifts in the structure of the range of goods offered, even as it was proving more and more difficult to find an analogous price on the world market.[162] But even these are not sufficient to explain the extremely complicated, barter-like conditions of mutual CMEA trade, in which the motive of supply plays a much greater role than any cost-benefit analysis. Terms of trade are difficult to calculate for total trade, but the determinations are already complicated enough for some commodity groups. This is indeed evident from Table 17 of Soviet "price subsidies" in trade with the East, calculated by Marrese and Vanous, and by Raimund Dietz.

Although both estimates are based on sound premises, the results are different. Although the authors expended considerable effort in determining the "subsidies," the new information they come up with is limited and can hardly be seen as an evaluation of the advantages and disadvantages of trade between the Soviet Union and its allies. Marie Lavigne and Raimund Dietz justly point out that the experts and economic policymakers in the East do not make much of the "Soviet subsidies." The Soviet representative in the CMEA Executive Committee,

Table 17

"Price subsidies" in Eastern trade in 1973–1978
(in millions of transferable rubles)

	Statistics from: Marrese and Vanous	Statistics from: Raimund Dietz
1973	1019	251
1974	5163	2704
1975	5065	2007
1976	5906	2287
1977	6150	1731
1978	5851	889

Source: Raimund Dietz, *Advantages/Disadvantages in USSR Trade with Eastern Europe*, Report 97 of the Vienna Institute for Comparative Economic Studies, August 1984, Table 12.

K. Katushev, who should know best, estimated Soviet price reductions in the years 1976 to 1980 at 5 billion transferable rubles.[163] But, however high or low Soviet subsidies to its CMEA partners may be, the advantages and disadvantages of its economic relations should not be evaluated without taking into account the costs of participation of the smaller countries in Soviet major projects. The participation in the trapping of new deposits of raw materials and fuels or in the ambitious pipeline was justified in that it guaranteed supplies of scarce goods for some time. As a capital allocation, however, it was certainly not favorable for the small countries; indeed, it even incurred losses. The project-earmarked credits give the lender only a nominal interest rate, as van Brabant pointed out, usually 2% annually, and this is much lower than the marginal capital productivity in the domestic economy. On the other hand, as van Brabant pointed out, the credits are granted in kind, in machinery, equipment, consumer goods, and materials, which for the planned economies, with their chronic shortages of goods, must certainly mean less resources for domestic capital investment projects or consumption. In some cases the smaller countries were also forced to borrow on the world market through the International Investment Bank to procure up-to-date technology, large piping, etc. The Orenburg pipeline is a good example of this form of participation on the part of the smaller countries. This 2750 km long pipeline, with a diameter of 1420 mm, was constructed through the cooperation of seven CMEA countries and the International Investment Bank. The heads of government of the participating countries signed the agreement in 1974 in Sofia. The project was realized with material means, technology, and construction of Bulgaria, the GDR, Poland, Czechoslovakia, and Hungary. Each country delivered building materials and participated in the construction either independently or in cooperation with other countries. Romania participated with financial funds in the construction of a complete refinery in Orenburg; the pumping stations were equipped with modern turbines and compressors.[164] The International Investment Bank provided credits raised on the world market to an amount of 1950 million dollars. The Soviet Union was to begin repayments of the credits with gas deliveries in 1978. Deliveries were to reach 15.5 billion cubic meters annually after the projected capacity was reached in 1980.[165] The CMEA partner countries were to participate with 3.5 billion transferable rubles of the total value, 6.5 billion transferable rubles, of the major projects built in the Soviet Union between 1976 and 1980.[166]

If the Soviet representatives in the CMEA are of the opinion that their country is a kind of raw materials colony for its CMEA partners, Laszlo Csaba is thoroughly justified in commenting that the foreign trade policy currently in operation, namely, Soviet raw materials and fuels in exchange for finished products from the smaller countries, is a product more of economic considerations than of altruistic ones. We might round out this opinion by saying that the heavy industry model, oriented toward a considerable material-intensive input, with gigantic steel foundries in every small CMEA country, is also no invention of Eastern and South-eastern Europe.

The resolutions of the 29th Council session of 1975 in Budapest introduced a new turn in relations between the Soviet Union and its allies in the context of the price adjustment made in that same year. In particular, it redefined the functions of the previous isolated bilateral agreements on participation into a multilateral concern of the CMEA. The Soviet Union had accumulated some experience in relations with Czechoslovakia and the GDR in this respect: on September 23, 1966, the Soviet Union agreed to supply 5 million tons of crude oil between 1973 and 1984 at a constant price of 15 transferable rubles per ton to Czechoslovakia to pay off a credit of 500 million transferable rubles which was to be granted in the form of goods (70% machinery, 16% construction materials, and 14% industrial consumption goods). A similar compensation agreement was concluded in April 1967 with the GDR. The size of the loan, 500 million transferable rubles, the delivery, namely 5 million tons of crude oil, and the price of 15 transferable rubles per ton were the same as in the case of Czechoslovakia, and the interest rate of 2% per annum was also of the same order.[167]

The 29th Council session of 1975 reduced the Comprehensive Program of 1971 to feasible dimensions. The goals of integration, which could only have been realized by general functioning communication mechanisms and by organic cooperation relations among economic units in the production process, were to concentrate in one area, albeit a very important area, namely, major joint projects in the energy sector. These were to be built mainly in the remote regions of the Soviet Union, in Siberia, and in the Far East, with the aid of the smaller countries. Of course one could apply the term "subsidy" in view of the material and financial participation, e.g., in the form of loans in foreign currency and lower interest rates. But this time it was a subsidy of the smaller countries to the Soviet Union. And then one might attempt to determine the scope of the material and financial assistance provided by the smaller countries and then compare this with Soviet "price subsidies." However, this would be meaningless since even these two determining factors in CMEA events of the '70s are not sufficient to ascertain the advantages and disadvantages of relations in economic policy between the Soviet Union and its allies. But a gigantic composite factor, which towers above all else, namely, the costs of defense, with considerable mutual deliveries at arbitrarily set prices, is left out of consideration. Differentiated allocations in this area are capable of overshadowing all the advantages and disadvantages in every other area of cooperation within the CMEA.

The adjustment in price-setting practices introduced in 1975 in connection with the decisions of the 29th Council session introduced a new phase in relations between the Soviet Union and its CMEA partners; as the Soviet economist J. Motorin put it, this Congress "made possible the expanded production of raw materials and fuels solely on the basis of long-term plans with participation of the CMEA countries interested."[168]

Of course the smaller countries were not happy with this form of cooperation. Kalman Pecsi, Hungary's expert and, at the time, department head in the CMEA Research Institute, wrote: "This type of cooperation can lead to a growth of barter in CMEA trade, where wheat will be traded against crude oil or other raw materials," and "if this form of trade becomes the rule, barter transactions will expand to become an instrument of restricted foreign trade."[169] Kazimierz Barcikowski, member of Poland's Politburo, called attention to the considerable deliveries of raw materials to the fraternal countries in 1984: 14 million tons of coal, 11 million tons of coke, 17,000 tons of copper and 1.8 million tons of sulphur, and pointed out that "the material means of the People's Republic of Poland are limited and the extraction of raw materials is becoming more and more capital-intensive. We cannot maintain production capacity and consequently deliveries of raw materials at the old level if the interested partners do not themselves participate with capital investments. We are counting on them especially in the construction of a coal mine in the Lublin Basin and in the creation of new capacities for the production of sulphur."[170] Poland has been seeking the participation of the CMEA partners in the tapping of the huge brown coal deposits in the Belchatow region and later the hard coal deposits in the Lublin Basin since the early '60s, but without success. Poland's interests were disregarded in the 13 major projects of the period between 1981 and 1985, e.g., the nuclear power station in Khmelnitskii and Konstantinovka in the Soviet Union, the high tension line from the Ukraine to Rzeszow in Poland, and a second line from Romania to Bulgaria, the fodder plant in Mozir in the Soviet Union. The 40th Council session of 1985 was the first one to address the question of participation in Poland's coal projects.

The 29th Council session at Budapest in 1975 marked a total victory for the advocates of institutional and organization integration instruments over the proponents of economic steering mechanisms. Henceforth the joint integration projects were to be considered organic parts of the national economic plans. Non-quota trade, proposed by the reformers, was rejected in favor of a progressive increase of trade in kind within the CMEA division of labor, e.g., compensation agreements in the form of participation of the smaller countries in the tapping of Soviet raw materials and fuels in payment for additional deliveries. This form of cooperation, together with the dramatic price rise, raised the share of raw materials and fuels in Soviet exports to Eastern and South-eastern Europe to one third to a half within a short time.

Foreign trade relations in the CMEA followed the principle of exchanging better goods for better goods and inferior goods for inferior goods rather than the principle of higher prices for goods of higher quality and lower prices for goods of lower quality. Laszlo Csaba, commenting on the '70s, said: "This was a period in which the concept of hard versus soft goods evolved; a second price-substituting system of devaluation became established in which a hard good could only be traded against a similar item, independently of the price of a soft item." And "the crucial point was that there was no longer a price-regulating mechanism (price mark-ups and mark-downs) which make possible the exchange of a product from one quality group for a product of another group, even with a price discount." Csaba's conclusion, which may be seen as an allusion to price developments since 1975, was: "A low price for an undervalued hard product must by definition never bring a loss, since the undervalued hard product will automatically cause a devaluation of the imported good."[171]

The CMEA in the 1980s

**The CMEA will be a community of interests or no
community at all**

The thesis that the advantages and disadvantages of CMEA cooperation was, is, and will continue to be dependent on how relations between the Soviet Union and its allies evolve is certainly not false. Still, the Soviet Union accounts for 70% of the domestic product of the CMEA, and its political dominance determines events in both the CMEA and the Warsaw Pact. But the advantages and disadvantages of the member countries cannot be unequivocally evaluated. The outstanding American experts on Eastern Europe are of the opinion that after the first ten years of exploitation, when most of the countries of Eastern and South-eastern Europe were forced to contribute considerably to the reconstruction of the Soviet Union in the form of variously motivated war reparations, the smaller countries have been beneficiaries rather than losers in their economic relations with the Soviet Union. John C. Campbell, citing Morris Bornstein, asserts that Eastern Europe has exploited Soviet resources since the '50s, although the extent of this exploitation cannot be evaluated.[172] Marrese and Vanous calculated that the Soviet Union had given a price subsidy of a total of 65.280 billion dollars to its allies between 1960 and 1980, with 22.776 billion dollars for fuels.[173] It may be objected that the profits and losses in these unique relations between a superpower and its allies cannot be so easily assessed. The advantages and disadvantages in relations between the Soviet Union and Eastern Europe have varied over the forty years of postwar history: the Eastern Europeans participate, following Soviet wishes, in the huge industrial-military complex, which is of superpower magnitude, and hence vastly exceeds Eastern Europe's needs. The overall concept of development, as well as the intra-CMEA division of labor and mutual exchange of goods between the Soviet Union and its partners in the CMEA and the Warsaw Pact are totally subordinate to this complex. No purely arithmetic cost-benefit analysis would be able to deal adequately with the manifold, complicated relations that are determined to a large extent by political and military motives. The terms of trade that have evolved in the CMEA are a consequence of the agreement, made at the 9th meeting of the CMEA in 1958, that the prices in intra-CMEA trade should be valid for five years. The Soviet Union has never considered itself a victim or even at a disadvantage. The tremendous monopoly prices for raw materials and fuels in the last twelve years which the Soviet Union has helped to impose upon the world market was gradually forced upon its CMEA partners as well, in contradiction to the provisions of the 9th Council meeting. Soviet "price subsidies" were partly offset by favorable terms of participation for the small countries in the major projects and since 1985, Soviet subsidies have been replaced by the subsidies of the smaller countries. The drain of Soviet raw materials and fuels is a consequence of the socialist iron and steel concept of development taken over by the Eastern Europeans and the curious "capitalist" price basis in "socialist" foreign trade is a consequence of the economic system forged in the Soviet Union which condemns the planned economies to setting their own prices autonomously, hermetically sealed off from the world market. The Soviet Union demanded the best possible goods in payment for its raw materials and fuels, and moreover this demand acquired the status of a directive in accordance with the provisions of the CMEA summit in June 1984. The small countries have of course learned how to defend their economic interests over the course of time, but the Soviet Union is not prepared to sacrifice its economic interests as a price to pay for political and military solidarity, and has itself learned with time what it can demand from the individual member countries. However, it too must, after many bitter lessons, take into account that this solidarity can only be assured if the smaller countries are able to perceive tangible evidence of the much-extolled superiority of the socialist commonwealth. The new Soviet leadership under Gorbachev seems to have a concrete concept for the future division of labor between the Soviet Union and its allies, and the new Kremlin leader indeed has quite openly put forth this new concept in the recent Party congresses in the Soviet Union and the fraternal countries, as well as on other occasions. The following sections will examine this concept in due detail, but first a brief retrospective look will be indispensable.

The Eastern bloc torn between a community and a sphere of hegemonic influence

The expansion of the Soviet sphere of influence to Eastern and South-eastern Europe has nothing to do with carrying socialism further or with the realization of the idea of world revolution. At the time when Stalin was considering incorporating Eastern and South-eastern Europe into the Soviet sphere of influence as a consequence of the victory in the Second World War, the Soviet Union was a country, not of utopian socialism, but of a real socialism bearing his name, i.e., a state administered by a huge semi-military bureaucracy to which the whole of industry and agriculture as well as every other social domain without exception was subordinated. Just before the World War, in the pact with the Nazi leader

Hitler, and during World War II, he replaced the exalted ideas of Communism by the ideas of Soviet patriotism, used the once scorned Tsarist heroes as military heroes in Soviet war propaganda, and subjugated the liberated areas of Eastern Europe to the giant Soviet empire, in violation of the Atlantic Charter accepted by him in August 1941. The intention was to surround the Soviet Union with a buffer zone of friendly countries. Since in Stalin's notions of things a friendly country could only be a country with like-thinking and identical system, he proceeded as the German princes in the Middle Ages in accordance with the principle *cuius regio eius religio*. The countries of Eastern and South-eastern Europe were not only converted to "communism," they were also exploited and drawn into Stalin's military-industrial complex. He behaved differently in only one case: Finland was neither converted to Communism, nor was a Soviet Stalinist state and economic system imposed upon it. The memories of 1940, when that small nation country offered a heroic resistance to the giant Soviet army for months were still too fresh in their minds for the Soviets to wish upon themselves a renewed resistance struggle from the Finns after the great victory in the Second World War. It was able in an astonishingly short time to create this huge sphere of influence, to administer it, and to create a national power elite in its own notorious and famous style. It functioned: it did so by recruiting the full-bodied population into the reconstruction of the destroyed economy after the devastating occupation; it regained freedom from the hated occupying power; through the agrarian reform, and through the hope, entertained by many, that the new social order would be better and more prosperous than the semi-feudal authoritarian regime of the interregnum period. Under Stalin, a community of free nations was impossible. The motherland was not free of oppression under his rule, and the sphere of influence commanded by him could also not be free of oppression. The great hope was once again resuscitated by de-Stalinization introduced by Khrushchev. He freed the Eastern countries from the burden of reparations, from deliveries at give-away prices, and institutionalized community existence by revitalizing the CMEA, which Stalin had erected as a political facade, and by the Warsaw Pact, created in 1955. But when the events in East Germany in 1953 and Hungary in 1956 placed the entire community in peril, he ventured a step further than Stalin did when Yugoslavia dissented. And Brezhnev followed Khrushchev's example in 1968 in the Prague Spring.

Stalin's epigones were compelled to look on impotently as Yugoslavia, followed by Albania, and especially China, countries which had carried out the historical, economic, and social transformations with their own forces, left the community. Without wishing essentially to change the system, they manifested their readiness to impart legitimate forms of community to the sphere of influence, to broaden the margin of maneuver for the leaders of Eastern Europe, and to distribute the costs of maintaining the huge empire more justly, but they were never willing to abandon Stalin's legacy in Eastern Europe. Clear limits were set to the extent of freedom allowed: the monopoly on power of the ruling Communist Party must remain intact and anchored in the Constitution as the state law; no institutionalized ideological pluralism was to be allowed, and above all the unquestioning loyalty to both community institutions, the CMEA, and the Warsaw Pact, had to remain intact. Brezhnev's thesis of "limited sovereignty" was never presented as an official state theory, just as earlier Khrushchev's secret report to the 20th Party Congress was never represented as an official Party or state document. To what extent sovereignty was limited and freedom was tolerated in East Europe was made clear in *Pravda* articles of September 26, November 13, and December 4, 1968, just after the smashing of the Prague Spring, as well as in the first years of the Gorbachev era in the *Pravda* articles of June 15 and June 21, 1985, which were not presented as the official standpoint either. That standpoint, however, was put forth in clear and unmistakable terms by Mikhail Gorbachev in his inauguration speech at the funeral of his predecessor Konstantin Chernenko: "The countries of Eastern Europe will remain a cohesive and irrevocable component of the Eastern community."

However much the political, economic, and social system of Eastern Europe may or must bear the unmistakable Soviet birthmarks, it would be an unpardonable mistake not to acknowledge the margin of freedom that had been purchased at such a high price: under Wladyslaw Gomulka, Poland gave permanent status to private peasant agriculture, and during the period in which he was in power the church regained its status as the ideological and spiritual superpower which it later was able to expand further. Poland had achieved a status with regard to plurality of opinion and speech that was the envy of the entire Eastern bloc. Romania's declaration of emancipation of April 1964 has also retained its force after many setbacks, and has been reinforced with new independent ventures. In 1968, Hungary began its noteworthy changes in the traditional economic system with its unmistakable positive implications throughout all of social relations, leaving a terrain of independent activity to the economic management of the country which created a new climate in economic management (in relations between it and the workforce) without altering the fundamentals of the system. Experts in East and West continued to conjecture whether the deviations introduced in Eastern Europe from the original model have enjoyed the blessings of the Soviet leadership or were at least within its limits of tolerance. But the US expert Sarah Terry is probably right that the Soviet contribution to the reforms introduced in Eastern Europe in the '60s was not in the form of a prior plan of implementation, but in fact the reforms were introduced in the absence of such a plan.[174] Nonetheless neither Poland's private agriculture and the universal influence of the church on public opinion, nor Romania's independent foreign policy, nor the extent of decentralization of economic powers or private initiative in Hungary, fit into the traditional Soviet system, and moreover are not to the liking of the Soviet leadership, which at most just tolerates them. However, they also show clearly that there are no clearly defined limits to Soviet tolerance, that it can be extended, and that above all untransgressable limits are set to the freedom of the smaller countries only in fundamental questions of the social system and their relations to the motherland of real socialism, and that all other remaining matters can be left to the populations of these countries and their leaders to decide. The considerable differences between the way power is exercised in Czechoslovakia, Romania, Hungary, or Poland are the best evidence that the tolerance or intolerance of the Soviet leadership are not the only factors which determine freedom or its limits in Eastern Europe. The events in Poland between August 1980 and December 13, 1981, i.e., after the signing of the Sczeczin and Gdansk agreements between the government and the free trade union Solidarity also show that Soviet tolerance of far-ranging transformations in the system and the stay of execution which the Soviet leadership is willing to accept in the bargain have become greater and larger than was the case at the time of the Prague Spring. But it should also not be overlooked that references to the limits of Soviet tolerance are often used by those in power in Eastern Europe to restrain the zeal of reformers. Zdzislaw Rurarz, who resigned his position as Ambassador to Japan after the state of emergency was evoked in Poland, and sought asylum, reported on how Edward Gierek rejected his reform proposals with the comment that a few reform projects could be implemented only if one were alone, because the Soviet leadership would reject them on the pretext that their purpose was to promote capitalism in Poland.[175] However, this argument was only an excuse for the Party leader, overthrown by the workers' uprising in 1980, who had never shown any serious intention of introducing genuine economic reform. At about the same time Hungary's reformers introduced their far-ranging reform, and continued it uninterrupted on the basis of internal developments without showing any concern for Soviet praise or censure.

Gierek's predecessor, Gomulka, ventured the most radical reform of his time in office, namely, the abandonment of the collectivization of agriculture, and restored to the church its status in society, but retracted the decentralization of economic activities and the rights of self-determination of factory workforces, begun in the early days of his leadership. It was by no means because of pressure from the Soviet leadership or his fear of it, but because of the logic of his authoritarian style of leadership, which he was disinclined to restrain by delegating any decision-making powers to the micro-level. But private agriculture or the challenge posed to official ideology by the omnipotent Polish church, with its extensive and self-aware hierarchy, is certainly a greater incursion into the fortress of the Soviet system than decentralized decision-making powers in a planned economy, which always in every instance leaves strategical decisions to the central level. The peoples and the governments of Eastern and South-eastern Europe have only themselves to thank for the greater range of freedom they have acquired, just as it is they who are responsible for restrictions on freedoms in society and in the economy. The total standstill in the reform movement in

Czechoslovakia and its devastating consequences for economic and social development are certainly not the work of the Soviet leadership. Both Khrushchev and Gorbachev knew that the planned economies had to be reformed if they wished to participate in world-wide scientific and technical progress. They also know that the reforms that had been introduced in the Soviet Union and the other Eastern countries would fail because they were half-hearted. The most radical and far-sighted reform, namely, the economic reform of the Prague Spring, was put down with brute force and Hungary's reform is much too radical for Gorbachev. The Soviet leaders also know the exorbitant price which they must pay for maintaining the existing unreformed economic and political system, and they no longer wish to pay this price, which is poor-quality goods, and low productivity of labor and capital. But Gorbachev as well, the most dynamic and far-sighted leader of the post-Stalin era, is not willing, at least not yet, to introduced reforms which could call into question the political universalism of the ruling Party apparatus. However, it should be noted in passing that in every phase of development when the Soviet Union's economic policy found itself at a crossroads the ideas of the well-known Western experts on Eastern Europe concerning the possibilities of reform in the Soviet Union went far beyond the reforms imagined by the Soviet leaders. Michel Tatu, one of the best observers of the Soviet scene, predicted in 1966 that the introduction of parliamentary methods of government seemed to be inevitable in the Soviet Union.[176] But even today there is slight chance that this prediction will be fulfilled. The same can be said about the prognosis of the world-famous currency expert Franz Pick in 1973: "In the not too distant future, the Soviet unit could become more convertible than the mini-dollar."[177] Finally, a number of notable US experts on Eastern Europe have ventured the rather implausible conjecture that Mikhail Gorbachev was contemplating a new edition of the New Economic Policy introduced by Lenin in 1921.

Close economic links to strengthen cohesiveness

Of course the Soviet Union would never permit Marxism-Leninism to fall into disrepute as the ideology of the community and a legitimation of its sphere of influence. However, it has been forced to look on as the purported ideological unity has degenerated into a thin mantle covering the ideologically totally alien conglomeration of peoples in its empire. The Soviet Union itself has replaced Marxist-Leninist ideology, loved so little by so few, by a primitive pride of the unmistakable achievements of Mother Russia, and has used this to justify the costly trappings of a superpower; but the leaders of the small countries have found themselves less and less able to find an ideological or any other kind of legitimation for their participation in the imperial costs. "Socialism" in Angola, Ethiopia, Nicaragua, or South Yemen, which are bases of influence for the Soviet Union within its constellation as a superpower, is more cause of sorrow than of joy for the peoples of Eastern Europe. They would like to be rid of this exotic "socialism" and save the costs of protection, estimated at 6% of the Soviet national income, for use for other more useful purposes within the Eastern community.

The legitimacy which Khrushchev created for the Eastern community by, for instance, getting rid of the discriminating conditions of socialist division of labor for the smaller countries, suffered considerable damage during the Brezhnev era. Many factors played a crucial role here: the brutal smashing of the Prague Spring with the assistance of four other Eastern countries and with it the hope for an untroubled socialism with a human face; or the unmistakable failure of the Comprehensive Program of 1971. The economic integration it had envisaged has not only made no progress, it has even suffered a setback through an expansion of the division of labor with the Western countries. The Eastern community, which has never had any great power of attraction, faded not only because the economic mechanisms that had been targeted had never become a reality, but also because the community projects contemplated were mainly on Soviet territory. John Campbell's view that the ends of the community were Soviet ends, and vice versa, and that in practice the question was how the East European allies could best abet the implementation of Soviet policy, either through the Warsaw Pact, the CMEA, or individually,[178] was truer of the Brezhnev era than of Khrushchev's regime. The people of Eastern Europe, who had enthusiastically entered into economic cooperation with the Soviet Union, inclined more and more to the conclusion that it had only one aim, namely, incorporating the national economies of the smaller countries into the vast economy of the Soviet Union and to make them dependent on it for raw materials and fuels. The opinion was frequent wherever anyone was permitted to write about it that the price explosion in October 1973 had been made possible only by the Soviet Union's support of the oil-producing countries, and it was regretted that the CMEA representatives had proven themselves unable to negotiate better prices for oil and petroleum products. It was unacceptable that the Soviet Union should demand the best goods for its crude oil from the other Eastern countries at a time when they were forced to cut back on their Western imports owing to their heavy indebtedness to the West, with grave consequences for economic growth and consumption. The Eastern countries, which had an interest in detente, considered the provisions of the Helsinki Conference of August 1975 to be a grave setback for their aspirations to independence. Dissatisfaction grew as during the course of time it became apparent that the de facto recognition of their belonging to the Soviet sphere of influence was not compensated by the freedoms promised in Basket 3 of the Helsinki Agreement, and that their share in the arms race was steadily increasing, instead of diminishing, owing to Brezhnev's project of catching up with and surpassing the United States. The progressive circles of Eastern Europe looked on with growing displeasure as the Soviet Union, after the defeated uprisings in the GDR in 1953, Hungary in 1956, and Czechoslovakia in 1968, forced the millions-strong Solidarity movement in

Poland to its knees five years after the Helsinki Agreement, with undisguised threats, military exercises, etc., and ultimately brought it to a standstill with the hands of the Polish military without the Helsinki Agreement being activated or annulled.

Poland's mass uprising and the way it was combated without direct intervention was without a doubt the greatest and most instructive lesson in the recent history of the Eastern community. It showed the resolve to regard the Eastern community primarily as a military alliance and to treat it accordingly, and that under no circumstances was the Soviet Union prepared to leave the destinies of the countries of Eastern Europe, which they had incorporated into its sphere of influence in the aftermath of World War II, in the hands of the popular masses. At the Congress of the United Polish Workers Party, held in June 1986, Mikhail Gorbachev made it clearer even than Brezhnev had done after the smashing of the Prague Spring that no attempt by an Eastern country to go its own way would be tolerated. Nevertheless one is unable to agree with the opinion of Zygmunt Zagorski, the American expert on Eastern Europe, that this position of the Kremlin leader was a proclamation of a new Gorbachev doctrine that would be harsher than the Brezhnev doctrine.[179] There has been no other doctrine in the Soviet Union from Lenin down to Gorbachev, and there has been no other practice than that of the old Russian superpower, engaged in expanding and maintaining the Russian state. The ideology and the motivation have changed: Russia's victorious Revolution behaved in the northern Caucasus and the Ukraine in 1918 in the same way as Khrushchev in 1953 or 1956 in the GDR and Hungary, or Brezhnev in 1968 in Czechoslovakia. But the lesson of Poland is not only that it showed how a resolute mass rebellion can be defeated by national or hegemonic power, but also to whom the heart of the second largest nation of the Eastern bloc belongs. The ideology of the rebels in 1981–1982 was more Christian socialist than real socialist, just as that of the rebels of 1863. The resistance was broken, but the moral and spiritual strength of broad layers of the population was not. It was also brought home to the other leaders of Eastern Europe that even accepting the inevitability of their subordination to the "geopolitical factor," their links with the people could subsist only so long as the people regarded them as true defenders of their economic interest. Soviet sociologists have also often expressed an opinion most clearly expressed by Fedor Burlatskii: "The actual concept of socialism is becoming more complex for every social group considers the socialist ideal in the light of its self-interest, its own cultural standard, and its own philosophy.[180] The Soviet Union which has been unable to establish a stable, cohesive, and efficient system in Eastern Europe in more than thirty years,[181] is also aware that it will be able to derive political and economic benefits from its sphere of influence only if it promotes the common aspects of the alliance and plays down its hegemonic qualities, and that its global strategy will only be successful if the success of the community members is regarded as the success of all.

No ideological internationalism and no international economic mechanisms

Never before were all other external economic factors of integration so emptied of their content as in the '80s. The situation is all the graver in that the community has become richer in its quests for effective means to maintain cohesion and has discarded many illusions. The signs of crisis in the domestic steering mechanisms have had their effects on management of CMEA cooperation. It was realized from the outset that the mechanisms of the international division of labor could be no more efficient than the economic infrastructure of the domestic economies. But that a planned economy was fundamentally introverted was something realized only later when efforts to stimulate CMEA activity were begun in the '60s. The stability of the currencies of the planned economies, much acclaimed as a token of the superiority of socialism, the autonomous price-forming practices, with the heavily subsidized prices shielded from the world market; the exchange rates, which bore no real relationship to other currencies, not even to the currencies of the CMEA countries or to the collective CMEA currency; the systemic inconvertibility of the national currencies, which as means of settlement and payments reduce foreign trade to a kind of barter transaction, created a handicap that has never been overcome or even replaced by other effective steering mechanisms specific to a planned economy. In the '80s, in which CMEA countries have entered into expanded economic relations not only with one another, but also with the other countries of the world, this systemic handicap is becoming more visible than ever before in CMEA history. Two experiences which nullified years of effort on the part of the best CMEA experts were especially instructive: namely, the preparations for realizing Khrushchev's imaginative proposal for implementing a super-plan and establishing a supranational executive body to administer the national economies as one single super-economy, and, secondly, the failure of Brezhnev's Comprehensive Program of 1971, aimed at tailoring economic mechanisms to the level of integration so far achieved. Forms of cooperation were much more broadly conceived than earlier, but no progress was made in developing the mechanisms of integration that had been instituted much earlier, in the Khrushchev era. Nor was any progress made in the practice of price formation or in the development of monetary relations necessary for multilateral trade and the shaping of an international division of labor that began in the production process. Again and again, whenever all other integration factors threatened to break down, the Soviet leaders would turn to economic integration as the one common cementing factor left, supported by those smaller countries which would never be able to bring their relations of production up to par with their level of production: examples that may be mentioned are Khrushchev after the collapse of Stalin's reign of terror, Brezhnev after crushing the Prague Spring, Chernenko and Gorbachev after the onset of an economic recession, and the insolvency of Poland and

Romania, especially after the grave economic and political crisis in Poland in 1980–1982.

There was no proletarian internationalism and there is no socialist internationalism. The inclination of proletarians of all countries towards one another which Marx and later other Communist leaders had evoked is as illusory as the inclination of the countries of Eastern Europe towards one another and all of them together towards the Soviet superpower from whom they had received its particular brand of real socialism. Even more dilute is their love of the developing countries of the CMEA. These are the distant Soviet bases which had nationalized their backward means of production, and established a one-party regime led by a strong man and adopted Marxism-Leninism as their state ideology, although that ideology was little understood by the leaders themselves and was totally alien to the deeply religious Catholics or Moslems of these countries, which however would like to present themselves as "real socialist" in the best meaning of the term and receive the commensurate military and economic help from their new sponsors.

Socialist internationalism has become a vacuous term. As ineffective as it is empty, it is replaced by a naked, sometimes violent nationalism, by totally forgotten ideologies, above all by the ideology of the Catholic or Protestant religion, which is enjoying a greater popularity in Poland, but also in a number of other Eastern countries, than was the case before the establishment of Marxist-Leninist ideology as the state ideology, ergo the state religion. The most violent and chauvinistic nationalism is more pronounced there than anywhere else, since the borders that were drawn after World War II are satisfactory to few: about half of Hungarians live either in Romania or in Czechoslovakia, many Germans live in Romania or in Poland, but want to emigrate to the Federal Republic of Germany rather than to the neighboring GDR; Polish resentment, while still alive, is addressed more to the fraternal GDR than to the Federal Republic, from which they can expect more, even much more economic aid than from the East Germans. During the economic and political crisis of 1980–1982, the GDR had practically sealed off its borders, previously open, to Poland's "tourists," while millions of packages, food, and other consumer goods streamed in from West Germany. The Romanians have never forgotten the amputation of their state territory by the Soviet Union, which occupied Bukovina, rich in sugar, in 1940, with the beautiful city of Chernovitze, and the larger part of Bessarabia with the beloved city of Kishinev, after World War II on the pretext of reunification with the Soviet Republic of the Ukraine or Bessarabia. Nor can the Poles forgive the fact that Lemberg—Leopolis Semper fidelis—is no longer Polish. Marxism-Leninism continues to be presented as the ideology of the community, but for the broad layers of the population of East Europe it is all the saints of the new and old testaments which count, not the protagonists of their postwar history, who quickly fell into disrepute. The courageous and evil generals and sublime or nefarious kings and ecclesiastical princes are receiving a new life in the dust-covered encyclopedias which suddenly have acquired a better memory for the half-forgotten heroes of their glorious histories; GDR historians are also zealously returning to the traditions of the once so reviled Prussian king Frederick the Great, whose monument is being restored at considerable cost. The 500th anniversary of Martin Luther was more solemnly celebrated than the 100th anniversary of the death of Karl Marx, the father of socialism. The 100th anniversary of Ernst Bloch, who resumed his scientific career after World War II in East Berlin, and ended it in Gottingen, and had something to say to both parts of his fatherland, was solemnly celebrated as if the disobedient Bloch had been a faithful Marxist and not a dissident. In the GDR people still tell the popular joke that the Marxist legacy was very unjustly distributed between the two parts of Germany since the West Germans got Capital but the East Germans got the Communist Manifesto.

May 3, Constitution Day, is still dear to Polish hearts. On that day they have celebrated for almost two hundred years the most progressive constitution of the times, which was created in 1791 under the influence of the great French Revolution, although it had been absolished as an official holiday after World War II because of the reminder of the struggle against the Russian occupation at the time. However, it is still celebrated two days earlier, on May 1, as the state holiday of the workers; and 150,000 Czechs and Slovaks spontaneously celebrated the one-thousandth anniversary of Cyril and Methodius, shouting out praise for the pope Wojtyla and not allowing representatives of the Prague government to speak.

As those before him, Gorbachev stresses the integrity of the Eastern bloc which, as he says, must be irreversible. The majority of the population of Eastern Europe have never had any illusions about the true content of this undesired community. They have never understood the fact that they were liberated only to fall into a new dependence to create a cordon of security for a superpower whose borders stretch 67,000 kilometers and necessarily became an issue of superpower policy. And indeed they understand it even less in these times of strategical weapons, long-range missiles, which can bring death without any intermediate way-stations to the most remote corners of the globe. The new social order has never been able to convince them on its own behalf. The surfeit of propaganda has had the opposite effect. Only resignation, the hopelessness and dead end of any resistance, and the growing conviction that neither detente nor an open confrontation between East and West could bring emancipation holds this community together which is disliked or even hated but from which there can be no leaving. Gorbachev proclaims ideological unity but he knows that reliance on ideology is a thing of the past. He would like, therefore, like Khrushchev before him, to establish the irreversibility of this alliance by an interlocking and interlinking network of economic relations, by making the economies of Eastern Europe dependent on the Soviet Union in a way which would make "every separatist attempt the equivalent of a national catastrophe."[182]

The Soviet Union has come closer to this goal under Gorbachev than ever before in the history of the Eastern bloc. The mutual dependency for supplies, created by the imposed iron-and-steel concept of development, was made even deeper by the price explosion in 1973, abetted by the Soviet Union. In two decades, between 1960 and 1980, the consumption of hydrocarbons in East Europe increased by eightfold, while energy consumption increased by 150%. The share of hydrocarbons in the energy balance sheet increased from 14% to 40% in the same period. Eastern Europe was transformed from a net exporter to an importer of one-third of its energy needs, namely, in the form of crude oil and natural gas, 90% of which comes from the Soviet Union. But the value of the hydrocarbons imported from the Soviet Union has increased by almost eighteenfold by the dramatic price increases.[183] Between 1974 and 1980 the volume of Soviet exports to the countries of Eastern Europe increased from 8,795 million transferable rubles to 20,919 million transferable rubles, including the value of fuels from 1,577 to 8,585 million transferable rubles and other non-food raw materials and semi-finished products from 3,185 million to 5,478 million transferable rubles. In the period between 1971 and 1973 the countries of Eastern Europe had a surplus of 1.7 billion transferable rubles in their trade with the Soviet Union, but between 1974 and 1980 they had built up a cumulative deficit of 6 billion transferable rubles, and this figure almost doubled in the first half of the '80s[184] despite the fact that the six countries of Eastern Europe increased their exports to the Soviet Union from 8,600 million transferable rubles in 1974 to 19,095 million transferable rubles in 1980.

The Soviet Union has achieved its objective of binding the smaller countries of Eastern Europe more closely to its own economic structures and has involved them in implementing its major projects, but it has still not been able to transform this achievement into real values. In early 1975 its CMEA partners declared themselves willing to pay exorbitant prices for fuels imported from the Soviet Union, but they were unable to raise the necessary money for this. The cutbacks in imports from the West had a negative effect on production, and this in turn had repercussions on the export program which was already meager. Although the aim was clear, the means necessary to achieve this aim were unclear. Khrushchev's concept of a supereconomic plan and a supranational executive body had been abandoned once and for all, not only because, as generally claimed, of Romania's declaration of emancipation on April 26, 1964, and its subsequent policy of independence, but because of the unwillingness of all the other Eastern countries to adopt a "uniform" international socialist economic policy which would inevitably have conflicted with their own ambitious national plans. The international economic bureaucracy which was created in the meantime is certainly not small, but it has been unable to develop into an international administrative executive board.

**Friedrich von Hayek's opinion that it is
presumptuous of men to aspire to manage an
economy finds confirmation**

When the economic mechanisms in Brezhnev's Comprehensive Program of 1971 no longer had any prospects of being fulfilled, CMEA experts inclined increasingly to the conclusion that a supranational executive body was compatible only with market economies steered by authentic market mechanisms, but not with planned economies steered by state directives. The decision-making powers of an economic community which has no authentic economic steering mechanisms would have to be much greater than is the case in a market economy. None of the six Eastern European countries wanted an inordinately powerful executive. The pessimism contained in Hayek's comment, which was coined with the planned economies in mind, became increasingly widespread: the astonishing cooperation and capacities which human beings had effected over the course of the centuries in the form of adaptable economic mechanisms are imperiled by man's presumption to be able to steer the economy by means of state directives. The history of CMEA activity has shown that the opinion which von Hayek wished to limit to internal economic relations was fully valid at the international level.

**Modern forms of cooperation and an antiquated set
of instruments**

The term "integration" was introduced in the 1971 Comprehensive Program to define economic cooperation in its latest stage of development; like the theory of "comparative cost advantages" before it in foreign trade, it had been dubbed a term of bourgeois economic theory for alien capitalist conditions of the division of labor. Fifteen years after the Comprehensive Program was adopted it had become clear that neither of these two categories of cooperation could be realized with socialist labor methods and the instruments proper to a planned economy. The term "integration" was supposed to have designated the transition from the international division of labor and foreign trade to the developed stage of economic interrelations between production units in the production process. The limited economic steering mechanisms which had proven themselves ineffective in foreign trade showed themselves also to be ineffective for developed integrational ties. The considerable differences in the steering systems of the member countries made impossible any direct links between production units of, say, the Soviet Union, which had no powers to conduct foreign trade transactions, and the production units of Hungary or Poland which advocated direct contacts. Fifteen years after the Comprehensive Program had been adopted Academician Oleg Bogomolov, the leading Soviet CMEA expert and co-author of many CMEA documents, said: "The Comprehensive Program contained many sound postulates, but major value was attached to coordination problems in the course of its implementation, and little or no value was attached to the development of the contemplated economic mechanisms.''[186]

What Professor Bogomolov said to Polish economists in June 1986 had already been clear in the early '80s, namely: neither the national steering system of the CMEA member countries nor the CMEA cooperation system, which was dependent on it, were able to bring economic efficiency of the CMEA countries to a higher qualitative level corresponding to world standards. The stepped-up imports of modern Western technology and Western know-how in the '70s had not helped to create a linkup with the dynamically progressing scientific and technical revolution. The use of modern technology on a backward foundation by an obsolete management functioning in a backward steering system worsened rather than improved the economic situation of the CMEA countries. The technology gap grew greater rather than smaller, the gigantic mountain of debt that had in the mean time been accumulated, the insolvency of Poland and Romania, as well as the refusal of further loans even to the solvent countries and the dramatic cutbacks in Western imports brought about the first economic recession in the history of the Eastern community—and this occurred in the Soviet Union also despite the windfall profits which Paul Marer estimated at about 50 billion US dollars between 1973 and 1980.

As always in a difficult situation, the way out was sought in closer CMEA cooperation, and as always, without having a concept of cooperation which was suitable to both the superpower and the smaller countries. As always, the problem lay not in the choice of forms of work, but in the creation of adequate cooperation mechanisms which had not even been created in the fifteen years following the adoption of the Comprehensive Program, nor was there any illusion that such mechanisms could be created at all. The fact that it was the traditionally dissident Romania that proposed a summit meeting of the CMEA countries at the 34th meeting in 1980, and was later vehemently supported by Poland which had fallen into insuperable difficulties, was clearly not received by the Soviet Union with enthusiasm. But it had basically achieved everything it had wished to achieve in relations with the smaller countries: extremely high prices for petroleum and petroleum products, and above all their participation on very favorable terms in joint major projects built on Soviet territory that enabled the Soviet Union to link up its CMEA partners to a network of oil and gas pipelines and made supplies of Soviet oil an indispensable condition for their normal economic activities. But the Soviet Union also had a good reason for second thoughts on the continued cohesiveness of the Eastern bloc. The economic integration envisaged in the 1971 Comprehensive Program had become weaker rather than stronger in the '70s, thanks to the dynamic expansion of economic relations with the West. The extremely grave economic and political crisis in Poland and the extraordinary activities of the free labor unions that had been released in that country had taken a heavy toll on the political image of the Eastern bloc, especially in the Communist parties of France, Italy, and Spain, which extended their sympathies to the free trade unions rather than to the ruling parties in Eastern Europe. One motive was more important than all others for the Soviet Union, namely, to divert the meager range of exports of the smaller countries away from the West and redirect it to the Soviet Union in order to reduce the growing, price-conditioned trade surplus with the best products possible, which were usually earmarked for export to the Western countries. Brezhnev, severely ill, already bearing the signs of his approaching death, reacted to Romania's proposal at the 26th Party Congress of the CPSU in February 1981. His advisors had also found a fitting catchword for the new forms of cooperation: in his report he proclaimed that "life itself demands that the coordination of the national economic plans of the member countries should be buttressed by harmonizing their economic policies." The 26th Party Congress repeated the postulate, proposed years ago by Poland and Hungary, that direct links between the economic ministries, associations, and enterprises of the CMEA countries be intensified, that joint ventures be introduced, etc. One thing was clear from Brezhnev's proposal: the Soviet leadership, which had never had confidence in developed economic mechanisms and the invisible hand of the market, had revived their conviction that the postulates which had been included in the 1971 Comprehensive Program under pressure from the market-oriented proponents, such as authentic exchange rates, market prices, convertible currencies, and similar heterogeneous categories of the capitalist market, had no prospects of being fulfilled either in the national planned economies nor in their community. The links between production units at the international micro-level were therefore to be cultivated on the basis of a "harmonized," i.e., uniform and "common" (in the sense given the term by John Campbell) economic policy and not on the base of an ordinary economic infrastructure. The notion of cooperation which Konstantin Chernenko and above all Mikhail Gorbachev would attempt to realize was becoming increasingly clearer.

Brezhnev's illness, his immobility in his last years in office, and the lack of a general policy that hallmarked the invasion of Afghanistan, as well as the crisis of leadership that resulted from the brief reigns of Andropov and Chernenko, created a standstill and a phase of uncertainty among the CMEA authorities. Romania's 1980 proposal to hold a CMEA summit was accepted, but was not implemented until four years later. Direct economic ties between production units became the prime goal and the principal means of CMEA cooperation. The Comprehensive Program approved in 1971 already addressed this issue, but the goal could not be fulfilled owing to the lack of the proper instruments. The 37th Council session, the summit meeting of June 1984, and the 41st Special Session of December 1985 addressed this possibility anew without discussing what circumstances had prevented it from being realized for so many years. However, experience suggested that direct cooperation at the micro-level is as impossible as it is indispensable, since the economic steering mechanisms envisaged fifteen years previously are still lacking. But Mikhail Gorbachev had pointed up the importance of such links at the April Congress of the Socialist Unity Party of

Germany in 1986, and stressed that direct ties between production units in the CMEA countries would acquire a crucial importance in the upcoming phase of development and that decisions concerning such ties ought to be made not at the macro level but at the micro level. His CMEA advisor Oleg Bogomolov stressed in the abovementioned interview for Poland's weekly *Polityka* that direct international ties between production enterprises would enable reserves of international cooperation and specialization and of scientific and technical cooperation to be found where they are usually discernible, i.e., at the micro-level. Poland's vice-premier and representative in the CMEA Executive Committee, Wladyslaw Gwiazda, expressed this even more clearly in his interview with the Polish weekly *Polityka* on June 21, 1986: "The yardstick of the Comprehensive Program of scientific and technical cooperation among the CMEA countries, approved by the 41st Special Session of the CMEA in December 1985, shows that the condition for its realization was the pooling of all forces and means of the CMEA countries, and above all the abandonment of the practice of dealing with problems at the upper levels of economic management, the delegation of the nucleus of decision-making powers to lower levels and the debureaucratization of the decision-making of producers."

No two do the same thing the same way

The main difficulty of CMEA management is that, while all the member countries as a rule seem to be pursuing the same end or at least define that end in the same way, they usually give it a totally different content. This was the case with the establishment of the international CMEA banks: some wanted merely a clearing house or a source of financing for "joint" (in Campbell's sense) investment projects, while others wanted full-fledged banks in the traditional sense of the term. This was further the case in drafting the 1971 Comprehensive Program: some wanted to initiate joint projects in all the participating countries and establish international cooperation by means of authentic prices, exchange rates, and traditional functioning currencies, while others wanted to establish "joint" projects by top-level decisions, to engage the Eastern European countries in the development of the raw materials and fuels bases. They regarded the economic mechanisms contemplated in the Comprehensive Program as an issue to explore, but not a realizable undertaking. Finally this has been the case in the currently relevant question of direct contacts between enterprises in different member countries. Gorbachev has so far shown no particular understanding of economic mechanisms even internally, and it is hardly imaginable that he would be ready to place the management of the CMEA in the hands of the anonymous instrument of the market. When he said that decisions on cooperation measures should be made at both the macro- and the micro-levels, he did not define the relationship between decision-making bodies or the extent to which those powers should be exercised, and presumably would not accept being a *primus inter pares* in CMEA management. Oleg Bogomolov, his CMEA advisor, knows quite well that international links between enterprises can only become a reality if economic mechanisms are authentic and not merely declared. He criticizes the fact that the mechanisms contemplated in the Comprehensive Program were never established, but has said nothing about the instruments that would be necessary or could be created under the given conditions if these direct relations, endlessly invoked, are ever to be taken seriously. But therein lies the fundamental controversy implicit in almost every CMEA document which contains everything the member countries would like to see, but only realizes what the power relations in the CMEA permit. And the controversy has if anything become greater with time rather than subsiding. In the '60s there were lively disputes in national and international CMEA boards to clear up differences of opinion and reduce decisions to a common denominator, and arbitration sometimes required the intervention of top-level decision-making bodies; however, later on the tendency was rather to take into consideration all the proposals of the member countries in the document under discussion if it was to be realized at all. Decisions reached beforehand at the national level, with a rather narrow margin for compromise, were difficult to bring together into a plausible international CMEA document, when it was already known which decisions had chances of being realized and which would fall into oblivion as time passed. So it was with the 1971 Comprehensive Program, which included the proposals of Poland and Hungary that mutual economic relations should be placed on real economic bases. Research was begun which resulted even in determining exchange rates for the national currencies of the member countries, but these exchange rates were never able to be used since they had diverged so greatly from purchasing power parity in the course of time that they were suited neither as a clearing instrument nor as an authoritative parameter for cost-benefit analysis. Of course the Soviet Union was already aware in 1969, when the development of the Comprehensive Program was placed on the agenda, that the proposed economic mechanisms had no chances of being realized because in the first place its national steering model could not create the conditions for this. But the proposers as well had too great illusions that their proposals could be realized without the cooperation of the largest and most influential member country. And so it was with the major joint projects specified in the Comprehensive Program. They were constructed jointly with the assistance of the smaller countries, but remained the property of the country in which they were situated, i.e., mainly the Soviet Union.

And so it seems to be also at present with the currently fashionable term "direct links between production units." The Soviet leaders who once in the past had had to abandon their proposal to establish an economic super-plan for the community and a "supranational" CMEA executive, had to accept the failure of their integration program. With growing concern they followed the expansion of economic relations with the West and the dependency that resulted therefrom; the growing emancipation tendencies of the smaller CMEA partners; and the resistance related to any slighting of the latter's own interests in the name of an opportunely interpreted common interest. They are not sure that extensive economic links between the production units of the smaller countries and their own can over the long term secure the cohesiveness of the Eastern bloc. But they also know quite well that they have not invested their economic units with either decision-making powers nor with a set of economic instruments that would enable them to enter into foreign transactions. A world market price has no meaning for them since they receive the domestic price for the goods they sell to the foreign company, while exchange rates or a foreign currency have no meaning since they receive payment for the goods they export in their own non-convertible domestic currency, even in intra-CMEA trade. Between them and foreign markets—the CMEA markets included—stands the foreign trade enterprise which settles and clears all foreign trade transactions. Gorbachev may speak of decision-making at both the macro- and micro-levels, but he knows quite well that his micro-level has very little authority to enter into economic relations abroad. If he even mentions the micro-level as the seat of decisions, he does so just as his predecessor Brezhnev did when he included economically realistic prices and exchange rates as well as currency convertibility into the 1971 Comprehensive Program—namely, in response to the wish of his partners, but not because he was taking them and their proposals seriously. The case is different when W. P. Gwiazda, Polish authority for CMEA affairs, speaks of direct links between production units. In Poland and in Hungary especially, large enterprises have the powers to enter into direct business relations with foreign firms and carry out such transactions on a commission basis via the competent foreign trade enterprises. But the advocates of direct relations between production units on the basis of economic mechanisms are mistaken if they think that their proposal concurs with the Soviet Union's proposal, just as they were mistaken in 1971 when they thought that the fact that their proposals on "economic mechanisms" had been taken into consideration meant they they had a chance to be realized. Therein rests the principal problem of CMEA cooperation: the Soviet Union, which has the overriding word in the CMEA thanks to its superior economic and political strength, is extremely conservative with regard to the question of decision-making powers in the domestic economy. The proponents of progressive instruments for establishing direct links, on the other hand, have very little final say, however, measured in terms of their economic and political strength. It should be noted in passing that there is no CMEA country that has developed its internal economic mechanisms so far that they could serve as a necessary basis for an international economic infrastructure, and no planned economy has so far answered the urgent question of whether such an economic infrastructure domestically could also serve as a condition for developed and modern means of communication in international relations. Economic integration of countries with different steering mechanisms has no great prospects for transforming existing foreign trade relations into relations originating in the production process itself, especially when a single member is able unilaterally to set the limits of reform in the other member countries—a very limited sovereignty in practice, despite the adjurations of sovereignty given at every opportunity. Brezhnev's appeal at the 26th Party Congress of February 1981 to standardize the economic policies of the CMEA countries will therefore be repeated in later CMEA decisions. The final communiqués of the CMEA meetings still speak of the superiority of socialist cooperation, but an undisguised pessimism reigns in inner circles of CMEA workers.

Nine months before the June 1984 summit, the 37th Council meeting indicated no serious problems

The 37th Council session took place between October 18 and October 20 and was headed by the host, Willi Stoph, the GDR head of government. It was to earn a worthy place in CMEA history in that its long-time secretary, Nikolai Fadeev, who had headed the CMEA bureaucracy and left his mark on the Eastern community for almost thirty years, was retired with thanks, and a new CMEA secretary, Viacheslav Sychev, also a Soviet functionary, was appointed in his place.

The permanent observers from the People's Republic of Angola, the Afghan Democratic Republic, the Yemenite People's Democratic Republic, the Laotian People's Democratic Republic, the People's Republic of Mozambique, and Socialist Ethiopia, as well as a deputy from the Republic of Nicaragua, followed the course of the deliberations attentively (the latter country on the basis of an agreement between the CMEA and this Central American pro-Soviet republic). None of these popular democratic republics have anything important to offer the CMEA members economically; they expect from the CMEA more than it can give, however. This is the reason that the application of one of them, namely, Mozambique, for full membership in the Eastern community, was rejected. Three developing countries, Cuba, Mongolia and Vietnam, which are dependent on abundant economic assistance from the CMEA, are apparently enough for it.

One will seek in vain in the final communiqué for those problems which have accumulated since the last summit on April 26, 1969, e.g., the failure of the integration program taken up at that time, the quest for a way to bridge the technology gap, which had been rendered unsuccessful owing to the expansion of trade with the West, the mountain of debt that has in the mean time accumulated, the catastrophic economic and political crisis in Poland, etc. The reader of this final communiqué will rather wonder what the purpose of this meeting of the leaders of the CMEA countries is, since it seems that they are unable to deal with any serious questions. The document literally beams with undisguised optimism, just as the documents of the 36 previous meetings. There is no trace of the debates which as always took place behind closed doors, no trace of differences of opinion or of interest. But first a brief summary: ". . . the 37th meeting examined the report of the Executive Committee on the activities during the time since the last session and approved these activities as well as the activities of other

CMEA authorities. It notes that during the period between the 36th and 37th meetings the CMEA countries have continued their efforts to achieve the objectives of the five-year plan and find a solution for any problems that cropped up. Further progress was achieved in developing the economic and social basis . . .'' Of course there were also a few problems, but these were, according to the final communiqué, imported from the capitalist West rather than being caused domestically. It was found, in particular, that despite the worsening terms of trade and the rising prices of raw materials and fuels, a further increase in national income had been achieved and industrial output increased, especially in those sectors responsible for technical progress. Progress was also reported in agriculture, and the standard of living of the population has increased. Experts and co-authors of some CMEA documents were astonished by this progress in the art of compilation as well as by the progress in embellishing reality, considered rather gloomy even by Eastern circles. In the East bloc as a whole, it profited considerably by price developments on the world market. However, windfall profits were reaped only by one CMEA member. Only the smaller countries of the CMEA had been drawn into world developments. Professor Paul Marer estimated that the Soviet Union took home at least 50 billion US dollars, no less than a third of which was at the expense of its allies who had lost much more in their foreign trade with their big brother than in trade with the West. The average profit of one country and the losses imposed by this country on all the others, however, created a distorted picture of developments in the past year. The economic situation of the community was painted much too rosy. 1981 and 1982 were years of economic recession rather than boom, which Andropov, at that time head of the CPSU, attributed to ''accumulated inertia'' two months before the 36th CMEA meeting. This evaluation of the causes of the decline in performance was, however, just as well known to the authors of the final communiqué of the 37th CMEA session as it was to the world public. The growth of foreign trade was unclear. The dynamic growth of intra-bloc trade was estimated as positive compared with total trade. The drastic decline in Western imports from 49.9 billion US dollars in 1980 to 43.2 billion dollars in 1983,[187] which was only partially substituted in trade with the East, and then not with goods of equal value, was more forced upon the Eastern bloc by the difficult payments situation than willed, and caused considerable difficulties. Vital imports from the West were suspended because they could not be paid for, and Western banks were not willing, in view of the insolvency of Poland and Romania, to grant further loans. A more important factor for the shift of foreign trade toward the East was the fact that growth in intra-bloc trade was due not so much to physical growth as to the increasing value as a consequence of the rapid rise in prices for Soviet crude oil and petroleum products. The exports of crude oil to the four most important Eastern countries decreased between 1981 and 1983: from 18.1 million tons to 16.0 million tons in Czechoslovakia, from 22.7 million tons to 17.1 million tons (1984) to the GDR, from 13.5 million tons to 12.5 million tons to Poland, and from 7.2 million tons to 6.5 million tons to Hungary.[188] However, it would be unfair to the final communiqué of the 37th CMEA meeting if we were to restrict ourselves exclusively to the superlatives it contains. It also states that "there are considerable reserves which could deepen scientific and technical cooperation of the member countries." And further: "Measures have been pointed out which the member countries must apply to be able to deal with top priority problems in science and technology." The member countries are called upon to "be frugal with raw materials and primary materials, to develop energy-saving technologies, and to reduce non-productive losses." The communiqué also states that the 37th meeting had recommended the development of a cooperation program up to the year 2000 for the further development of the agro-industrial complex, in order better to provide the population with vegetables, food, etc. Member countries are called upon as part of the coordination of economic plans for the five-year period from 1986 to 1990, to take measures to ensure a better supply with foods. The 37th CMEA meeting also mentions the community's duty to take an active interest in the world political situation in order to assist the second community institution, the Warsaw Pact. The final communiqué states: "The 37th Council meeting expresses its solidarity with the Prague Declaration of the Warsaw Pact and states that the CMEA will do everything possible to improve international economic and political relations, and that it assesses positively the Madrid CSCE follow-up conference which subsequently foundered, and of course condemns the efforts of imperialist circles to increase international tension and to complicate East-West economic and political relations." However, it also expresses its will to "deepen economic and trade relations with the West on the basis of mutual advantage."

The decisions of the 37th meeting differ from previous decisions in one other respect as well; namely, the tendency to expand intra-bloc trade at the expense of trade with the West is clearly in evidence. In connection with the economic sanctions imposed due to events in Poland and Afghanistan, the CMEA countries are called upon to undertake an accelerated development and exchange of those products whose "imports have been prevented by the discriminating measures of a few capitalist countries." One decision also calls for solidarity with the developing countries and notes with satisfaction that their attitude toward questions of disarmament coincides with the attitudes of the CMEA countries.

As the final communiqué stresses, one important result of the 37th Council meeting was the signing of an agreement on the construction of the Krivoi Rog mine on Soviet territory, with the participation of the interested countries.

The traditional concluding sentence that "The meeting took place in an atmosphere of unity, fraternal friendship, and in total mutual agreement" must not be allowed to conceal the fact that the discussions concerning the upward trend of Soviet oil prices—the CMEA price increased from 15.67 dollars per barrel in 1981 to 21.91 dollars per barrel in 1982 and 25.89 dollars per barrel in 1983[189]— were continued at this peaceful congress as well. In 1983, the Soviet price for crude oil delivered to the smaller countries was nonetheless still 11% lower than the world market price, but a downward trend [in the latter] was already evident. These countries, which were hit heavily by the rapid and considerable price rise, had little understanding for this monopoly price, which stood in crass contrast to the price-setting practice established at the 9th Council meeting in 1958, and were even less able to absorb it. One would not be wrong to assume that the decision to construct a new "joint" project on Soviet territory with the economic and financial help of the smaller countries was not greeted with much enthusiasm by the latter.

Although the published decisions of the 37th Council meeting provide little information about actual CMEA problems and on the CMEA's capacity to solve them, nonetheless an analysis of its final communiqué would seem to be warranted since this session took place only nine months before the CMEA summit which had been awaited for a long time, but which was continuously being postponed, first due to the crisis in the leadership in the Soviet Union, but also due to the economic and political crisis in Poland. A fair analysis of this final communiqué also seems justified by the fact that it shows perhaps more clearly than the others in the last phase of development how great the gap between the optimistic tone of the communiqués and an ever-more complicated reality has become through the course of time.

The 1984 June summit under the leadership of the gravely ill Konstantin Chernenko did not favor the smaller nations

The CMEA summit was urged by a number of the smaller countries because of troubled waters: terms of trade with the Soviet Union were deteriorating, solvency in trade with the West had become severely problematic, leading to a dramatic cutback in imports of important goods for which it was impossible to find a substitute on the CMEA markets. The Soviet Union also had good reason to call its allies to account. Although it was able to impose the world price for oil and petroleum products on them, it was still unable to obtain top quality goods from them for its hardware.

An abundance of unsolved problems had accumulated since the last summit meeting, April 22, 1969, for which no solution had been found. There had been lacking effective ways to deal with these problems, especially because the Soviet Union was experiencing the gravest crisis of leadership—and of the system in general—in its entire history, under the last representative of the Soviet gerontocracy, after eighteen years under Brezhnev's leadership and fifteen months under Andropov. Poland's and Romania's insolvency, the mass protests in Poland against the existing regime, the calm political situation in Czechoslovakia which had caused a chronic stagnation in the economy and in society, and the decline in economic growth in all the Eastern countries indicated that the creative forces in the steering instruments of the planned economies were exhausted and that the reserves of a former dynamic growth had reached an insurmountable barrier. The price explosion and the unfavorable conditions imposed upon the smaller countries for participating in major projects within the Soviet Union as a precondition for deliveries of raw materials and fuels had troubled relations between the Soviet Union and the smaller countries.

The summit came too late for those who had uttered their desire for a new one much earlier, in the early '80s, in the hope that it might find a remedy for their unfavorable terms of trade, payments difficulties with the West as well as in trade with the Soviet Union, the decline in economic growth, the stagnating specialization measures, and costly and unfinished capital investment projects. The summit, which the Soviet Union had postponed as long as it could, came too early, however, to find a solution for the seemingly insoluble problems of cooperation. It should be recalled that the June 1984 summit took place nine months before the governing Soviet gerontocracy was replaced by a dynamic, young, ambitious leadership headed by Mikhail Gorbachev. The search, in the published joint declaration of the leaders of the CMEA countries on the "principal questions on the further development and deepening of economic, scientific, and technical cooperation," for the conflict-ridden issues which had induced the leaders of the Eastern bloc and their closest advisers to call a summit meeting will be in vain.[190] A careful reading of the declaration of the community leaders leads one to the conclusion that they had not come to Moscow in June 1984 to discuss the grave problems of the economic community, and to find a viable solution for them under the given conditions which would overcome the serious discord between the Soviet Union and its allies in respect of the fundamental questions of future cooperation, the disputed terms of trade between the Soviet Union and the smaller countries, the specialization measures, a just choice of location for joint capital investment projects, etc. Rather, there was a vain atmosphere of sheer rapture which reigned in the community and that the meeting had been called to solemnly proclaim urbi et orbi a state of utter prosperity, the superiority of socialist cooperation, and untroubled unanimity. The declaration states: "The states of the socialist community have consolidated the economic, scientific, and technical potential and thanks to the unselfish labor of the peoples and the leadership of the Communist and workers' parties, have completed important social programs and ensured continuous growth in the standard of living, the further development of science, education, culture, health, and social security."

Of course the CMEA countries have recorded definite achievements for which they can thank the conscientious effort of their populations, but also community cooperation within the CMEA. However, when the unbearably poor quality of goods, their unsaleability on the international markets, chronic difficulties in supply, low productivity, and simple negligence and disregard are constant themes in almost every CMEA country, the self-praise of the Eastern leaders seems somewhat exaggerated. If one also reads declarations of other communities, the EEC for instance, one gets the impression that all they have are problems, in contrast to the CMEA where there are only successes to report.

In view of the CMEA's undisputed inferiority to the industrial states of the West in scientific and technical progress, labor productivity, and quality of life, and in view of the growing dependence on modern Western produced technology and Western credits for which no counter service can be found in the Eastern banks, the following statement in the declaration of the Party leader is especially astonishing: ''The experience and activities of the CMEA member countries demonstrates the fundamental superiority of socialism over capitalism,'' or by the successive mention of such themes as social and national freedom, confidence in tomorrow, ideological unity of the society, a constant concern for people, and the all-round development of the individual. This sounds as if there were many people in Poland, Hungary, and elsewhere, who were quite happy with the official state ideology; as if the roughly 20,000 priests in Poland did not have a greater influence on the souls of its citizens than the entire Party apparatus; as if there were fewer churchgoers than participants in Party meetings; and as if the church and not the Polish United Workers' Party was obliged to complain of the loss of a million believers in the past few years. As for equality, has it existed, or can it exist at all between the very big and the very small member nations? Whether there were not, and are not, some who are more equal than others, as the great Satan of Orwell put it so well; whether in a world in which every country is plagued by blatant contradictions, that ideological unity is really the great virtue and not the greatest disadvantage, and whether a regime which demands ideological unity and persecutes dissident thinking really does it contribute to the all-round development of the individual? To take the words of the great martyr of the socialist movement, Rosa Luxemburg: ''Let freedom always mean freedom for dissidents.'' Dissidents of course also have the right to think their dissident thoughts in the Eastern countries, but of course only insofar as it is possible given the uninterrupted brainwashing that takes place. They do not have the right to speak or to act differently quite openly. Hence the following statement in the joint declaration is the least convincing of all: ''Socialist democracy, which in practice guarantees the most extensive rights and freedoms, is continuously being perfected.'' Yet, as we know, other means than the means of ideological persuasion had to be employed in the second largest country of the socialist community to maintain social cohesion; namely, martial law on December 13, 1981, which was suspended just before the June summit. The following contrast of socialist success with capitalist failure is not much more convincing: ''The scientific and social progress of the CMEA countries stands in bold contrast to the crisis situation in the capitalist countries.'' It is unconvincing if for no other reason than that at the time of the June 1984 summit conference the industrial countries of the West had achieved just as much of an economic recovery as the socialist countries and still, as the Soviet leadership has stressed innumerable times, play the role of pioneers in the world scientific and technical revolution. So now the main concern of Mikhail Gorbachev is to find ways and means to become part of world technical progress since, as the experiences of the '70s shows, imports of modern technology and other factors of the rapidly progressing scientific and technical revolution have as few prospects of success and are just as costly as the export of world revolution.

The June summit, under the leadership of the mortally ill Konstantin Chernenko, regretted the "inability of capitalism to extricate itself from deep economic crises and acute social and political problems with its own forces" and praises the "correct and timely, collectively worked-out guidelines for deepening cooperation and developing socialist and economic integration" which, as it is stated, "contribute to the important factor of the all-round progress of every fraternal country." Naturally the obligatory marginal comment is not lacking: "Every CMEA member has contributed to strengthening unity and concord, especially the Soviet Union." Thus in this matter did Konstantin Chernenko honor the great work of his sponsor, Leonid Brezhnev, who wanted him and not Yurii Andropov as his successor, as an expression of his loyalty to the late Soviet leader. However, the 1971 Comprehensive Program was a complete failure, and Academician Oleg Bogomolov regarded it negatively. The statement on the insuperable economic and political crisis in the capitalist West is also striking. Unfortunately, this opinion was not only that of the Soviet gerontocracy, which had now been pushed into the background, but also of all Communist leaders of every period since the Communist Manifesto in 1848, and is also reflected in the 27th Party Congress, the new edition of the 3rd Party Program adopted in February 1986. The economic crisis for the past a hundred and forty years has been dubbed the last crisis of capitalism. But after every crisis came a recovery, and further economic and social progress, even after the extremely severe and protracted crisis following the oil shock. Nevertheless, it is best to clean one's own house. The Poles have always had a witty, if a bit exaggerated, joke in comparing the socialist achievements with the capitalist crises: "Under capitalism there are social problems, but under socialism there are capital problems." The June 1984 summit as well as the preceding 37th Council meeting seems to have concluded that the occasional difficulties are not homespun, but a result of pressure from aggressive imperialist circles, blackmail and discrimination. It adds, however, that it has been possible to alleviate these difficulties through community cooperation. The actual reasons for the summit meeting are stated somewhat later. But less attention is given to them in the joint declaration than to commonplaces. Once again, as in the final communiqué of the 37th Council session, mention is made of the considerable reserves which can be drawn on to expand economic cooperation and mutual trade as a precondition for more efficient utilization of the productive, technological, and scientific potential of the fraternal countries and for raising the standard of living of their populations.

A number of prime areas are mentioned in which cooperation among the member countries should be concentrated in the upcoming period. These are areas which were designated priority areas in the majority of earlier CMEA documents. But the decisions of the June 1984 summit did introduce one novelty into the coordination of national economic plans. Economic plans in those areas which are given priority in the given planning period are coordinated. As for other areas, they may be regarded as an object of coordination only by the wishes of the countries with an interest in doing so. According to the summit decision, this type of coordination should create conditions for a stable economic, scientific, and technical cooperation. Another novelty is also to be found in the decisions of the June summit: emphasis is placed on using those economic areas in which international coordination takes place as a basis for developing the one-year and five-year plans of the member countries, and—even more importantly—it is stated that these areas should become an organic component of the plans. It should be remember that the Soviet Union was the first CMEA country to include the following indices of community cooperation in its 1981–1985 five-year plan: realization of major projects on Soviet territory with the participation of other CMEA countries; construction of major projects in other CMEA countries with the participation of the Soviet Union, and related mutual deliveries; international specialization and cooperation, in which the Soviet Union participates in the domestic economies and national economies of the other CMEA countries; cooperation in science and technology. The summit declaration mentions machinery construction as a top priority area of crucial significance for the CMEA. The purpose of expanding cooperation in this area is to be able to equip key branches of industry and other economic areas with top-quality machinery and equipment of world standard. It was agreed that the countries participating in the area of machinery construction should deliver finished products, semi-finished products, and whole assemblies. They must also be equippped with the appropriate spare parts. One of the most important problems of the CMEA countries would then be solved, namely, often the entire normal production process has to be halted owing to the lack of some small part.

The June summit placed special stress on the most progressive branches in machinery construction, namely, electronics, microprocessors, and industrial robots. Closer cooperation in this area should help to modernize the production process in all economic sectors. But the June summit gave special attention to the expansion jointly of the raw materials and fuel base. The opinion was stated that the CMEA countries will create the best possible conditions for overcoming energy problems by mobilizing their own resources and intensifying cooperation. The summit conference repeated the decisions and measures taken at the 37th CMEA conference with regard to ''making frugal and rational use of raw materials and fuels,'' and to equip the energy sector with modern technology and know-how. Absolute priority was given to atomic energy, but also to the development of non-conventional sources of energy, and the drafting of a development program for nuclear power stations up to the year 2000 is recommended. According to the statistics of the International Atomic Energy Authorities, there are now 51 nuclear reactors in the Soviet Union, 28 of which are of the Chernobyl type. Total capacity at the end of 1985 was 27,756 megawatts (MW); 26 reactors with a capacity of 29,258 MW were under construction at this time. The share of atomic energy in electricity production was 10%. However, the nuclear power station construction plan was not fulfilled. In the five-year period from 1981 to 1985, 15,800 MW were installed, but 25,000 MW were planned. According to the International Atomic Energy Authorities, 16 nuclear reactors with a capacity of 6,131 MW were installed in the smaller countries. Poland and Romania have as yet no nuclear power stations. Bulgaria covers almost a third of its electricity consumption with atomic energy, followed by Hungary with 19%, Czechoslovakia with 15%, and the GDR with 10%. All Eastern countries with the exception of Romania employ Soviet technology.[191] The nuclear energy expansion program envisioned by the June summit was developed shortly afterward and left unchanged even after the Chernobyl disaster. Certain safety precautions were specified to avoid such damage, which according to TASS figures was 12 billion dollars at the official exchange rate.[192] The needs of the population were also taken into account. The summit declaration recommends that the agro-industrial complex be built up and the food industry be expanded.

Aid to the developing countries of the CMEA is stressed more emphatically than in preceding CMEA documents. The summit decisions state that ''The CMEA countries consider it their duty to provide economic assistance to the Socialist Republic of Vietnam, the Cuban Republic, and the Mongolian People's Republic to accelerate their economic development and raise their efficiency, as well as to intensify their participation in the international socialist division of labor.'' The three developing countries receive about 60% of the total aid of the Eastern community to the third world, according to statistics published in *The Economist*. Rather than an explicit promise of development aid, a detailed political declaration is dedicated to the third world in which it states that the provision of economic aid was the affair of the imperialist countries who were guilty of the economic misery in the third world. This topic will be dealt with in the following section.

There were very few problems to which the June 1984 Summit devoted much more attention than the preceding congresses, conferences, and deliberations at various levels of the thirty-five years of community activity. Some problems were brought up to date, some were expanded, but only very few new ones were taken up. One area, however, was rather neglected compared with other programmatic CMEA documents. This was the question of economic steering mechanisms, to which the Comprehensive Program, resolved at the April 1969 Summit Conference and approved at the June 1971 Special Session, had devoted a whole compendious section, section VII. The June summit, on the other hand, had only three rather vacuous and non-binding statements on this question. The declaration states: ''. . . The organic connection between planning activity and the effective utilization of commodity and money relations retains its timeliness. The price system in mutual trade as well as the currency and financial instruments of economic cooperation should be further developed, and the collective CMEA currency, the transferable ruble, should be strengthened.'' The June 1984 summit, as mentioned earlier on, paid its due respects to Brezhnev's 1971 Comprehensive Program. But no words were lost on the failure of the economically realistic exchange rates for national currencies and prices, based on internal cost relations, nor was even a limited convertibility contemplated in this program. The reasons for the failure are not so much as mentioned, and nothing is said about the possibilities of actually perfecting commodity and monetary relations, as referred to in the three very important statements of the June 1984 summit decisions, fifteen years after the adoption of such a historical document. These were important statements, but such similar statements can be found in the decisions of almost every council meeting since the founding of the International Bank for Economic Cooperation in 1964. Interestingly, apathy and formalism found expression even in the most important CMEA documents in times of all-embracing mobility.

The summit declaration contained a resolution concerning "the direct connections between production units," and Hungary, which has enjoyed some decentralization of decision-making since 1968, and Poland, which began to undertake decentralizing measures after martial law was lifted, both regarded this as a victory of their negotiating abilities. They were also able to put through the measures necessary to implement this project, such as granting appropriate decision-making powers, creating instruments for a cost-benefit analysis of the cooperating firms, and joint ventures, etc. It is nonetheless striking how such important integration resolutions were formulated in an unconcrete and non-binding form. At the time of the 1984 June summit, however, it was known well enough which CMEA countries had prevented such direct connections, fifteen years after the resolution put forth in the 1971 integration program, by doing nothing to establish the requisite powers and economic mechanisms; and which countries were in the process of creating foundations for such connections through reforms in their system. Brezhnev and Kosygin were not prepared to establish the necessary decision-making powers at their micro-levels in the economic reform of 1965 and its new edition of 1979, and Andropov continued this tradition by doing nothing to create the necessary mechanisms and powers after the July 1983 Party and government resolution. Chernenko, the initiator of the June 1984 summit, was the least prepared to take such measures considering that he had always emphasized strengthening central economic management in all reform measures. Two and a half years after the June 1984 summit, far-ranging reforms were introduced into management of the Party and the economy during the course of 1985 and 1986, and, as mentioned, Gorbachev also spoke of the necessity of establishing direct contacts among production units of the CMEA member countries at the April 1986 Congress of the Socialist Unity Party of Germany. Yet not even the rudiments of the decision-making powers necessary for this are discernible in his ambitious reforms. What, then, do all these CMEA resolutions mean when the economically and politically most important CMEA country does nothing to create the conditions necessary for such interrelations? Gorbachev's CMEA advisor, Oleg Bogomolov, dwelt on the conditions that were lacking for such contacts during his visit to Poland in June 1986, and observed that Poland's enterprises were also not so independent. And he was certainly right. Poland's economic experts and journalists have a similar opinion, but would hardly agree with the further observation of the Soviet professor, who went on to say: "If Poland's enterprises were truly independent, Poland would not have achieved the successes it has in fact achieved despite everything." This additional observation is in accord with the opinion of the Soviet leadership which would like to strengthen central management, but also to give the micro-level certain decision-making powers, to free it from the stifling hold of the central bureaucracy. Bogomolov also had this implicitly in mind when he said in the same talk[193] that Soviet enterprises had less freedom than the Polish ones, in that there were no enterprises in the Soviet Union which were also involved in foreign trade matters; that under the given conditions there could be no direct contacts between Polish and Soviet enterprises. He then went on to say that this matter was currently being dealt with intensively.

Of course in view of the prohibitive conditions existing above all in the Soviet Union, the proponents of direct production contacts have no special grounds for rejoicing that they were able to put through a pertinent resolution in the declaration of the June 1984 summit, as indeed they were able to do many times before. On the other hand, Chernenko, in permitting the resolution, made a compromise, as his predecessors did many times before, that was extremely favorable for the Soviet Union. He accepted a proposal of some of the smaller countries that was absolutely unrealizable under the given conditions, and in return received a collective CMEA decision that was important for the Soviet Union. The summit declaration makes a commitment "to create economic conditions for the continuation of Soviet deliveries of raw materials and fuels, which meet the import needs of the other CMEA countries within the framework of their coordinated economic plans and the long-term agreements; the interested member countries will gradually and systematically initiate the indispensable measures for modernizing their production and export structure, and for altering their capital investment policy in accord with the agreed-upon economic policy, in order to enable them to provide the Soviet Union with top quality, world-standard construction materials, machinery and equipment in return for Soviet raw materials and fuels, foods, and industrial consumer goods."

Of course the Soviet Union has a right to demand "hard" goods from its trading partners in the CMEA in return for its "hard" raw materials and fuels. This accords with CMEA practice of exchanging "hard" goods for "hard" goods and "soft" goods for "soft" goods. "Hard" goods for which no appropriate countervalue can be found are exchanged for hard convertible foreign exchange and not for "soft" non-transferable IBEC-transferable rubles. This unwritten rule of barter-like intra-CMEA trade has been functioning for a long time. But for the first time in CMEA history, this practice, nowhere officially sanctioned, was raised to the status of a CMEA law, specifically in relations between a large group of smaller countries in trade with their biggest economic partner, i.e., the Soviet Union. This is therefore a fundamentally new strategy of trade between the Soviet Union and its smaller CMEA partners. The latter were required to deliver the best possible goods of their rather meager range of exportable goods to the Soviet Union. The smaller countries have an export goods structure which would be difficult to amend in an historically brief period. They divide up their range of export goods between the CMEA and the West in accordance with their economic policy. Of course perhaps they were forced to export a larger portion of their exportable goods to the West to cover their debt service, and in order to import top-quality machinery and equipment of world standard which cannot be obtained in any CMEA country. It was also probably taken into account that indebtedness to the West was at least seven times higher than to the Soviet Union. The resolution of the June summit can therefore only be interpreted as an attempt to divert the qualitatively best portion of the exportable goods of the smaller countries from the West to the East.

Of course the June summit declaration speaks of maintaining normal economic relations on the basis of mutual advantage with the industrial states of the West. However, there can no longer be any doubt that the priority granted to the Soviet Union in participation in the range of exportable goods of the smaller countries will have a considerable influence on the future geographic structure of their foreign trade. The Eastern European leaders realize quite well that the commitments they had undertaken had very little to do with the platonic wishes and unrealizable decisions to which sufficient space is invariably accorded in any programmatic CMEA document. They realized that the Soviet Union knew quite precisely what it could demand from each ally, and also has persuasive means to realize that demand. The importance of this resolution, and the scope of the concession wrung from the smaller countries induced the Soviet CMEA giant to venture a commentary. Academician Bogomolov, one of the best CMEA experts and government advisor for many years, published a statement (as he always does in special matters) in the theoretical journal of the CPSU, *Kommunist*.[194] The commentary is more detailed than is usually the case. He refers to all international relations in the community. The commentary deserves to be quoted extensively in view of the author's prestige and political and professional competence: "Community economic interests can only be fulfilled within the family of sovereign states of equal status on the basis of the voluntary agreement of each and every member. Of course one cannot call those decisions optimal which reduce everything to the lowest common denominator. The agreements of national interests can, it seems, be fulfilled through a voluntary renunciation of many current economic conveniences for the sake of a considerable strategic advantage, on the basis of a sober evaluation of the individual interests in the light of common needs or in the light of the general situation.'' Bogomolov continues to speak about the importance of voluntary concessions as a basis for expanding the identity of interests among the individual participants, and then goes on to speak in more detail about the conclusion of the summit meeting: "For example, an agreement was made at the Economic Summit Conference of CMEA members in 1984 which committed the fraternal countries to supply the Soviet Union gradually and regularly with top-quality goods of world standard[195] [referring to the range of goods mentioned above] in order to create economic conditions for the realization and continuation of Soviet deliveries of a number of raw materials and fuels.''

Bogomolov's example of renouncing short-term national interests for the sake of strategic community interests, namely, that the states of East and South-east Europe should renounce certain advantages of trade with the West in order to create more favorable conditions for the Soviet Union in intra-bloc trade, seems to suggest that John Campbell's interpretation of community interests as those which are in consonance with the existing balance of power, has prominent supporters in the Eastern bloc.

The June 1984 summit paid more attention than previously to the interest announced some time before in CMEA documents in international affairs. There was, in addition to the declaration on intra-CMEA cooperation, a declaration on international relations. A number of passages are more informative and more interesting than in preceding CMEA documents.

The Gorbachev Era

Gorbachev's influence on events in the Soviet Union and on CMEA activities

The June 1984 summit took place eight months before the historical change of power in the Soviet Union, which could have an important influence on the history not only of his country but of the entire Eastern bloc. The new, more youthful, and more dynamic Soviet leadership does not lack goodwill, resolve, and ability. In the time since Mikhail Gorbachev and his team assumed power, much has been undertaken, both in the CMEA community and in international relations, that can arouse hope that economic activity will be stimulated and relations with the West will improve. There have been many commentaries published in the East and in the West. No CMEA study can be considered complete if it does not take a position on this important event in the history of the Eastern bloc and East-West relations.

Mikhail Gorbachev is the seventh Party leader in the roughly seventy years of Soviet history. The first four, who ruled the country for sixty-five years, had a tremendous effect on its history: Lenin, the great leader of the October Revolution, and the person who shaped the country's power structure; Stalin, who ruled the country in an authoritarian manner for thirty years and reduced the sublime revolutionary ideals to the conditions of the backward Russia, the great victor in the Second World War and the founder of the Soviet Union as the second superpower in the world; Khrushchev, who freed the country from Stalinist terror, attempted to decentralize the economic system and to promote coexistence by withdrawing Soviet troops from Austria and organizing the Geneva conference of the four in 1955, but who demonstrated the unbending determination to keep the great empire together by crushing the Hungarian uprising, and who was the first and only leader in the Soviet Union's history whom the Party apparatus succeeded in overthrowing; and then Brezhnev, who in the eighteen years of his government brought about an unprecedented stability, but who began the extremely dangerous armaments race, neglected to put to good advantage the impulses from the scientific and technical revolution led by the West, and brought the country its first economic recession in history.

A de facto interregnum set in after these big four. First came Andropov, many years the head of the KGB, but already bearing the marks of his imminent death, who attempted to regenerate the government with his harsh campaign of purges and discipline, and attempted to breathe new life in the hardened arteries of the state organism, but effectively was in power only nine months; then came Chernenko, who was in even poorer health and three years older, and governed the country, and its serious economic and political problems, from his bed.

The crisis of leadership in the country was finally surmounted with the choice of the youngest, most dynamic, and most ambitious of the country's politically powerful figures, Mikhail Sergeevich Gorbachev, long considered the crown prince. No leader after Stalin was bedecked with so many laurels beforehand as he.

Of course the leader of a one-party regime is more powerful than a head of government in a pluralistic society. The times of omnipotent leaders are also gone in the Soviet Union as well. Looking back, it is now clear that only Stalin's rule was dictatorial and unlimited, and even then only twenty years of his thirty years in office. Lenin, the undisputed leader of the October Revolution, enjoyed an unlimited authority, but was continually having to defend his rule, which was marked by civil war, foreign intervention, deprivation, and starvation, in a bitter struggle against the right, left, and ultra-left wings, against the workers' opposition, against the democratic centralists, etc. Within a short time Lenin was able to suppress every legal opposition, and establish the absolute rule of the Bolshevik Party. But still, this was not a Party of unimpaired unity.

Stalin had to struggle for ten years against a variety of opposition groups until he finally succeeded in reducing the Party and society to total uniform submission, and instituted a reign of terror without parallel. He shaped and reshaped the power structures after his own image, but took only himself seriously: thirteen years passed between the 18th and 19th Party congresses, and in the most difficult time of Soviet history, between 1939 and 1952, he held only six meetings of the Central Committee. His will triumphed in politics, economics, and philosophy, in historiography, in biology, and in linguistics. He was surrounded by a genuinely idolatrous cult. Nine months after his 70th birthday in 1949, the greetings from within the country and abroad filled a fourth of the edition of the central Party organ *Pravda*. Seventy million copies of the short history of the CPSU were published under his editorship and made into basic doctrine for every Soviet citizen.

No one described Stalin's reign of terror more dramatically than his successor, Nikita Khrushchev. But Khrushchev was also not inclined to make his own autocratic rule statutory even without the idolatrousness of his predecessor. He had undermined the conditions for this himself by the demythologizing of Stalin's cult. After he had shifted a large segment of the central apparatus to the regional administrations he had set up (''Sovnarkhozy''), and attempted to reform the sacrosanct structures of the Party organization, the most powerful Party leader was overthrown for the first time by the Party apparatus. The apparatus proved to be stronger than its First Secretary. Khrushchev's successor on the Kremlin throne, Leonid Brezhnev, eliminated many politicians from the Party and state leadership, e.g., the Party boss of the Ukraine, Shelest, KGB chief Shelepin, Politburo member and agricultral advisor Polianskii and Podgorny, head of state, whom Brezhnev replaced in 1977 as chairman of the Presidium of the Supreme Soviet. But Brezhnev was never confronted with an opposition, as were his predecessors. He avoided a serious confrontation with the Party apparatus, sought its consensus, and recruited the heads of the most important state administrations: defense—Grechko (later replaced by Ustinov), foreign affairs—Gromyko, and the KGB—Andropov to the Politburo.

Brezhnev aspired to no radical reforms. During his rule the central apparatus flourished as never before, all the while it nipped in the bud every initiative and desire for innovation from below. As he found his physical and intellectual powers declining he was forced to loosen his grip on state affairs, just at the time when the country was entering into a grave economic recession. Brezhnev was an authoritarian leader, but within a collective state leadership.

The helm was placed in the hands of the head of the mightiest secret police in the world, Yurii Andropov, to tighten the reigns of state administration. Andropov proceeded to purge, with hands of iron, the Party and state apparatus of corrupt and incompetent functionaries. One-third of local Party secretaries, a fourth of the 90 ministers, and nine of the 23 Central Committee department leaders fell victim to this campaign of purges, unparalleled since Stalin's rule. However, Andropov's time in office was too short for him to have instituted a thorough change in the leadership and in the country's difficult situation. The Party apparatus was deeply intimidated by the General Secretary's zeal in his purges. When he died in February 1984, the Party elite passed over Gorbachev, fifteen years younger and long considered the crown prince, to elect Chernenko, three years older, who was Brezhnev's favorite. The state returned to the immobility that characterized the last years of the Brezhnev era. The protracted crisis of leadership was finally overcome in March 1985 when the ailing Chernenko died and Gorbachev was elected his successor.

How great is Gorbachev's margin of maneuver?

Gorbachev, an erudite jurist and agronomist, is a man of the Party apparatus. At 39 he became the first Party Secretary of the regional committee of Stavropol; at 40, member of the Central Committee; at 47, Secretary of the Central Committee; at 48, Candidate; and at 49, full member of the Politburo. When Foreign Minister Andrei Gromyko proposed him as the most suited for the highest office of the country in March 1985, he was referred to as the man with the "iron teeth." Gorbachev's very first steps as the new ruler of the Kremlin showed him to be a strict, dynamic, self-aware and resolute Party leader who did not shy from decisions. Whereas Brezhnev needed nine years to eliminate his greatest rivals and create his own power base, Gorbachev needed only four months to send his most dangerous political opponent, Grigori Romanov, healthy as a bear, into the political desert, "for reasons of health." The next step was to promote Andrei Gromyko, who had been in his office longer than any other foreign minister in the world, to the decorative office of Head of State, and replace him with Edward Shevardnadze, the head of the Georgian Communist Party, who was totally inexperienced at foreign policy. Yet Shevardnadze immediately revived the planned and abandoned summit meeting with Reagan, which actually took place in November 1985, and planned three subsequent meetings. Gorbachev inundates Party and economic managers with passionate speeches, travels throughout the country, comes into direct contact with the population, has proclaimed a bitter struggle against the country's most dangerous pestilence, alcoholism, and continued Andropov's campaign of purges with undiminished severity. His victims have been members of the Politburo and the republican leaderships, nineteen ministers of the Russian Republic, and many many others.

However, the question is still open whether Gorbachev has a suitable concept for restructuring the backward economic organization of the country, whether he is disposed to forgoing "fraternal aid" from all corners of the world, and to replacing confrontation with coexistence as a lasting model for relations to the world outside, and thereby make his contribution to the de-escalation of the perilous and costly armaments race.

Gorbachev has a reform of economic management in mind. His predecessors also attempted reforms, but later retreated by applying patchwork to a discredited continuity: Khrushchev decentralized the steering of the economy, and placed it in the hands of regional administrative authorities; Brezhnev and Kosygin restored decision-making powers to the central authorities, but granted some decision-making powers to enterprise managers in the 1965 reform.

This half-hearted reform was as ineffective as its second edition in 1979. In July 1983, Andropov began a new steering experiment which, however, emphasized discipline and rigor. Can Gorbachev's reforms go further than those of his predecessors? And if so, will he be able to realize them under the given conditions?

The basic problem is not that enterprise managers have few decision-making powers, but that they are reluctant to use those they have been given. T. I. Zaslavskaia, the author of the famous "Novosibirsk Report," writes that a significant portion of the powers available have not been made use of in the last ten years.[196] It is after all easier to expand production through capital investments subsidized by the state budget than to modernize production procedures through one's own responsibility. It is easier to produce steel than to manufacture technically sophisticated products out of steel.

Economic mechanisms, the constraints of the market, thinking in profit terms, world-wide competition, an indispensable cost-benefit analysis for every economic activity and the conscious and purposeful actions of hundreds of thousands of entrepreneurs is proven to be stronger and more beneficial than a command economy in which the administrators of state enterprises must fulfill plan directives on command from above.

It is easier to evade the commands of a state executive, however powerful it might be, than to dismiss the material constraints of a well-functioning market economy. Whether Gorbachev will be able to redefine the functions of a planned economy at this level is questionable.

How does Gorbachev see the Soviet economy?

Gorbachev appears in public more often than his predecessors did. He speaks his mind and sharply criticizes inefficient economic performance and the captains of industry. In his many speeches—at the funeral of his predecessor on March 11, 1985, in his programmatic speech to the Central Committee on April 23, in his statements before the conference and Party and economic managers on June 11 of that year, in his speech to the economic and political management of the largest industrial center of the Ukraine, Dnepropetrovsk, but above all in his speeches at the 27th Party Congress on February 26, 1986, and the Party Conference on June 28, 1988—he has not concealed the fact that he is unsatisfied with the economic performance and management, and has said what he expected of it and how he would like to change how it is managed. The picture the General Secretary paints of the Soviet economy is anything but rosy. Although these and many other statements are not free of repetition, the modifications Gorbachev has in mind for the existing steering system assumed definite contours in his later speeches.

The economic situation of the country is not catastrophic. The recession of the early '80s and the difficulties of the first months of this year seem to have been surmounted. The malaise that is plaguing the West—high unemployment and inflation—are not what ails the Soviet Union. Although Gorbachev said at the April 1985 meeting of the Central Committee that "the historical fate of the country and the position of socialism in the contemporary world depends on how we pursue our purpose,"[197] and two months later he chided the population by saying "We must act together, all of us, to bring all the links in the chain together into a uniform economic current in which there must be no place for conservativism, indifference, lack of organization, waste, bureaucracy, and neglect,"[198] there was good reason in the urgent admonitions of the Party leader, which he straightforwardly stated in his dramatic speech of June 11: "Since the beginning of the '70s, the country has neglected to adapt the forms and methods of economic management, and the actual psychology of economic activity to the needs of the times."[199]

The Soviet Union produces more steel than any other country but, as Gorbachev noted in his book *Perestroika*, it has a chronic shortage of metal, because its quality is low, the range of goods available is insufficient, and much too much is wasted. The problem is not that too little money is invested in the steel industry. "Quite to the contrary!" said the Party leader in his June 11 speech: "In the past fifteen years the iron and steel industry invested 50 billion rubles, but mainly in unsophisticated structures, giving no heed to technical redesigning."

He used the example of Krasnoiarsk, the most promising region of Siberia, as an example of how inefficiently capital investment funds are used. The capital investment funds were scattered among 500 projects, the completion of which dragged on and on, with vast quantities of resources being wasted. The construction of one huge hydroelectric power station was taking twice as much time as the similar project. "We will spare no money in developing Siberia," stressed Gorbachev, "but we have the right to demand that the money invested brings a corresponding return and is not put into deep freeze." He directs his principal criticism against the inefficient capital investment structure, which is oriented toward building new capacities rather than modernizing those that exist: 32.4% and 34.8% of money for capital investment projects in 1980 and 1983 respectively were used for modernization and reconstruction, but 63.3% and 61.5% respectively were used for expanding old and constructing new capacities."[200] No more than 7% of industrial capital stock, including 8% in the electrical engineering industry and 8.2% in the chemistry and machinery industries, was renovated in 1983. This investment structure is not only counterproductive—modernization investments are twice as effective as investments in new constructions according to Gorbachev—but also costly. Despite stable prices, the costs of capital investments increase 5–8% annually.[201]

The failure to adapt the forms and methods of economic management to the needs of the worldwide scientific and technical revolution is the reason for the considerable backwardness compared with the production structure of the Western industrial countries, which are developing into societies based on informatics. In the early '80s, the share of industry and construction in the national product was 34% in the United States, 40% in France, 48% in Austria, but still 61.4% in the Soviet Union.

The Soviet Union is still a net importer of modern technology. The computer industry is hopelessly backward. US studies show that the Soviet Union is still currently producing copies of computer designs which IBM ceased producing six or seven years ago; that the best computer a Soviet manager can obtain is the ES–105 S from the GDR, which corresponds to the third IBM generation (system 370); and that in 1984 only one-third of large concerns (more than 500 employees) had computers, compared with 100% in the United States.[202]

The backwardness in agriculture seems to be insuperable. 20% of the population is still employed in agriculture, but the Soviet Union is still a net importer of grain (57 million tons in 1984–1985). Imports come mainly from the United States where only 3% of the employed population works in agriculture.

No revolution but far-ranging organizational measures

Mikhail Gorbachev is not Peter the Great or Stalin. It is not his intention to change the existing social order. However, he does want to make it more efficient in order to deal better with three principal components of the trinity of distribution strategy—consumption, capital formation, and armaments. He does not have Khrushchev's ambition of overtaking the United States in per capita income. He would like to provide the food program, begun in 1981, when Khrushchev's fanciful objective was to have been achieved, with qualitatively better goods, but will not make any cutbacks in the armaments program, and will maintain the priority of heavy industry. Investments in machinery construction will be increased by 1.8 to 2-fold.

Gorbachev announced his economic strategy on June 11, 1985: "Not only accelerated growth, but a new quality of economic development is the goal to intensify progress in strategically important areas of industry, to effect a structural reorganization of industrial output, to make the transition from extensive to intensive labor, and to deal more completely with the country's social problems."[203] The General Secretary also mentions the most important measures necessary to achieve the objectives staked out.

The economic experiment, adopted under Andropov's leadership on June 27, 1983, and expanded from five to six union ministries and fifteen ministries of the republics under Chernenko, will be maintained. The comprehensive reform program adopted in June 1987 calls for placing detailed planning in the hands of enterprise managers, who will also have to decide on the deployment of capital investment funds, and further top-quality goods of a world standard or higher, an increase in salaries and bonuses, etc. The emphasis will be placed on central planning. The central planning commission (Gosplan) will be transformed into an effective scientific and economic authority and bring together the best scientists and experts. The binding indices will be reduced to a minimum and will be focused on quality; for example there will be efficient utilization of resources, modernization of capital stock, and an enhancement of the labor and production process; the central economic apparatus will be considerably reduced, and overall day-to-day economic activities will be made the responsibility of enterprises and associations of enterprises. The General Secretary attaches great value to direct contacts between production units. "The hope that the Gosplan or the economic ministries are capable of choosing the optimal form of mutual relations is an illusion," he says, and proposes that administrative authorities of large industrial complexes be formed. He calls upon the Academy of Sciences to give their institutions more research tasks of "direct technical relevance."

Anyone who has expected Gorbachev to establish some modification of market socialism will be disappointed. The existing steering system is subordinated to the military and industrial complex, the priority of which he cannot leave to the invisible hand of market mechanisms. A precondition for transforming the economic and political system would be the dismantling of this huge complex which consumes almost a fifth of the gross national product, and the country's best potential. All this depends on relations with the outside world, and on the easing of East-West tensions.

Gorbachev's unsolved CMEA problem

Gorbachev and his team know that the objectives posited at the founding of the CMEA have not been achieved, and moreover that efforts so far to bring the international division of labor in the CMEA into line with present needs have failed and that under the given conditions these efforts have no chances for success. In making international economic ties irreversible, it was hoped that they would become the backbone of a political alliance. However, it is understood well enough that interrelationships through foreign trade alone are not irreversible. The share of intra-bloc trade decreases and trade with the West increases as a function of the political climate in East-West relations, as was the case in the '70s, or conversely, as is the case in the '80s. The new Soviet leadership understands quite well that the traditional trade concept of Soviet raw materials and fuels for Eastern European finished products, which increased in importance as a consequence of the oil shock of the '70s, is in the process of losing its dynamic effect; it is also understood that the involvement of the smaller countries in Soviet major projects in the raw materials and fuels industry can have no lasting effect. It is being realized increasingly that progress in economic interrelationships can only be achieved through more streamlined international steering mechanisms than hitherto. However, no progress has been made in this area since the '60s. The steering mechanisms proved to be inadequate for a mature foreign trade and absolutely unsuited for extensive ramifications and cooperation in production. The new leadership also knows quite well that the notion of a universal economic plan for the entire community which could be fulfilled like an individual state plan through commands from an international executive, is even less realizable today than in the early '60s.

After the unmistakable inferiority the CMEA countries manifested in trade with the West, when they were dependent on the prices, clearing currencies, credits, and above all the modern technology and knowhow of the Western partner, without being able to offer anything equivalent in exchange, these countries plunged into a payments crisis which some have not yet overcome even today. The Soviet leaders were forced to swallow severe losses in prestige in their negotiations with the European Economic Community. The EEC, once scorned as a miscarriage of imperialist circles, has been solicited unsuccessfully for cooperation efforts since 1974. An agreement on mututal recognition was signed in June 1988, but not mutual cooperation. The EEC rejects the ministrations of the CMEA on the grounds that it does not possess the requisite authority.

Whereas the EEC authorities, and only these authorities, are empowered to conclude foreign trade treaties with third countries and basically control the overall trade of its members, the CMEA embraces only intra-bloc trade with no authority to conclude any economic agreements with third countries in the name of its members. Gorbachev and his CMEA First Secretary, Viacheslav Sychev, were compelled to recognize this fact only after Romania, Hungary, and Poland had concluded agreements with the EEC authorities in specific areas of their economic relations. Bilateral relations may now been concluded with the EEC authorities without the mediation of the CMEA.

The superiority of socialist cooperation which has always been publicized outwardly has fallen into discredit in an unprecedented manner. But there is no doubt that the political coherence of the East bloc is greater than elsewhere. In no other economic community is the influence of a single member country so great as is the case in the CMEA, yet the EEC has proven itself to be more coherent and above all in possession of greater authority than its Eastern counterpart. It is becoming apparent that the economy can no longer be subordinated to politics, in any case not as greatly as has been imagined and desired hitherto. Economic capacities increasingly exceed the capacity to administer them. The ability of the planned economies to consciously steer the production process through the decisions of vast administrative authorities has turned out to be inferior to the cumulative traditional collective wisdom of mechanisms created over the course of generations. The confrontation between these antagonistic forms of management appears to bear out the German social democrats who in their Bad-Godesberg progam inscribed the slogan: "Market as far as possible, plan as far as is necessary." Gorbachev and his talented economists see the relationship between these two steering mechanisms in the opposite manner, but are unable to find the right proportion, perhaps because it is beyond human powers to do so with conscious intent.

The following question is often posed in economic circles in East and West: "Can Gorbachev fundamentally alter CMEA relations, as he would like to change economic relations within the Soviet Union itself? Can he mold CMEA relations in such a way that they can be brought into the services of his far-ranging ideas of restructuring?" One thing seems quite certain: the smaller countries have their own economic needs which cannot easily be made to coincide with a superprogram designed by a superpower. The new Soviet leadership will find it more difficult merely because the leaderships in the smaller countries have become more self-aware, and have learned to put up resistance and where possible to put through their national interests. The clear-defined opinion—especially in Hungary—that there is no international interest for which national economic interests should be sacrificed is shared by the others, if not always so clearly expressed. The leaders of the smaller countries are under growing pressure from a more knowledgeable population which demands more than their governments are capable of providing under existing international commitments. The question is raised: "Will the new Soviet leadership be willing to transform the CMEA from a fundamentally politically motivated community into a fundamentally economically motivated community, which would also involve a restructuring of its composition; and do justice to the circumstance that the incorporation of remote developing countries may serve the interests of a superpower, but not the purposes of economic integration?" No one in Eastern Europe is ready to believe the often-repeated CMEA declaration that the distance between Vietnam, for instance, and an underdeveloped country of Eastern Europe such as Romania, or between Romania and the most developed country of the East bloc, the GDR, could essentially be eliminated within the course of a few generations.

A more important question is whether the new Soviet leadership would be willing to free the CMEA countries of Eastern Europe from its military-industrial complex, which is subject to the interests of superpower policy, and to which the overall concept of development and growth, as well as the structure of production and foreign trade, seems to be subordinated; and whether the Soviet Union would be willing to consider that critical circles in Eastern Europe are uninterested in the concept of proletarian internationalism, and would like to see their own national economies developed for peaceful purposes; that long-range goals in the name of a proletarian revolution which were not brought about at home, and which they do not particularly like, do not interest them; that they have even less understanding for totally alien superpower interests, and bear no distinctions between these two definitions of interests, although they must help to bear the costs, which are a growing prohibitive. These circles would also like to see their governments themselves deciding on the development of the national economy, and their foreign economic relations so structured that they benefit the national economy in the first instance rather than the latter being subordinated to some joint policy, however it is defined. They would also like to see their own governments and only their governments, with no other supranational or supra-state center, to determine national and international priorities. But above all, the question is whether under the new Soviet leadership, they will be able to keep a distance from superpower conflicts and shape their economic relations with the West on the basis of their own national interests and not in dependence on brief periods of detente and long confrontations on which they have no influence. They like detente; they do not feel threatened from the West, and do not want to call into question their social system. They are oriented more to the West than to the East by tradition. They have their Catholic religions, their Enlightenment ideas, and have even taken their Marxism from the West, and so wish no surrogate from the East.

Of course they value economic contacts with the neighboring Soviet power with its vast market where they can sell in great volumes, and where many things can be purchased cheaper than elsewhere. But they would like to shape these relations on the basis of the tried and true principle of comparative cost advantage without discrimination and special advantages. They would like to shape friendly relations on the basis of favorable economic relations rather than on the basis of a disputed political alliance with a superpower whose political and military interests can never coincide with the interests of the smaller countries.

Will Gorbachev and his team recognize the unmistakable signs of the times and the ineluctable trends toward emancipation, as well as the historical developments of all superpower structures, and release the Soviet Union's political embrace of its allies, and structure bilaterally advantageous economic relations as a foundation for a lasting friendship? Will the Soviet Union give consideration to the fact that the Eastern countries, with their growing demands, are in the process of being transformed from an asset to a liability, and that martial law, as for example in Poland in 1981 through 1983, is prohibitively expensive—and not only for the country concerned—and finally that the renunciation of an all-embracing and binding tie is politically more far-sighted than the expansion of it?

Another crucial question for CMEA cooperation is whether the new Soviet leadership will be willing to acknowledge that the existing production capacities and economic interrelations cannnot continue to develop without the help of new international means of communication; that the contemplated direct contacts between economic units in the different member countries, as experience hitherto has shown, cannot be shaped on the basis of commands from the macro-level; and that the precondition for the development of these contacts must be modern economic mechanisms. An even more important question is whether the Soviet leadership under Gorbachev is willing to acknowledge that the smaller countries have in the past mounted a vigorous resistance to supranational bodies, in order to administer CMEA cooperation without an official superexecutive, through the appropriately interpreted community factor corresponding to power relations; finally, the question arises whether the Soviet Union will be willing to meet the requirements of international cooperation in the restructuring of its economic system, since it has after all suppressed reforms of greater scope, for instance, in Czechoslovakia in 1968, and still sees itself as a supreme arbiter for political and economic reforms. Under Khrushchev, Brezhnev and Andropov, the Soviet Union has shown the same inclination to alter the parameters of management just so long as everything remains as it is and creates no preconditions for the elaboration of functional means of international economic cooperation. Will things be different under Gorbachev?

Gorbachev's CMEA concept

Gorbachev would like to achieve more in the CMEA than his predecessors. However, the new Kremlin chief is a few illusions poorer and a few experiences richer than they were, and is quite aware of the limited possibilities of realizing the far-ranging integration projects. For him too, the Warsaw Pact and the CMEA are the supporting pillars of the socialist world community. On March 11, 1985, at the funeral of his predecessor, he proclaimed that no departures from the interests of the Soviet Union and its allies would be permitted. He stressed the organic relation between these two community institutions more clearly than his predecessors, and, as reported, the historic meeting of the Warsaw Pact on April 26, 1985, also dealt with economic problems, while the 40th meeting of the CMEA on June 27 went beyond purely economic problems. If, however, the military alliance could be cemented for another twenty years by prolonging the Warsaw Pact, and if roles and quotas were carefully distributed and there could be no leadership problems, the situation would be different in the economic community. The inability that it has shown since the early '60s to fulfill a collective economic plan by means of a supranational executive has become a certainty for Gorbachev. But he, like his predecessors, is not prepared to accept proposals which are based on an expansion of the economic mechanisms of a market economy. Hungary's economy cannot serve as a model for the Soviet Union or, at the other extreme, for the smaller countries in the CMEA. There will continue to be no uniform steering system. But the more differentiated the steering system becomes, the more difficult it will be to profile the steering mechanisms in the CMEA, and the deeper will be the gap between the demands of integration and the possibilities of realization of it. No collective economic plan and no supranational executive, but rather the involvement of the smaller countries into the farsighted restructuring projects of the Soviet Union seems to be the aim which the new Soviet leadership would like to achieve in the CMEA. It is granted that this concept has greater chances of being realized today than in the early '70s, merely because there is a convincing air about the argument "in the contemporary world, no single country is able to institute all types of production to an economically optimal degree and to maintain a world standard of quality; however, a community which has a solid material and technical basis and rich experience is able to do so." Another reason that closer economic cohesion seems to have greater chances of realization is that the path chosen in the early '70s for finding an alternative on the world market was unsuccessful and made economic relations with the West even more complicated by the accumulation of a considerable debt. However, it is no accident that the most enthusiastic advocate of economic integration is Poland with its heavy debt, and that even dissident Romania is attempting to deal with its difficult economic problems by closer cooperation within the CMEA.

The new Soviet leadership differs from the previous leadership also in the fact that it revealed its intentions clearly and unequivocally to the world at large. In his programmatic speech at the April 1985 meeting of the CPSU, Gorbachev defined the principal task of the Soviet leadership as follows: "A thorough perfection and enrichment of cooperation with the fraternal countries in socialism; a closer cooperation in the areas of political and ideological defense, and elsewhere; as well as a concern for achieving an organic concord between the national and international interests of all participants in the great alliance."[205] He goes on to say that "the Soviet leadership would be willing to strengthen and consolidate relations with other socialist countries, including the People's Republic of China.'' It should be noted in passing that the present pragmatic leadership of China, the triumvirate Deng Hsiao-ping, Zhao Zi-yang, and Li Hsien-nien prefers to learn from real capitalists rather than from real socialists, and sends 14,000 students to America, 6,000 to Japan, and 5,000 to Western Europe, but only very few to Eastern Europe.

The social and political framework of CMEA cooperation

The ideas of the new Soviet leadership on the political and economic conditions of the Soviet Union's cooperation with the smaller countries are defined more precisely in *Pravda* articles of June 16[206] and June 21, 1985.[207] After the due denunciation of the imperialists, their intent on destabilizing the Eastern alliance, and those who have not renounced their ''crusade against Communism and in favor of the export of counterrevolution,'' reference is made to the misuse of notions of the ''specific role'' and ''peculiarities in the development'' of a number of Eastern countries, the aim of which is to weaken the alliance of fraternal countries, to carry them away and separate them from the Soviet Union, and ultimately to erode and even change the social system. Of course the Eastern countries alluded to are not named by name. But anyone can imagine which country is meant. The alliance with the Soviet Union has lasted only forty years, but the written history of the Eastern countries is over a thousand years old. More rigorous criteria for fidelity to the alliance and priority for general interests of socialism are demanded. In some Eastern countries, priorities are set differently. Matyas Szuros, Politburo member of the Hungarian Socialist Workers' Party, rejects the view that national interests should play a secondary role and pleads for methods which give priority to national characteristics.[208]

The lively criticism of ''nationalist and revisionist views'' gives an idea how narrow the margins for realized or contemplated economic reforms have been set. The power of the toilers under the leading role of the working class, the leadership of society by a Marxist-Leninist Party, and social ownership of the most important means of production . . . are named as inviolable laws of the socialist community. Of course these programmatic slogans, which have never been realized in real socialism, are regarded as utopian and antiquated by critically thinking intellectuals in Poland, Hungary, and elsewhere. The unrealizable thesis of the hegemony of the working class in Eastern socialism is compared with the trenchant phrase of Raymond Aron, who says that the proletariat rules under real socialism to the same extent that ''God rules in France,'' namely, through the economic and political elite of the country whom no one has elected. The famous British historian Arnold Toynbee is more precise when he says that the worker is quite indifferent over who pays him his salary. A Polish joke makes this undeserved promotion of the proletariat to the ruling social class somewhat more ridiculous. To the question "What is champagne?" it is replied "It is a splendid drink which the society's elite drinks to the health of the proletariat." And: "The productivity of labor is not so high in Poland; what ruling class likes to work?"

The proletariat is being more rapidly liberated in the highly developed industrial states of the West by the rapidly progressing scientific and technical revolution than by the Communist revolution in the economically underdeveloped countries of Eastern Europe. The number of workers and farmers is decreasing, and the transformation of blue-collar workers into white-collar workers is taking place much more rapidly in the industrial states of the West, which are being transformed into information societies, than in the East, in which basic industries still set the pace. The share of heavy industry and construction in the gross national product of the United States is no more than 35%, while agriculture and forestry make up only 3%; in the Soviet Union, however, the corresponding figures are still 61.4% and 15.2%. The thesis of the mediating role of the smaller countries in "developing a compromise between the two superpowers" put forth in some of the countries of Eastern Europe, comes under fire. Again no names are named, but with good reason, for they are no less than Erich Honecker and Janos Kadar, pleading for the intervention of the "smaller and medium-sized states of Europe to limit the damage caused by American-Soviet tension." "But the mediation of any socialist country in dealing with the controversies between the Soviet Union and the United States is out of the question," states the *Pravda* author, "since in the key questions of foreign policy, the views of the Soviet Union and the Marxist-Leninist core of world socialism are identical."[209]

A sharp attack is levied against those in Eastern Europe who, in view of the difficulties arising in the late '70s and early '80s, in shifting the economy to intensive growth factors, as well as in trade and payments relations with the West, have asserted the superiority of the "free market and free enterprise and have attempted to bring state ownership into discredit and contrast it with other forms of ownership." Criticism is also levied against scholars who would like to weaken the state management of the economy and central planning, and have advocated introducing market competition as well as the expansion of the private sector. The nation in which such apostases have been put forth and in part also realized is not named. But it would not be wide of the mark to presume that Poland and Hungary are the countries meant, where the private sector in small crafts, trade, and services has some importance. Allusion is made to the "serious economic, social, and ideological consequences and the resultant negation of the content of the principles of socialist economic management, and finally to the violation of social justice and to the creation of social tensions."

Observers of events in the Eastern bloc who had expected more liberalism from the new Soviet leadership in relations with its CMEA partners will consider the above-outlined framework to be limited.

The basic framework of economic cooperation

The necessity of "intensifying economic activity of the fraternal countries" is stressed in this rather limited political and social framework, and a "far-ranging utilization of the advantages of the international division of labor and economic integration" is called for as a precondition for this. Reference is made to the role of integration factors in the evolving scientific and technical revolution as well as to the necessity of "giving international cooperation a new quality" because, as Gorbachev is always stressing, "there is no other way," and because "the West often makes use of the language of decree and uses embargoes, boycotts, and other discriminatory measures against the socialist countries."

When it is stated emphatically that the Communist and workers' parties themselves determine their economic policies and the methods for implementing them, as well as the forms of the fundamental laws of socialist economic management, it is of course demanded "in one's own well-understood interest that a social and economic strategy be agreed upon, and that the economic and administrative mechanisms are subjected to joint verification." After reference to the "revolutionary restructuring in scientific and technical progress and the transition to fundamentally new technical and technological systems promising optimal efficiency and to the contemplated reorganization of all economic spheres" that is being introduced in the Soviet Union, similar measures in other Eastern countries are referred to. Great value is attached to the "electronization" of the economy, complex automation, flexible automated systems, atomic energy, new production technologies, and biotechnology.

Principal stress is placed on machinery construction which is supposed to increase its growth rate by 150% in the next five-year planning period. New generations of machinery technology are to be developed which would be capable of revolutionizing production procedures, and raising labor and capital productivity rapidly. Cooperation in the enlargement of the raw materials and fuels basis, and especially in atomic energy, will have a no less of an important role. Recent agreements for ten years has already linked together fifty enterprises and associations in a unified technological cycle capable of creating power units with a capacity of 440,000 and 1 million kilowatts. By the year 2000, nuclear power plants in the CMEA should be able to save 200 million tons of bituminous coal units.

The construction of major projects with the participation of all the CMEA countries with an interest in them is contemplated as a component of the joint raw materials and fuel base; the mining combinate in Krivoi Rog, with a capacity of 13 million tons of iron units, and the Yamburg gas pipeline to the Soviet Union, are examples of such projects. A few joint projects will also be undertaken in other CMEA countries, such as the expansion of the mining of coal in Poland, of magnesite in Czechoslovakia, of cobalt and nickel in Cuba, of bauxite in Vietnam, etc. Of course these small projects in the smaller countries stand in no comparison to the major projects which are being planned or carried out in the Soviet Union with the help of the smaller countries; as Politburo member Kazimierz Barcikowski reports, Poland alone is participating with 1 billion rubles in projects in the Soviet Union. The decisions of the 40th Council session, which was held just after Gorbachev assumed power, show, however, that after many years of impediments some of the smaller countries of the CMEA have been able to put through their wishes. Just before the 40th CMEA Congress Barcikowski wrote: "We cannot maintain production capacities and hence raw materials deliveries at the same level if the interested partners do not participate with capital investments."[210]

Major value is attached to the competitiveness of the goods traded in foreign trade. The desire to hold delivery dates and to maintain product quality is expressed, and it is made clear tht the CMEA countries are not autarkically inclined, and that they would be willing to expand economic relations with all countries regardless of their social system. However, they will attempt to manufacture goods whose export to the East bloc has been prohibited by the Western countries. Intra-bloc trade reached a share of 60% of total trade in 1984 (313 billion transferable rubles), and will grow more rapidly than trade with third countries. The share of socialist countries in Poland's total imports increased from 49.7% to 62.9% between 1981 and 1984.[211]

Emphasis on "intelligent" commodities within the entire CMEA

Gorbachev hopes to make up for the neglect of the '70s within the next five-year period, and to link up with the worldwide scientific and technical revolution as rapidly as possible. The direction will be successively, but also consistently, developed. A selective and dynamic development of the branches that are crucial for technical progress is supposed to make the economy the most modern in the world as it enters the new century. The contemplated projects are impressive if one considers that in the period between 1986 and 1990 more than 100,000 robots, 4,000 automatic and semi-automatic production lines, 110,000 digital control machines, 2,000 flexible automatic production systems, and 3,000 automatic design systems are scheduled to be produced.[212] Gorbachev would also like to include the CMEA partners in this truly revolutionary structural change. Mutual deliveries of computers, electronic and information devices between the Soviet Union and its CMEA partners are set to constitute 15% of total deliveries of the machinery construction branch in the next five-year period. The Soviet Union will step up the production and export of high-efficiency mining and highway construction machinery, passenger planes, with consideration of the needs of the fraternal countries and at the same time, in accordance with already-existing agreements, order technologies for extracting oil and gas, ships, electrical locomotives, railroad cars, specialized means of communication, farm machinery and other types of machinery from the CMEA countries.[213] More than 60 middle-term and long-term multilateral agreements on scientific and technical cooperation have been concluded on the fulfillment of delivery plans.

The reform in the steering system will play a considerable role in this revolutionary restructuring of the economy. Contours of the reform are already known. The experiment initiated in accordance with the Party and government decision of July 27, 1983, to improve steering mechanisms has been in operation since 1984, and at present affects 12% of industrial production and will be extended to the whole of heavy industry in 1987. Supplementary measures to promote quality and modernize the production process were promulgated on August 4, 1985. Production enterprises and heavy industry which improve the quality of the goods they produce will be given the right to raise the price of these goods by 30%, but enterprises which do not meet quality requirements will be forced to reduce prices by 5% the first year, 10% the second year, and 15% the third year, and to cover up to 70% of their losses from the bonus funds. Enterprise powers in the area of capital investments are being expanded: investment plans will be presented to the competent ministries for approval only if their cost exceeds 4 million rubles in heavy industry and 2.5 million rubles in other industrial branches.

"These quite considerable reform measures must, however, be realized without any deviations toward a market economy and private enterprise," said Egor Ligachev in late June 1985 before the Academy of Social Sciences.[214]

The references above to the changes being undertaken by management in the Soviet Union are important in the context of this study, not only because it will have a not inconsiderable influence on the profiling of the steering systems of other CMEA countries, but above all because it is the Soviet and not the divergent steering systems of the small countries that will be decisive for shaping the steering mechanisms of the CMEA.

The 40th and 41st Council sessions begin a new era in CMEA history

There was nothing in the 40th CMEA meeting, which took place in Warsaw in late June 1985, under the chairmanship of General Jaruzelski,[215] that would have indicated that a historical turning point was approaching in the Eastern economic community. Nikolai Tikhonov, the oldest of the Soviet gerontocracy, who in 1979 at the age of 74 replaced Aleksei Kosygin, the best technocrat in Soviet history, assuming the office of Prime Minister, headed the Soviet delegation. Tikhonov was a man of the "Dnepropetrovsk-Brezhnev mafia," as people were accustomed to say deprecatingly in the Soviet Union in an allusion to Brezhnev's leadership methods. Brezhnev was the man in command in Dnepropetrovsk, Bessarabia, and Kazakhstan, and he was accustomed to choose his assistants from the most intimate circles around him. The greatest purge in the post-Stalin era, which would also claim the graying Prime Minister as one of its victims, had just begun. As usual, the session listed the achievements between June 1984, the date of the Economic Summit Conference, and June 1985: the economic results of 1984 were better than in the preceding two years. "An end to the economic recession was in sight: the national incomes of the fraternal countries increased by 3.6% compared with 1983, industrial output increased by 4.4%, agriculture output increased by 3%, the housing construction program was realized, the material basis of education and culture were strengthened, and medical care and social security improved."

However, the new ideas of the young Kremlin leaders were nonetheless reflected in the tone-setting speech of the old man. They were wholly oriented toward the quality of production: "Acceleration of scientific and technical progress and an increase in production efficiency are inseparable from improving the quality of output overall, and the solution to the problem of quality is at the same time a solution to the problem of quantity," said the Soviet head of government. "And this strategy," he continued, "is the most hopeful way to satisfy the needs of our country and to alleviate the shortage of goods. Therefore we must regularly compare our goods with the best analogs on the world market." The Soviet head of government then mentions measures taken in his country to improve those goods which could be competitive on the world market, and then stresses that the problem of product quality is a common problem of the entire community; he ends with the emphatic statement: "It is high time to stop producing goods which no longer meet world standards."

The second most important problem which refers to mutual relations between the Soviet Union and its smaller partners in the CMEA is supplies of energy and raw materials. The Soviet head of government gives his partners no false hopes: "Additional deliveries must not be expected. Frugality with material resources is the most rational way to deal with the problem of raw materials and fuels." An example from the Soviet Union reinforces the opinion of the head of government: in 1985, consumption of fuels was reduced by 117 million tons of bituminous coal units compared with 1980, and in machinery construction and construction in general 7 million tons of rolled steel was saved; three-fourths of the increase in the consumption of fuels and raw materials should be covered in the upcoming five-year period by savings. The Soviet head of government would like to involve the fraternal countries in the effort to make more economical use of material resources—the input per production unit is at present at least one-third higher than in industrial countries of the West. A relevant program of economizing measures to the year 2000 was presented for the approval of the 40th Council meeting. Resource-conserving technologies, machinery and materials, will be used with growing intensity in all CMEA countries. This measure, from which the Soviet head of government expects quite a bit, will be implemented under the organizational supervision of the CMEA Committee for Cooperation in the Area of Material and Technical Supply.

Of course the speech of the Soviet head of government must not give the impression that he regards increasing production and its efficiency, improving the quality of goods, and frugality with scarce resources merely as art for art's sake. By no means, he knows the joke from Radio Erevan: "What does our prosperity signify?"—"It is something miraculous; it grows steadily without anyone noticing it." This time things really must change. The society's problems are to be dealt with more resolutely: in the five-year period from 1986 to 1990, deliveries of foods and industrial consumer goods will be expanded, and cooperation in this area, which has not been so thorough, says Tikhonov, will be put to better use. "Much more can be done for technically re-equipping light industry and the food industry as well as for expanding mutual trade and the exchange of services," he commented, and thus proposes that in the final phase of coordination of economic plans, supplementary measures be undertaken to better satisfy food needs and for better technological equipment of the corresponding industrial branches, and that cooperation in the remodelling and modernization of industries producing for mass consumption be strengthened. He suggested that some projects, which presuppose the construction of turn-key enterprises, have already been submitted to the fraternal countries for their inspection.

Soviet ideas on future cooperation with the developing countries of the CMEA and the Third World suggest that the new Soviet leadership would like to deal with or at least formulate a number of CMEA problems differently from what had previously been the case. Tikhonov observed: "International interests of the alliance require that we activate joint effort and cooperation with Vietnam, Cuba, and Mongolia. These countries are building socialism under especially complicated conditions and require our help and support." Of course Tikhonov then goes on to say: "This aid must be put to efficient use and these countries must use their own resources to the fullest." To make aid palatable to the countries of Eastern Europe as well, Tikhonov gives the good example of the Soviet Union, which intends to provide these countries with economic aid in the next five-year period to develop vitally important branches of their economy, including those producing goods for export. "Cooperation within the CMEA to deal with this problem must clearly be expanded," he stated. The Soviet delegation therefore supported the proposal—without mentioning who put it forth—to deepen the division of labor with these three countries at the next Council session. Of course the fraternal countries had also been encouraged earlier to intensify their economic aid to the developing brothers of their community, but in a somewhat milder form. The leaders of the smaller CMEA countries still did not understand, however, what the "socialism" in Vietnam, Cuba, or Mongolia has in common with their "socialism." They are quite aware that the contribution required from their populations in the name of international interests will arouse no great enthusiasm. They have already learned to distinguish between international interests and superpower interests, and have not too many illusions about either.

The Soviet Prime Minister used the presence of observers from other developing countries to give them his best greetings and assure them that the path that had been embarked upon, the cooperation at many levels with the liberated countries should continue, that they will be supported in their struggle against imperialism, and to strengthen their dependence and develop their national economies. Unfortunately Tikhonov did not say whether his government was ready to increase its share of economic aid to the Third World—its share is at present the smallest of the total aid of industrial countries of this world—and not, as always reiterated, to leave economic aid to the former colonial nations, and reserve for itself the support of the struggle against them.

The tone of the Soviet head of government sounded rather peaceful and conciliatory when he spoke of relations with the Western countries: "The Soviet Union and the fraternal countries are unconditionally in favor of normal and equitable relations with the capitalist countries and their economic groups in the spirit of the Helsinki Final Act." In this context he mentioned the recently undertaken new initiatives to establish mutually advantageous relations with the European Community. Tikhonov was referring to the May 1985 talk between Gorbachev and the Italian Prime Minister Craxi, as well as the memorandum which the chairman of the 40th Council meeting had sent to the Brussels authorities. Tikhonov rated very highly the initiative and its possible consequences: "We are convinced that cooperation was in accordance with common interest and could be useful for improving the situation in Europe and in the entire world."

The last representative of the Soviet gerontocracy ended his attentively received speech with the traditional homage to the Marxist-Leninist policy of the Communist and Workers' Parties of the fraternal countries, to their ideological unity, and their efforts to contribute a due effort to a common cause, "which is a secure guarantee that the new historical tasks of the building of socialism and Communism will be successfully realized." Perhaps the old man already had a premonition that the Marxist-Leninist policy he had pursued was coming to an end, and that a young generation of leaders would initiate a new Marxist-Leninist policy not only based on the past.

The Council session, inspired by Tikhonov's speech, came to the conclusion that both internal and worldwide conditions urgently required a greater dynamic in the development of national economies, and an intensification of production on the basis of the latest scientific and technical achievements. The speakers from the smaller countries also spoke in this connection, saying that the reports of the Central Committee of the CPSU on accelerating scientific and technical progress were being studied intensively by them.

Decisions were adopted on further CMEA activities and a number of important agreements were signed in the course of the Council session: one cooperation program of the fraternal countries on the "frugal and rational utilization of material resources up to the year 2000" was approved. It included "measures on the manufacture and use of energy-saving and metal-saving machinery, equipment, control instruments, automation systems, and progressive technologies." A first step toward the realization of these measures was taken in the course of the

Council meeting in an agreement on multilateral cooperation on the use of natural gas as a fuel for transport vehicles.

The Council session noted with satisfaction that the CMEA member countries were consistently fulfilling the measures taken to expand the fuel, raw materials, and energy base. Construction had begun on the ore-concentrating plant in Krivoi Rog for providing raw materials for the metal-processing enterprises of the member countries. The construction of the first reactor in the Khmelnitskii atomic power station was in its final phases. Powerful power transmission lines were being constructed in Bulgaria, Poland, and Romania, and new reactors had been put into operation in the atomic power stations of Czechoslovakia and Hungary. Conditions for building the long Yamburg gas pipeline and extending it to the western border of the USSR had been agreed upon.

The 40th Council session, however, would not go down as one of the most important events in CMEA history by virtue of the routine decisions and declarations made or its agreements on the continuation or initiation of new joint projects. In this respect it differed little from previous Council meetings. It enters into CMEA history as a congress of historical dimensions because it aspired to serve as a bridge between the basic industry stage of the old CMEA, as an international cooperation authority, and the stage of entry into the worldwide scientific and technical revolution. The Council meeting carried further the initiatives of the June 1984 summit conference on the development of a Comprehensive Program for scientific and technical revolution to the year 2000. It was noted that the three hundred scientific production organizations existing at present within the CMEA were creating new or more sophisticated machinery, instruments, and construction materials which were already having a tangible influence on the overall economy, and that international teams of scientists were working on research projects in top-priority areas of scientific and technical progress in the five most important industrial branches of the CMEA countries, which would be included in the Comprehensive Program. All this was taking place, it is stated, under conditions of a tense political situation which is "continuously being inflamed by aggressive imperialist circles, especially American." This aggressive policy is contrasted to the peace-loving policy of the socialist community, which undertakes everything possible to maintain peace on earth.

The Comprehensive Program of scientific and technical cooperation which the next 41st Special Meeting of the CMEA adopted, was conceived as the great friendly initiative of the East bloc in contrast to the strategic defense initiative, SDI, of the United States.

Gorbachev's alternative to SDI: the CMEA Comprehensive Program of December 1985

Gorbachev returned to Moscow from his summit meeting with Ronald Reagan without having been able to dissuade him from his SDI program. He had been in a hurry to present a counter-program of his alliance program, which he had already presented to his own country, and which was to have been approved by the upcoming 27th Party Congress. The entire CMEA was to be brought into this ambitious development plan. The June 1984 summit planned to prepare a Comprehensive Program to accelerate scientific and technical progress to the year 2000. However, at that time the gerontocracy still ruled in the Soviet Union, and it was in absolutely no hurry, especially when the issue was such a turning point with long-range consequences. The young leadership has no time to lose. The Comprehensive Program increased in its political timeliness after the meeting with Reagan. The Kremlin clocks have a different rhythm after the lethargy of the omniponent impotent gerontocracy. The young Party chief is in a hurry to make up as rapidly as possible for what has been neglected and to take the giant leap into the modern world.

In this respect he is not unlike Peter the Great, or Sergei Witte, the far-seeing and skillful Finance Minister of the last Tsar, or even from Josef Stalin, who initiated his momentous five-year plans for accelerated industrialization of the hopelessly backward country with the following words: "We are decades behind the industrialized West, and weak as we were we have always been defeated in our battles with the strong, by the Polish nobility, the Japanese Samurai, the German princes, and everyone else."

So too does he resemble Khrushchev, whose third Party program of the CPSU, adopted by the 22nd Party Congress in 1961, set down the objective of achieving a higher per capita income than the United States by the year 1980, in order then to make the utopian dream and passionately longed-for Communism a reality on earth.

The great leaders had brought some progress to Russia with its centuries of backwardness. However, Russia has also remained backward in its economy and in the amenities of civilization compared to the West, which has been shaken by crises but has rapidly moved forward nonetheless. The same may be said about the real socialism in the Soviet Union, whose revolutionary development has failed to link up with the worldwide scientific and technical revolution of the greatest economic and social revolution of our age. Gorbachev bitterly noted at the April 1985 Central Committee meeting that the Soviet Union had failed to create this linkup and proclaimed that it must accomplish this within an historically short time of fifteen years if it is to enter the 21st century as the most industrially developed nation of the world. Gorbachev also has good reason to fear the consequences of the backwardness of his country. Reagan's SDI program worries him. Backwardness in science and technology means backwardness in the armaments industry. And that he something he cannot afford. The military which is supporting him could never forgive him for this.

The question is posed in all quarters: Will Gorbachev be luckier than his predecessors who brought the country further, but left eternal Russia in a backward condition? To answer this question correctly, another question must also be answered: namely, why his great predecessors had failed in their attempts to resolve these historical tasks. The answer is as simple as it is complicated: because they had tried to surmount perennial backwardness with the ways and means of Peter the Great: in other words with the force of the state, with stern discipline, and with coercive methods. The great leaders have not brought the economic and political system much further compared with the rapidly modernizing West. The Soviet leaders also allowed production capacities to develop more dynamically than the relations of production.

Peter the Great cut the beards of his Boyars and imported foreign engineers and the most modern technology of the time, to bring the military strength of his country up to the top standard of the time. Stalin built up the industrial base of the country by nationalizing the entire economy and the society as well through the discipline of terror; Khrushchev took over a backward country which he had freed from Stalin's reign of terror, but despite many attempts did not create a new system; even then he was not up to the rapidly progressing scientific and technical revolution. Brezhnev did not succeed in bridging over the ever-growing technology gap through imports of modern technology and knowhow.

Gorbachev will be luckier than his great predecessors in carrying his country forward if he is successful not only in strengthening economic discipline, but also in adapting the existing economic and political system to the requirements of the times. So far, the measures taken have not been adequate to the task, and many years of observation of developments in the Soviet Union have shown that even if this is Gorbachev's intention, he will not be able to realize it. For this a new social revolution would be necessary. The overthrow of the gerontocracy and the assumption of power by a younger generation does not mean that this generation is a generation of revolutionaries. It is not. It would like to improve the existing system, infuse new energy in the calcified arteries of the social mechanism, but is not about to allow any basic changes in the social structures and mechanisms that might place its rule at risk. However, the existing economic and political system is itself incapable of adapting, since it is not integrated into the world economy and does not receive impulses from it. The economy is administered, and its driving forces are the increasingly sophisticated technology of administration. But this has always been less effective than the accumulated traditional wisdom of communication mechanisms formed in the course of mankind's history—mechanisms which fail only when they are distorted and there is too much state intervention, or at least more than they can bear.

Of course Gorbachev will improve steering mechanisms and above all management. However, his great predecessors also carried out half-hearted reforms. But there has been no transition from the quality of reform efforts to a new quantity of an effective, efficient steering system. The principal driving force of his policy of renewal will be the impressive energy of his and his younger team, strict discipline, the struggle against the perennial pestilence of his country, namely, alcoholism, which is driving the productivity of labor, already weak, into the ground, and a consistent system of rewards and penalties. With these measures he will be able to carry his country and perhaps the entire Eastern community forward, but not very far.

According to experts, the technology gap is about ten years. Gorbachev allows fifteen years for overcoming it. He will be able to overcome the backwardness with the means at his disposal if capitalism, whose inevitable death had been predicted well over a century ago, succumbs to its own social diseases, or at least brings its scientific and technical progress to a halt in this century, i.e., within the time Gorbachev has allowed for carrying out his Comprehensive Program. But hopes such as these have never been fulfilled and nothing indicates that Gorbachev will be able to fulfill his proclaimed goals by virtue of strengthening the socialist economic and political system, rather than because of a weakening of the capitalist social system.

**Reorganization of the institutional framework
of integration**

A supranational integration is the "economic method for the coming millenium" Gorbachev is fond of repeating at every opportunity when he speaks with leading personages of his smaller partner countries in the CMEA. The first milestone in this direction was reached in this century, however: on December 18, 1985, the historical Comprehensive Program for scientific and technical cooperation of the member countries to the year 2000 was adopted at the 41st Congress of the CMEA. The smaller partners approved the Comprehensive Program, for they see in it a major chance for the further development of their national economies. They know quite well that they will be unable to revolutionize their hopelessly backward production capacities by going it alone. Every CMEA country has its own priorities which they would like to fulfill through the common Comprehensive Program. This is especially true of crisis-ridden Poland, which in 1986 was almost 15% behind its level of production in the pre-crisis year of 1979, with a 39 billion dollar indebtedness to the West and about six billion dollars debt owed to the Soviet Union, and whose vehicle stock is only 63%, and transport capacities only 58% in usable condition (as General Jaruzelski reported to the 1,776 delegates to the Party Congress held at the end of June) and whose production capacities are already very closely interlocked through coproduction with Soviet enterprises. Next comes Romania, suffering severe crises of supply, which cannot use its expanded petrochemical foundry capacities sufficiently, and which has hopelessly neglected agriculture by placing exaggerated stress on heavy industry. After the crushing of the Prague Spring, Czechoslovakia, once a highly developed country in Europe, has stagnated economically and socially, and is currently in the process of becoming even more backward relative to the industrial states of the West, with which its development was once on a par. Hungary, alone in its reform course, has changed much, but has not found a suitable path to dynamic development. Bulgaria, which once had achieved some substantial progress and economic development with the help of the Soviet Union, would like to overcome the economic difficulties that arose in the '80s with the aid of a common economic program. Finally, the GDR expects stimuli for the progress of its economy from the Comprehensive Program that would enable it to maintain an equal pace with West Germany.

Gorbachev's Comprehensive Program of 1985 is much more far-ranging and thorough than Brezhnev's ill-fated Comprehensive Program of 1971. It is not limited to the creation of a raw materials and fuel basis for the overall Eastern bloc and coordination of several other economic areas of the member countries. It concentrates on five progressive industrial sectors to bring the entire economy up to the highest world standard. It is a program for reaching the world level in scientific and technical progress and aspires to carry the Eastern economic community into the 21st century as a modern economic community. Its organizational design creates a perfect framework for a perfect interlocking of the Soviet economy with those of its smaller CMEA partners in the selected progressive industrial sectors and, with their help, in the overall economies of the member countries. The new Soviet leadership has proposed the best possible form of integration which, if successful, could make the economic interlinkings in the Eastern bloc and hence its political cohesion irreversible.

Many compare the level of integration aspired to by the 1985 Comprehensive Program with the Stalinist concept of alliance in the postwar period. But appearances deceive: Stalin imposed the uniform notion of heavy industry on the smaller countries of Eastern and South-eastern Europe, made them dependent on Soviet raw materials and fuels, and held them together with his iron Stalinist discipline of terror, set up obedient leaders, and irrevocably paralyzed them politically and physically. His program was concerned with the first great phase of industrialization, restoring or creating basic industries, and realizing the Stalinist economic model, based on iron and steel. Gorbachev's Comprehensive Program is different: it is a program of scientific and technical revolution of the modern era. Not much can be achieved through commands and discipline. The leaders of the smaller countries have accepted it, but they will implement it only insofar as it accords with their national economies. They have no other recourse. Gorbachev does not have Stalinist instruments of discipline. Those times are past and cannot be repeated. The emancipation and self-awareness of the people of Eastern Europe have come too far to be able to impose upon them something which is contradictory to their interests. Stalin's concept of industrialization and integration is also unrepeatable because Gorbachev no longer has Stalin's resources, he does not have deposits of raw materials and fuels situated in abundance near industrial areas, nor does he have immeasurable reserves of labor power and overpopulated agriculture at his disposal. Agriculture can no longer serve as a source of primitive accumulation for accelerated industrialization as it did during Stalin's time. The measures necessary to restore it to its status as a source of food for an undernourished population were much too costly. Considerable investments must be made today in agriculture in order to reduce grain imports to tolerable dimensions.

Political and economic aspects of the 1985 Comprehensive Program

The proposal of the Comprehensive Program to accelerate scientific and technical progress to the year 2000 was presented by the new Soviet Prime Minister Nikolai Ryzhkov to the 41st meeting of the CMEA which began on December 17 and ended with the adoption of the historic Comprehensive Program on December 18, 1985.[216] The actual reason for this was mentioned by Gorbachev at a reception in the Kremlin for the Prime Ministers of participating member countries (only Cuba and Vietnam were represented by their vice-heads of government): the Comprehensive Program just adopted was designed, said Gorbachev, to make the community independent of Western technology and also to make it invulnerable to pressure and blackmail from the forces of imperialism. The program was therefore a political task of prime importance for strengthening the unity and cohesion of the fraternal countries, said the Soviet Party chief. The Prime Minister presented its economic aspects and the mechanisms of its realization. Its connection with the ambitious projects of the new Soviet leadership is beyond doubt. The involvement of the smaller countries in the Comprehensive Program, so important for the Soviet Union, but for them as well, was presented clearly and straightforwardly: "The October meeting of the Central Committee of the CPSU (1985) presented the project for a new edition of the Party Program as well as basic guidelines for economic and social development of the USSR for nationwide discussion" and further: "This documents sets forth the strategy of accelerated social and economic development of our country, a strategy based on extensive use of the achievements of the scientific and technical revolution." The fraternal countries as well, Ryzhkov noted, "hope that the establishment of the Comprehensive Program and its implementation will bring solutions to fundamental problems of their national economies and in particular the intensification of social production, and a sharp increase in economic efficiency in order to reach new frontiers of science and technology." In this part of his speech, Ryzhkov pays tribute to the great services of leading scientists and experts, representatives of the fraternal countries, and expresses his gratitude to the fraternal countries for their rapid and positive reaction to the Soviet proposal as well as for their active participation in the development of the Comprehensive Program. He concluded by saying that the way the program was prepared reflected the good comradely cooperation of the countries in the socialist alliance.

Ryzhkov is an outstanding technocrat, no diplomat, has served only a brief time in the office of Prime Minister, and has had little to do with the fraternal countries in his managerial practice. Therefore he does not conceal the fact that his concern is a far-seeing Soviet development program in which the fraternal countries—of course in their own well-understood interests—are to be involved. The Soviet Prime Minister said that according to the description of its basic principles by the chairman of the CMEA Committee for Scientific and Technical Cooperation, N. Marchuk, the Comprehensive Program aspires to provide the foundations for the unified actions of the countries of the socialist alliance in making use of fundamentally new techniques and technology. His arguments sound convincing: "The majority of our countries have exhausted the resources for extensive growth but where they do still exist they must be made use of efficiently, with a maximum return." Under the existing conditions, says Ryzhkov, the newly proposed course has not only an economic but also a political significance; Ryzhkov then quotes his Party chief: "There is no alternative to scientific and technical progress." The Soviet Union has therefore posed itself the task of doubling production potential by effecting a qualitative renewal of the means of production, and raising the productivity of labor by 2.3–2.5-fold.

The Soviet Union, says the head of government, has taken due account of both internal and external economic factors, and the circumstance that the world is in the process of entering into a new technological stage of scientific and technical progress, a stage marked by the "complex restructuring of production, quality, and the skills of the workforce, as well as methods of management, and by the transition from selected progressive technologies, to an all-embracing technological system of new generations. The prime minister does not lack examples: "The exchange of technologies is growing dynamically, and in the last ten years the technology and knowhow market has increased by fourfold, and the volume of licences granted exceeds 28 billion dollars." To convince his audience, the delegations from fraternal countries, of the value of international cooperation, Ryzhkov takes an example from the imperialist West: "The centers of powers of imperialism—the United States, West Germany, and Japan—have learned methods that are unusual for capitalism, and which basically must be regarded as a borrowing from socialism: they develop state and international programs for scientific and technical development." Examples from the imperialist West are always convincing in a socialist environment. However, it remains unclear what the state has to do with socialism, which rejects it, and why state programs and international programs are a borrowing from socialism. But theoreticians of Marxism-Leninism also identify, in a more nuanced manner than Ryzhkov, state socialism, i.e., real socialism, with Marxist socialism, with which it has long had nothing in common. The Soviet head of government is thinking not so much of what imperialism has borrowed from socialism, but rather the obstructions to socialism's borrowing from capitalism. For the United States, and some of his allies, says Ryzhkov, are conducting "a technology war against the world of socialism with the aid of embargoes, various prohibitions and restrictions, as for example Cocom lists, with the aim of cutting the socialist countries off from modern technologies, impeding their economic development, and undermining military and strategic parity." The Soviet Prime Minister is not engaging in vacuous propaganda against the hostile system, but rather appealing to his allies to step up the efforts of the socialist alliance and make use of the means of the possibilities of the scientific and technical revolution on the basis of the superiority which the socialist system enjoys, namely: "The planned steering of the economy, highly developed scientific and technical potential, qualified cadres of workers, experts, and scientists." However, he has not mentioned why even with all this superiority the socialist alliance has fallen behind progressive imperialism.

The gap is considerable and immanent to the system

The nationalized planned economy has a major superiority. It is able to concentrate material and financial resources of the economy as a whole on the construction of top priority major projects and itself determine their selection. It has done this throughout its history. The results are the mammoth steel and power plants in the Soviet Union, and even in Poland, Hungary, or Romania; and also the giant raw material and fuel basis and second largest military-industrial complex in the world. But this advantage, namely, that of being able to manage the overall economy as a huge state concern, turned into its opposite when it was necessary to make the transition from basic industries to the complicated sophisticated production of the modern world in which quality, decision, and skills play a decisive role. Central planning authorities have information about what the economy needs, but they have no reliable parameters for measuring efficiency in a standard way. This tightrope walking on false, often heavily subsidized prices, the unreal exchange rates, the rules of the state monopoly on foreign trade and currency which shield producers from the foreign markets, the chronic sellers' market which has no competition on the domestic market, to say nothing about on foreign markets, all have a devastating effect on quality, the cost of production, and the productivity of labor and capital. The manager of a state enterprise who must answer to his superiors in the economic hierarchy or to a Party representative and not to the market ceases to be an entrepreneur. The same process which causes economic mechanisms to degenerate into instruments of economic accounting reduces the manager of a state enterprise to the level of a state official. Although he meticulously fulfils the indicators of the state plan, he has learned over the course of time to do this without taking into account the needs of the consumer. That is the reason for the chronic shortage of urgently needed mass consumer goods which every Soviet leader and above all Mikhail Gorbachev complains of so bitterly, and that is the reason for the low productivity and low quality. Adam Smith's theses that the sum of individual advantages which promote the advantage of the society as a whole is confirmed beyond dispute in the results of a planned economy, in which the sum of the state authorities decides what is of advantage to society. The state, which administers the economy as a single giant concern, transforms the presumed superiority, of being able to dispose over the whole of society's resources, into a disadvantage. The planned economies moved forward at tremendous growth rates as long as they had an abundance of cheap human and material resources. It was extensive but not intensive factors which carried them forward. They have never reached a leading position in productivity or quality. They have never taken over the leadership in the production of advanced technologies and knowhow. Since their genesis down to the present they have imported progress-promoting technologies from abroad. This fact has been known to the Soviet leadership for some time. Gorbachev like his predecessors would like to alter the course of history of the planned economies. He and his team speak of the superiority of the socialist planned economy and the superiority of socialist international cooperation, but are quite well aware of the gap between the socialist nations and the developed capitalist countries of the world.

According to American estimates, about 30,000 large computers were operating in the Soviet Union in 1986, and at least half of them are in the command centers of the Ministry of Defense. In the United States there are 170,000 giant computers functioning. Only 3,300 of the 44,000 Soviet industrial enterprises are hooked up to computerized data centers or themselves have data processing systems for which printers are imported from the GDR and diskettes from Bulgaria.[217] The Soviet standard computer Esa carries out 5 million operations per second, but comparable Western instruments do 10 million operations per second. Whereas Soviet small computers with storage chips have a capacity of 4,000 bits, comparable Western devices have 256,000 bits. The telephone network is hopelessly backward. Two computers only a few kilometers from one another cannot be connected with the existing transmission lines in the Soviet Union. In other countries, however, computers thousands of kilometers apart are in communication with one another.[218] The Soviets order ancient computer work done abroad. Many Moscow foreign trade organizations as well as the planning authorities in the Baltic cities of Riga and Vilnius use Siemens computers; all Soviet grain imports are coordinated with computers from a Munich concern.[219]

The fifth progressive area of cooperation

It must be admitted with all due frankness, said the Soviet head of government in his speech to the delegates from the smaller countries, that the socialist countries are far from utilizing all the possibilities of scientific and technical progress and dealing jointly with scientific and technical problems. Therefore the Comprehensive Program for scientific and technical progress has a strategic significance. Ryzhkov mentions the five principal areas of the Comprehensive Program: electronization with comprehensive computer systems and modern information devices; complex automation with flexible production systems; atomic energy; new progress-promoting materials and technologies; and biotechnology. He expresses his belief that the priority given to these main areas is fully correct. The most important tendencies of the present-day scientific and technical revolution, as well as the potential directions of the development of science, were taken into account in selecting them. The Soviet head of government returns once more to the projects of his own country and to the task posed in the main areas of the economic and social program: reducing manual and physical labor—at present its share in total performance is almost twice as great as in the developed industrial countries of the West—and then goes on to add: "It is one of the principal aims of socialist society to make men's labor easier, and to give it a creative character." He then goes on to concentrate on measures which will be necessary to fulfill the ambitious program. The principal themes were taken into account earlier in the "Draft of the principal areas of economic and social development of the USSR," and the development of specialized production of new products in accordance with the Comprehensive Program would begin with the revision of the draft of the five-year plan for 1986 to 1990. He therefore appeals to the other CMEA countries to include the tasks of the Comprehensive Program in their five-year plans. Ryzhkov attaches special value in this connection to atomic energy and biotechnology. It should be pointed out that the Comprehensive Program was adopted a half year before the Chernobyl disaster. At that time it was possible really to believe his comments that atomic energy owed its great success to the development of socialist integration. The promise of the CMEA secretary Sychev, that in the future atomic power stations in the CMEA will be based on water-cooled nuclear reactors and that the WWER–440 reactors will be gradually replaced by much stronger WWER–1000 reactors does not sound so impressive in this context.[220]

The Comprehensive Program is contingent upon the availability of adequate instruments to fulfill it

It is the main task of the member countries to undertake the appropriate measures to fulfill this programmatic CMEA document, said the Soviet Prime Minister. The Soviet Union has already undertaken measures in this direction, he said to the delegates of the partner countries. The entire system of planning and administration of science, technology, and production has been brought to bear. A special system for providing statistical reports on the results of fulfillment of the program has been initiated. Almost 700 scientific organizations will participate in the implementation of this gigantic program. It is therefore extremely important, said Ryzhkov, to avoid the dissipation of energies and to concentrate the efforts of the teams of experts on the ultimate goal, and to strengthen cooperation within the CMEA. Ryzhkov commented that the Soviet Union had recruited the strongest and most competent workers in research, designing, science, and production into the program.

Ryzhkov revealed the true purport of the Comprehensive Program when he described organization methods. There is no longer any doubt that the aim is to involve the best scientists and production forces of the smaller countries in the development projects of the most powerful CMEA country. "We have jointly proposed the concept of leading organizations to guarantee an efficient and meticulous cooperation between Soviet organizations and the organizations of other countries. This form of cooperation will help us to deal with the principal problem of creating contacts between the various agents and actors responsible for carrying out the program in the individual CMEA countries." The Prime Minister informed his audience that the Politburo of the Central Committee of the CPSU had adopted a resolution to create fundamentally new types of designs for technical organizations which would extend beyond the individual branches. In the next sentence, the Prime Minister revealed something which should be of crucial importance for the interrelations between Soviet organizations and the corresponding organizations of other member countries: "Almost all of the Soviet organizations will be the leading organizations for problems of the Comprehensive Program."

Of course it is only correct that the powerful research, designing, and production centers of the Soviet Union, equipped with all the appropriate research instruments, and not the relatively weak institutions of the smaller countries, which are usually poorly equipped, should be leading the way in implementing the ambitious themes of the Comprehensive Program. It should be recalled that the branch commissions, hitherto the most important coordinating centers of a number of the economic areas of the member countries, have their seats in the individual CMEA countries, in particular, where there is a special interest in the particular area: e.g., in Poland for coalmining, in Czechoslovakia for machinery construction, in the GDR for the chemical industry, in Mongolia for geology, etc. The institutions which lead the way in fulfilling the Comprehensive Program, which undoubtedly have pushed the CMEA branch commissions into the background, or have at least narrowed the area of their activities, will, however, have their seats in the Soviet Union. The organizational form for linking the crucial command centers of the smaller countries with the giant institutions of the Soviet Union is certainly not without its own logic.

The densely interwoven organizational network is, however, not enough to fulfill this far-seeing program for cooperation. It can only be efficiently implemented if it is fuelled with the appropriate material and financial resources of the member countries. The Soviet Prime Minister is thinking about forms of cooperation for the future, and joint scientific and production associations which would work on the basis of unified practical plans. Two Soviet-Bulgarian associations in the machine-tool industry are already operating, he reported. A second organizational form proposed by the Prime Minister was joint enterprises. "Relevant studies are being carried out in this area," he stressed, and went on to say that in the future "efforts will also be undertaken to construct joint designing and experimental offices." Ryzhkov is not very familiar with CMEA matters. His older colleagues might have pointed out to him that these efforts have been going on for three decades, but have so far succeeded in building only one joint small-scale Hungarian-Polish coal-concentrating works, Haldex, and a joint German-Polish textile plant in Zawiercie in Poland. The ambitious plans foundered on problems of ownership, clearing, and transfer. We might note in passing that the Polish-Hungarian firm Haldex was forced to determine hundreds of conversion factors to evolve a comprehensible clearing practice that was of use to both Poland and Hungary.

The organizers of the 41st Council meeting were also concerned with giving the themes of the Comprehensive Program the binding form of cooperation agreements. Sychev, the CMEA Secretary, reported that these procedures had already come into force. The heads of government signed three very important agreements that made concrete the program's provisions during the course of the meeting: one agreement on multilateral cooperation on the designing and establishment of glassfibre means of communication, an agreement on an automatic designing system (SPAR), and an agreement to establish the international scientific and technical association Interrobot. The intention was in the next half-year to conclude 67 agreements and to make concrete another 84 existing agreements. Ryzhkov informed his audience that half of the 92 topics in the Comprehensive Program should lead to the preparation and manufacture of sample products and technologies within the next three years. Over the following years, the scale of creating new projects should increase gradually. The Comprehensive Program "will contribute to the institution of penetrating structural changes in the economies of the member countries and to a renewal of their production base," said Ryzhkov. In his opinion the best path in the right direction would be the conclusion of agreements with a complex cycle, which would include both scientific research, as well as production and sales.

The greatest surprise of the 41st meeting was the declaration of the Soviet Prime Minister that his government had adopted a resolution to permit the organizations, called upon to play leading roles in implementing the themes of the Comprehensive Program, to conclude agreements with corresponding organizations of other countries, and to pass on the results within the framework of cooperation in the implementation of the particular themes of the Comprehensive Program.

It was known from the outset that the three developing countries of the CMEA, Cuba, Mongolia and Vietnam, had no special place in the implementation of this Comprehensive Program, with its sights set on new horizons of scientific and technical progress, the aim of which is to make possible the entry of the Soviet Union and its allies into a modern worldwide economic network. The approximation of the less developed countries to the level of the industrially developed countries of East Europe, stressed in every programmatic CMEA document, is convincing to no one, and hence was not included in Gorbachev's Comprehensive Program. However, it was not completely forgotten. The 41st Council meeting resolved to increase the efficiency of scientific and technical aid as well as economic aid from the European CMEA countries and to Vietnam, Cuba, and

Mongolia. Of course the Comprehensive Program also speaks of continuing support to the developing countries of this world as well as to the expanding and deepening of mutually advantageous cooperation with all other countries.

One other important problem came up at the 41st Council meeting, namely, the organizational structure of the CMEA, which was created during Khrushchev's time and had been later expanded quantitatively, without however altering the principal structures. The 41st Council therefore expressed the intention of perfecting the activity of the CMEA authorities and especially its secretariat, and to bring it up to a level commensurate with the tasks posed in the Comprehensive Program; important changes in its structure, its style, and its working methods have been outlined.

The following statement in the speech of the Soviet Prime Minister gives some idea of the value attached by the architects of the Comprehensive Program to that program: "The whole of mankind will make the results of the scientific and technical revolution the yardstick for their comparison of the socialist world with the capitalist world." To emphasize the peaceful nature of the Comprehensive Program it is stressed that: "We can already see that we have adopted a program for a peaceful creation in the name of mankind. We have no intention of creating a privileged club of states claiming a monopoly over the latest achievements of science and technology." However, the Eastern bloc at present seems too far behind the world level to speak of a club of countries, whether they claim a monopoly or not, which would be able to assume leadership in science and technology in the foreseeable future.

The second Comprehensive Program of the CMEA and the third revised program of the CPSU

Soviet Prime Minister Nikolai Ryzhkov informed the 41st session of the CMEA that the Central Committee of the CPSU had approved two fundamental documents: the new version of the third Party Program of the CPSU; and the guidelines for economic and social development in the five-year period from 1986 to 1990 and in the period up to the year 2000, which indicated the ways and means for the development of Soviet society to the end of the present century.[221] The delegates of the smaller countries to the 41st session understood the Soviet Prime Minister correctly: these documents also indicate ways and means which the CMEA will initiate in the next fifteen years to carry the economies of the Eastern bloc into the 21st century as a progressive economic bloc in accordance with joint and national interests.

The Central Committee of the CPSU approved a draft of the revised Third Party Program and the guidelines for the economic and social development of the Soviet Union on October 15, 1985. These documents, as the Soviet Prime Minister stressed, served as a foundation for the Comprehensive Program decided upon on December 18, 1985 by the 41st CMEA meeting, but were not adopted until March 6, 1986 by the 27th Party Congress of the CPSU as Party documents. There seem to be certain discrepancies in this chronology, but only at first glance. The fundamental documents approved by the October Congress of the Central Committee of the CPSU served as an inviolable law for the 27th Party Congress, as well as a firm foundation for the Comprehensive Program approved by the 41st CMEA meeting. Gorbachev had a good reason to adopt the Comprehensive Program of the CMEA after the October meeting of the Central Committee and after the November summit with Reagan, rather than wait for the March 1986 CPSU Congress. After all, not since the 16th Congress of the CPSU in 1934 has any ruling Communist Party congress been convened to draft or amend a Party Program. They have confirmed Party documents that have already been voted upon by the highest Party committees. And that is the way it was this time at the 27th Party Congress, the first under Gorbachev's leadership. The 4,993 delegates of the roughly 19 million members of the CPSU listened; the most prominent of them read their prepared speeches, applauded Gorbachev and his assistants from time to time, and got bored. A Polish joke gives a good idea of the course of Party festivals: The head of the secret police, who has called the Party leader's attention to the presence of an enemy of the people in the conference hall, apprehended the latter within a few minutes, and was awarded with the boss's praise. "Not worth talking about," says the secret policeman. "It was quite easy to expose the enemy. He was the only one who wasn't asleep."

The 27th Party Congress, which took place thirty years after the 20th Party Congress, at which Khrushchev expressed his uncompromising condemnation of Stalin's reign of terror, was also "historic" just like the February 1956 Congress. The omnipotent yet impotent gerontocracy was overthrown and a new generation had come to power that had experienced neither the romanticism of the October Revolution and the great historical disappointment of Thermidor nor the horror of the crushing defeats of the first phase and the intoxication of victory in the final phase of World War II. At this 27th Party Congress, the new leader of his country and his personally chosen team also passed a merciless judgment on the eighteen years of Brezhnev's reign, just as Khrushchev had harshly condemned Stalin's method of rule and Brezhnev those of Khrushchev's. Gorbachev himself endeavored to draw a direct connection between himself and Lenin's methods of leadership, as he declared to *Time* magazine on September 8, 1985: "It is not my personal style," he said referring modestly to his own methods of rule, "it is what we learn from Lenin." Many American experts drew from this statement the conclusion that the new lords in the Kremlin would introduce a new strategy that would be equivalent to that adopted by Lenin in the early '20s under the name of the New Economic Policy (the NEP). However, this opinion diverges widely from the decisions of the 27th Party Congress and the two years of practice of the new leadership. It should be borne in mind that Gorbachev is not the only one to attempt to trace his roots directly back to Lenin; each of his predecessors had done the same. None of them has claimed a continuity with the methods of rule of his immediate predecessor. The methods of rule of each of Lenin's successors are invariably severely deprecated by the official Soviet history such as "Stalin's cult of the personality," "Khrushchev's voluntarism and subjectivity in making decisions." Brezhnev, as the Moscow joke says, enjoined his people to call him by his patronymic Il 'ich, i.e., the same patronymic which the protagonist of the Great October Revolution called their highly esteemed and respected leader Lenin. Gorbachev's judgment of Brezhnev's methods of rule was, however, no more sparing than Brezhnev's judgment of his precedessor whom he and his accessories overthrew in October 1964.

The mid-'80s bear no point in common with the NEP of the early '20s. We should remember that the NEP was a departure from devastating war Communism, imposed by the ideals of utopian Communism and the bitter reality of the postrevolutionary years, which reduced the Soviet economic production to one-third the prewar level. There was certainly no abundance of goods to remunerate everyone according to his needs, as is stipulated in the Communist Manifesto; rather, hunger and destitution were evenly distributed because there was very little to distribute at all. It should also be remembered that during the NEP only the commanding heights of industry, i.e., heavy industry, was in state hands, and that small businesses and services as well as half of domestic trade and almost the whole of agriculture were in private hands. The share of state ownership in the total economy of the Soviet Union was not much greater at that time than was targeted by the Mitterand-Marchais coalition in 1981.

It was this mixed economy which Lenin wanted to steer with a mixed set of instruments of market and state mechanisms, using functional monetary prices, exchange rates, etc., that were a part of the world system; a thoroughly realistic undertaking. However, between Lenin's NEP and Gorbachev's reform plans is the real socialist system established by Stalin, with its totally nationalized industries, domestic trade and foreign trade, a nationalized or collectivized agriculture planned and administered by the state, since the traditional economic mechanisms have been sapped of their economic content and reduced to instruments of economic accounting.

Gorbachev's economic program; no privatization

The Party Program speaks in an unmistakable language about the projects of the new leadership. We read: "The historical mission of socialism in the economy consists in the use of the achievements of progressive science and perfect technology. Its task is to create the material basis for the objectives of the Communist Party, and for a steady rise in prosperity, as well as to strengthen the economic and defense capacities of the fatherland." Like the Comprehensive Program accepted by the 41st session of the CMEA, the newly drafted Third Party Program postulates the "technical reconstruction" of the economy on the basis of the highest level achieved by science and technology, the renovation of the production apparatus and its technology, an orientation to complete automation, completely automated departments and enterprises, the gradual spread of electronics, chemistry, robotics, and computers and biotechnology.'' Like the CMEA Comprehensive Program, the CPSU Party Program stresses economy in the use of material resources: ''Frugality will be the principal source for covering the needs of the economy in material resources,'' we read. The Soviet Prime Minister informed the delegates of the 41st Council session that half of the Soviet Union's industrial growth will be accounted for by savings, and encouraged them to initiate a similar austerity policy.

A similar emphasis was placed on labor productivity, and Lenin is quoted in this context: ''No transition to a Communist society is possible without a considerable increase in productivity.'' Labor productivity is to be increased by 2.3–2.5-fold by the end of the century. It should be possible to overcome the present gap relative to the Western industrial states. The results of competition will be dependent on developments in the West. However, the Party Program demands far-ranging restructuring in the decisive areas of activity of Soviet man, the switch from extensive to intensive factors in production, steady improvement in the quality of goods, and efficient utilization of production capital. One other important aspect of the Party Program, which may have an appreciable influence on events in the economies of the Eastern bloc is noteworthy: namely, the proportions governing distribution of the targeted above-average economic growth. After the introduction of accelerated industrialization in 1928 and Stalin's five-year plans, industrial production increased much more dynamically than consumption. It should be remembered that bread coupons were introduced in the years of unprecedented growth rates. Inordinately high growth rates presuppose high investment rates. Frugality and restructurings of investment policy are not sufficient to restore the above-average growth rates of the '50s and '60s. High rates of investment mean relatively low rates of consumption. The authors of the Third Party Program understand this, and prefer not to pin themselves down. An ''optimal relationship between investments and consumption, perfection of the relationship between the production of capital investment goods and mass consumption goods, as well as goods of the agro-industrial complex'' is postulated. The programmatic goal of doubling industrial potential, already highly developed, within fifteen years is ambitious, and it is thoroughly justifiable to fear that no great growth rates are to be expected in the satisfaction of human needs. One thing is to be expected from the restructuring of existing investment practice, namely, the transfer of investment money from costly and inefficient concrete new constructions to reconstruction and modernization. With modernization comprising 34.8% (1983)[222] of total investment expenditures, the Soviet investment structure is the strangest in the world economy since the relationship between new construction and modernizations is the converse in the Western industrial countries. However, expectations will only be able to be fulfilled if Soviet managers alter their attitude toward modernization. This too is peculiar, as is to be devined from the following statement to the delegates of the 27th Party Congress by the General Secretary: "[The managers'] principal aim is to create new capacities under the pretext of modernization, and to outfit them with obsolete equipment."

Anyone who expected that the new Party leadership wanted to initiate a privatization of certain areas of the economy as part of an NEP strategy will be deeply disappointed. It does not even think of such things, and the new version of the Third Party Program leaves no doubt that the Party leadership has no such intentions. We can read the following: "The strengthening and expansion of socialist ownership of the means of the production is the principal objective of the socialist social system." And even more clearly: "The degree of socialization as well as the structure of property are to be steadily improved." Of course, the means of production of industry are not meant here, since statization, wrongly identified with socialization or nationalization, and hailed as the most suitable form of property for mature socialism, is the only form of property at all in Soviet industry. Agriculture is meant. Most observers have had inordinate hopes that Gorbachev will begin with privatization in just this area. However, something rather the opposite is to be inferred from the programmatic statement above, namely, that the restructuring of collective into state property, initiated by Khrushchev and Brezhnev: between 1940 and 1981 collective farms decreased from 235,500 to 25,300 and the number of state farms increased from 2,300 to 21,600.[223]

Gorbachev, who had the post of Central Committee Secretary for Agriculture for some time, proposed other measures instead of privatization. These have to do with improving agrarian output, the methods of sale, and the organization of the division of labor, but leave property relations intact. The day-to-day supervision is to be abolished. Every collective farm shall henceforth be assigned a delivery quota, set for five years, for grain, cattle, and other agrarian products, and will be able to dispose of the surplus itself. That means the collective farms may sell to the state or on the free collective-farm market, or use the surplus for their own purposes. They are also to obtain higher prices for farm products. It should be remembered that agriculture is highly subsidized by the state: state subsidies increased from 17 billion rubles to 37 billion rubles between 1970 and 1980, and this covered more than half of the value of production manufactured in agriculture.[224] One of the most important measures seems to be the higher status given to brigades. They are to play the principal role in the division of labor in the collective farms. The brigades will conclude contracts with the collective farm administrations, assume responsibility for proceeds, and be paid in accordance with what has been achieved. But no privatization and no quasi-privatization are in sight in agriculture.

More state administration than economic mechanisms

Now there can be no doubt: the new Party leadership will not abandon economic steering to factory managers nor to the "invisible hand" of the market. Quite to the contrary. The final resolution of the 27th Party Congress states: "The principal area of activity of the Party was and is the economy." This declaration determines everything beforehand. Anyone who entertains any illusions about future steering methods will be disabused by the speech of Ryzhkov, Prime Minister, at the 27th Party Congress on March 3, 1986. He stated: "The hopes of bourgeois ideologs that we will depart from the principles of democratic centralism and central management and planning of the economy have not been fulfilled and will not be fulfilled."

Of course the new Party leadership wants to reform economic steering mechanisms. Ryzhkov further explained the above tendency with the following words: "The Party will work to expand independence of industrial associations and enterprises and to strengthen their responsibility for the end result." The new Party leadership will perhaps go further in this direction than Brezhnev and Andropov. Gorbachev has described his projects more passionately and more resolutely than Brezhnev did. At the 26th Party Congress in 1981, Brezhnev spoke of a "further perfection of the economic mechanism and improvement of the planning system"; at the 27th Party Congress five years later, Gorbachev said: "Comrades, we are standing before what is undoubtedly the most significant restructuring of the socialist economic mechanism." The Soviet leadership must currently however deal with the consequences of the economic negligence of the Brezhnev era, just as Brezhnev and Kosygin had to cope with the grave consequences of Khrushchev's horizontal decentralization of economic management, the destruction of the central economic apparatus, and the transfer of economic leadership to the newly formed Sovnarkhozy (regional authorities of economic management). Gorbachev has no better estimation of Brezhnev's economic leadership than Brezhnev did of Nikita Khrushchev's. He reproached the Brezhnev era for not having assessed "changes in world economic development promptly or politically correctly, and not recognizing that the transition of the economy to intensive economic methods could not be put off." Egor Ligachev critized the governing methods of the past with Lenin's words. "We have fallen into a bureaucratic swamp of paper-writing, degrees, draft bills, and our work is disappearing into this sea of paper."[225] And on March 3 the new Prime Minister Nikolai Ryzhkov said "Discipline and order have sunken to an intolerable level, unfavorable tendencies are growing steadily in economic development, no one drew the corresponding conclusions from the fact that the factors of extensive growth are now exhausted and when discipline was strengthened after 1983 [under Andropov and Chernenko] there was no more time to fulfill the goals of the five-year plan for 1981–1985"; Boris Yeltsin rounded out these bitter words with the comment: "The errors of a few people have damaged the prestige of the Party and socialism."

The new Party leadership promises that it wants to change a lot in the steering mechanism, but only with a framework of the existing economic system. The Party program formulates the basic principles of the reform steering system as follows: "Conditions for a growing contribution of every social unit must be created for optimal satisfaction of social needs with a minimizing of the social costs and the rational utilization of resources." The term "democratic central-ism" is redefined. The organic unity and special value of each component of the term are stressed. And an accent is placed on the necessity of "strengthening the efficiency of central management as well as autonomy for day-to-day operations and responsibility for the results of the enterprise." The central authorities are to "concentrate mainly on strategic tasks and social problems." Day-to-day plan-ning and monitoring by Gosplan is to be reduced considerably. As Gorbachev said at the 27th Party Congress, the central planning authority should function as a "chief of staff of the economy and an effective economic center and not be involved in the day-to-day management of the economy." Other central authori-ties should also not be concerned with the day-to-day management of economic enterprises and should concentrate solely on strategic tasks of the economic branches under them, without interfering in their internal affairs. The focus of all economic activities, states the Party Program, is to be shifted to the factory and enterprise workforces. Industrial plants are to go over to "true economic ac-counting covering costs and self-financing." Gorbachev understands that the principal problem that must be solved is that of finding an adequate combination of "centralism and democracy." But the reform projects of all his predecessors as well as of the leaderships of the People's Republics have all foundered on this task. What he promises to his country sounds very passionate, but in the light of experience hitherto not very convincing. Gorbachev said that a law is being prepared that gives every citizen the right to legal defense in matters arising out of conflict with the authorities" and that "we will not rest until we find the right path, until servility to the authorities is eradicated."

The existing economic mechanisms are to be perfected, however, without altering their content appreciably. The Party Program provides for strengthening monetary and credit relations and increasing the buying power of the ruble. Of course there is no thought of integrating the ruble into the world monetary system by means of an economically justified exchange rate, as the NEP strategy and the 11th Party Congress of 1922 had contemplated, since the Party Program points out that his measure is being taken "in accordance with the new socialist con-tent." However, more margin of freedom is being conceded to price policies. Henceforth prices will not only express the socially necessary costs of produc-tion, but will also create forces for manufacturing top-quality goods and become more consistently an "active instrument of economic and social policy," and give due consideration to "the social requirements of public demand." The fulfillment of this objective, however, will make it necessary to raise prices for basic foods. As Mikhail Gorbachev said on September 8, 1985, in Tselinograd, state subsidies for meat alone amount to 20 billion rubles.[226]

The binding indices of the State Plan are to be reduced in number and where possible replaced by long-term "economic norms" in order to "promote the readiness for initiative and innovation among the managers as well as the workforces of enterprises," as the Party Program states it. However, this quite interesting method of planning is not new. It was used a few years before the Prague Spring in Czechoslovakia as well as to some extent in Poland, but had no perceptible influence on economic practice. On the other hand, as the Berlin economist Hans Herbert Götz correctly comments: "The proposal to do away with binding plan indices and to replace them by economic norms—i.e., establish price ratios which after all must also be determined by someone—are not sufficient to prevent continual misuse and misdirection of resources and the much criticized disproportionalities."[227]

"120 professors? Fatherland, you are lost!"

This quotation is attributed to Otto von Bismarck. Today the number of professors who could bring their fatherland to ruin is much greater. The Soviet Union alone has over 1.5 million scientists, one-fourth of the world figure. Many, very many of them, are sociologists and economists. Soviet Party leaders have often used and still make use of their advice in making important decisions. Lenin took counsel from the best economists of his time, e.g., Bukharin and Preobrazhensky, when he had to take the historical decision on the New Economic Policy (NEP). Stalin was an exception. He had the illusion that he was the best scientist in every area of science; wrote the "best" book on economics of his time, *The Economic Problems of Socialism in the USSR*, and shaped economic policy himself without making use of or taking seriously any counsel. He murdered the greatest economic advisors of his great predecessor.

Khrushchev took the economic theories of Liberman and Novozhilov, and Brezhnev the theories of Kantorovich, Nemchinov, and Trapeznikov very seriously, but acted otherwise. Gorbachev, as did Andropov and Chernenko, has made use of the capacities of the Siberian section of the Soviet Academy of Sciences in Novosibirsk, the director of its economic division Abel Aganbegian and the sociologist Tatiana Zaslavskaia; as well as the director of the Economic Institute of the Socialist World System, Oleg Bogomolov, on CMEA matters. Soviet scientists have a good reputation in the world. The achievements of some of them are world-renowned. If their overall results are rather modest this is not because there is a lack of talented persons in the Soviet Union but because the economic bureaucrats are unable to translate the results of research so easily into practice. The path from the research laboratory to production is a phony one. The book by Vladimir Dudintsev *Not by Bread Alone*, which describes this rocky road, aroused passions, but since then nothing has changed. Nonetheless the Americans are wrong to measure the performance of Soviet scientists by the number of Nobel prizes received. Of the 370 Nobel prizes awarded since 1901, scientists of Russia and the Soviet Union have received only ten, and only one in the last decade, while the Americans have received 137.[228] The Nobel prize is a measure of recognition and acknowledgement of achievement, but it is not without its subjective undertones. Soviet scientists are too remote from world public opinion and the gap between performance, utilization, and recognition in the Soviet Union is much too great. The writings of the late Soviet Nobel prize laureate, Leonid Kantorovich, and of many other economists have achieved world acclaim (Nobel prize-winner for economics Wassily Leontief is considered an American).

However, more is demanded of Soviet economists and sociologists than they can give. It is demanded that they produce a closed system of economic management thoroughly thought out in all its detail. They cannot do this, because neither God nor any genius has ever anywhere created a closed economic system: the great Adam Smith and David Ricardo were the best interpreters of a classical market economy. Ricardo was also a talented practitioner in that he made use of his knowledge not only to enrich Great Britain but to enrich himself with lucky speculation in shares on the London Stock Market. However, none of them created or changed any market mechanisms. But market mechanisms have not stood still over the centuries. They have adapted continually to expanding and self-differentiated production and division of labor and become more refined. They were created not by an individual or a team of individuals, but by generations of men over the entire course of human history. Primitive exchange instruments, cattle, mussels, coins, etc., developed into the transferable paper money and complicated credit facilities of the large banks of the modern era. This long and tortuous path has been handed down by producers, traders, and bankers from generation to generation and become more sophisticated in the process. Scientists were also involved. But Karl Marx no longer wanted any part of the riches of his time; poor but full of genius, he wanted to overthrow the capitalist world with its riches and its money, its exploitation and oppression, and brought to the world his somewhat modified vision of a society in which equality existed for all, in which man ruled over things and not over other men, in which everyone would take from the stores of his society as much as he produced and needed, of course without the mediation of the much-coveted money, which he hated so passionately, but rather on the basis of coupons which indicated how much time was spent on productive labor.

This vision seems somewhat primitive. But Marx gained his fame not through his vision of a future society, but through his great criticism of capitalism in the mid–19th century, which no longer exists in the civilized world. His dreams of a just egalitarian society remain a utopia, even where his theory has become the ideology of the protagonists of the Great October Revolution. The economic system created by Stalin resembles Luddendorff's war economy, a prototype of Lenin's, much more than it does Thomas More's Utopia, Charles Fourier's Phalansteries, or Robert Owen's production cooperatives. The notion that a modern industrial society can be steered more purposefully by planning and administration than by economic mechanisms created over the course of centuries by the accumulated collective human reason proved to be as illusory as the utopia of a just and egalitarian society. The first and second phases of industrialization were accomplished by commands from the state authorities with an inordinate expenditure of capital and labor power; but the scientific and technical revolution, heralded by the present Soviet leadership, cannot be accomplished with the obsolete extensive growth factors of the past.

It was no accident that the sociologist Tatiana Zaslavskaia had the following to say in her now famous "Novosibirsk Report": "The complexity of the economic steering mechanism is much greater than in all other existing social systems. In contrast, the research work being done for a new steering model has been no more than amateurish." In the light of our reflections above, however, the following comment of the sociologist seems even more important: "The complexity of modern economic structures has long ago passed the level where a planned economy can still be steered from a center."[229] And even more clearly: "The system of centralized administrative steering has reached the limits of its performance." Zaslavskaia's conclusions are right on mark: an economy in the phase of the scientific and technical revolution of the modern era cannot and must not be administered by directives from a central authority. Moreover, there is no science which could create steering methods for a planned economy based on intensive development factors. It is a systemic problem which the ruling Party is not ready to take on. The consequences are for the politicians and not scientists to draw. The politicians of the planned economies have to decide how these economies are going to be steered in the phase of the scientific and technical revolution, taking into account the requirements of the international division of labor as well, especially in the CMEA; mechanisms which have become dysfunctional nationally cannot provide a basis for complex relations in the CMEA in the modern period. Nonconvertible money, intended for the purposes of economic accounting, is of no use here. The effect of the traditional economic mechanisms, and their need for their own sphere of influence narrowing the range of maneuver of politicians in the economy is known well enough. If the political leadership wants to leave some room to economic mechanisms, then it must give up some of its administrative powers, and some of its politics in the economy, as much as the "invisible hand" of the released market will demand. The combination of these two components of economic management can be found but on the condition that the fundamental principle of the Party Program "the main area of activity of the Party was and is the economy" is fundamentally changed. There is no place for economic mechanisms and economic rationality in the economy, which the Party has made its principal domain of activity. This is reduced to the rational thinking of politicians and economic policymakers.

The premise that somehow scientific socialism is the ideology of an egalitarian and just society is false. It is also false therefore that scientific mechanisms would create a non-existing scientific socialism. What has been created is real socialism, based on a centrally administered state economy. The diagnosis of the disease from which the Soviet and the other planned economies are suffering has been correctly defined by the new leaders. The scientists from Novosibirsk have also prescribed a correct therapy, namely: less state and more self-initiative for entrepreneurs and their workforces. But the 27th Party Congress contemplated another therapy: a stronger central administration and a stronger self-administration. In whatever way the relationship between these two components of democratic centralism might be shaped, no state control, creates adequate conditions for giving sufficient play to economic mechanisms. The conclusion would therefore be justified that the economic reforms introduced by the new Soviet leadership will provide no inspiring impulses from the countries of Eastern Europe; and that the Comprehensive Program accepted on December 18, 1985, will be fulfilled by means of administrative decisions at the macro-level rather than by means of organic contacts at the micro-level and hence will have limited possibilities of achieving its ambitious targets.

Opinions differ appreciably on the path the new Party leadership will embark upon in the new economic reform. In addition to those observers who expect an unlikely NEP strategy, there are skeptical opinions such as presented by two prominent US experts[230]: "Gorbachev's goal is not a socialist revolution; he is striving for scientific and technical evolution; a convinced technocrat promises a reformed regime, technological expertise, managerial experience, and political art," but not much more. But the British Soviet expert Alex Nove thinks that the difficult situation will force reforms upon the new leadership. "They will want to maintain their *political* monopoly, but will use it to introduce far-ranging economic reforms which will also have significant sociopolitical consequences, out of their fear of the consequences of doing nothing." Time seems to be bearing out the first prediction.

The reform projects in the light of the historical prospects of development in domestic and foreign relations

The answer to the question of how far the new leadership can go in reforming the existing economic and political system cannot be answered without taking into consideration the prospects of development of the Eastern community and the contemplated strategy for relations to the world outside. The new version of the Third Party Program gives sufficient information on both aspects of development. One can say with confidence that the new Party leadership has shown itself to be much more realistic in evaluating the current phase of development as well as the long-term prospects of development of the Soviet society than Nikita Khrushchev was in his day. If the Soviet Union had developed as the Party Program adopted in 1961 by the 22nd Party Congress had diagnosed, the present Soviet generation would be living in a Communist society in which each Soviet citizen would have a higher per capita income than each US citizen. There would be an abundance of products which would have made it possible to compensate every working person "according to his needs" and not according to his performance, as all Communist manifestoes since 1948 have promised.

In the 25 years between the old and new versions of the Third Party Program, i.e., between 1961 and 1986, Soviet society has neither developed in the direction of an egalitarian Communist society nor does the new Soviet leadership intend to lead it in this direction in the next 25 years. The revised version of the Third Party Program is a fundamentally new program in respect of the definition of the phase of development of the 25 years that have passed since the 22nd Party Congress, as well as in the definition of the future historical phase. As is discernible from certain statements of prominent Soviet politicians, e.g., Konstantin Chernenko, a new version has become indispensable not only because Khrushchev's vision of a Communist society had not been realized in the last 25 years, but because there will be no preconditions for it in the foreseeable future. The revised program, like the CMEA Comprehensive Program adopted on December 18, 1985, speaks of entering the 21st century as an economically and scientifically progressive world system, but contains no indications of the intention to overtake the first economic power of the world, the United States. Even the end specified in the original program of 1961, namely, to enable the next generation or the next one after it to live in Communism, can no longer be found. Instead we find the phrase which speaks a very clear language: "The path from socialism to Communism is determined by objective laws of development; any attempt to introduce the principles of a Communist society without consideration of material and intellectual maturity is destined to failure." The revised Third Party Program defines the next phase of historical development of Soviet society not as "communism" but as "developed socialism," i.e., in the same way as the present phase is described, in which everyone is compensated not according to his needs but according to the quantity and quality of his performance. The new Soviet leadership wants to create a differentiated distribution rather than an egalitarian one.

As we see, Gorbachev will not embark upon the path to Communism. The ruling stratum lives fairly well, even under real socialism. The revised Party Program aspires only, like all Party leaderships hitherto, to create a material basis for the transition to a new phase of civilization. This is regarded as achieving the level of science and technology which a few Western states have already achieved by other means. As prior experience has shown, an intensive economy cannot be managed with "socialist" means, and hence no qualitatively higher production and distribution system can be created. The Western nations, which have achieved a high level of development and have provided their "proletariat" with much more than would be possible in the East, are called capitalists or imperialists. But the intention is not war but coexistence with these countries, although they are still regarded as a hostile environment, the fall of which will be brought about in other ways. The costs of armaments have become prohibitively high and promise to become even higher, and in this respect the dynamically progressing scientific and technical revolution in the West augurs nothing good with regard to keeping pace with the Western level of armaments. An arms reduction is the desired objective, and proposals and summit meeting follow one after the other. The revised Party Program, as in fact all other Party programs, defines coexistence impeccably. It is stated literally: "The historical difference between the different world systems can be solved by peaceful means." Or: "Every nation has the right to live in a society free of oppression in which each has equal rights and democratic laws are made." And further, and even better: "The Communist Party rejects the export of revolution and of counterrevolution, because it sees in this phenomenon a contempt for the right to live in peace and to choose freely one's path of development." This phrase is to be found in the Atlantic Charter of August 14, 1941. The Soviet Union accepted it one month later. But Stalin would not honor it after the victory in World War II. The cult of his person was condemned, but the fait accompli was not made reversible. His successors have expressed their desire to expand what they have conquered to keep together with weapons where necessary and to expand with fraternal aid. Gorbachev swore his loyalty to the socialist alliance on the grave of his precedessor Konstantin Chernenko, and a few months later called "Stalinism" an anti-Soviet invention.[231]

The revised Party Program wants no confrontation with the West. Each sentence is correctly formulated and beams with the love of peace. The renunciation of war is solemnly proclaimed, as well as the threat of war, and even the use of force as a means to solve conflicts which must, so says the program, be solved through negotiations. Coexistence is formulated correctly as "non-interference in the internal affairs of nations and the right of every nation to decide on its own destiny," and "sovereignty and national borders must be strictly respected." One reads with satisfaction the sentences in which the Party Program stigmatizes every attempt to "expand ideological contradictions to international relations in which the United States is reinforced." However, the following sentences are a bit disappointing. This outstanding notion of coexistence is conceived as a state without war, but also without peace. It is a notion of living together with an eternal enemy, with the capitalist world, which not only is described in the same way as in the First Party Program of 1903, the second of 1919, and the third in 1961, but also in an identical way with the Communist Manifesto of 1848. The Western world of the present, with its relatively high standard of living, social security with free trade unions, a pluralistic *ergo* democratic political system with a scientific and technical progress and level of productivity the Eastern countries seek in vain to emulate, is still regarded to be the eternal enemy of the working class. Imperialism of today, now with no colonies, is still described as

Lenin did in his famous work *Imperialism as the Highest Stage of Capitalism* in 1916.

The Western proletariat of today, whose standard of living far exceeds that of the Eastern proletariat, which has militant trade unions and the right to strike to defend its class interests, is still described as 140 years ago and invested with the same historical mission, namely, to overthrow capitalism, as it was viewed 140 years previously. As if it had been the proletariat of a Western country and not the proletariat of the Polish Peoples Republic in 1981 and 1982, or in the GDR in 1953, Hungary and Poland in 1956, Czechoslovakia in 1968, that had entered into a classical class war and had been driven to its knees with martial law, as occurred with the Chilean proletariat in 1973. As if the worker cares whether his salary is paid by a businessman or by the state, as Arnold Toynbee observed. As if the quasi proletariat of the industrial states of the West that are developing into information societies had not solved its historical mission, namely, of bridging the gap between physical and intellectual labor and between the proletariat and the peasants, and between the standard of living in the countryside and in the city, better than the proletarians and peasants of the East have. The industry and agriculture of the United States employed about 28% of all those employed in 1980, while the figure for the Soviet Union was 49.7%.[232] Of course Mikhail Gorbachev can no longer shoulder the burden of greatness and indeed is also serious about his disarmament plans. But these plans cannot be taken seriously so long as he and his Party continue to educate their peoples and the people of the Eastern Europe in the spirit of eternal hostility and are reluctant to reinforce the physical disarmament with a spiritual disarmament.

The hope of the smaller countries of Eastern and South-eastern Europe that the CMEA Comprehensive Program adopted on December 18, 1985, will free them from the military and industrial complex of the superpower and give their populations a higher standard of living can therefore prove to be a pure illusion. Nor is there much contained in the program statement that every country has the right to participate in the relief of international tensions independent of its status, geographical situation, and social system. What is meant is all the other countries of the world who do not need the approval of the superpower. But this is not the case with the smaller countries of Eastern Europe, which have not, nor can they have any basis for differing from the Soviet position.

The major Soviet share in the 1985 CMEA Comprehensive Program

The Soviet share in the 1986 CMEA Comprehensive Program corresponds to its share in the economic capacity of the Eastern bloc. In the final analysis the program is an economic and social program of the new Soviet leadership to which the other CMEA member countries were linked in accordance with the decision of the 41st Council meeting on December 18, 1985. The 12th five-year plan of the

Soviet Union for 1986 to 1990 is aimed wholly at modernizing and developing the progressive branches of industry.[233] Seventy percent more capital investment funds, namely, 232 billion rubles, than in the five-year period 1981 to 1985 will be used for reconstruction and modernization; 165 to 205 billion rubles, i.e., more than 80% of the total growth in investment capital compared with the previous five-year plan, will be used to modernize machinery construction and the expansion of the use of electronics and chemistry, etc. Machinery construction will increase by 43%, but the growth rate of total industry will be only 25%. The accent is on updating the range of products offered in machinery construction, apparatus and instruments, and vehicles, and in these branches the renovation rate will increase from 3% to 1985 to 13% in 1990. The production volume of progressive technology will increase by twofold to tenfold in the course of the 12th five-year planning period, processing centers will increase from 2,500 in 1985 to 10,700, i.e., by 428%, flexible automated manufacturing departments will increase by 298% from 183 to 546, the number of industrial robots will increase by 217% from 13,200 to 28,600, machine tools with digital program controls will increase by 193% from 17,700 to 34,200, microprocessor controls for technological processes will increase by tenfold from 200 to 2,000; program control units for all types of equipment will increase by 254% from 20,400 to 51,800; the output of electronic data processing and process computers will increase by 140% and the proportion of machinery and equipment equipped with microprocessors and other control technology will increase from 5% in 1985 to 27–32% in 1990.

The second most important industrial sector of the 12th five-year plan which will receive considerable capital investment is the fuel and energy sector. Capital investments of 180 billion rubles are envisioned for the development of the fuel and energy sector; this is 35% more than in the five-year period from 1981 to 1985. All production capacities of 25 million kilowatts will undergo a thorough modernization, and uneconomical power plants and equipment of 15 million kilowatts will be shut down. The projection is to save 20 million tons of bituminous coal units in the 12th five-year planning period through renovations, including 6.5 million tons in 1990. Power production will increase from 1,545 billion kilowatt hours in 1985 to 1,860 billion kilowatt hours in 1990, including nuclear energy from 167 to 390 billion kilowatt hours. The increase will be 129 billion kilowatt hours greater in the 12th five-year planning period than in the 11th planning period. Crude oil output will increase from 595 million tons to 635 million tons, whereas in the 11th five-year period there was a decline of 8 million tons. The production of natural gas will increase from 643 billion cubic meters to 850 billion cubic meters, i.e., a growth rate equal to that in the previous five-year period. Coal mining will increase from 726 million tons to 795 million tons, 59 million tons more than in the 1981–1985 period. Ten percent more will be invested in the crude oil industry than in the previous five-year period. In the period from 1986 to 1990, seven more transcontinental natural gas pipelines will be begun in connection with the development of the Yamburg and Yamal deposits. Further development of coal deposits in Kansk-Achinsk (eastern Siberia) and Ekibastuz in north Kazakhstan will be speeded up. Extensive restructurings are planned in the iron and steel industry. The planned growth of rolled iron will be 10%, and the production of semi-finished materials made of low-alloy steel varieties will increase by 39%, while rolled steel products will increase by 73%. Fourteen technologically obsolete furnaces will be shut down in the 12th five-year period. Eighty rolling mills will be modernized and 38 will be shut down. Special emphasis will be placed on the chemical industry in which 50% more will be invested than in the 11th five-year planning period.

Like the Comprehensive Program adopted at the 41st CMEA meeting in December 1985, the 12th five-year plan of the Soviet Union is oriented toward a dynamic expansion of every top priority branch that is earmarked to serve as a vehicle of the Soviet Union's and the entire East bloc's linkup with worldwide scientific and technical progress. The 12th five-year plan initiates a fifteen-year period in which the entire Eastern bloc will be made independent of imports of progressive technology from the West by restructuring and modernization. The smaller countries of the CMEA will enter into this renovation process, already begun in the Soviet Union, by adapting their five-year plans to the requirements of the CMEA Comprehensive Program.

The new leadership of the Soviet Union introduced an economic policy which makes an extensive economic integration, especially in the five top-priority sectors, a precondition for the scientific and technical progress of every CMEA country. The interlocking of the economies of the Eastern bloc and especially the smaller countries of the CMEA with the Soviet Union will become more closely knit than ever before. Successive modernization by integration will depend however not only on the economic and political development of the Soviet Union but also on the development of the smaller countries of the CMEA.

Factors of Integration and Disintegration in Eastern Europe

The countries of Eastern Europe have accepted the 1985 CMEA Comprehensive Program to deepen scientific and technical progress. They know quite well that technical progress comes from the West, but are little integrated into the world economy as a consequence of the geopolitical factor, the regulations of the foreign trade and currency monopoly, etc. Although they are immune to the negative phenomena on the world market, they are also far removed from the worldwide international competition, which compels a continual modernization of the production process. They also know quite well that they will never be able to link up with worldwide scientific and technical progress alone considering the real possibilities of managing their extensive obsolete production potential, with their modest, poorly equipped research capacities, their limited investment possibilities, and their considerable debt to both the West and the Soviet Union. However, they also take into account that the steps initiated in the '70s to diminish the interdependence within the Eastern bloc by expanding economic relations with the industrial countries of the West and to bridge the technology gap, not only failed to achieve the effect envisaged, but also made them even more dependent on Western banks and on the Soviet Union.

The leaderships of the smaller countries of the CMEA know the price that they must pay for accepting the 1985 Comprehensive Program. Their economies will be integrated into the overall system, perhaps to the point of no return, and national economic interests will be subordinated to international and "common" interests more than before. The political implications of their economic integration as a component of the organic integration of their smaller systems into that of the socialist world system dominated by the superpower are also known well enough. But they also know that the geopolitical factors, as experience has shown, will continue to be decisive for their economic policies in the foreseeable future, and hope to reap certain advantages from closer cooperation between their modest scientific and technical potential with the great potential of the East bloc taken together. It is of course too early to know whether the Soviet Union will actually be able, as hoped, to integrate the smaller countries into CMEA history with the help of this extremely ambitious Comprehensive Program, and at the same time reap certain advantages for its own economy, or whether the Soviet Union will help the smaller countries rise to the worldwide scientific and technical level without sacrificing their own national economic interests to "common" interests. But one thing is clear: the two integration instruments contemplated, namely a supranational executive body and functional economic mechanisms, the lack of which was responsible for the failure of the 1971 CMEA Comprehensive Program, continue to be lacking. It was also clear that the leading personages of Eastern Europe who accepted the 1985 Comprehensive Program did not have much time left. The Party leaders of Bulgaria and Hungary, Todor Zhivkov and Janos Kadar, respectively, had been in power for thirty years; Gustav Husak, General Secretary of the Communist Party of Czechoslovakia since 1979, was 73 years old; and Erich Honecker, General Secretary of the Socialist Unity Party of the GDR since 1971, was 74. Nicolae Ceausescu, General Secretary of the Communist Party of Romania since 1965, was thought to be in poor health. Poland's Party chief Jaruzelski, General Secretary since October 1981, was only 63 years old, but any number of factors could bring the seemingly calm situation in Poland to the brink of turmoil again. A change of leaders was imminent in five of the Eastern countries. Persons could come to power who interpret the relationship between national and international interests differently and furthermore want to realize them differently. Today, when the traditional national component is increasingly gaining the upper hand over the international component, never very strong, in shaping consensus, the leading persons of Eastern Europe have much less range of freedom in their decisions than in the first decade after the War. The 1985 CMEA Comprehensive Program is much too capital-intensive for this. However, the people of Eastern Europe are no longer prepared to make sacrifices for the military-industrial complex program and for the benefit of future generations. Of course, one can no longer speak of a uniform Eastern Europe. Integration-promoting factors are much weaker in Romania and Hungary than in Bulgaria, the GDR, or Czechoslovakia.

Poland, Romania, and Hungary in the force field of integration policy

Poland

Poland's leaders, from Gomulka and Gierek to Jaruzelski, have always supported the integration projects in the Eastern bloc. However, Poland's Party leadership has never had much support among the Polish people, especially in the later periods. Far-ranging integration projects were always undertaken at times when the leadership was still fumbling among the debris of the failed economic policies of its predecessor. Gomulka in 1956 as a consequence of the economic political crisis of the bankrupt Stalinist regime of the postwar period; Gierek in 1970 as a result of the economic and political crisis of the last years of the Gomulka leadership; and Jaruzelski as a consequence of the severest crisis the country had ever gone through, in 1981–1982. Poland's leadership has always had interesting cooperation proposals to present in the CMEA: proposals of its economic experts who took the reform plans of their Party leadership more seriously than the Party leadership itself. Modernization measures have been proposed in the CMEA for the realization of which the necessary preconditions were lacking at the time of presentation, and in other CMEA countries had never been even begun. So it was in the early '60s when Poland's delegation in the finance and currency commission of the CMEA proposed convertibility for the transferable ruble, when the economic reform initiated in Poland itself after the Gomulka comeback in the mid-'50s had already faded and no other CMEA countries were even thinking about accentuating monetary relations so much as to create the conditions for convertibility of the collective currency. After dropping the proclaimed reform plans, Poland's economic leadership was even ready to support Khrushchev's daring integration proposals in order to find a solution for the chronically complicated economic situation of the country within an integrated CMEA. Poland's representative in the CMEA Executive Committee, Piotr Jaroszewicz, explained before leaving for Bucharest to participate in the 17th Council session on December 14–20, 1962: "The upcoming meeting will modify CMEA cooperation to make the creation of a central planning institute for the entire CMEA possible."[234] A uniform economic plan was created neither then nor later, not only, as generally claimed, because of Romania's opposition, but because the mechanisms for realizing it were lacking. Gomulka had found in the CMEA neither the economic help his country needed nor political support for himself. The workers' uprising on the Baltic coast overthrew the leader of the Polish United Workers' Party on December 20, 1970. His successor, Gierek, vigorously supported the 1971 CMEA Comprehensive Program and presented proposals to make cooperation more efficient by the expansion of economic mechanisms. However, he immediately instituted a closer cooperation with Western firms and banks, stepped up capital investment activities, and allowed the incomes of the population to rise sharply, all with the aid of Western credits. But after the inflow of Western credits stopped, and the gap between supply and demand had become unbridgeable, and he attempted to initiate an austerity policy as had his unfortunate predecessors, he was overthrown by the workers' uprising in historic August 1980. Geberal Wojciech Jaruzelski, leader of the Polish United Workers' Party, had no other choice than to support the integration attempts of the new Soviet leadership to bring his crisis-ridden country out of its predicament. Poland was in favor of calling the June 1984 summit conference, the Comprehensive Program of December 1985, and the integration proposals of the Soviet Union that were contained in it. Jaruzelski had a more cogent reason than his predecessors to seek a way out of the insoluble situation in the CMEA. The problem was not only the mountain of debt of 39 billion US dollars to Western banks and the approximately 7 billion US dollars debt to the Soviet Union, but above all the capital investment project ruins which Western credits helped to finance, and whose completion would require more money than the money already invested in them, money which Poland would never be capable of raising. These uncompleted, abandoned capital investment projects are so obsolete that it would make no sense to throw good money after bad. But the Soviet Union has begun to complete a few incomplete capital investment projects to be able to receive their products. It is hoped that the economic interlocking envisioned in the Comprehensive Program will stimulate investment and economic activity and thereby create a way out of the protracted economic crisis. An annual average growth rate of 4.9% was achieved in 1983 to 1985, but the gross national product in 1985 was still 13% lower than in 1978.[235]

Wladyslaw Gomulka, General Secretary of the Polish Workers' Party, said in a speech on December 7, 1945: "Poland can initiate social restructurings without revolution in view of the presence of the Red Army." This sentence of the former Party leader and later victim of the Stalinist regime could be further qualified: "A real-socialist revolution would not have taken place without the Red Army." Poland was the number one bone of contention in Yalta, Teheran, and Potsdam. The history of the Eastern bloc began with Poland's incorporation into the Soviet sphere of influence. Its withdrawal or expulsion could mean its end. Poland's Western border is with the GDR, which separates the Eastern bloc from the Western world through the Elbe river. The Polish people have had bad experience with Russia and are not inclined to make an absolute distinction between Russia and the Soviet Union, and between their old and their new experience. "The Soviet Union and Poland are the largest socialist countries in Europe," said Mikhail Gorbachev at the Party Congress of the Polish United Workers' Party in late June 1986. The 1,776 delegates to the 10th Party Congress understood this emphasis correctly. Without Poland there would be no Eastern community, which the Soviet Union will never renounce. The Soviet Union has never had a great confidence in the loyalty of the Polish people. The Soviet troops were never withdrawn as, for example, from Romania in 1958. They remained stationed in Lignitz from the very beginning. Even during the most difficult times, however, they were not used to bring peace and order to restless Poland once again. The Poles have never had confidence in the Soviet social system which the Red Army had brought with it from the Soviet Union. The restless people on the Vistula have never rebelled so passionately as after World War II. Three popular uprisings were started against Russia's occupation at respectable distances: in 1794, 1830, and 1863. But after World War II, the uprisings, though weaker and more poorly organized, were more frequent and more class-related. In no country in Europe has the struggle of the working class assumed such classically Marxist forms as the struggle of the millions-strong trade union Solidarity in the years 1981 and 1982. Nowhere was the political crisis so complicated and the country's government so helpless as the Polish Party leadership in 1981, which saw no other way out of the confused situation than to impose martial law on December 13 with mass arrests, curfews in the late evening hours, prohibition of meetings, etc. At the June 1986 Congress the general leader of the Polish United Workers' Party called this war against his own people a "means to pave the way toward socialist renovation," finding full sympathy from the guest of honor at this Congress, Mikhail Gorbachev, who praised the leader of the Party and army for the courage he showed to defend the achievements of the revolution with his own resources, and naturally placed the blame for the economic crisis on the imperialists. He said: "The Polish crisis has shown how dangerous an economic orientation to the West is." His conclusion was just as logical: "So that something similar is not repeated, a close cooperation between Poland and the Soviet Union, the two largest socialist states in Europe, is indispensable." It should be noted that economists of both countries agreed even before the Party Congress to increase Poland's exports to the socialist countries by 6.7% annually for the five-year period from 1986 to 1990, but its exports to the West by only 3.5% annually.[236] Eduard Shevardnadze, Gorbachev's foreign minister, announced during an official visit to Poland before the 10th Party Congress that if the Polish government had not shown the courage to have done with rebellious workers "through its own resources" it could have counted on fraternal help from the big neighbor in the name of proletarian internationalism.

From the very beginning the Soviet Union did not conceal the fact that it was not prepared to tolerate free trade unions and the revolutionary changes in the economic and political system of Poland which they advocated and which deviated from real-socialist practice. A month after the Gdansk and Szczecin agreements were signed, came the first warning.[237] With reference to Lenin it was averred that trade unions independent of the state were incompatible with the principles of socialism. The 1968 scenario used in the conflict with the Prague Spring had recurred, but the Soviet leadership drew a much longer breath. It could not want to intervene directly with force of arms because it feared that the resistance would be stubborn and that fatalities would be unavoidable. On December 5, 1980, came the appeal of the Warsaw Pact to Poland's leadership to put an end to the rebellion with its own forces. Maneuvers of the Soviet, East German, Czech, and Polish troops were announced for the second half of March 1981 under the code name of Soiuz 81. On April 7, 1981, came Brezhnev's passionate appeal from the podium of the Czech Party Congress to put an end to the free trade unions. On April 23, 1981, the chief ideologue of Soviet real socialism, Mikhail Suslov, visited the gravely tormented country without, however, being able to find a constructive solution. Sharp attacks from the Soviet, Czech, and GDR press followed a few days later. On June 5, 1981, came the hitherto sharpest memo of the Central Committee of the CPSU to Poland's Party leadership; invoking the summit meeting of December 1980 and the March 1981 warning of the 26th Congress of the CPSU it referred in unconciliatory attacks to the continuing grave situation in Poland. This was interpreted throughout the country as a precursor to a military intervention. A few months later on July 31,

1981, eleven days before the 9th Party Congress of the Polish United Workers' Party, Andrei Gromyko, Soviet foreign minister and Politburo member, visited the country in order to exert an influence on the decisions of the Party Congress. It was agreed in the final communiqué that the defense of socialism was a common concern of the socialist community, but the 9th Party Congress, under the leadership of the reform-inclined Stanislaw Kania, had voted out of office 90% of the Central Committee members who had been elected at previous Party Conferences. Only sixteen members and eight representatives were reinstated to the newly appointed Central Committee of 200 full members and 70 representatives.[238] Extensive economic and political reforms were contemplated, such as limiting the time in office of the political leadership, rotation, extensive involvement of the micro-level in the decision-making process, etc. The unconditional fidelity to the Soviet Union, adjured at the same time in the Congress decisions, was not enough to appease the Soviet leadership.

The next four months went more poorly than expected. The economic crisis grew deeper, the situation with supplies became intolerable, and strikes and demonstrations complicated the economic and political situation, which was complicated enough anyway. The Congress of Solidarity in September and October 1981 issued demands that were deemed provocative: e.g., free elections, self-determination, access to the mass media, and legalization of the trade union Solidarity. In addition an appeal was made to other Eastern countries to permit free trade unions as well. On September 10, 1981, the Soviet embassy in Warsaw issued its sharpest protest of all against the anti-Soviet wave in Poland which in its opinion had exceeded tolerable limits. Rumors became increasingly frequent that the feared Soviet intervention was imminent. These rumors were spread by the country's official authorities, and with good reason, since under the threat of foreign intervention, steps were initiated to encourage a home-grown solution. Unlike in the GDR in 1953, Hungary in 1956, and Czechoslovakia in 1968, the growing opposition was to be crushed by Poland itself with its own forces. Alongside the compromise-inclined Party leader Stanislaw Kania, the powerful defense minister, Jaruzelski, stood out. On October 17, 1981, the General assumed the position of General Secretary of the Party and on December 13, four days before Solidarity's announced mass protest on the anniversary of the uprising on the North Sea coast in 1970, the general invoked martial law.

The general succeeded in smashing the Solidarity movement in an almost two-year war against the people, as the martial law imposed in December 1981 is called in Poland. The general and Party leader attempted in vain to present himself as the executor of the August 1980 demands of the workers. Poland enjoys much more freedom than most of the states of East Europe. In addition to the official public there is also a second public which can no longer be driven to silence. The Polish press is critical and readable. One amnesty of political prisoners follows another. The Poles can travel almost unhindered to the West. But the hope that the Party leadership under General Jaruzelski would be able to attract the approval of the Polish people to introduce a true renewal remains slight. The general has reintegrated Poland into the Eastern community. However, between 1980 and 1982 the Polish United Workers' Party had lost over a million members, i.e., a third of its total membership. There is no one who believes that this Party, which has lost its ideological effect, will be able to govern again as it did before the great crisis of 1980–82. There are four generals, including the political General Jaruzelski, in the newly elected Politburo. There are generals in leading positions in the economy and in political life. However, the forty years of real socialism have made the country more deeply Catholic than was the case in all of Poland's previous history. The Party leader calls the Pope a "glowing Polish patriot." He knows that the Poles will deeply appreciate his praise for the warmly loved Karol Wojtyla. But the great handicap remains the Polish economy. It has recovered somewhat in the last few years, but has not reached the level of the pre-crisis year of 1978, which was itself not too high. The Polish leadership supports Gorbachev's integration plans because they know that the economy is backward and is not competitive on world markets.

After five years of negotiations Poland succeeded in June 1986 to renew its membership in the International Monetary Fund and the World Bank which it had broken off in 1950. However, it did so on the basis of Article 14 of the IMF for developing countries and not Article 8 for industrial countries of the West. Article 14 seemed in this case to be more suited than the 8th Article, not only because Poland has no chances in the foreseeable future of restoring the convertibility of the Polish zloty, but also because the country, like Romania and Hungary, raised loans from the World Bank which can be useful for building up the backward infrastructure, for regulating the Vistula River, and for ecological measures, etc., which have become absolutely necessary. The special drawing rights of the IMF would be able to provide financial assistance which can at present be found neither in the West nor the East. However, the economy is recovering so slowly that the creditworthiness of the country is still assessed as low as that of the most indebted countries of the world. After many reschedulings of Poland's debt, on September 6, 1986, a new debt rescheduling agreement of the loans (95%), which had already been rescheduled in 1986 and were due in 1987, was granted—15% of the 1987 loan[239] as a credit line. The inflation rate—15%–20% annually—remains the highest in Europe even after prices for foods and industrial consumer goods were doubled in 1982. In early September 1986, Poland's government found itself once again forced as so many times before to devalue the Polish zloty by 17.6% against other currencies (the zloty was devalued by 15.6% in that February). The new official exchange rate of 200 zlotys per dollar (until September 1 it was 170 zlotys per dollar) still remains much higher than the black market rate, which at present is 1500 zlotys per dollar. In relation to the transferable and Soviet rubles the devaluation is only 4.4%. The Polish National Bank calculates 95 zlotys for 1 ruble[240] at an official exchange rate of 1 transferable ruble = 1.39 US dollars at the International Bank for Economic Cooperation.

After the dynamic per capita growth of 5.7% annually, financed with Western credits, in the first half of the '70s, economic growth was reduced to 0 per capita in the second half of the decade. In the crisis years, it fell to −2.3% in 1979, −4.1% in 1980, −6.2% in 1981, and −1.8% in 1982, but rose again in the next two years to 3.7% and 2.5%.[241] In absolute figures, the national income grew by 6.0% in 1983, 5.6% in 1984, but only 3% in 1985. Agriculture had negative growth rates from 1976 to 1980 of 1.7%, and 2.7% in 1979 through 1982; in 1983 a growth of 1.6% was reached, followed by 5.7% in 1984 but only 0.9% in 1985. A drastic reversal is discernible in the trend in foreign trade. Unlike the '70s, when trade turnover in relations with the industrial nations and above all imports increased more than intra-CMEA trade, Poland's foreign trade with the Eastern countries has grown more in the last few years than its trade with the West. Exports to the East increased by 3.8% annually in the years 1979 to 1982, by 11.8% in 1983, by 16.5% in 1984, and by 27.8% in 1985; imports showed even more vigorous growth rates, namely an annual average of 7.9% for the period between 1979 and 1982, but 10.6%, 24.8%, and 31.4% in the next three years. Imports from the Eastern countries, which have shown a dynamic growth as a consequence of the sharp price rises for Soviet crude oil, are intended to replace at least in part the decline in imports from the West due to a shortage of foreign exchange. Imports from the West decreased by 0.1% in the second half of the '70s, and by as much as 9.6% between 1979 and 1982.[242] However, the cutbacks in imports from the West have had a devastating effect on the economy. Another path was therefore attempted: repaying credits which had fallen due after having been rescheduled, and postponing a considerable portion of the interest due to finance Western imports that had become indispensable. After many years of decline, an increase in Western imports of 4.2% in 1983, 27.4% in 1984, and even 43% in 1985 was registered.[243]

However, the rate of recovery in the post-crisis years is no grounds for rejoicing. Work morale and discipline leave much to be desired especially because the standard of living is at least one-fifth lower than in the '70s, although private consumption has increased by 5.2% in 1983, 2.8% in 1984, and 1% in 1985 after a catastrophic decline in the crisis years. The delegates to the 10th Party Congress of June 1986 told the Party and army general that the industrial workers did nothing for 1.5 days per week, that 37% of the machinery stock and 32% of transport capacities were either out of commission or not usable. There was a quite tolerable growth of 3.8% in 1985 in industry, even though this was somewhat lower than in the preceding year (5.2%); however, some branches of industry of importance for the state showed a decline, such as mining by 0.5%, building materials by 2.8%, iron and steel by 1.5%; growth was lower than in the preceding two years in the electrical industry, chemical industry, and fuels industry. Machinery construction showed a somewhat higher increase than the overall national average (+ 7.7%), and precision instruments showed an increase of even 13.2%. The most important industrial branches such as shipbuilding and mining have been able to show a relatively favorable efficiency owing to the above-average wages. A miner or a dockworker receives a monthly salary (including overtime) of 75,000 zlotys, three to four times as much as a teacher or a physician. The low labor discipline is, it should be noted in passing, in no sense a result of the events in the first half of the '70s. The specific expenditure of energy in raw materials was already the highest in the world earlier in Poland. In 1979, energy input per 1,000 US dollars of the gross national product was 1,515 kg bituminous coal units, or 153 kg more than in Eastern Europe and 955 kg more than the West European average. The consumption of steel per 1,000 US dollars of the gross national product was 135 kg in 1980, 24 kg more than in Eastern Europe and 93 kg more than the West European average.[244]

Discipline in the capital investment sector has remained low. In 1985 a growth of 6.4% was reached, but the completion plan for previously begun capital investment projects was only 65.7% fulfilled, which was worse than in the preceding year when the fulfillment rate was still 70%.

The balance of payments is still hopeless. The debt to Western banks was 31 billion US dollars on September 1, 1986, that to the Soviet Union was 5.6 billion rubles, or 7.7 billion US dollars at the official exchange rate. The planned excess of 1.5 billion dollars in 1985 in foreign trade with the West was not fulfilled. The actual figure was 1.077 billion US dollars, which was 397 million dollars less than in the preceding year. The current account balance showed a deficit of 0.9 billion US dollars.[245] This was despite a 3.3% improvement in the terms of trade. The trade deficit increased by another 684 million transferable rubles in trade with the East, and the terms of trade decreased by another 1.2%. The country was unable to pay 550 million US dollars in interest due on state guaranteed loans. A trend similar to the preceding year was in evidence in the first half-year of 1986: exports to the Eastern countries increased (at constant prices) by 8.8%, and imports increased by 11.6%. Exports to the Western countries decreased, however, by 3% while imports increased by 3.2% (at constant prices). The export structure remained extremely differentiated: the share of products of the electric machinery construction industry was 60.2% of total exports to the East and 22.1% of total exports to the West.[246] The planned 1.6 billion dollar surplus for 1986 in trade with the West was only fulfilled to a figure of 420 million dollars in the first half-year, and there are, as Poland's foreign trade expert Stanislaw Gruzewski asserts, no prospects that the planned surplus will be reached. In 1985 and in the first half of 1986 Poland was the only CMEA country that had no access to new consortium loans and even supplier credits were granted very sparingly, mainly by Austria and the Federal Republic of Germany.

Membership in the International Monetary Fund could mean 200 million dollars annually in special drawing rights. Credits in excess of this are earmarked to an austerity program which the country will scarcely be able to carry off. If it is taken into account that the interest payments alone are about 3 billion US dollars and that the foreign trade surplus can be no more than 1–2 billion dollars, a further postponement of the term of payment, on loans that have already been rescheduled, will be unavoidable. About 95% of the credits falling due in 1986, i.e., 3.7 billion dollars, would have to be rescheduled.[247]

On July 25, 1988, according to Reuters, the Soviet Union agreed to postpone for ten years the repayment of $1.5 billion in hard currency debts. The rescheduling followed an agreement reached on July 20 under which Western banks rescheduled the payment of $9 billion. The Soviet Union also offered Poland new ruble credits equivalent to $640 million.

The reform embarked upon in 1982 bears a broad resemblance to the experimental reform measures introduced by Andropov in June 1983 in five Soviet industrial ministries. State enterprises were declared to be the principal cell in the economic structure, which were fundamentally self-administrating and self-financing. Production was to be regulated by five-year and ten-year plans divided into four components: (1) prognosis of production and distribution of the national product; (2) the main areas of scientific and technical progress; (3) scientific cooperation with foreign countries, with special consideration for relations with CMEA countries; (4) capital investments with a long-term cycle of realization (tapping of raw materials, energy, infrastructure, etc.). Planning takes place in two stages: a central planner sets down the guidelines for planning at the enterprise level. A major value is attached to economic mechanisms, and appropriate credit policy, benefits for good performance and sanctions for poor performance, etc. The planning procedure is to be considerably improved: 186 material balances for products of importance to the state, and for raw materials and fuels are being prepared; of which 50 were approved by the Council of Ministers, 30 by the Planning Commission, and 106 by the Central Supply authorities. The prices shall be centrally set only for products important for the state. Other prices will be agreed upon contractually between the producer and the consumer. Thirty percent of prices for agrarian products and 50% of prices for consumer goods were agreed upon contractually between the producer and the buyer in 1983. The existing regulations for the foreign trade and currency monopoly have been modified: henceforth foreign trade enterprises will cultivate their relations to exporting or importing enterprises on a commission basis. Mixed export-import companies with limited liabilities have been created in which specialized foreign trade enterprises and the production enterprises participate with 51% and 49% shares in the total capital. If the export volume reaches 25% of the volume of the goods produced, or 1 billion zlotys, the production enterprise will be authorized to enter independently into relations with foreign markets; 50% of proceeds in foreign exchange may be kept for import purposes. A similar solution was found for joint ventures: they pay no taxes for three years, and after three years they pay 40% of profits.

The chronic shortage of goods and foreign exhange has, however, forced the central authorities to impose restrictions and ad hoc regulations which nullify the reform measures. The experiences of the past few years seem to bear out those who from the outset claimed that so long as there was the acute shortage of resources a far-ranging decentralization of decision making would have no prospects for success. The state is forced to concentrate scarce resources on priority objects. Poland's economic reform seems to resemble less Hungary's decentralized economic system than the reform model of the GDR in which large combinates have certain economic authority while decisions on the development of strategically important areas are reserved to the state authorities. The GDR model, with its combinates with certain decisionmaking powers, fits wholly in with the specifications of the CMEA Comprehensive Program of December 1985, since according to this program combinates with decisionmaking powers will assume the leadership in realizing the joint CMEA projects. As already mentioned, Soviet large combinates, which have been selected to lead the most important CMEA projects, are authorized to enter into agreements with competent combinates in other CMEA countries.

The 10th Congress of the Polish United Workers' Party, which ended on July 3, 1986, announced a reform of the reform. Henceforth income differentiation rather than equality was to promote labor productivity; more state pressure and less liberalism would force the fulfillment of economic plans. The general said to the delegates: "People who are inefficient must lose so that the society overall can win. These are the realistic conditions of the sui generis social contract which the Party presents to the nation." The government declaration says: "Different criteria and standards must be used in wages policy. Everyone has a stomach, but unequal knowledge, the amount of labor expended, initiative, and an enterprising spirit vary."[248] Former vice-premier Rakowski said in his speech to the Congress delegates: "In the poor and backward country which Poland was thirty years ago, a distinct contradiction arose between the efficiency and rationality of economic performance which protected the weaker and the poorer," and further: "We have not resolved this contradiction without mistakes—generally in the spirit of social justice—and it is this circumstance which we have to thank for the cultural progress of our nation. This contradiction is rooted in social consciousness and influences behavior." He then concludes: "Today we must boldly and daringly apply a new policy: justice primarily through efficiency."[249] It should be pointed out that the income differentiation that has now been introduced in Poland was not an isolated phenomenon: on September 1, 1986, the Soviet press announced a similar reform in wages policy, geared to performance, in the Soviet Union. Social security was also scheduled for an essential modification. Jaruzelski said in his report to the Party Congress: "Fewer social services for those for whom this has a marginal significance, and more for those who really need it. In a word, restrictions on services in order to deepen and expand their effectiveness."

Zbigniew Messner, the Prime Minister, announced stringent measures in carrying out plan directives to the Party Congress delegates: "Efficiency cannot be achieved easily. Historical experiences show that it must also be coaxed through pressure.'' Although he knows quite well, as he said, that such measures will bring the government no popularity. The Prime Minister corrected a skilled worker delegate from the textile city of Lodz, Stefan Delbowski, as follows: "This policy might cause social tensions, but there is no retreating. . . If we are unable to achieve higher efficiency, economic results will deteriorate further, and workers' situation will be even more difficult.''

This new course, with its contemplated price rises, wage freeze, and ''revision of cadre policy'' (in many areas people are in the wrong jobs; ''musicians and theologians have assumed positions within the economy,'' said the Party chief to the Party Congress delegates) found support with the guest of honor Mikhail Gorbachev: ''Radical reforms are necessary to prevent reversion to the uncontrollable situation of the pre-crisis period,'' and directed an unexpected praise to Jaruzelski, who had previously been eyed with mistrust: ''This outstanding statesman with a political eye for finding solutions to very complicated problems,'' he called him. The Soviet Party leader did not come to Poland with empty hands. On October 7, 1985, two agreements were signed between Poland and the Soviet Union: one on cooperation in the period between 1986 and 1990 which set the conditions for utilizing certain production capacities, and a second, which rescheduled loans of over 5 billion rubles up to the year 1990 and specified tolerance of a trade deficit for Poland to the end of 1987.[250] In early September, after three years of negotiations, the details of Poland's participation on the Yamburg gas pipeline were agreed upon. In return for Poland's equipment and the labor of construction companies, the Soviet Union will deliver two billion cubic meters of natural gas over a period of twenty years. The Soviet Union will modernize the passenger plane fleet of Lot and buy four times more fruit and vegetables from Poland up to the year 2000.[251]

It is known quite well in Moscow that Poland is not a reliable partner in the Eastern European community and cannot be trusted even after the suppression of the Solidarity movement. Although Poland's government valued highly the official election results of October 1985 in which the government received 78% yes votes, this result, which was challenged by the opposition, was still 21% lower than the election results in other Eastern countries. The new Soviet leadership sympathized fully with the Polish Communist leadership in this totally un-communist country. Poland supplies coal, sulphuric acid, copper, ships, railroad cars, and many other important raw materials and finished products to the other CMEA countries. However, people know that Poland's economic situation will continue to be a serious problem for its CMEA partners, and that the country is a burden rather than an asset. But, as Mikhail Gorbachev said, ''Without this second largest socialist country in Europe there is no CMEA and no Warsaw Pact. The Soviet Union is prepared to pay the economic price to maintain the political alliance with Poland.''

Romania

This author has always been of the opinion that, even though Romania has prevented a few CMEA decisions, its presence in the CMEA has resulted in a better fit between the basic conditions and the real possibilities of the community than would have been possible without Romania's dissent. The experience acquired in cooperation with the experts of this country indicate that with their opposition to certain utterly unrealistic proposals that went far beyond the existing possibilities of realization, the competent Romanian specialists have been practising a kind of argument for argument's sake, to the delight of official circles. It should be pointed out that the signature of the Romanian state leadership is present on all important CMEA documents—the Basic Principles for the International Division of Labor, the decisions of the 9th Council meeting in 1958 on price-forming practices, the agreement on multilateral clearing in transferable rubles, and the agreement on founding the IBEC, the Comprehensive Programs of 1971 and 1985, and many others. Romania also participates in the most important international CMEA enterprises. It is often stressed that Romania prevented the development of a uniform economic plan for the entire CMEA, as well as the creation of supranational decision-making bodies in the CMEA. But other countries as well have opposed these unrealistic projects. Poland's longtime representative in the CMEA and outstanding specialist on integration, Henryk Rozanski, wrote: "Poland supports the convoking of the June 1961 summit, but the objective conditions for a uniform economic plan embracing the entire community do not exist."[252] This opinion could be expanded: if the CMEA countries had initiated a central CMEA plan, the indispensable mechanisms for fulfilling the plan would have been lacking. It is not Romania's fault that the ambitious and far-sighted Comprehensive Program on deepening economic integration of the member countries approved by Romania and adopted in Bucharest in July 1971 could not be fulfilled. Further, even Romania's agreement could not make the transferable ruble convertible. Romania's resistance to certain integration projects in the CMEA, and especially in the Warsaw Pact bodies, is stronger, and in a certain sense more complicated and more institutionalized than that of the other community members. But the other members have resisted and continue to resist measures that are in contradiction to their interests as well, although this resistance is usually voiced behind closed doors. The thesis that Romania's dissent is the principal cause of all the problems in the CMEA makes any analysis of the real causes of failure of CMEA projects impossible. Such failures are above all the consequence of the peculiar composition of the CMEA community, consisting of a motley amalgamation of a superpower with hegemonic aspirations, and other industrially developed countries with different structures, as well as underdeveloped and developing countries. But they are also a consequence of the fact that planned economies do not have adequate contact mechanisms owing to their underdeveloped economic infrastructure, and are basically introverted.

Their foreign trade and currency monopolies, which shield exporting and importing production enterprises from the external markets, were tailored to the needs of an autarkically oriented super-economy. And very little has changed in the foreign trade mechanisms of this economy, which has had a decisive influence on all CMEA decisions, since the very founding of the CMEA. It was not Romania's opposition to a uniform CMEA economic plan and to a supranational executive which prevented the administration of all the economies of the member countries as an overall economy, but rather the progressive emancipation and differentiation of national economic policies and domestic steering systems which made a uniform planning and steering system impossible.

The CMEA regulation that every member has the right to manifest its disinterest in any joint project of the other countries has made the veto of any one country totally meaningless. It is inconceivable that a single country of minor economic importance could prevent serious integration projects of nine other member countries.

Although the Romanian opposition has relatively little effect on CMEA events, the fact that it exists at all is all the more astonishing in that the Romanian economic and political system is more centralized than that of any other steering system in Eastern Europe. The reasons for this dissent, with its ebbs and flows, are manifold. The Soviet Union annexed areas which were of vital importance for Romania. In its pact with Hitler, Romania's dictator General Antonescu advanced to Odessa and re-took this area. Despite the fact that the royal coup d'état of August 23, 1944, overthrew the dictator, took the country out of its coalition with Hitler, and placed it on the side of the Soviet Union, and despite the fact that in March 1945 a government friendly to the Soviet Union was formed under the leadership of Petru Groza with Communists in important positions in the state, the Soviet Union has never annulled its annexation of the Romanian part of Bessarabia with its capital Kishinev or Bukovina with its capital Chernovitse. But even after Petru Groza's friendly government was replaced by an even friendlier Communist government, King Michael went into exile on December 31, 1947, and the Romanian Socialist Republic was proclaimed on January 1, 1948, and within a short time created a Soviet-like regime, heavy reparations were demanded of Romania and in addition mixed Soviet-Romanian companies ("Sovroms") were created, inflicting considerable damage on the country's economy.

The Soviet Union has always stressed its own feat of liberation, giving no recognition to the role of the Romanian people in the fateful month of August 1944. Both the first Communist leader of the country, Gheorghe Gheorghiu-Dej, as well as the second and present dictator Nicolae Ceausescu, felt themselves humiliated by this disparagement of the liberating feats of the Romanian people. In 1955 Gherogiu-Dej wrote: "In August 1944, under the victorious and liberating conditions of the advance of the Soviet army, the Romanian people overthrew the fascist dictatorship; the Romanian army turned its weapons against the Nazi aggressors and fought together with the Soviet army against the Nazi hordes."[253]

His successor Ceausescu was even clearer: "On August 23, 1944, our Party initiated, organized, and carried out an armed uprising which led to the overthrow of the fascist dictatorship; Romania turned its back on Nazi Germany and Romania joined the anti-Hitler coalition."[254] The role of the Communist Party, which at that time had not many more than 2,000 members, was highly overestimated, but the role of the Soviet army is not even mentioned.

Nonetheless the Communist leadership of Romania was more pro-Soviet and the Romanian regime more like the Soviet regime in the first decade after World War II than any other Communist leadership and regime in East Europe. No one therefore could have guessed that there were any emancipatory impulses at work when Romania's leadership petitioned for the withdrawal of Soviet troops in 1958 on the grounds that Romanian workers considered the presence of Soviet troops on their state territory an affront and a sign that the Party could not govern the country without them. The Soviet Union heeded the request, perhaps because the invasion of Hungary by Soviet troops in October 1956 had left a bad aftertaste, and perhaps also because Romania's Party leadership justified the Soviet invasion. The official Party organ stated: "The unity of the countries of the socialist camp and their friendly association with the Soviet Union—whose sons once again spilled their blood to defend the freedom of the Hungarian people—made it possible to counteract the formation of a reactionary fascist Hungarian state with chauvinist and revisionist tendencies aimed against all neighbors."[255]

However, if one looks back it seems that Romania's demand that Soviet troops be withdrawn from its territory was one of the most important components of its emancipation policy. But this was not the first step in that direction; it had to do with the systematic elimination of the Communist group under Ana Pauker that had returned from the Soviet Union. The symptoms of emancipation multiplied: in December 1959, the following startling statement was to be read in the theoretical organ of the Central Committee of the Communist Party: "The transition of the socialist states to Communism will not take place at the command of a supranational executive body, but under the leadership of the Communist or workers' Party of every socialist country, without any intervention in internal affairs from without."[256] There was as yet no open opposition. In November 1960, Gheorghiu-Dej visited Moscow and supported Soviet policy toward China, and at the 22nd Party Congress in October 1961 Romania supported Soviet policy toward Albania. Romania's resistance to Khrushchev's integrational measures in the early '60s became more and more perceptible. Romania's opposition to a unified economic plan for the CMEA was made known to the world public in a confidential speech of Walter Ulbricht's before the July Plenum of the SED in 1963. He reported that Gheorghiu-Dej had obstructed multilateral measures to coordinate economic plans at the March Congress of the CMEA in 1963, and opposed limited specialization possibilities of his country in the machinery construction industry.[257] On April 26, 1964, the emancipation declaration appeared, generally interpreted as the Magna Carta of each country's "own way to socialism." It states: "No Party has a privileged position, and cannot have such a position. . . . It is the exclusive right of every Party to establish independently its political line, its concrete aims, the ways and means to its development. . . ."[257] Gheorghiu–Dej's successor continued Romania's independent policy in the CMEA, in the Warsaw Pact bodies, and in relations with the West and the third world, without, however, initiating any departure from the Soviet-like economic and political system.

In 1967, Romania did not follow the other Eastern bloc states in their decision to break off diplomatic relations with Israel, and on January 31, 1967, the foreign minister Manescu agreed to an exchange of ambassadors between the Federal Republic of Germany and Romania. In that same year, Ceausescu refused to participate in the conference of the Communist Parties of Europe at Karlovy Vary, and his resistance to the suppression of the Prague Spring was the most vehement. Ceausescu had no intention of supporting Dubcek's ideas of freedom, socialism with a human face, but rather opposed the foreign intervention in the internal affairs of another Eastern country. On August 15, 1968, six days before Warsaw Pact troops invaded Czechoslovakia, he visited Prague to manifest his friendship with the Dubcek government. Romania was the only country in the Warsaw Pact which did not invade Czechoslovakia on August 21. Twelve hours after the beginning of the Soviet intervention, he said to the hundreds of thousands who had gathered before the building of the Central Committee the following dramatic words: ". . . It is inconceivable that a socialist state, that socialist states, should trample on the freedom and independence of another state. . . . It has been said that there was a danger of counterrevolution in Czechoslovakia, and there will perhaps tomorrow be some who say that counterrevolutionary tendencies had been proclaimed at this meeting. We all answer: 'The entire Romanian people will never permit the territory of our fatherland to be violated. . . .' "[259] Romania has continued its independent policy, but no one has invaded Romania, for well-known reasons. The strategic importance of this country is not so great, and the economic and political system remains more "real-socialist" than that of any other Eastern bloc country. During the '60s the country succeeded in playing an active role among the developing countries of the third world, beginning at the very first congress of UNCTAD. In 1972, Romania was the first Eastern bloc country to become a member of the IMF and the World Bank on the basis of Article 14. In the '70s, Romania developed an active foreign policy toward third countries that deviated from official Soviet opinion. Its foreign policy was more similar to the Yugoslavian foreign policy than to that of the other Eastern countries.

In the '70s, Romania expanded its foreign trade relations with the West more than any other country, came into payments difficulties, and in 1980 was the first CMEA country to call for a CMEA summit conference.

The Western share in Romania's total exports was 32.3% in 1970, 35% in 1975, and 36.9% in 1980. The Western share in imports increased even more sharply: in 1975 it was 39.6%, rising to 42.2% in 1980. This discrepancy between imports and exports from the West led to a dramatic rise in debt to Western banks of 1.6 billion dollars in 1970, 3.1 billion dollars in 1975, 9.3 billion dollars in 1980, and 9.7 billion dollars in 1981 (net).[261] In 1982, Romania was compelled to stop its payments and apply for a postponement of the credits that had fallen due. Romania is not dependent on Soviet oil deliveries. Hence insofar as the country was dependent on imports for its refining capacities, which had in the mean time been expanded to far beyond its possibilities of supply, it did not experience the oil shock, like the other Eastern countries, in its relations to the Soviet Union, but in its relations to third countries as a supplier of crude oil and to the industrial states of the West as an importer of petroleum products. The terms of trade deteriorated, especially in trade with third countries. A drastic turn was initiated in trade with the West. The Western share decreased to 31.4% in 1980, 28.2% in 1981, 19.9% in 1982, and to 16.2% in 1983.[262] Western imports decreased by 45.5% in one single year, 1982, and in the next year they decreased by another 25.1% compared with 1982. Western imports began to rise again in 1984, but only by 7.3% compared with the preceding year. In 1985 they remained at the 1984 level. This drastic cure enabled Romania to raise its positive balance of payments from 0.5 billion dollars to 1.5 billion, 1.4 billion, and 1.5 billion dollars in the next three years[263] and to reduce its debt to Western banks to 6.7 billion dollars in mid–1986,[264] but the economy suffered gravely. The distributed national product decreased by 0.2% and 0.5% in 1981 and 1982 respectively, but in the next few years recovered somewhat. The produced national product increased by 3.8%, 7.7%, and 5.9% in 1983, 1984, and 1985 respectively compared with the preceding year in each case.[265] Growth in the machinery construction industry and the consumer goods industry was above average, 7.9%, in 1985, but oil production decreased by 6.6% and gas extraction by 3.2%. Coal production was 46.6 million tons, short of the plan target of 64 million tons. Crude oil production was 10.7 million tons compared with a plan target of 12.6 million tons, and natural gas extraction was 27 million cubic meters, compared with a plan target of 32.8 million cubic meters. The energy supply to the population was reduced drastically and power plants were placed under military control. Because of the low grain harvest, which was 2.3% lower than in 1984, and low sugar-beet harvest, which had fallen by 27.5% compared with 1984, the supply of the population with basic foods deteriorated drastically. In 1986, ten million tons of corn and barley was harvested, but as the Party leader said, this was three million tons less than could have been harvested. "Responsible comrades have exercised self-criticism, but one does not become a revolutionary through this alone,"[266] said Ceausescu in criticism of the agricultural officials. The population continues to suffer shortages. The heavy industry model of development, in which agriculture suffered for years from underinvestment, was just as much to blame for the poor harvests in the last years as the weather conditions. The consequences of the iron and steel growth concept proved to be devastating not only for agriculture. It has led to an expansion of capacities which are a long way from being fully utilized. The steel production potential of 20 million tons produces no more than 12 million tons, and oil refiners, which have a capacity of over 30 million tons, deliver no more than 11–12 million tons of their own oil. The situation decreased perceptibly when the flow of Western credits was reduced to a minimum. Capital investments decreased by 7.1% in 1981 and by 3.2% in 1982 compared with the volume of each preceding year, and when they increased in the next three years by 24%, 6.1%[267] and 1.6%, Romania was unable to stop the decapitalization of its basic stock. Payment difficulties set in anew in 1986.

Romania intends to return to the dynamic growth rates of the '60s and '70s. In the second half of the '80s, national income is projected to increase by 9.9% to 10.6% yearly. In the first half of the decade, however, the annual average increase was only 4.4%. Like the CMEA Comprehensive Program of 1985 or the 12th five-year plan of the Soviet Union, the remaining five-year plan attaches value to intensification of economic performance: labor productivity is to increase by 7.4%[268] in five years, and the degree of utilization of raw materials and fuels as well as energy is to increase by 30% to 32%. Priority is given to modernization of the industrial structure. Romania has posed itself the goal of achieving a medium level of development in the upcoming period. Energy, expansion of the power network, utilization of water power, and making use of reusable sources of energy are focal points for economic planners. The "technically matured" industrial sectors will be expanded, i.e., those which process raw materials and fuels with the greatest effectiveness. Deep sea, and offshore oil and gas deposits will be exploited more, and the quality of top-grade steels is to be increased with less consumption of alloys. A central concern of the five-year plan is to raise the technical level and quality of machinery construction. Electronics and microelectronics, automation of the production process, and precision mechanical products are major areas of emphasis.

Capital investments are to reach a value of 1,400 billion lei in the five-year period from 1986 to 1990, with 841 billion lei going to industry but only 210 billion lei to agriculture, forestry, and waterways. As in the Soviet Union, stress will be placed on modernization and the completion of already-begun projects rather than on new capital investment projects. Investments in agriculture will be relatively slight, but the growth rate is estimated at between 6.1% and 6.7%. Grain harvests are targeted at 32.5 million tons, sugar beets at 11.6 million tons, and potatoes at 8.3 million tons. Ambitious growth rates are targeted for foreign trade. The turnover of volume is to be 52.7% greater, and exports even 75% greater compared with the volumes in the first half of the decade. The contemplated changes in the commodity structure are also considerable: the share of high-grade products of the machinery construction industry will make up one-third of total exports in 1990. The exports of steel, chemicals, and construction materials, on the other hand, will be reduced. The foreign exchange earnings from foreign trade are to increase by two thirds. The top-priority goal is to pay back Western credits. Imports from the West will therefore increase much more slowly than exports to the West.

The five-year plan for the second half of the '80s is an ambitious growth and modernization program. In view of the partial retreat from the West, and the lack of financing sources for capital investment purposes, the possibilities of fulfilling the plan will be just as limited as for the preceding one-year plans. Romania is participating in the CMEA Comprehensive Program for 1985 not as a member country that has much to offer, but rather as a potential beneficiary. It will also not abandon its dissent with regard to far-ranging integration plans. Emancipation remains a constant component of state policy. It was also clearly emphasized in Bucharest that "a distinction could be drawn between desired cooperation and undesired economic integration." [269]

Hungary

Hungary has gone much further than the other CMEA countries in decentralizing its steering system. Industrial enterprises are authorized to retain more profits for their own targets, and carry out more capital investments on their own responsibility. Large enterprises have the right to enter into direct contacts with foreign markets, and have informative trade parameters, as well as more or less real prices and exchange rates. Hungary has been able to organize its agriculture in such a way that Janos Kadar was able to say in an interview with *Time* magazine in late July 1986 that the structure of agriculture now met the needs of the farmers.

Hungary, like some other Eastern countries which broadly expanded their economic relations with the West in the '70s, has not had the best experience. It was unable to build up a competitive range of export products in order to be able to pay back debts and finance necessary imports.

Hungary is therefore interested in deepening CMEA cooperation and thereby creating conditions for linking up to the progressive scientific and technical revolution. However, Hungary is a champion of modernized contact mechanisms and an advocate at least of convertibility of the collective CMEA currency in order to be able to initiate multilateral trading relations and direct contact between cooperating enterprises of the member countries in this way. But Hungary's proposals for modernization in the CMEA are based on its continual efforts to perfect the national steering mechanisms.

The hope that Hungary's modernization proposals in the CMEA will be accepted is slight, however, as is the hope that any other CMEA country would introduce its reform measures. The leadership is willing to acknowledge that Hungary has improved supplies to the population, given greater freedom to enterprises, etc., and that this constitutes a positive balance. But there is little approval for the fact that a small but steadily growing layer of newly rich is developing who, on the basis of their own initiative and effort, but also often at the cost of the state economy, are accumulating wealth. This has happened at the same time as the incomes of officials, pensioners, etc., which were already low, have stagnated for years. According to statistics Hungarians have had to accept a decline in real wages of about 5% since 1980. But the strongest objection to the reforms of the Hungarians is that they have not been permanent, they have not enabled the economy to grow more rapidly, and have not freed it from the traditional flaws of all planned economies, such as low quality and low productivity, insufficient competition on the world market, etc.

The statistics published on February 5, 1986, by the Central Office of Statistics show that the national income in the five-year period from 1981 to 1985 increased by only 7% compared with 1976–1980; the planned targets were 14% to 17%. But in the past five-year period as well, the economic growth rate was no more than 2.6% annually, and in the period from 1981 to 1985 the annual growth rate (1.4%) was 50% lower than in the preceding five-year period. After a 0.3% growth in 1983 and 2.5% in 1984, a minus growth rate of 1.0% was registered in 1985. Industrial output increased by 12% in the first half of the '80s, but remained far below the plan target (19–22%). A growth of 2.7% was reached only in 1984, while in '83 and '85 growth was only 0.8% compared to the preceding year. The country has little money for capital investments. New loans are used primarily to pay back due commitments. In the past few years, investment activity decreased by 4.9%, 5.2%, and 4.6% in the state sector compared to the previous year in each case. Reform in agriculture, which created much better working and income conditions for farmers and brigades, was unable to increase harvests owing to bad weather. In 1983, farm output decreased by 2.7% compared with the preceding year. A growth of 2.9% was registered in 1984, but there was again a decline by 6% in 1985 compared to 1984.

The balance of current accounts is crucial for assessing the economic situation of this highly indebted country: in none of the last four years was Hungary able to achieve a surplus with its Western trade partners. The deficit varied between 1.2 billion US dollars in 1982, 0.6 billion dollars in 1983, 0.8 billion dollars in 1984, and 0.9 billion dollars in 1985.[270] The shift to closer trade relations with the CMEA countries at the cost of Western trade was already in evidence in 1985: ruble exports increased mainly in relations with the Soviet Union by 13.9%, while imports increased by only 5.5%. A ruble surplus of 255 million was reached for the first time since 1980 in CMEA trade.[270] This helped to decrease the previously accumulated debts to the Soviet Union. A contrary trend was registered in hard currency trade: imports increased by 4.6%, but exports decreased by 5.6%. The foreign trade balance with the West was –543 million dollars in 1985 against a positive balance of 159 million dollars in 1984. Debts to Western banks increased by 8.8 billion dollars in 1984 to 10.4 billion dollars in 1985 (gross) and 18 billion dollars in 1988, while the net debt increased by 5.1 billion dollars to 6.9 billion dollars.[271] In 1985, Hungary took out further middle-term and long-term loans to an amount of 1,578 million dollars.[272] In 1986, loans amounting to 1 billion dollars will be taken out according to Lajos Faluvegi, chairman of the planning commission.

Hungary has no raw materials and fuels, and was perhaps the Eastern country hardest hit by the price shock in the '70s. The losses registered between 1973 and 1980 were almost 1 billion dollars yearly.[273] This estimate can be confirmed by a simple calculation: to purchase 1 million tons of oil from Soviet Union, Hungary had to sell 800 Ikarus buses in 1973, but by 1981 this figure was 2,300.[274] However, this loss was partially covered by increased prices for Hungary's exports and the remainder was financed with Western credits. The causes of economic stagnation therefore lie elsewhere, and in this respect the insufficient effect of the economic reforms should be considered.

The new economic mechanism introduced in 1968, its effect, and the problems associated with it, were presented in detail in my books *The Economies of Eastern Europe in a Time of Change* (1983) and *Market, Plan, and State* (1987). A few new aspects and above all the importance of the Hungarian reform in connection with the integration measures introduced in the CMEA in 1984 to 1986, are discussed. The new post-Stalinist social contract envisioned by Janos Kadar with his economic reform remains in force. New measures were taken within the basic framework of the reform of 1968, and decision-making powers were further decentralized. The turn away from the original iron-and-steel and large-plant production activity became increasingly evident. In 1983, 26 trusts were reorganized into 167 medium-sized plants with a good result. Profits increased by 6% to 9%.[275] In the years 1984 to 1986, a far-ranging reform was undertaken in the banking system.[276] The National Bank lost its monopoly position in the economy. Two development funds with a total capital of about 544 million US dollars were reorganized into independent banking institutions, and two sections of the National Bank with assets of about 15 billion dollars were reorganized into commercial banks for industry and agriculture. A third trade bank, the Budapest Credit Bank, was founded. The foreign trade bank will receive more independence than hitherto (80% of foreign trade has been financed by the National Bank). The commercial banks have been given more freedom in establishing their interest policies. The National Bank sets the minimum rates for deposits as well as the interest rates for borrowing, but the interest rates for borrowers are then agreed upon on the basis of these reference rates with one condition, namely, that the deviation from the reference rate must not be more than 1.5%. A stock-exchange market with bonds has been functioning since 1983. A hundred bonds are in circulation, 80% of which was initiated by central and 20% by community banks. They are eagerly acquired by the population who in this way can increase their interest on savings (7% at the savings banks) to 11%. A stock market with 40 joint stock companies is active in Hungary. But the shares are primarily in the possession of the National Bank and the Minister of Finance. Only four of the forty joint stock companies resell their shares. There is no capital and money market in the normal sense of the term in Hungary, and the issue of securities is extremely slight. In 1985, it was 1.1 billion forints (23 million dollars). The freedom of the commercial banks in formulating credit and interest policy is limited. This activity continues to be reserved for the National Bank. It should be noted in passing that a similar experiment with the restructuring of the National Bank into a bank of banks and the shift of business activities to commercial banks was initiated in the late '60s in the GDR and somewhat later in Bulgaria, but after a few years was abandoned. A market economy banking system, with credit and interest policies left to the workings of market forces, can simply not be integrated into a traditional centrally administered planned economy. However, a centrally steered banking system with market features in an administered economy would make no sense. The pursuit of the bank reform in Hungary will therefore be dependent on the progress of the economic reform, the "marketization" of the economic system, and the "reform of the reform," as this process is called in Hungary. But the progress of the reform seems to have encountered insuperable obstacles. It has come further than in any other Eastern country, and has been more consistent than elsewhere. Since 1968, when the new economic mechanism was initiated, similar measures were introduced in other Eastern countries, such as the decentralization measures of the Brezhnev-Kosygin leadership in the Soviet Union in 1965 and 1979, the changes in planning and administration introduced in Poland in the early '70s by Gierek, and the new economic system introduced in the GDR in the second half of the '70s. But none of these reforms lasted. After a few years, a return to traditional administrative methods took place. In Hungary as well, the reform was suspended in 1973 after the oil shock and losses were absorbed by the state, but in 1978 Hungary returned to the basic principles of the reform. The price system began again to function, subsidies were cut and prices were increased drastically by 35.5% by 1976 and 1980; the income of the population increased by only 8.1%, however, and in the following years prices were increased by 4.6% in 1981, 6.9% in 1982, 7.3% in 1983,[277] 7.5% in 1984, and 7.0% in 1985. Realistic exchange rates were introduced on the basis of buying power parity and are regularly adjusted. A differentiated exchange rate for hard-currency trade of 1 dollar = 50.64 forints and 1 transferable ruble = 26.00 forints for CMEA trade was established. Production enterprises have received far-ranging powers to engage in foreign trade on their own account or on a commission basis.

The reform has powerful opponents; its advocates, on the other hand, are calling increasingly loudly for a "reform of the reform" in the direction of more decentralization of decision-making powers and liberalization of the existing regime. The opponents point out that the reform has neither brought economic progress nor solved social problems. The economy is stagnating; the quality of goods and efficiency have not improved. A small layer of private persons, making up 3–4% of the total population who either have a small enterprise, provide a service, or are part of a work commune, as they are called, have profited from the reform. The majority of the population, especially state officials, physicians, teachers, and pensioners, have lost more than they have won, and 15% to 20% of the population is still living below the subsistence level. A study of the Institute for Economic Trends and Market Research shows that more than half of the employed population is working in the private sector. Most of these are in agriculture, in which there are 1.7 million family enterprises, members of which also work in the cities. In addition there are 140,000 small craftsmen, 10,000 economic work communes with 55,000 blue-collar workers and 7,000 white-collar workers who work in many areas, from arranging marriages to programming. There are more than 21,000 work communes with 230,000 members in industrial factories who continue their work after official working hours using the means of production belonging to the plant. In addition, there are specialized cooperative groups with 90,000 members. The work done in the private economy is mainly in second jobs. Thus, recently a "luxury taxi" cooperative was set up with taxi drivers of over forty cars manufactured in the West, and who take 10 forints for every extra kilometer. These luxury taxi drivers are mostly from the free professions. Not infrequently, they are addressed as "Professor." Twelve hundred citizens apply every year to the Office for Wages and Labor for permission to work abroad. Thirty-five countries have been specified, but most people work in East and West Germany and in Austria.

Not only has the reform brought nothing to the majority of the population, it has even taken from them. Prices are rising, sometimes faster than wages. Most people are unable to find a second job. The gap between the small group of the newly rich and the majority of the population whose income has been stagnating or declining for years has become deeper. The post-Stalinist social contract, which was intended as a restructuring of the economic system in the direction of expanding the food and consumer goods industries by a greater decentralization of decisionmaking, and greater initiative to enterprises and workers as a precondition for improving the quality of life, is in danger. The majority of employees have no motivation to perform better. A small layer of enterpreneurial individuals seek additional earnings in the second economy and not in the state economy, where wages are little differentiated and provide no incentive for higher labor productivity. The reform has created better living conditions for a small group of the population which is envied by the overwhelming majority: 56% of respondents welcome clandestine work or side jobs, but just as many are unwilling or unable to find a job in the second economy.[278] Frankfurt journalist Viktor Meier found that "A psychological uncertainty seems to be spreading among the population as to what social values now apply in Hungary, capitalist or socialist. The argument that it is better to have the privilege of a split mind than a unified soul may seem rational, but it does not always solve the dilemma."[279] However, at present the important issue in Hungary is not so much moral values as scientific and technical progress as a precondition for improving the relatively low quality of life of the majority of the population. The reform, as it has proceeded, has not created such preconditions. Although one hears a lot about progressive decentralization of decision making, and this has in fact in part occurred, 70–80% of total output is still concentrated in 50–100 large combinates.[280] Hungary's new economic mechanism, which Kadar called "a socialist planned economy which gives heed to the market," seems more like the GDR steering system, which has shifted economic powers to the large combinates, and the decentralized steering system of Yugoslavia. One part of the social contract has definitely been fulfilled: the population is better supplied with top-quality goods than is the case in other Eastern countries. "Between 1979 and 1982 100,000 passenger cars, 300,000 televisions, 20% of which were color TVs, were sold each year, and 82,000–83,000 apartments were made available each year," observed Ferenc Havasi, Hungary's Central Committee Secretary for Economic Questions.[281] However, cars and color televisions are bought only by those who have a relatively high income, i.e., mainly those who have found some work or a second job in the second economy and not those who work in the state economy and receive an average wage of about 5,000 forints.

As regards the quality of goods, Hungary is still a planned economy, and still stresses quantity and not quality. Tibor Vamos, director of the Institute for Computer Research, points out that Hungary's share in German imports of electric motors was 20% in 1938. Today, however, Hungary is negotiating with West Germany over the sale of furniture. Hungary, says Tibor Vamos, does not always make advantageous use of cooperation with the Soviet Union: "we try to sell the Soviet Union everything in the belief that we are selling good things, goods which it cannot obtain elsewhere, in exchange for goods which we also cannot sell elsewhere."[282] Tamas Bauer, of the Karl Marx University in Budapest, says that in terms of growth rate, Hungary's economy is not doing any better than the other CMEA countries which have not had a reform program.[283] However, this opinion can only apply to the first years of the present decade. In the mid-'80s, the traditional centrally planned economies grew more rapidly than Hungary's economy. But again, the quality of goods does not appear to be any better.

*　*　*

Is Hungary's reform a model for other CMEA countries? CMEA decisions over the last few years have referred increasingly more often to a unified economic policy and economic system. In most cases, reforms have been initiated in the unchanged economic system, and everywhere the reform catchword is: decentralization of decision making. Hungary has given its production units more freedom in taking decisions than the other Eastern countries. This brings up the question to what extent Hungary's present steering system may be regarded as a model for other CMEA countries. It is of course important to know to what extent this system is accepted by the Soviet Union. There are certainly an abundance of direct or indirect references. Grigorii Romanov, the former Polit-buro member of the CPSU, participated in the 13th Congress of the Hungarian Socialist Workers' Party in late March 1985, and expressed not his own, but the opinion of the Soviet Politburo: "There is no other way for a socialist state to safeguard its own interests than by strengthening the entire community and expanding the traditions of proletarian and socialist internationalism."[284] Of course Romanov also said that there was no place in this community for subordi-nation and command, for imposing the will of one nation on another, or a purely mechanical standardization of relations, etc. He was positive concerning the exchange of experience in improving methods of management and expanding democracy, but warned very clearly against shaping relations with the West in a way that could enable imperialist forces to use economic levers as means to exert political pressure, and for interfering in the internal affairs of sovereign socialist states. Romanov's speech to the 13th Party Congress of the Hungarian Socialist Workers' Party was interpreted as an acceptance by the new Soviet Party leader-ship of the Hungarian way. Nothing has changed since then, even after Romanov was purged from the Politburo of the CPSU. Since then Janos Kadar has been to Moscow, and in June 1986 Gorbachev visited Budapest. After this visit, Kadar himself referred to the opinion of his prominent guest from Moscow in a *Time* interview as follows: "I think that many things which we are doing in our country cannot be borrowed by Gorbachev, and that is understandable. The conditions and possibilities in the Soviet Union are quite different from those in our country. But I can say that the Soviets understand and appreciate our search for new solutions for present problems."[285] Some aspects of the Hungarian reform have been vehemently criticized in the Soviet newspaper *Pravda*, especially the private economy, which *Pravda* thinks is very much expanded, and the differentiation in income relations that this has caused. However, the Soviet leadership definitely does not see the present development of the Hungarian economic reform as a danger to the political system of the country or as a reason to interfere in Hungary's internal affairs. It knows quite well that the political monopoly of the Hungarian Socialist Workers' Party under Kadar's, and now Karoly Grosz's, leadership is safe and sound. Hungary's ruling party supports Soviet foreign policy almost without reservations. In the Soviet Union, Hungary's reform is seen more as a problem of rationality of the initiated decentralization measures than as a political problem which might be cause for concern to the Soviet leadership. A statement by Georgii Arbatov, Director of the Soviet Institute for the Study of the USA and Canada, is very clear in this respect. He has the following to say on the Hungarian steering system: "It has been recognized as successful although it is not free of complications; the Hungarians speak about these. However, no one can automatically adopt and introduce a model from another country. I think the Hungarian comrades themselves would be shocked if we had accepted their model and implemented it."[286] As it is with the reform at present, it is quite certain that its fate will be decided in Hungary, and nowhere else. It seems to have exhausted the progress-promoting factors before it was able to restructure the economy and raise labor productivity and quality, and in the process has caused a number of difficult social problems without being able to raise the income of the population perceptibly in the last few years. The demand for a "reform of the reform" is becoming ever louder, and the opinion is becoming increasingly stronger that an effective decentralization of economic powers can only take place in a liberalized political system. Imre Pozsgai, General Secretary of the Patriotic People's Front and since May 1988 a member of the Politburo, who is more on the mark than many others in assessing the relation between economics and politics, says that the bureaucracy is too cumbersome and the hierarchical pyramid too steep. Pozsgai does not think that the deterioration of the economic situation of broad layers of the population is the essential reason for the dissatisfaction; rather it is the growing conviction that Hungary's problems cannot be solved with existing methods. It is certainly not true that Hungary's leadership has done nothing to democratize the political regime. Not only official candidates chosen by the Party, but also candidates proposed by free voters' assemblies, ran for parliament in 1985. But what does such a measure signify when the parliament meets only eight days per year to pass laws which have already been decided upon part and parcel in the executive bodies of the state? These laws are usually unanimously approved in the parliament. The upper house of the Hungarian people has become more representative but has not gained any responsibility in the leadership of the country. Pozsgai, who was elected to parliament on the basis of the national list of 35 candidates, said that he would have been more content if he had been elected with 60% of the votes in a normal voters' district with one or several opposing candidates than with 99% of the votes on a list of prominent personages.[287]

The post-Stalinist social contract contemplated by Hungary's political leadership aimed at an economic reform which would stimulate the economy and raise the quality of life in order to bring peace and order following the extreme turbulance the country had experienced after the October 1956 uprising. Kadar and his assistants believed that decentralized decision-making was possible in a state economy led by a single Party and that this could achieve a higher level of efficiency than a centrally administered planned economy. There is also no doubt that the new economic mechanism brought about considerable improvements. Culture especially profited. The restoration of the peasantry in a collectivized agricultural system is one of the country's greatest achievements, and has ensured the supply of the population with basic foods, as well as the export of farm products on a much greater scale than had been possible before. The gap between supply and demand no longer exists. Citizens of other CMEA countries also come to Hungary to buy consumer goods at favorable prices. A much more liberal atmosphere than formerly has been created in the economy. Economic managers have suddenly realized that they have quite a bit of freedom, that they can invest a considerable portion of their profits on their own responsibility in capital investment projects, and that they can also engage in foreign transactions. After eighteen years of reform, Kadar rated the effect of the new economic mechanism highly. In his noteworthy interview to *Time* magazine he said: "The Hungarian reform policy has proven itself. Before 1975 Hungary was growing, and since then it has at least maintained its position despite difficulties throughout the world economy." However, this assessment by the former Party leader is questioned on many fronts. Until 1975, other countries also had high growth rates. After 1975, and especially after 1983, the growth rates in the East and in the West were higher than in Hungary's stagnating economy. Although private initiative which developed under the favorable reform conditions was able to close certain gaps in supply, it also gave rise to social problems that have made the contrast between rich and poor clearer. That is what a country which calls itself socialist finds difficult to tolerate. Ferenc Havasi, Central Committee Secretary for Economic Affairs, referred to the new conflicts as follows: "The new social conflicts that were to be expected after decentralization were not given due consideration."[288]

The orthodox Party wing, which has never been happy about the reform, which calls into question the monopoly position of the Party in the management of the economy, believes that it has been borne out in its view that central steering by Party and government is the only adequate steering form in a one-party regime. Its call for a return to the status quo ante is consistent. This Party wing is quite strongly represented in the Party hierarchy, but cannot count on a large following. However, those who from the very outset claimed that decentralization of economic powers was doomed to failure in a centralized antipluralist political regime because the governing bureaucracy retained its hegemony in the economy and society and stifled every initiative at the micro-level, also feel they have been proven right. This contradiction between economics and policy is most clearly expressed by the research economist Mihaly Bihari: "In the relationship between the economic and political system the latter has played a decisive role through specifically political directives; in the process, politics has descended into economics in order to integrate the economy into the political system; as a consequence of total politicization of the economic system, and total economization of the political system, the two systems have grown together to such an extent that the relative autonomy of the economy has wholly disappeared."[289] The reform introduced in 1968 was intended to eliminate the dominance of politics over the economy or at least to attenuate it. This was unsuccessful, as Tamas Bauer describes: ". . . The reform program of the '60s aimed not only at achieving better economic rationality, but was also more or less a component of the program of social democratization: the advocates of the reform wanted not only to prevent a further deterioration of economic conditions, they also thought that the reform would create a more democratic, more humane, and more socialist socialism. Such considerations," concludes Bauer, "have, however, now almost wholly disappeared."

The course of the reform shows the limits of "taking into account the market in a socialist planned economy'' (Kadar). The Hungarian state economy, led by a single Party which will not give up its monopoly on power, is not more efficient; social conflicts have rather become more acute. Hungary's eighteen-year-long experiment has not convinced other planned economies since it has not proven that in a one-party system a relatively decentralized steering system can be successful and less conflict-ridden than a centrally administered and centrally planned economy.

The GDR, Czechoslovakia, and Bulgaria

The German Democratic Republic

A half year before the CMEA Comprehensive Program of 1985 was adopted the GDR included its objectives, which were still being drafted, in its national economic plans at the 10th Plenum of the Central Committee of the SED in June 1985. The introduction of microelectronics into the construction, administration, and production sections on as broad a front as possible was made the most important goal of the economic plan for 1986. The tapping of key technologies, which, in the words of the Politburo member Günter Mittag, are of crucial importance for the economy, is to become the vehicle of the further development of the GDR economy. An 8.1% rise in labor productivity was targeted for 1986. Priority was given to electric engineering and electronics, in which a growth of 13.2% was targeted for 1986. The tool and machine-tool industries were to increase by 13.2%, production in the chemical industry was to increase by 9.3% compared with the preceding year. The production of construction elements in microelectronics was to rise from 85,750 to almost 100,000; expenditures for science and technology to increase by 10.6%.[290]

The projected economic growth of 4.4% will require more capital investments than previously. In 1986 capital investments were to reach 63 billion marks compared with 56 billion marks the preceding year. A perceptible burden for price subsidies was anticipated: they were to increase by 46.2 billion marks in 1986 compared with 40.4 the preceding year, and reach a level of 17% of total spending (236 billion marks).

The GDR is in a phase of intensive development which is just only beginning in the Soviet Union and in the other Eastern countries. It would like to raise its economic level to regain the technological level of West Germany—the level it had before the War and which it lost after it. It will make a pioneer service to the Eastern bloc and be able to contribute to the fulfillment of the CMEA Comprehensive Program in 1985.

Erich Kissner, director of the Commerzbank, said at a meeting of the Office for Undivided Germany in the Berlin Reichstag that the GDR's international credit rating had further improved. From September 1985 to March 1986, the GDR moved from 35th place to 32nd place on the world debtor list and achieved the same creditworthy level as Ireland, South Korea, or the United Arab Emirates. Of the East bloc countries, only the Soviet Union had a better rating. The GDR net debt, estimated at 6.8 billion dollars by the OECD, is no longer an issue for banks. "They would be standing in queues in East Berlin to get rid of their money." The improvement in their debt structure is especially important for assessing GDR creditworthiness. In the early '80s, the share of middle-term and long-term obligations in total debt was about 20%. Eighty percent was due within 360 days, and yet today the situation is the reverse. Only 20% are short-term, while 80% are middle-term and long-term.[291] However, as stated, the GDR is now more reticent about taking out loans after it had borrowed 1.2 billion dollars in 1985 on the Euromarket. If it is considered that GDR deposits in Western banks have now reached 5.3 billion dollars, there is good reason for such reserve.

The consolidation of the GDR's debt situation is due to a distinct improvement in the efficiency of economic activity. Developments in East Germany seem to bear out the thesis of the founder of the Soviet state, V. I. Lenin, namely, that a dynamic economic growth could be achieved with Prussian discipline and the promptness of the German postal system. Lenin was thinking about the Soviet Union. But this thesis seems only to be valid where Prussian discipline is an innate property. East Germany's start in the Eastern community was extremely unfavorable, not because this part of Germany was the poorest part, quite the contrary: 28% of the total population of Germany, who had lived in this territory before World War II, produced 30% of the country's national income.[292] But this part of Germany suffered considerably more damage from World War II than the Western part. War damage—15% of total assets of 1939—was much less than in Western Germany (21%), but the dismantling of factories after the war, 26% of the total assets of 1939, resulted in losses twice as high as those incurred in the Western part of the country (12%).[293] In 1938, the per capita national income of East Germany was 80% higher than in Czechoslovakia,[294] but in 1950 it was 21% lower. The decline to the second largest industrial state in the Eastern bloc was not overcome until 1967 when the per capita income in the GDR reached 1,476 dollars, while in Czechoslovakia it was only 1,421 dollars.[295] In 1980, the GDR had a per capita national income of 5,910 dollars, which is at the top of the Eastern bloc, followed by Czechoslovakia with 4,740 dollars and the Soviet Union with 4,740 dollars.[296]

The GDR's superiority in competition in the CMEA was manifested most distinctly in the first half of the '80s. While all the countries of the Eastern bloc were experiencing a perceptible economic recession in the first years of the decade for the first time in postwar history, the GDR suffered a decline in growth rate in only one year, from 4.8% in 1981 to 2.6% in 1982, after which it rose again to 4.4% in 1983 and 5.7% in 1984. In 1985 as well, the growth rate was only 0.2% under the 5% mark. The GDR is the only Eastern country which increased its annual growth rate from 4.1% in the five-year period from 1976 to 1980 to 4.4% in the period from 1981 to 1985, while the other CMEA countries suffered declines: Bulgaria from 6.3% to 3.7%, Czechoslovakia from 3.7% to 1.8%, Romania from 7.2% to 4.4%, the Soviet Union from 4.3% to 3.5%, Hungary from 2.8% to 1.4%, and Poland an absolute decline.

Industry contributed over 80% of the economic growth in 1985. The introduction of new key technologies played the decisive role in industrial growth. While net industrial production increased by 9%, electronics and the electrical engineering industry had an increase of 15.5%, integrated automatic production lines showed a growth of 34%, general machinery construction, farm machinery, equipment for transport increased by 14.1% in production, but mining and metallurgy also showed a considerable increase of 11% in 1985. The key technologies were also the focal point of capital investments in 1985. The share of rationalization investments increased by 78% in the processing industries. A total of 13,800 industrial robots were installed in the course of modernization. Fifty-seven thousand industrial robots are already in operation. Rationalization of the production process has made it possible to reduce the consumption of important raw materials and fuels by 3.5% compared with the preceding year. There was even a decrease of 7% in the consumption of rolled steel in the metal-processing industry.

A certain improvement is also to be noted in the energy sector, although mainly due to the expansion of brown coal extraction, which in 1985 reached a volume of 312 million tons, 54 million tons more than in 1980 and 22 million tons more than in the planned target. However, there are limits to a further expansion of brown coal production. Its share in energy production is already 70% and is creating serious environmental problems, since the thermal power stations of the country do not have filters. There are also limits to energy saving. Energy consumption per production unit continues to decline, but at a slower reduction rate: by 1.5% in 1985 after 1.8% in 1984 and 4.4% in 1983. Power production increased by only 0.8% in the previous year. The main goal of the government is to reduce oil, gas, and bituminous coal imports and replace them through the expansion of brown coal production and especially nuclear energy. The GDR recently obtained the appropriate equipment from the Soviet Union.[297]

The preceding year was a record year like 1984. Grain harvests reached an unprecedented volume of 11.6 million tons. The per hectare yield of 4.6 metric tons compares favorably with the results of Western industrial countries. Vegetable harvests increased by 18% compared with the preceding years, and fruit yields almost doubled.[298] Potato yield increased by 4.9%. The state was also able to buy more farm products than previously, since the prices were increased drastically. Supplies to the population have improved. Retail trade increased by 4.2% compared with the preceding year, including an increase of 5.6% in the sale of industrial consumer goods, but only 2.7% increase in food sales. After an increase of 4% in real income in 1984, an increase of 5% was reached in 1985. Almost every second household in the GDR has its own car.

In 1985 foreign trade turnover reached a total of 180 billion foreign exchange marks and increased by 3.6% in both Eastern and Western trade compared with the preceding year. The export surplus was 7 billion marks, including 4 billion marks in trade with the East. Two-thirds of total foreign trade were accounted for by CMEA countries, 38% by the country's largest trading partner, the Soviet Union, trade with whom reached the value of 70 billion foreign exchange marks in 1985, a growth of 4%. Trade between the two Germanies has developed actively. After a surplus of 1.3 billion foreign exchange marks in 1984, the GDR balanced its trade in 1985 despite an increase of 23% in its orders from the FRG. The GDR was also able to negotiate a favorable agreement on a swing credit of 850 million clearing units (1 clearing unit is equal to 1 DM) for 1986–1990. However, it must in return provide 70 million DM annually to offset the imbalance in non-commercial payments.[299]

The main thrust of the GDR economic reform was not a decentralization of economic powers, but rather a perfection of the organization of the economic system, methods of central planning, and industrial and investment policy. In contrast to Hungary, decision-making is concentrated in the central economic apparatus which controls and monitors production activity through a consistent system of economic planning and a hierarchically structured industrial administration. Binding plan indices were reduced in number in 1983. The most important are still regarded as state directives, and their fulfillment is rigorously monitored by a higher economic body and the Party apparatus through a "reward and punishment" system. A number of economic reforms have also been carried out in the GDR over the past twenty years. But their purpose was not, as in the other planned economies, to shift economic powers partially to the micro-level, but to perfect central planning and improve criteria of success, as well as the organizational structure of industrial administration.

The 11th Party Congress of the SED of 1981 made the industrial combinates the most important administrative cell in industry and construction. In 1985 there were 175 combinates operating, employing more than three million people. They comprise a closed system of production, sales, and research. A middle-sized combinate employed 20,000–40,000 people. Most combinates are managed by a leading plant in the particular industrial branch. Where the dispersion of production is great, combinate administrations are also formed. Combinates steer the entire economic activity of the economic area under them, have drafted 3,500 material balance sheets, and are fulfilling them. Economic strategy and the directions of development are determined by the central economic authorities in the branch ministries. Three hundred material balance sheets in the principal areas of the country's economy are approved by the Council of Ministers, and 600 are initiated by the Central Planning Commission.

The combinates were not only successful in production. Seventy-nine made considerable profits in the preceding years, and 61 of them showed a growth increment of 50%. This is partly due to an increase in labor productivity and a reduction in energy and materials input. Zeiss Jena (employing 58,000) reported a 20.2% increase in net profit for 1985 and an increase of 7% in sales. The Leuna combinate (employing 30,000) had a 38.5% increase in profits between 1981 and 1985 and an increase in production by 29.7%. The combinate Mikroelektronik Erfurt (employing 68,000) is above average with 29.4% increase in commodity production and 154.9% increase in net profits.[300] The substitution of Western imports by this combinate is also considered an economic success. The electronic element combinate in Treptow (employing 28,000), the Party chief tells us, has begun the production of top-quality materials for microelectronics and thus has broken the US embargo policy.[301]

The government decree of March 1983 introduced an improved system of plan indices: industrial output was eliminated as a principal index since it caused a waste of materials and an inflation of cooperation. It was replaced by the indicator "net output," which expresses actual value added (production value minus material consumption and write-off into the amortization fund). Net profit, products, and services for the population, as well as exports, also serve as principal indices of "performance evaluation." Other "important qualitative indicators" are connected with labor productivity, costs (especially material costs), production of economically important products (especially newly developed products with the quality symbol "Q") as well as material costs per 100 marks commodity production.

However, the East Germans are aware that the best system of plan figures cannot express success and failures, and cannot reward or punish performance appropriately. "Sold output is not automatically equivalent to covering demands," say well-known economists[302]; and Günter Mittag, Politburo member responsible for economic affairs, maintains that the accounting system should be organized so that higher profits can serve as an "expression of progress in quality, needs, decline in costs, and export profitability."[303] Attempts are being made to prevent unavoidable manipulations to obtain larger or unjustified profits by changes in the range of products offered by making it mandatory to pay any profits that result from violations of plan targets in determining the range of products into the state budget. The state planning system cannot function without a comprehensive state control and the application of administrative measures.

All investment activities in the GDR are centrally planned and centrally steered. However, funds for financing have become scarcer. After a growth rate of 2.7% in 1981, a decline was registered of 5.2% in the next year, there was no increase in 1983, and another decline of 4.9% occurred in 1984. In 1985 the investment volume was 62 billion marks, 6 billion marks more than in the preceding year. Thus more and more value is attached to frugal use of capital investment monies. The money can only be assigned if the investment contributes to intensification and modernization of production, less labor, and the production of top-quality goods. Every capital investment project must present a detailed information on efficiency, technical parameters, and supply with construction materials and equipment.

The government decree of September 1, 1985, obligates the central and regional authorities to test whether the proposed capital investments are necessary and whether they might not be replaced by other measures such as modernization of existing production capacities. To make the use of basic capital more difficult for industrial plants, the tax on it will be changed as of January 1, 1986. The net value rather than the gross value (balance value minus amortizations) will be taxed, and not at a constant rate of 6%, but at a variable tax rate. About three-fourths of the capital investment volume in 1985 went toward modernizations and rationalizations, a singular case in the East bloc where these proportions are usually reversed.

The efficiency and standard of living in the GDR are still much lower than in the Western part of the country. However, the GDR is the pace-setter in the Eastern community with regard to both productivity and the level of supplies to the population.

Czechoslovakia

The economic data published on the eve of the 16th Party Congress[304] state that CMEA countries account for 74% and the Soviet Union alone for 45% of Czech foreign trade. The interlocking seems to be permanent since a good portion of foreign trade relations are based on specialization and cooperation agreements. Thirty-six percent of exports in intra-CMEA trade and 72.5% of exports in Soviet trade are covered by middle-term and long-term industrial cooperation agreements, while only 16% and 19.7% are the figures for imports. This difference is understandable if one considers that raw materials and fuels are the most important Czech imports from the Soviet Union.

Czechoslovakia is the only CMEA country which did not take part in the vigorous expansion of economic relations with the Western industrial countries in the '70s. The Western share in total exports increased from 20.6% in 1970 to 22.0% in 1980, and then declined to 19.9%, 18.0%, 17.7%[305] in the next three years, and to 15.9% in 1985. The share of the developing countries in Czech exports also decreased from 7% to 5.3%. The foreign trade turnover of Czechoslovakia increased by 48.5% from 161.7 billion foreign exchange crowns to 240.1 billion foreign exchange crowns in the five-year period from 1981 to 1985. However, Western industrial countries and the developing countries accounted for only 4.3% of this growth, reaching a total turnover of 50.8 billion crowns. There is no inordinate gap between Western imports and Western exports permitted in Czechoslovakia. In 1980 the debt was no more than 4.9 billion dollars gross and 3.6 billion dollars net, the lowest in the CMEA with the exception of Bulgaria.[306] There was a surplus of barely 20 billion foreign exchange crowns in the five-year period from 1981 to 1985 in trade with the West, and the balance on current accounts in the last four years was positive at 0.1

billion dollars in 1982, 0.65 billion dollars in 1983, 0.7 billion dollars in 1984, and 0.5 billion dollars in 1985.[307] Debts to Western banks decreased from 3.3 billion dollars gross and 2.3 billion dollars net in 1985. The Federal Republic of Germany was the biggest Western foreign trade partner of Czechoslovakia in 1985 with a share in total trade of 10 billion foreign exchange crowns, followed by Austria with 5.8 billion crowns, Switzerland with 3.6 billion crowns, and Great Britain with 2.7 billion crowns.[308]

In 1985 and 1986, the tendency for foreign exchange with the CMEA countries at the expense of Western trade continued to grow: exports to the socialist countries increased by 6.2%, imports from them increased by 6%, while exports to non-socialist countries increased by 0.6% and imports from them increased by 5.1%. Foreign trade turnover with the CMEA countries was 3.4% lower, and trade with the Soviet Union 2.3% higher in the first half-year of 1986 than the volume in the comparable period in the preceding years; exports to the socialist countries accounted for 80.2% of Czechoslovakia's total foreign trade in the first half-year of 1986.

Czechoslovakia intensified its foreign trade with the Soviet Union for more than simply political reasons. Because of the rise of oil prices, its terms of trade between 1970 and 1974 deteriorated by one-third, mainly in trade relations with the Soviet Union. Czechoslovakia must therefore export one-third more to the Soviet Union to be able to finance the same import volumes as previously. However, in 1985 it had another deficit of 607 million transferable rubles.

The country's leadership under Gustav Husak steered a normalization course. It reduced its political and economic relations with the industrial countries of the West to a minimum and has not made use of the opportunity to renew its hopelessly obsolete machinery stock with modern Western technology and Western credits. Nor does Czechoslovakia have a range of exports with which it could enter the Western market, as was the case between the two World Wars. It has therefore been endeavoring all the more to build up the position it had lost in the West on Eastern markets. Czechoslovakia has been able to carve out for itself a place in CMEA specialization agreements. It has not only become the most important subcontractor for nuclear reactor construction in the Soviet Union, it has also built up its own reactor market in the CMEA. It provides technological supplies for the chemical industry, for food production, and for pumps and machine tools. The data prepared for the 17th Congress show that Czechoslovakia has concluded 323 bilateral and 146 multilateral specialization and cooperation agreements with CMEA countries. It has concluded 101 such agreements with non-socialist countries, which, however, account for only 1.25% of the foreign trade turnover with this group of countries. Czechoslovakia plays a decisive role alongside the Soviet Union in the newly founded Interatomenergo. Reactors are manufactured in the Skoda works in Pilsen. Twenty one reactor units of 440 megawatts of the WWER type (different from those in use in Chernobyl) will be built between 1981 and 1988. Ten of these are for Czechoslovakia, four for Hungary and Poland, and three for the GDR. Ten reactors have already been delivered.[309] The Chernobyl disaster could, however, have grave consequences for Czechoslovakia's production plans. It is assumed that supplementary safety equipment will be necessary both for existing nuclear reactors as well as for those in the process of construction. For these it will be mostly imported technology from the West that will be used. In addition, a delay is feared in the manufacture of the 1,000-megawatt reactors which are supposed to be delivered in the late '80s. A hesitation on the part of the buyers will put a hitch in both the manufacture and the export plans.

The sharp rise in Czech participation in specialization in machinery construction and especially in reactor construction is reflected in production data for the first half-year of 1986. Industrial product increased by 3.2% in comparison with the first half-year of 1985. Deliveries of heavy machinery, mainly equipment for atomic power stations, increased by 36.2%, manufacture of pipes increased by 45%, production of cranes by 23.2%, and the production of compressors and pumps increased by 7.7%.[310] Large orders from the Soviet Union such as 6,500 diesel locomotives or 50,000 trucks[311] make large-scale mass production possible.

The 17th Party Congress of the Communist Party of Czechoslovakia, with 1.67 million members, began only three weeks after the 27th Party Congress of the Communist Party of the Soviet Union ended. Gorbachev, who later participated in the congresses of the Socialist Unity Party of Germany and the Polish United Workers' Party, was represented at the CPCz Congress by Politburo member Solomentsev. He praised the achievements of the host country, but not the Party leader. In Moscow, it is open knowledge that Gustav Husak, the outstanding administrator of normalization, has not earned himself the love of the people in his seventeen years in office, after having crushed the Prague Spring and restored peace and order. There is more peace in Czechoslovakia than the present Kremlin leadership would have liked. The creative forces proclaimed by the 17th Party Congress as necessary to put life into the stagnating economy, adapt the economic structure to the needs of the times, and bring morale and labor productivity up to the standards of the industrial states of the West, and to give the Czech economy the status it had in prewar Europe, were conspicuous by their absence in this tranquil atmosphere.

"One of the principal obstacles to the recovery of the Czech economy," as Poland's observers at the 17th Party Congress said, "is the unwritten law of economic egalitarianism, in which a poor enterprise has a share of the good results of the other enterprise, and in which the wage difference between a successful and a failed enterprise is no more than one hundred crowns."[312]

Gustav Husak knew the customs reigning among the fraternal parties. "The experiences of the fraternal parties and especially the CPSU are a source of inspiration," he said. Due reverence was offered to the 27th Party Congress and the new version of the Third Party Program, as well as the Guidelines for Economic Development to the Year 2000. The talk by Gorbachev was called a "worthy enrichment." Husak said, "Czech and Slovak Communists will, however, rely on the experiences accumulated since the 14th Party Congress in 1971." What this experience had taught was presented by the Party leader nine months before in unequivocal terms to the Plenary Session of the Central Committee in June 1985: "We will not adopt the path of a market-oriented concept which weakens the system of socialist collective property and the leading role of the Party in the economy. We have had bad experience with this concept."[313] But the country has also not had good experience with the normalization initiated by the 14th Party Congress. The economy is stagnating. Economic growth is declining. In the second half of the '60s, the average annual growth rate was 6.2%, in the first half of the '70s it was 5.7%, in the second half of the '70s it was 3.6% and in the first half of the '80s it was only 1.6%.

Since 1980, the Czech economy has achieved the growth targeted by the plan in only one year, 1984, with 3.49%. The growth rates for 1980 (2.39%), 1981 (−0.11%), 1982 (0.24%), 1983 (2.25%) and 1985 (2.43%), were under the plan target, and in 1981 and 1982 no growth was achieved. The Party did not attempt to play down the economic difficulties, and only in part blamed adverse external conditions, the unfavorable terms of trade and the growing pressure of the capitalist countries. The Party leader presented the economic development of the last fifteen years, however, as a proof of the correctness of his normalization policy. Only in this way was he able to show that the economic policy pursued was successful. The results of the last six or seven years were certainly not suited to this purpose. He did not attempt to embellish the symptoms of malaise in the society. He assailed the ever-growing parasitism, theft of state property, corruption and bribery, the striving for the easy life without a commensurate performance, and the lack of consistency in combating these adverse phenomena in the social life of his country. Husak could draw on the results of a recent survey in his assessment of the quality of life in his country. According to this survey, half of the population thought that the standard of living has improved; 90% of those questioned have a black and white television, 54% have a stereo, 50% have automatic washing machines, 54% have their own car or have access to one, and 26% have a summer house. Nonetheless half of the respondents in this country, the best-developed industrial state of Eastern Europe after the GDR, still dream of a color television, automatic washing machine, a summer house, and a telephone.[314]

One cannot reproach Husak for not recognizing the signs of the times. He studied carefully Gorbachev's report three weeks earlier. Such tones could not go by unnoticed. In the economic and political part of his three-hour talk, he put forth the demand for economic thinking and a higher moral consciousness among the citizenry, for increased responsibility on the part of leading cadres, and spoke of the necessity of a "socialist spirit of enterprise." Gorbachev's call for criticism and self-criticism, on which such stress was placed, also found its due place in Husak's report to the 17th Party Congress. This part of the talk, as Polish observers report, received the greatest applause from the delegates. The Party organ *Rude Pravo*, one week before the Party Congress, had struck up critical tones with the cry of indignation that not one major project of the past few years had been completed on time.[315] But Husak not only criticized the flaws in economic activity. He was also dissatisfied with the ideological work which neglected economic propaganda, and did not give sufficient place to the "crisis of capitalism" and its effects on the socialist system. Husak knew that the followers of Charter 77 are not too many in number. However, he did not underestimate both their effect and the influence of the Catholic church. A church which brought 150,000 persons to Velehrad in the year before for devotions, and which brings thousands every year to the Holy Mary pilgrimate in Slovakian Levoca is not to be underestimated. However, he sought a constructive dialogue neither with the dissidents nor with the church. "We will never permit anyone to violate law and order even if he makes use of such exulted words as freedom, democracy, and human rights."

The decisions of the 17th Party Congress of the CPCz differ from the decisions of the 27th Party Congress of the CPSU in one area. All previous presidium members and Central Committee secretaries of the CPCz were confirmed in their positions. Three Party functionaries were promoted to candidates to the Party Presidium. But it is only the Party leadership which shows such stability. At the local level, 40% of Party functionaries have been dismissed since the 16th Party Congress, and in the ministries 45% of all vice-ministers, directors, and principal section leaders have been replaced.

The new Party leader, Milos Jakes, would rather perfect than reform economic management. But, as he stressed, and as Andropov, the late CPSU head, stressed in June 1983: "There are no patent recipes; every CMEA country seeks its own way."

Prime Minister Lubomir Strougal called for a reorientation of the economy. However, he did not offer any fully developed concept of a new economic mechanism. The productivity of labor and the quality of goods should be promoted more than hitherto with expanded incentives, the principle of democratic centralism, in which central planning is to concentrate on the most important economic areas and the crucial areas of production activity and sales, is to be maintained. A considerable number of binding indices will be eliminated. However, any attempts to reduce central steering will at first be only of an experimental and tentative nature. The head of the planning commission (Potac) spoke of four areas of production in which the size of taxes to be paid into the state budget and payments for social services will be set centrally. Some agricultural cooperatives, which are steered in similar ways, and above all the Suslowice cooperative at Gottwaldow, have been showing good results. The responsibility of managerial personnel will be increased by giving industrial enterprises more independence.

The perfection of the steering mechanism proposed by the 17th Party Congress is rather modest. Although the Congress called for adroitness in new methods, the "renewal concept" resembles more the steering methods of the last years of the Novotny era than the far-ranging decentralization measures of Hungary. The reformers are cautious. After eighteen years of normalization, factory managers can not only not be won over for far-ranging reforms, the leading stratum itself has become a victim of normalization methods. It no longer has courage. The middle levels and lower levels are more apathetic than inclined to reform.

As in the preceding five-year period, national income is to increase by 3.5% annually. Growth will come not from a further pile-up of material input, but on the basis of the existing input rates of raw materials, energy, and semi-finished materials; industrial production is targeted to increase by 15–18% by the end of the decade, construction will increase by 10%, and growth in agriculture will be 6–7%. Higher labor productivity will account for 92% and 95% of economic growth (in the preceding five-year period it was 80%). Three-fourths of growth in the national income is to be used for individual consumption and capital investments. The growth rate of individual consumption will double, collective consumption will increase by 22%, and capital investments are scheduled to increase by 10%. In the five-year period from 1981 to 1985 individual and collective consumption accounted for a fourth of the growth achieved. "The rest was used to pay back foreign debts and to mitigate the consequences of decreasing efficiency of foreign trade," commented the head of government Strougal.

The obsolete machinery stock is to be renewed, partly through Western imports. However, the conservative, reticent debt policy will be retained. Modernization of whole branches, the use of progress-promoting technologies, increased capital investments to save on energy and materials, and for environmental protection as well as improvement in the transport system, are high on the list of priorities. In the machinery construction sector, Czechoslovakia will continue to specialize within the CMEA, but will also conclude cooperation agreements with the industrial states of the West. The range of products offered will be pruned. Consumer goods production will be switched to manufactures with a high added value.

The focus of specialization will continue to be nuclear energy, and growth in this sector will be both for domestic purposes as well as for deliveries to the other CMEA countries. The share of nuclear energy in power output will increase from 14.6% in 1985 to 28%. Of the planned 88 billion kilowatt hours, no less than 25 billion kilowatt hours will come from nuclear power plants in 1990. Nuclear energy will be the source of the entire increase in power production in the last decade of this century, and moreover will replace a considerable portion of the power that is now produced from coal and natural gas. Sixty percent of power output in the year 2000 will be covered by nuclear energy. Czechoslovakia claims to have no other choice but to build more nuclear reactors. No further growth is contemplated using natural gas and coal. According to the five-year plan, 94 million tons of brown coal and 25 million tons of bituminous coal will be mined in 1990, somewhat more than in the preceding five-year period. The plan target, however, will not be fulfilled and there is not too much hope that it will be filled in the current five-year period either. The fuel industry mined 63.4 million tons of coal and lignite in the first half of 1986; this was a decline of 2.6% compared with the first half-year of the preceding year. The growth rate for 1989 was reduced in July from 3.5 to 2.2%.

Czechoslovakia has problems similar to those of other CMEA countries: the share of new products in industrial output has hardly risen. The level of innovation is extremely low, and stockpiles are inordinately large. The industrial potential of Czechoslovakia is the greatest in Eastern Europe after the GDR. It has more experience in machinery construction than any other CMEA country. However, the normalization course has had unfavorable effects on relations with the West. The conservative debt policy has prevented the introduction of modern technologies from Western industrial countries. The machinery stock is obsolete. Normalization has already lasted nearly two decades and will be continued. But it creates no preconditions for breathing life into economic activity, stimulating creativity, or increasing work morale and labor productivity. Czechoslovakia should be able to contribute considerably to fulfilling the 1985 CMEA Comprehensive Program. However, it is itself dependent on imports of modern technology from the West.

Bulgaria

Four weeks after the 27th Party Congress of the CPSU and one week after the 17th Party Congress of the CPCz, the 13th Party Congress of the Bulgarian Communists took place on the first days of April in 1986. Gorbachev did not grace this Congress with his presence either, but sent someone high-ranking to represent him, namely, the head of government Nikolai Ryzhkov. It is uncertain whether he was endeavoring thereby to give expression to his dissatisfaction with the closest ally of the Soviet Union. There is, however, some evidence to support this conjecture. The Soviet Union is not satisfied with the quality of the goods provided by Bulgaria or with its low productivity of labor. The Soviet ambassador Leonid Grekov spoke about this problem in July 1985 for the first time in the postwar history of this country. The devotion of the workers to their country is not so simple. Many of Bulgaria's workers have country houses, gardens, vineyards, or raise livestock. When they return to their factories, it is quite natural that they must also rest a bit after working on their private plots, and more clearly: "Bulgaria's workers are not sufficiently proletarianized."[316] Shortly afterward Stanko Todorov, a member of Bulgaria's Politburo, visited Moscow and assured the Soviet comrades that the workers of his country would undertake everything to improve the quality and reliability of the goods delivered to the Soviet Union.[317] On October 10, 1985, Bulgaria reacted to the criticism of its great ally with a decree on measures against youths who violated socialist morals, in particular, youths between the ages of 16 and 19. The decree made it mandatory for students to carry identity papers and to wear school uniforms.[318] A campaign against corruption, incompetence, and lack of discipline was started.

In preparing the 13th Party Congress, Todor Zhivkov, 74 years old, proceeded in exactly the same way as the eighteen-years younger Mikhail Gorbachev. He rejuvenated and altered the Party and government leadership in two major episodes, in January and in March 1986 before the Party Congress, and he then had himself confirmed as Party leader and all other Politburo members and Central Committee secretaries in their functions by the Party Congress. The changes he carried out were certainly no slighter than those in the Soviet Union. Several functionaries of the Gorbachev generation entered leading positions. The head of government Grisza Filipov was dismissed as head of government and replaced by the dynamic Georgi Atanasov. Chudomir Aleksandrov, Ognian Doinnov and Georgi Jordanov became Politburo members and assumed important positions in the state leadership. The 43-year-old economist Stoian Markov was appointed the first deputy of the head of government and chairman of the Commitee for Research and Technology.

The changes carried out before the 13th Party Congress and scheduled by the Congress in the existing economic system and organizational structure are more important than the changes among the leadership. The times of Sturm und Drang in the Bulgarian economy are past. The annual growth rates decreased from 7.8% in the period between 1971 and 1975, to 6.1% in the second half of the '70s, and 5.0%, 4.2%, 3.0%, and 4.6% in the years 1981 to 1984 and as low as 1.8% in 1985. Bulgarian agriculture suffered grave setbacks after two successive years of drought. In 1983, farm production decreased by 7.2% and in 1985 by 9% compared with the preceding year in each case. Food exports declined by 20% in the first nine months of 1985, while imports of farm products increased by 50%. Everything possible was undertaken to fulfill delivery commitments to CMEA countries: exports in the socialist countries increased by 7.5% in 1985, and by as much as 8.2% to the Soviet Union, but imports increased by only 3.5% and 2.1% respectively, and the trade deficit in relations with the Soviet Union was reduced by half to 240 million foreign exchange levas. Exports to the Western industrial countries, on the other hand, decreased by 6.6% in 1985, and to the developing countries by 12%. Debts to Western banks, which decreased by 8.2% in 1982, and 8.6% in 1983 compared with the preceding years to 2.8 billion dollars (gross) and 1.4 billion dollars (net) in 1984 thanks to drastic cutbacks in Western imports, and then increased to 3.7 billion dollars gross and 1.9 billion dollars net in 1985.[319] The share of the Western industrial countries in Bulgaria's total exports was on the average no more than 12% in the last three years. Reducing the debt will therefore cause considerable difficulties.

The poor economic results of 1985, as well as the breakdown in energy supplies, impelled the Bulgarian Party leadership to modify the planning and organizational structure even before the Party Congress. The official Party organ *Rabotnichesko Delo* called for more extensive use of economic categories such as prices, profit, interest rate, credit, and taxes. Contractual relations between socialist enterprises, self-financing, profit orientation, and improving economic accounting were set down as basic guidelines for the contemplated modernization of economic management. But the definition of the workers as "the possessors of socialist property," with more decision-making powers than previously in organization and production, was introduced into the vocabulary. It must be remembered that this also entails personal responsibility for the results of production as well as sanctions for factory managers in cases of failures. As in the Soviet Union, the central planning authorities were in the future to concentrate on "strategic planning of the main development areas."

Changes in the organizational structure of economic management undertaken in January 1986 are the most important. Three councils were formed in the Council of Ministers: one for the economy, one for social welfare, and one for intellectual and cultural development. Their task is to realize the goals of the state leadership and coordinate the activities of the corresponding ministries and other state organs. The decisions of these councils have the same legal force as decisions of the Council of Ministers. Two months later, on March 21, 1986, the ministries for machinery construction, metallurgy, energy, the chemical industry, and forestry, as well as the National Agrarian Industrial Association, were dissolved. "Self-administrating socialist organizations" were created headed by a president rather than a minister. Six such organizations were created by the end of the first half-year of 1986. As Todor Zhivkov stressed at the 13th Party Congress: "These are placed under the control of employees and will make independent decisions in planning and development. Enterprises will however remain state property and the state can also impose requirements on them. They will become authentic producers of goods, function in accordance with the law of value, and will have to be guided by economic competition on both the internal and external markets." He expressed his conviction that if the barriers of monopoly in industrial production can be eliminated, bottlenecks in supply will also be eliminated. As was also to happen three months later at the Congress of the Polish United Workers' Party, Todor Zhivkov also announced a revision of the existing wage system. The work code would be revised to make room for more flexible forms of compensation for work done. Enterprises that work better will be allowed to pay higher wages. Bulgaria's economic system will not go so far as the Yugoslavian. The factory and its means of production remain state property, but the self-administering socialist organization will have full right to make use of the state assets with which it has been entrusted. However, Bulgaria's production relations will also differ from Hungary's: workers will not be allowed to form work brigades to raise their incomes. The organizational structure of Bulgarian economic management will also differ considerably from the Soviet structure.

The Party leader dwelt especially on the scientific and technical revolution. He critized Bulgaria's scientists for not taking sufficient advantage of discoveries domestically and abroad, impressed upon them the need to work more closely with reality, and announced the founding of technological centers as well as essential changes in the pay and promotion of scientists. The whole of the country's manpower in science was to be placed on a new basis so as to be able to achieve the technological goals set up for the year 2000. He stressed the translation of the achievements of science into the practice of economic activity. "We must all overcome the typical Bulgarian discrepancy between words and deeds." The 13th Party Congress of Bulgaria called for closer economic cooperation. Three recently founded joint ventures in electronics and machinery construction were mentioned as models for such cooperation. A joint mixed management was assigned to production and sales. This form of cooperation resembles the organizational forms for scientific and technical activity in the five most important industrial areas of the CMEA countries as put forth at the 41st meeting of the CMEA. Important changes were stipulated in the existing foreign trade system. An "economic bank" that would take over some of the functions of the foreign trade banks was to be founded. It would provide credits and foreign exchange for the import of modern technology. The price of the credits will be set in accordance with an enterprise's efficiency. A struggle was proclaimed against the migration of workers from enterprise to enterprise. An employee will be obliged to work for a legally set length of time in an enterprise. If he leaves his job prematurely, he will lose the social services otherwise coming to him.

The theoretical foundation for the project link-up with the worldwide scientific and technical revolution was presented one year before the 13th Party Congress at the February meeting of the Central Committee in 1985 by Party leader Zhivkov in his talk on some new views and solutions in carrying out Bulgaria's scientific and technical policy.[320] "Tremendous changes have taken place between the base and superstructure. The objective laws of building up a mature socialist society were however underestimated. The superstructure has fallen behind the base." Zhivkov named four laws which will play a decisive role in the present stage of socialist construction: the first and most fundamental law is, in his opinion, the carrying out of the scientific and technical revolution. All other laws are contingent upon its realization. The second law is the perfection of socialist social relations, which are supposed to create favorable conditions for the development of the means of production through the utilization of the latest achievements of the scientific and technical revolution. The third law is the specific effect of the law of value under socialism. Anyone who neglects this law or attempts to replace it by administrative directives would have to pay dearly for it, as historical experience has shown. "The fourth law is the growing role of the people as the creator of history." In this context Zhivkov demanded more democracy and the perfection of the political system of socialist society. The February meeting of the Central Committee came to the conclusion that the scientific and technical revolution is a key, or even more, a "superkey to social and economic development," and that the "realization of the scientific and technical revolution under present conditions means the building of a mature socialist society."[321]

The most important conclusion of the February meeting of the Central Committee of the Bulgarian Communist Party is directly related to the Comprehensive Program accepted at the 41st meeting of the CMEA on December 18, 1985. The success of the scientific and technical revolution in Bulgaria is, it is stated, dependent on the continuation of socialist integration. The precondition for the success of this is an all-round deepening and enrichment of cooperation in science and production with other socialist countries, and above all with the Soviet Union, whose science and technology has a mighty industrial potential and manpower and is in the front ranks of the worldwide scientific and technical progress. As Jordan Jotov states, "There is no more reliable and secure precondition for the successful development of our science and technology than an even closer organic linkage of them with Soviet science and technology."[322]

The realization of the scientific revolution in close cooperation with the CMEA countries and above all with the Soviet Union has priority over measures to perfect the steering and management system, adopted before and after the 13th Party Congress. As Party leader Zhivkov stressed, Bulgaria has also no patent recipe. Like every other CMEA country, Bulgaria is also seeking for an adequate concept of development which will enable the Bulgarian economy to adapt to the needs of the rapidly progressing worldwide scientific and technical progress. However, Bulgaria will not copy the solutions of other CMEA countries, but is developing its own highly original concept of management within the framework set by the laws of socialist construction.

Poland, Romania and Hungary, who are always presenting original proposals of their own to the CMEA, are just as interested in the Comprehensive Program adopted by the 41st Council meeting on December 18, 1985, as Bulgaria, the GDR, or Czechoslovakia, who supported the Soviet proposals. The countries of Eastern Europe know quite well that they will never be able to effect the linkup to the steadily progressing world level alone, given their introverted steering mechanisms and limited scientific and economic potential.

Efforts are being made to adapt the existing steering system to the requirements of the times. However, there is no longer any paradigm to follow. The present Party leadership in the Soviet Union is itself looking for a steering concept that would be able to help the country out of its economic difficulties. The smaller countries are directed to the "laws of socialist construction," vaguely defined as the tolerable deviations from the existing economic and political system.

The Comprehensive Program approved at the 41st Council session in 1985 is directly connected with developments in the second community organization, namely, the Warsaw Pact. These will be discussed in more detail in the next section.

The CMEA and the Warsaw Pact

History

The Council for Mutual Economic Assistance was founded in January 1949 during Stalin's time. The Warsaw Pact was founded two years after his death in May 1955. Both community entities of the Eastern bloc were in the first instance a response to economic and political developments in the West at the time. The founding of the CMEA was a reaction to the Marshall Plan in which some of the Eastern countries such as Poland and Czechoslovakia wanted to take part, while the Warsaw Pact was a response to the prepared entry of the Federal Republic of Germany into NATO. The CMEA seems to have fulfilled its historical mission only insofar as it created a counterpart to the Marshall Plan. No Eastern country participated in the Marshall Plan. However, the CMEA was unable to evolve any noteworthy activities during the first years after its establishment. Stalin needed no international economic authority to steer the Eastern economies and needed no international military authority to coordinate the defense policy and foreign policy of the Eastern bloc. Stalin was the sole judge and the only law both in the Soviet Union and in its sphere of influence. His concept of integration was made complete by the imposition of the social system formed in the Soviet Union and his own interpretation of Marxist-Leninist ideology; by concentration of the whole of power in a single Communist Party; by nationalization of the means of production and collectivization of the economy, and by the iron-and-steel oriented concept of development and the consequent dependence of the Russian sphere of influence on Soviet raw materials and fuels. The CMEA functioned without statutes and without clearly defined powers and responsibilities. The founders seemed to have forgotten that they had created an international economic coordinating authority.

The national armies of the countries of Eastern Europe were to become components of the Soviet army, the largest army in the world. Units of the Soviet army which brought the Soviet system to Eastern Europe were to remain there and watch over the newly created social system. A network of political, military, and economic advisers was supposed to aid and abet the newly created national authorities in the Soviet sphere of influence. Stalin had least trust in Poland, the most restless and most populated of the Soviet Union's neighbors with its key position in Eastern Europe. In 1949, he sent his faithful Marshal Konstantin Rokossovskii, who won a permanent place in the history of his country as the savior of Moscow in 1941, to Poland as defense minister. The Polish-born marshal returned to the land of his birth not only to take over the leadership of the Polish army, but also to enter into the Party leadership as a member of the Politburo. A Soviet general with a Polish name, Bordzilowski, was made chief of staff, and Soviet officers were placed at the head of the country's four armies.

The Warsaw Pact was founded by a new Soviet Party leadership which could not and perhaps did not want to wield its power in Eastern Europe as Stalin had done. After the June uprising in 1953 in East Berlin it was ready to contemplate a new geopolitical constellation in Europe. A united but neutral Germany, excluded from the Western alliance, and the withdrawal of Soviet troops from Austria were envisaged. The incorporation of West Germany into the Western military alliance was in the Soviet Union's view the greatest danger to it and to its Eastern European sphere of influence.[323] It did everything possible to prevent the Paris Agreement. On October 23, 1954, the Soviet foreign ministry protested in a sharp note against the rearmament of Western Germany. Three weeks later, on November 13,[324] it issued a sharp note against the prepared ratification of the Paris Agreement and invited the 23 countries of Europe as well as the United States to an all-European conference in Moscow or Paris. In late November 1954, a conference of the future members of the Warsaw Pact was called at which the then Soviet foreign minister Molotov issued a declaration that the entry of West Germany into NATO would give the Western military alliance a superiority and force the Soviet Union to take counter-measures. On February 8, 1955, Molotov proclaimed that the ratification of the Paris Agreement would mean a grave danger for the independence of Austria. However, the preparations for ratification of the Paris Agreement were already complete. On March 22, 1955, the Soviet foreign ministry announced that the eight countries of the East had reached a complete accord on a military pact and a unified command, and that China had also participated in the deliberations.[325]

The Paris Agreement was ratified on May 5, 1955. On May 14, 1955, the agreement establishing the Warsaw Pact was signed. The Soviet Union was unable to prevent West Germany's entry into NATO. By the establishment of the Warsaw Pact, it thus wanted to bind its sphere of influence more closely and show unity outwardly. The Warsaw agreement did not however prevent the withdrawal of Soviet troops from Austria. It was not only strategical considerations that were decisive for Austria's status of neutrality, which was proclaimed the day after the signing of the Warsaw Pact, May 15, 1955. The Soviet Union was obviously well aware of the dramatically escalating situation in its sphere of influence and wanted to prevent a new source of conflict in Austria at any price. The Soviet Union was more interested in legitimating its power in Eastern Europe than in provoking new confrontations. In Poland and Hungary, the political clouds which would soon burst into a violent storm were already noticeable. The ratification of the Paris Agreement on May 5, 1955, and the signing of the Warsaw Pact ten days later did nothing to hinder the contemplated measures to normalize relations with the West and the four-power conference scheduled for July 1955 in Geneva. Detente with the West was needed to defuse the increasingly acute situation in the Eastern bloc.

As with the economic community founded during Stalin's time, the Warsaw Pact seemed also to have exhausted its range of maneuver in a demonstration directed against the West. But things were to be different. Both community institutions would later play a not insignificant role in the reshaping of relations between the Soviet Union and the countries of Eastern Europe. Not only events in Eastern Europe, but the power constellations within the Soviet Union itself had contributed to this. The 20th Party Congress of the CPSU in February 1956 and especially Khrushchev's "Secret Report," had created a new situation in the Eastern bloc. The Stalinist regime had received its irrefutable assessment as a reign of terror from its highest authority. The governing elite in Eastern Europe were themselves deeply shaken. A political crisis that had gotten out of control shook Poland and Hungary. It showed how weak the political structures, built up with great effort under a hegemonic power, were. In Hungary, the political and military power structures totally collapsed. The violent protest against Stalinist methods of government in two countries at the same time threatened to destroy the constellations of political power in Eastern Europe. Events developed precipitously: on June 28, 1956, the Poznan workers mutinied in Poland, and three weeks later, on July 18, 1956, Hungary's leader Matias Rakosi resigned under popular pressure. In October, Poland's First Party Secretary Edward Ochab resigned, a half year after he had taken over the Party leadership after the sudden death in February 1956 of his predecessor Boleslaw Bierut. Wladyslaw Gomulka, martyr of the Stalinist regime, was appointed First Secretary of the Polish United Workers' Party. On October 17, the Polish Party leadership declined Khrushchev's invitation to Moscow. The security forces under Waclaw Komar (faithful to the regime and to the new Party head, a prisoner of the Stalinist regime) mined suburbs of Warsaw to prevent the entry of Rokossovskii's troops. However, the Russians did not risk invading. In his memoirs, Khrushchev has the following to say about the reasons: "Rakowski, who had remained more faithful than the political leadership, was ready, if necessary, to arrest the swell of counterrevolutionary forces with weapons, and that was all well and good. But when we began to consider whether the Polish regime would be ready to obey Rokossovskii the situation began to seem somewhat grimmer."[326] On October 19, 1956, Khrushchev, Mikoyan, Kaganovich, and Molotov (the last two were dismissed from the Party leadership nine months later) travelled to Warsaw where they were able to find a peaceful solution. In time, Poland's Party leader Gomulka became Khrushchev's, and later Brezhnev's, most faithful ally, and one of the most zealous advocates of economic integration.

The situation was different in Hungary. After the Nagy government declared, under the pressure of the rebels, that it no longer respected the Warsaw Pact, the Soviet leadership felt itself compelled to crush the revolt with force. Order and calm were restored to Poland and Hungary. The Soviet government, however, recognized that hegemonic power in Eastern Europe had to be replaced by an institution resembling an alliance. The transition from total hegemony to an alliance was, however, not easy. Like the CMEA, founded in 1949, the Warsaw Pact also had still had no meaningful activities and no corresponding organizational structure several years after its establishment. A. Ross Johnson, an expert on these matters, observed "Until 1961, the Warsaw Pact was devoid of any political and military substance."[327]

The surveillance network of Soviet advisers established to safeguard the fidelity of the regimes in the Soviet sphere of influence had collapsed. The Soviet Union was unable any longer to withstand the pressures of the smaller countries toward emancipation. Rokossovskii was voted out of his position as Politburo member at the historic 8th Conference of the Central Committee of the Polish United Workers' Party and had to return to the Soviet Union. He was followed by other officers of the Soviet army. However, chief of staff Bordzilowski and his deputy General Czaplewski, also former Soviet officers, kept their posts until 1965 and 1968, respectively. But alongside of them was the personality of the Polish patriot Zygmunt Duszynski and many nationally conscious officers who replaced the Soviet generals and military advisers. Not only army and secret police advisers, but also advisers in the finance and economic ministries, in the central planning authorities, etc., returned to the Soviet homeland from all the Eastern countries.

The armies of the peoples' democracies were renationalized. The Soviet troops who had brought real socialism to Eastern Europe were, however, to remain where they were stationed as guardians of order. Their status was to be regulated by bilateral agreements. On December 18, 1956, the Soviet Union concluded a bilateral agreement about the stationing of troops with Poland. On April 15, 1957, an agreement was signed with Romania, another agreement with Hungary on May 27, 1957, also with related specific stationing locations, as well as non-interference in internal affairs. However, an important amendment was made in 1958 when the Soviet Union withdrew its troops from Romania.

The return to calm after the serious test of power in 1956 had created the possibility to rethink the activities and organizational structure of the two community institutions. The statutes of the CMEA, the International Bank for Economic Cooperation, and many other CMEA bodies were established in the early '60s. The Berlin conflict in 1961 and the steadily exacerbating situation with China accelerated the development of an overall conception for activating the Warsaw Pact and giving it an organizational structure. Khrushchev intended to draw the Eastern European armies more extensively into his strategy of confrontation with the West. He understood that they had to be given greater autonomy in shaping their armaments policy and especially their personnel policy, as well as a greater say in the bodies of the Warsaw Pact.

Stalin's concept of a great unified army was replaced by Khrushchev's concept of a coalition defense strategy. In March 1961, a new strategic concept and a new organizational structure for the Warsaw Pact were approved: regular conferences of the minstries of defense, joint multinational manoeuvers, and a schooling program were to form the backbone of the interplay between the unified armies. The first joint manoeuver under the code name "fraternity of arms" was carried out in connection with the Berlin crisis in Autumn 1961. The development of new strategic weapons would have an influence on the armaments strategy of the Warsaw Pact. Some of the ground troops would be replaced by middle-range missiles and modern aircraft. Adjustments were made in the armaments industry of some of the countries. The production of military aircraft was discontinued in the GDR in 1961 and in Poland in 1969.[328]

An interesting parallel with CMEA events developed. A selective arms integration, rather than a comprehensive one, was contemplated. Only the airforces were to be completely integrated. However, they were to be subordinated to the Soviet armed forces directly rather than to the Warsaw Pact. Thus, just as the CMEA did not succeed in creating a supranational executive body, the Warsaw Pact was unable to establish an operative unified central command either. The CMEA differs from the EEC executive body, and the central command of the Warsaw Pact differs from NATO, in the same respect: namely, limited executive powers.

August 21, 1968, altered the concept of how the CMEA and the Warsaw Pact functioned

The two community bodies—the CMEA and the Warsaw Pact—were conceived as pillars of cooperation of the countries of Eastern Europe with the Soviet superpower. There was also an organic link between the two. The military alliance and the military-industrial complex formed an inseparable whole. The basic strategy of the two community institutions is coordinated at the highest political level. The specialization and cooperation programs initiated in the CMEA develop in direct connection with the defense strategy of the Warsaw Pact. However, modern weapons have increased the costs of arms and placed a severe burden on the economies of the CMEA countries. The small countries have had to bear greater armaments costs than their defense needs required, and are forced to share the burden of the superpower. Their resistance to the heavy costs of arms, and to the risk of being drawn into a new conflict, this time with remote China, shook the entire laboriously built-up economic and defense concept. In its emancipation declaration of April 1964, Romania expressed what the others did not dare to express. Romania opposed a unified organizational concept in both community bodies insofar as it might limit national sovereignty: in the CMEA this was the concept of a supranational body and a unified economic plan. In the Warsaw Pact, Romania resisted the demand that the other countries should share the burden of the superpower, as well as the concept of a unified central control that would command the national armies.

The view stated in the preceding chapter, that Romania's opposition had no crucial influence with regard to limiting the framework of CMEA integration, is confirmed by A. Ross Johnson as regards the activity of the Warsaw Pact. He states: ". . . Romania's dissent alone could not be the only cause of the lack of progress, evident since 1965, in the creation of a permanent political mechanism of coordination or the lack of progress in expanding the military institutions of the Warsaw Pact. The other Eastern countries have also put up similar resistance. However, Romania dared quite early on, in late 1964, to reduce the time of service of soldiers from 24 to 16 months and to reduce the army by 40,000 men."[329]

The new leadership under Leonid Brezhnev sought in vain to overcome the accumulating contradictions. For the first time in many years after being expelled from the CMEA and the military alliance in 1961, Albania was invited to the session of the Political Advisory Council of the Warsaw Pact scheduled for January 19, 1965. However, Albania demanded an apology from the Soviet Union for its earlier attitude and a condemnation of Soviet practice with regard to the Warsaw Pact. Neither of these things were granted and Albania remained outside the community institutions.

Cooperation and the strength of the community were demonstrated. In January 1965 the summit bodies of the Warsaw Pact and the CMEA met at the same time in Warsaw and Prague. The Soviet government organ *Izvestiia* stressed that the Warsaw and Prague conferences served the same purpose, namely, "the success-ful construction of a new society in the socialist countries."[330] Brezhnev praised the solidarity and strength of the Warsaw Pact at the 23rd Party Congress in March 1966: "If it were to become necessary, the joint strength of the members of the Warsaw Pact would set a mighty force into motion to defend the socialist system and the free life of nations. . . ."[331]

However, the symptoms of dissatisfaction multiplied in the Eastern bloc. In mid-June 1966, Chou En-lai was received with a 21-gun salute in Bucharest, and Romania's Prime Minister Ion Maurer spoke of an unshaken friendship with China. In February 1967, Romania all alone established normal relations with the Federal Republic of Germany. In April of the same year, the country refused to participate in the international conference of the Communist Parties in Karlovy Vary, since it was known in Bucharest that its purpose would be to condemn the People's Republic of China.

Romania's resistance to the hegemonic claim in both community bodies was openly stated. But other Eastern countries were also dissatisfied with this policy. However, their resistance was not so well-known: in April 1965 a few high-ranking officers and Party functionaries in Bulgaria mutinied with clearly anti-Soviet slogans, as the American military expert Jeffrey Simon reported.[332] The situation in Czechoslovakia was growing increasingly acute. In mid-April 1968, the dean and some of the staff of the Gottwald Academy signed a memorandum on the army policy, which had been distorted for twenty years, and had been conceived "devoid of any rational criteria," as they put it.[333] Developments were moving more and more clearly in one direction: namely, that the "collective forces of the Warsaw Pact," as Brezhnev put it at the 23rd Party Congress, would not be necessary against the imperialist enemy, but to reestablish peace and order in the Soviet Union's own sphere of influence. The central point of support on the north flank (Poland, Czechoslovakia, and the GDR) seemed to be threatened by the progressive democratization of the Czech regime. The Warsaw Pact troops (without Romania's participation) under the command of Ivan Pavlovskii, commander of the Soviet ground troops, marched into Czechoslovakia on August 21, 1968 (not, it should be noted, under the command or under the leadership of the Warsaw Pact) to crush the fighters for "socialism with a human face" and restore real socialism in its classical form. Five Soviet divisions remained and are there to this day, despite the promise that they would be withdrawn after the situation had returned to normal. Nor have they been withdrawn after two decades of normalization and the advent of Gorbachev.

The thwarters of the Prague Spring knew quite well that Czechoslovakia or the East bloc was not threatened by any danger from without. Brezhnev said to the Czech Party leadership after they had been brought to Moscow: "Your country is on territory occupied by the Soviet soldiers in World War II. We paid a high price for this; your borders are our borders. The entry of our troops into your country is justified so that we can feel secure within your borders. . . . It is a secondary question whether a threat from any quarter exists. . . ."[334] This makes clear without any equivocation that the entry of Soviet troops into Czechoslovakia was meant to secure the cohesiveness of the territory conquered in World War II, as well as the inviolability of the political regime in its classical real socialist form, as it was a guarantor of this cohesiveness. S. Kudriavtsev, a journalist on the government newspaper *Izvestiia*, made it even clearer. Four days after the invasion of the Soviet troops he addressed Yugoslavia and Romania as follows: "Don't you know that the Warsaw Pact was established not only with the purpose of defending the borders of its signatories, but also to create an instrument which defended Communism from the machinations of aggressive imperialist forces."[335]

After the dramatic events in 1956 in Poland and Hungary, and after August 21, 1968, measures were taken to secure the cohesion of the Eastern bloc by strengthening economic and military integration. In the CMEA, preparations were begun for the summit meeting which took place in April 1969 to discuss the fundamentals of the Comprehensive Program for the further deepening and perfection of socialist economic integration approved in July 1971. On March 17, 1969, the Political Advisory Council of the Warsaw Pact met in Budapest. To underscore that nothing out of the ordinary had taken place between August 1968 and March 1969, this conference was chaired by Alexander Dubcek, the instigator of the Prague Spring. In an interview for the Party organ *Rude Pravo*, he ventured the opinion that the discussions were concerned with more efficiency rather than higher armaments costs.[336] Ceausescu, on the other hand, stressed, as he did many times before, that the national army could be employed only in accordance with the constitution.[337]

The Budapest conference coincided—undoubtedly not by accident—with the armed conflict on the Ussuri river. A conflict on two fronts, in the West and in the

Far East, seemed likely. Within three years, the number of Soviet divisions stationed on the Chinese border had been increased from 15 to 45.[338] The Soviet leadership was considering replacing the Soviet troops withdrawn from the Western border with units from the smaller countries. Once again, as so many times before, the autonomy and equality of the CMEA members and those of the Warsaw Pact was stressed. No supranational bodies were contemplated in either of the two community organizations. The reorganization of the Warsaw Pact was carried out under this slogan. The formation of authentic mixed staff organizations, with greater participation of the military elite of Eastern Europe than formerly, was contemplated. The joint training program would be expanded. The military elite of the national armies of the smaller countries were to receive their education to a greater degree than previously in the renowned military academies of the Soviet Union. The relationships between the Soviet army and the armies of the smaller countries were to be institutionalized in an organic way, whereby the deputies of the ministers of defense of the countries of Eastern Europe would be appointed deputies of the Soviet chief of staff of the Warsaw Pact. The newly reorganized united staff of the troops of the Warsaw Pact was granted greater decision-making powers than before. The generals of the smaller countries— most of whom had been trained in Soviet military academies—were to have more say than previously in decisions on weapon deliveries, training, and war planning. A joint committee for science and technology was to coordinate the training of military cadres and logistics.

But the decision to place only the entire GDR army under the unified command of the Warsaw Pact was of greatest significance. In contrast, only selected units from the armed forces of Bulgaria, Poland, and Hungary were placed under the joint command.[339] Three tank divisions, three motorized divisions, one airforce division, and one marine brigade of the fifteen Polish divisions; four of the ten Czech divisions, and only a small portion of the Bulgarian and Hungarian armed forces and all six GDR divisions were incorporated into the military units of the Warsaw Pact.[340]

The new organizational structure of the Warsaw Pact introduced by the March 1969 conference in Budapest gave the military elite of the smaller countries broader powers. However, it also required adapting the armed forces of Eastern Europe to the most modern world standards. Brezhnev had begun an unprecedented arms race in the '70s, and carried the smaller countries along with him in it. The costs far exceeded the security needs of the smaller countries, which did not feel threatened, and overstrained their economic capacities. The relative expenditure for armaments in the Soviet Union is the highest in the world. Although its per capita income is half that in the United States, it aspires to a parity, if not superiority, in its competition with the greatest economic power of the world.

It is generally claimed that the Soviet Union has realized this aim. But at what price? According to authoritative estimates, Soviet military spending increased

Table 18

Defense spending in relation to gross national product

	1965	1970	1975	1980	1982
Bulgaria					
GNP in million US dollars 1981	19,787	25,363	31,863	33,392	35,336
Defense spending in percent of GNP	11.1	9.4	9.9	9.2	10.1
Czechoslovakia					
GNP in million US dollars 1981	89,993	106,584	125,689	139,640	138,761
Defense spending in percent of GNP	6.3	5.1	5.2	4.8	5.2
GDR					
GNP in million US dollars 1981	103,578	120,913	143,262	160,883	165,611
Defense spending in percent of GNP	4.4	5.6	5.6	5.4	5.8
Poland					
GNP in million US dollars 1981	112,396	136,748	187,326	194,070	176,274
Defense spending in percent of GNP	6.0	5.9	5.3	5.3	7.0
Romania					
GNP in million US dollars 1981	44,800	57,026	78,874	95,753	98,908
Defense spending in percent of GNP	8.0	6.7	5.6	4.3	4.6
Hungary					
GNP in million US dollars 1981	42,316	49,138	57,809	63,879	65,209
Defense spending in percent of GNP	5.6	5.6	4.5	4.5	4.5
Eastern Europe total					
GNP in million US dollars 1981	412,871	495,772	624,823	687,618	680,098
Defense spending in percent of GNP	6.1	5.9	5.6	5.2	5.9

Source: Thad P. Alton, Gregor Lazarcik, Elizabeth M. Bass, Krzysztof Badach: ''East European Defense Expenditures 1965–82,'' in *Selected Papers*, U.S. Congress, pp. 476–479.

Table 19

Defense costs 1980 to 1982, in millions of dollars (current prices), and share of personnel and material costs (%)

	Defense costs	Share of personnel and material costs	
Bulgaria			
1980	2,822	73.8	26.2
1981	3,146	73.3	26.7
1982	3,766	75.9	24.1
Czechoslovakia			
1980	6,131	44.5	55.5
1981	6,854	43.2	56.8
1982	7,637	45.6	54.4
GDR			
1980	7,999	37.1	62.9
1981	9,107	35.6	64.4
1982	10,249	37.1	62.9
Poland			
1980	9,472	57.1	42.9
1981	10,287	57.8	42.2
1982	13,012	53.9	46.1
Romania			
1980	3,776	73.2	26.8
1981	4,057	73.7	26.3
1982	4,798	80.7	19.3
Hungary			
1980	2,612	58.6	41.4
1981	2,883	58.7	41.3
1982	3,096	59.1	40.9
Eastern Europe (total)			
1980	32,813	53.3	46.7
1981	36,334	52.7	47.3
1982	42,559	53.7	46.3

Source: Thad P. Alton, Gregor Lazarcik, Elizabeth M. Bass, Krzysztof Badach: "East European Defense Expenditures 1965–82," in *Selected Papers*, U.S. Congress, pp. 491, 492.

in the '70s from 12% to 14% of the national income at the beginning of the decade
to 15% to 17% at the end of the decade.[341] According to estimates of the
American Department of State, the Soviet share in worldwide military spending
in 1983 was no less than 258 billion dollars in a total of 810 billion US dollars,
followed by the United States with 217 billion dollars, and then China far down
the scale with 34.5 billion dollars, Great Britain with 27.4 billion dollars, Saudi
Arabia with 27.2 billion dollars, France and the Federal Republic of Germany
each with 23.8 billion dollars and 23.6 billion dollars. Poland is also among the
ranks of the big spenders, with a by no means negligible expenditure of 12.3
billion dollars.[342] Other Eastern countries have also spent more than other countries on a comparable level. The well-disciplined armed forces of Eastern Europe
are half the size of the American armed forces, and their spending for military
purposes is one-fifth that of the largest economic power of the world.[343] The
relatively high growth rate of defense costs in Eastern Europe is striking: it has
increased at an annual average rate of about 6% since 1970.

Table 18 shows the development of defense spending for the six countries of
Eastern Europe, as well as the relationship to national income between 1965 and
1982. The defense costs are estimates, and the gross national product, given in
US dollars, is for a variety of reasons unable to reflect the exact value of the gross
national product in Eastern Europe. Nonetheless these statistics give the best
possible approximation of developments in relations in the individual Eastern
European countries. The relative costs in 1982 were highest in Bulgaria (10.1%)
followed by Poland (7%); the relative spending of Czechoslovakia (5.2%) and the
GDR (5.8%) were near to the Eastern European average, while spending in
Hungary (4.5%) and Romania (4.6%) was lowest. Compared with the reference
year 1965, relative armaments spending, measured in relation to the gross national product, has declined. The two exceptions are Poland and the GDR, where
it increased from 6.0% to 7.0% and from 4.4% to 5.8%, respectively. Romania
showed the greatest decline compared with 1965, from 8.0% to 4.6%. However,
compared with 1980, relative armaments expenditures increased in 1981 in all
Eastern European countries. The only exception was Hungary where it remained
at the same level of 4.5%. The relative and absolute increase in armaments costs
in Poland, caused more by internal than external developments, is noteworthy.

US experts have calculated defense costs in current prices, and broken them
down into personnel and material costs (see Table 19). The three countries on the
north flank of the Warsaw Pact, Poland, GDR and Czechoslovakia, bear 73% of
defense costs of Eastern Europe. However, these countries are also economically
the strongest and most populated countries in Eastern Europe. The share of the
south flank is less, although as stated above, Bulgaria's relative share is the
highest. The shares of Romania and Hungary are relatively lower than those of
the other Eastern European countries. The differing shares of personnel and
material costs are striking. The share of personnel costs is highest in the economically underdeveloped countries such as Bulgaria and Romania. They are the

lowest in the GDR and in Czechoslovakia, and about the same in Poland and Hungary. These differences are mainly due to differences in the level of armaments.

These estimates of defense costs show how burdensome they are, especially for the small countries of Eastern Europe. They also have no national motive of their own to demonstrate their military strength. Poland's defense costs, for example, are almost a half of the amount spent by Europe's strongest countries, e.g., West Germany or France. Multiplied activities, especially on the part of the GDR and Hungary, to reduce tensions between the superpowers may be attributed to the fact that their share in bearing the burden of the superpower has come into contradiction with their goals with regard to improving the quality of life. The small countries of Eastern Europe support every disarmament initiative, especially when they originate in the Soviet Union, since they know that their own efforts can only be realized within the existing geopolitical framework.

Long-term strategy of the CMEA and the
Warsaw Pact

Both community bodies have presented their long-term programs: the CMEA, the Comprehensive Program for promoting scientific and technical progress up to the year 2000 approved on December 18, 1985, by the 41st Council session; and the Warsaw Pact its agreement, signed April 26, 1986, to prolong the pact another twenty years.

There is a link between the economic and military objectives of the Eastern community. Armaments can be maintained at a world standard only if the efficiency also corresponds to the world level; but the gap is great. The new dynamic Soviet leadership has set itself the goal of closing the considerable technology gap by the year 2000. It would like to involve the other CMEA countries in the struggle for scientific and technical progress. The small countries are being given the chance of striving jointly for the world standard which would be unattainable if each country had to go it alone. This is a one-time-only chance which can only be taken advantage of if their economies are more closely integrated with the economy of the Soviet Union. A perfect organizational structure will help economic integration achieve success. In the five economic areas which are to serve as a vehicle for technical progress in the joint economies of the Eastern bloc, the leading large enterprises will assume leadership of each development program. However, Soviet large enterprises have the largest research staffs. They will therefore have the key position in the economic integration of the Eastern bloc. They had recently been granted the right to enter into direct contacts with corresponding production and research units in other CMEA countries.

The agreement to prolong the Warsaw Pact another twenty years offers no new work program. It extends the duration of the pact, concluded thirty years previously, and extends working methods, accepted in March 1961 and amended in

March 1969. The core concepts of the pact are collaboration of the armies of the member countries on a coalition basis instead of the previous unified army; subordination of selected units of the small countries to the unified command of the Warsaw Pact instead of to the aggregate army; a greater say in decision making for the small countries; common training programs, manoeuvers, etc.

The renationalization of the officers' corps of the Eastern European armies initiated after Stalin's death, with increased internationalization through a joint training program, manoeuvers, and other common activities, has thoroughly proven itself. The renationalized military elite seems to be more interested in maintaining real socialism than the hierarchy in the Party and the economy. This was made most clear on March 13, 1981, when General Jaruzelski, with his comrades in arms—almost all without exception graduates of Soviet military academies—introduced martial law in the name of national integrity and saving Poland from foreign invasion, and restored peace and order. The army elite, which is a component of the establishment in the power structure, is more strongly and firmly anchored in the existing social order and the existing geopolitical framework than any other social elite in Eastern Europe. The unified military and economic development concept has, however, reached the limits of its effectiveness. The growing demand of the military for modern and more costly weapons is obstructed by inadequate economic efficiency; the Soviet Union is unable to bear an armaments burden which is twice as high relative to its own economic potential than that of the number one economic power in the world, and the small countries of Eastern Europe are even less able to maintain as relatively a high armaments burden as the highly developed industrial states of Western Europe.

Voices of discontent over the burdensome armaments costs trickle through only rarely. Romania's dissent is generally known. The cutbacks that have been made are evident from the data in the preceding section. Some weeks after the agreement to prolong the Warsaw Pact for another twenty years was signed, Ceausescu announced that the member countries would decrease their armaments costs by 10% to 15% per year[344] in order to motivate the NATO countries to do the same thing. But, for the first time, statements of discontent over the much too high armaments costs were to be heard from high-ranking Hungarian politicians. The defense minister Lajos Czinege, his deputy Lajos Morocz, gave assurances that their country would meet the demands of the Warsaw Pact, but only "in relation to the capacities of the economy and to real possibilities."[345]

The conflict between national and international interests

The contradiction between the leading superpower and its allies is just as evident in the Warsaw Pact as in NATO, with the difference that the small countries of Eastern Europe can justify their large armaments burden in terms more of international than of national defense needs. This contradiction could lose its effect only if there were full identification between national and international interests. But such an identification is increasingly more complicated in a time in which the shortcomings of socialism must be replaced by authentic national and patriotic slogans, both in the leading country and in each of the smaller countries. Consequently national attributes are receiving more and more stress and international attributes are moving into the background. The contradiction between the national and international is growing in strength. The Tsarist generals, whose medals embellish the best of the bravest of the brave Russian officers have not left a good reputation behind them in the recent history of the countries of Eastern Europe. The renationalization of the past and the present arouses bad memories not only in relation to the superpower, but also among the countries within its sphere of influence. The GDR has a good reason to celebrate Frederick the Great as a hero of Prussian history. But he was the Prussian king who participated in the partition of Poland and incorporated a large part of this country into the Prussian Kingdom. At just the time when apologetics for Frederick the Great were reaching a high point in the GDR, Poland's most popular weekly *Polityka* published an article under the remarkable title "Why the Poles do not like Frederick the Great,"[346] with a few comments made by the king about Poles, the most flattering of which was: "One should not go out of one's way with the Poles, for then one spoils them even more; one should only take care that they obey orders and fulfill them promptly." The debate on the past is, however, harmless compared to the hard and momentous debate in the present, as for example the escalating controversy between Hungary and Romania on the situation of minorities.

In this conflict between national and international aspects of the long-term economic and military community programs the small countries support those aspects which are consonant with their national interest. They participated in the far-seeing CMEA Comprehensive Program of 1985 with the intention not of abetting the military industrial complex in the arms race of the superpowers, but to bring their own stagnating economies up to the world level. The small countries are more and more frequently seizing the initiative to reduce the tensions between the superpowers. Erich Honecker and Janos Kadar, antagonists in shaping the steering system, gave harmonious declarations on the role of the small countries in reducing the damage which the conflict between the superpowers has inflicted upon peace policy. Erich Honecker evoked the "coalition of reason" in the two German states in the interest of the "German people." The GDR head of party and state postponed his visit to West Germany, scheduled for September 8, 1984, but leading West German politicians travelled to the GDR and vice-versa, and Honecker himself made the trip in 1987. And not only international agreements are concluded: in a basic draft of October 20, 1986, a member of the Politburo of the SED Hermann Axen, and Egon Bahr, disarmament expert of the SDP, agreed on creating a nuclear-free corridor along the German-German border.

The small countries of Eastern Europe are also seizing the initiative in the Far

East conflict. After many not always successful visits to China by Soviet experts, an official state visit by the Party heads of Poland and the GDR took place in October 1986, setting an unmistakable Eastern European accent in the balance of international relations. Matyas Szuros, Hungary's Politburo member responsible for foreign affairs, stressed the national aspect of the international Eastern alliance even more clearly than the head of government did. He rejected the view that national interests must be subordinated to community interests; "There can be no talk of subordination," and further, "Historical traditions and current characteristics make thriving relationships between a socialist and capitalist country possible even when the general trend is rather toward a deterioration of East-West relations and a reduction in contacts."[347]

The Soviet Union needs peace just as any other country on earth. The Soviet Union and its allies need disarmament more than any other country because their armaments burden is greater relative to their economic capacity than is the case in most of the developed industrial countries of this world. The new Soviet leadership seems to take this circumstance seriously, as well as the will of the countries of Eastern Europe to develop their long-term economic programs for peaceful rather than for military purposes. Gorbachev seeks to give his words "The world is too little and too fragile for war and a politics of the mighty" a content insofar as he has already initiated four summit conferences with President Reagan. But despite some successes—such as the agreement on middle-range weapons—as long as the confrontation between the two world systems exists, a peace which presupposes a balance of deterrence is not a secure peace. A consistent physical disarmament would only be possible if there were a total disarmament in the minds of men as well. The greatest and most humane thinkers of this world have not given their sublime thoughts to the world to justify social systems which contradict them or serve as a basis for superpower interest. The utopian, antiquated, never realized, and unrealizable ideas of the 19th century must not be used as a fuel for the deadly weapons of the waning millennium. The East-West confrontation is the main cause of the arms race, which has gotten out of control. Its abolition is the sole precondition for an unarmed peace. There is no exportable universally adequate social system that is worth being carried further with arms.

It is inconceivable that a country which is struggling with major difficulties in its economic and social life and is dependent on the import of progressive technologies should all at once have an exportable social system. The West too has no social system to export. However, it has maintained an intellectual continuity with the irreplaceable values of the Enlightenment of the great French and American revolutions and it must take over the initiative for spiritual and physical disarmament without the least intention of offering a Western social system to the East. To conclude with the words of George Kennan: "Democratization can and must wait, world peace cannot."[348]

Postscript

**Gorbachev's *perestroika* and the programmatic 43rd
special meeting of the CMEA**

Gorbachev presented his book *Perestroika: The Second Russian Revolution* on
November 1, 1987. On November 2, he gave a three-hour speech on the occasion
of the 70th anniversary of the October Revolution before 5,800 invited guests and
119 delegations from around the world. In his speech he reviewed the history of
the Soviet Union and outlined the goal of his revolutionary restructuring. "Whatever emotions Soviet history may evoke," said Gorbachev, "it is our history and
it cost us dearly." He rated the achievements of the past seventy years as "enor-
mous" but said that the current economic situation was "on the brink of crisis."
He stated in his book: "Something strange occurred: the gigantic wheel of a huge
machine continued to turn, but the transmission belt to jobs began to slip. . . . In
the past fifteen years the growth rate of national income has decreased by more
than half, and since the early '80s, it has remained at almost stagnant level. . . .
Our country is drifting into crisis. . . ."

This failure to adapt to the requirements of the times is reflected not so much in
a slowing of economic growth, as in the underdevelopment of the economic and
social structure. The country of the first socialist revolution was lagging behind
the world's industrial countries in the real revolution of modern times, the
transition from an industrial to an information society capable of realizing just
those ideals which the October Revolution inscribed on its banners: to transform
agricultural labor into industrial work and the manual labor of those working in
industry into intellectual labor.

At a meeting with political and economic functionaries of Leningrad, Gorbachev described *perestroika* as follows: "Up until now, economic activity has been
administered; there were no economic mechanisms, so we were forced to make
use of administrative command methods and Party orders. Now, however, we
have worked out economic mechanisms and put them into practice." The plenary
meeting of the Central Committee of the CPSU approved Gorbachev's plans for
reform on June 25, and the Supreme Soviet on June 30, 1987.

Radical reform in a traditional system

Gorbachev called his notion of restructuring a direct continuation of Lenin's October Revolution. He criticized Lenin's successors, some of them even very violently: "Stalin's misuse of power and his genuine crimes," said Gorbachev in his anniversary speech, are "unforgivable." However, he stressed the achievements which "from the present vantage point are of historical importance," namely, "accelerated industrialization" and Stalin's achievements in World War II. He esteemed Khrushchev's "de-Stalinization" but criticized his "voluntarism and subjectivism" and concluded that Khrushchev's "lack of democracy" was the reason for the failure of his reform attempts. He had much criticism and little praise for the Brezhnev era.

But although Gorbachev refers to *perestroika* as revolutionary, the preamble of the Reform Law of June 30, 1987, indicates that the basic pillars of the social and political system will remain unchanged. It is stated with utmost clarity that "state (national) ownership of the means of production of industry, construction, and the agro-industrial complex will be strengthened" and that the "principle of central decision-making in questions of economic development will be deepened." However, the reform puts an end to the previous practice of state intervention in every area of production and sales of the enterprise, in the relations between management and enterprise personnel, between the enterprise and the state budget, as well as in relations between enterprises.

Profit shall no longer be seen only as an indicator of the success of an enterprise, a fraction of which was used for developmental purposes and for promoting employees, but rather as a fundamental source of financing for the growth of the firm and the aggregate income of its staff. The wage and average wage of individuals will be set, not determined by centrally established plan targets. As Prime Minister Ryzhkov stated in his report to the Supreme Soviet, there will be "no limitations on remuneration of personnel; equalization, in which the misfits were paid too much and successful workers paid too little, shall come to an end."

The right of an enterprise manager to one-man leadership, anchored in the traditional central administrative system, will be retained, but enterprise personnel will be given broad say. The newly stipulated type of management leaves no doubt who determines enterprise functioning and who has a say without having a determining voice. The law states the following: "Socioeconomic decisions on enterprise activity shall be worked out and implemented by the enterprise manager with the participation of the work collective, the Party, and the trade union and other social organizations active in the enterprise, in accordance with statutes and legislation."

The election of the enterprise director is new. According to the law, elections will take place through a competitive procedure to "raise the quality of leading cadres and to enhance their responsibility for the results of production." The enterprise director, the managers of the subordinate departments of the enterprise, and the association director are all to be elected, the enterprise director by a general assembly of employees in a secret or open ballot for a five-year term. The election results, however, are not decisive since they must be confirmed by a higher standing body.

The June 1987 law of the Supreme Soviet was especially important for the CMEA. In the past it was the Soviet Union, with its conservative steering model, which had opposed proposals from Poland and Hungary to modernize the obsolete economic infrastructure of the economic community. It was also the Soviet Union which had prevented radical reforms in some of the countries of Eastern Europe, often by force of arms.

However, Gorbachev is both a zealous reformer of the economic system as well as a passionate advocate of economic integration of the Eastern countries. Nine months after he took office as General Secretary of the CPSU, the Comprehensive Program to accelerate scientific and technical progress to the year 2000 was adopted in December 1985. Brezhnev needed seven years for his CMEA Comprehensive Program of 1971. Brezhnev's plan failed because at that time the planned economies, and especially the Soviet Union, were, as the department director of the Soviet Institute for the Socialist World Economy, Professor V. Dashitkev put it, "more like a gigantic military mechanism with battalions, divisions, and armies, enterprises, economic associations, general administrations, and ministries, with a supreme commander at the top."[349]

However, the new Soviet leadership seems to have made the same mistakes as Brezhnev, who adopted a broad integration program before he had established the necessary mechanisms for its implementation. But in contrast to his predecessor, who had never succeeded in creating a viable steering mechanism to the very end of his rule, Gorbachev has promptly attempted to correct his mistakes. A year and a half after the adoption of the Comprehensive Program of December 1985, the Supreme Soviet approved Gorbachev's reform law. In early September, the Central Committee secretaries for CMEA economic issues recommended the development of a consistent concept of international division of labor as well as a concept for the required economic mechanisms. On October 15, 1987, the 43rd special session of the CMEA followed suit.

The final communiqué of the 43rd Special Session showed clearly that two years after the adoption of the Comprehensive Program the CMEA still did not have a mature notion of cooperation, nor did it have any clear ideas of feasible mechanisms for its implementation. We read: "To determine the agreed-upon directions of cooperation it is recommended that a collective concept of socialist international division of labor be prepared for the period 1991–2005." The following statement in the communiqué is more sober: "It is deemed necessary to carry out the restructuring of the mechanism of cooperation and of socialist economic integration as well as the perfecting of CMEA activity in stages; the national economic mechanisms of the member countries as well as the measures they have taken to improve them shall be taken into consideration."[350] Evidently the member countries had arrived at the conclusion that the Comprehensive Program, just as the preceding ones of 1971 or 1985, was not sufficient in itself to bring about effective economic integration without the corresponding preconditions—i.e., adequate mechanisms—being created nationally and internationally in the CMEA.

The final communiqué also states that the activity of CMEA bodies shall undergo an essential reform. For instance: "To improve the effectiveness of CMEA activity, it has been considered necessary to improve the CMEA structure and to eliminate parallelism in its work." Economic, scientific, and technical policies in mutual cooperation shall be agreed upon between governments. The countries interested will also work together in other areas of economic and social development and adopt far-ranging programs of cooperation. Measures for developing international specialization, for the technical modernization of economic branches and areas of production, and for complete utilization of production capacities will be worked out at the economic sectoral level.[351]

This point of the communiqué indicates that the 43rd Special Session came to the conclusion that a far-reaching cooperation will be possible only for countries interested in it. This opinion was confirmed in a speech by the Soviet Prime Minister N. Ryzhkov: "Those member countries who at the present time are not ready to participate in any measures should not hinder the others in their efforts at cooperation."[352] The countries that were meant were those not prepared to accept the ambitious integration projects and the economic mechanisms of the market. The Soviet Prime Minister showed himself to be a zealous advocate of integration and of the economic infrastructure necessary for this. In his speech to the delegates of the special session he said: "We have so far not succeeded in overcoming the tendency toward stagnation. . . . The monetary value of Soviet foreign trade with the other CMEA countries has stagnated since 1985 despite the increase in physical volume. . . . The Soviet Union will give priority to intra-CMEA trade, but it will not tolerate that foreign trade with the CMEA countries should increase solely through an expansion of trade in fuels and raw materials against finished goods." The Prime Minister's speech shows how fundamentally the Soviet ideas of the economic CMEA infrastructure have changed. Ryzhkov proposed that the national currencies of the member countries be brought into play in their foreign economic relations, and he supports the agreement, reached by the majority of the member countries, to introduce a mutual convertibility of national currencies and of the transferable ruble. In his opinion this undertaking could help to expand direct production relations and innovative forms of cooperation. However, intra-CMEA trade has still to be cleared in transferable rubles. According to reports on the 43rd Special Session, the GDR, Mongolia, and Romania did not approve the convertibility projects extending far into the future. The following words of the Polish Prime Minister Zbigniew Messner were addressed to them and several other member countries: "Integration will entail certain costs, but the advantages will far outweigh them. The problem, however, is that the costs must be borne first."[353]

The process of reform is under way, but the economic situation is no better in the countries engaged chronically in reform than in those that hold back. No planned economy has yet succeeded in restructuring the dichotomy of the sacrosanct democratic centralism into an effective synthesis. The economic reforms will be more likely to lead to a differentiation among national steering systems than to their convergence. Therefore it cannot be expected in the foreseeable future that the Eastern economies, with more market, but still a good deal of planning, will be able to develop a functioning economic infrastructure for a modern economic community, or that the CMEA will have powers as adequate and as strong as those of the EEC.

The 19th Party Conference of the CPSU

The situation of the CMEA was radically changed by the resolutions of the Supreme Soviet of June 30, 1988, and of the July 2, 1988, Party conference. The Soviet Union, long the obstructer of reform of the inefficient framework of the community, took on the role of pioneer. The Party conference, for example, described the economic structure as "on the whole, cost-intensive. Scientific and technological progress is as yet slow, and the plans for increasing the national income and resource economies have not been fulfilled." There is no noticeable improvement in product quality. To overcome the bureaucratic methods of management "typical of the command style of administration," the conference resolutely supported the course of "transforming the functions and the style of work of the ministries and other central agencies, . . . transferring their rights to the local level" and completing the "construction of a new economic mechanism."[354]

While the framework of the economic reforms approved by the Party conference was mainly an elaboration of the Supreme Soviet resolutions of June 1987, the conference statements on the political system are new and of great importance. The conference gave top priority to "a fundamental reform of the political system," in order to "open up new possibilities for *perestroika* in every area of public life, and to guarantee its irreversibility."[355] The functions performed by the Party and state bureaucracies were to be cut back and the sovereignty of soviets from the lowest to the highest increased. A Congress of People's Deputies is to be convened to elect a president who will have broad executive powers, presumably similar to those now held by the Party general secretary. This will concentrate the joint power of the Party and the state in one person's hands—by all indications, those of Mikhail Gorbachev. Party functionaries are to be elected from among multiple candidates and their tenure in office is not to exceed two five-year terms. In accordance with the old rule *lex retro non agit*, this limitation will apply only to those elected *after* the Party conference.

Clearly a radical reform of the Soviet economic and political system could have a profound effect on the CMEA and its member countries. Gorbachev is received differently in different countries. While Hungary, Poland, and Bulgaria see validation of their own reform efforts, other countries are less enthusiastic. The leaders of the GDR declared themselves disinclined to copy another system; while once the GDR learned from the Soviet Union, now the Soviet Union might learn something from the economically more successful GDR. Czechoslovakia is prepared to reform its stagnating economy, but not to depart too far from the "normalization" process embarked upon in the wake of the Prague Spring. Romania under Ceausescu is not about to liberalize any aspect of its centralized system. To be sure, the majority of the ruling elite of Eastern Europe have held power for a long time and are not, like Mikhail Gorbachev, in a position to blame political predecessors for their economic misfortunes.

The main point, however, is that those Eastern European countries that made an early and ambitious start on economic reform have already seen much of the future. They have revitalized many market mechanisms, and permitted small private enterprise—and much *glasnost'*. But they have preserved intact the main features of the traditional regime, including the institutionalized monopoly of the Communist Party. These countries have been unable to achieve their goals. They have not significantly improved their economic and social situation, and internationally they remain in the status of developing countries, as indicated by their membership in the International Monetary Fund and the World Bank under Article XV. It is inconceivable that even these reformed mechanisms can support the ambitious integration program the CMEA adopted in December 1983. As the 43rd Special Session of the CMEA in October 1987 made clear, the *conditio sine qua non* for the realization of sophisticated specialization measures must be direct contacts between production units, for which the possibilities remain severely limited. It is likewise difficult to believe that the CMEA will be able to take much advantage of the June 1988 mutual recognition agreement with the European Economic Community.

The conflict between ambitious integration targets and the insufficient mechanism for their realization will dominate the CMEA for the foreseeable future. Moreover, with the official ideology—and the influence of its sponsor—losing force, and the national ambitions and self-confidence of the member countries growing, it will become ever more difficult to find a common denominator between the interests of the small countries and those of the superpower.

It is possible, of course, that in the process of democratization the Soviet leader will realize that equal rights and obligations are also a precondition for the economic success of the whole Eastern European economic community, and will curb political in favor of economic interests. Such a development could have a positive effect on the evolution both of the CMEA and of the economies of the member states.

Notes

1. *Industrialisation and Foreign Trade*, Geneva, 1945, p. 13.
2. *Ibid.*
3. *Monthly Bulletin of Statistics June 1971* and *Handbook of International Trade and Development*, New York, 1971.
4. Y. Kowalski, *The Communist Party of Poland 1935-1938*, Warsaw, 1978, p. 68.
5. *Encyclopedia of the State Science Publishing House*, Warsaw, 1973, p. 374.
6. W. Zolotarev, *Vneshniaia torgovlia sotsialisticheskikh stran*, Moscow, 1964, p. 169.
7. *Vneshniaia torgovlia SSSR za 1918-1940*, Moscow, 1960, p. 14.
8. Y. Giezgala, "Industrializacja krajów RWPG," in *Handel Zagraniczny*, Warsaw, 1969, p. 28.
9. Pawel Bozyk, *Wspólpracy gospodarcza krajów RWPG*, 1977, pp. 30 and 31.
10. *Ibid.*, pp. 30 and 31.
11. *Ibid.*, p. 31.
12. Giezgala, *op. cit.*, p. 28.
13. Bozyk, *op. cit.*, p. 43.
14. *Ibid.*
15. *Ibid.*, pp. 30 and 44.
16. Jerzy Kleer, *Integracja gospodarcza w RWPG*, Warsaw, 1978, p. 48.
17. J. Bielajew and L. Siemionowa, *Integracja socjalistyczna a gospodarka swiatowa*, Warsaw, 1971, p. 130.
18. *Ibid.*
19. *Handel Zagraniczny*, November 1973, Warsaw, p. 375.
20. Vulko Chervenkov, "The Activities of the Bulgarian Workers Party," in *For a Lasting Peace, For a People's Democracy*, 1947, no. 3, p. 2.
21. O. K. Flechtheim, "Kommunismus in Deutschland 1918-1975," in *Die Sowjetunion, Solschenizyn und die westliche Linke*, Rowohlt, 1975, pp. 98 and 99.
22. Quoted from Karel Kaplan, *Znarodneni a socialismus*, Prague, 1968, p. 211.
23. *Podstawowe dokumenty RWPG*, selected by B. W. Reut, Warsaw, 1972, pp. 13 and 14; *Ibid.*
24. L. Ciamaga, "Von Zusammenarbeit zur Integration," in *Probleme des Aussenhandels*, 1974, p. 7.
25. Quoted from R. Gardner, *Sterling-Dollar Diplomacy*, 1956, p. 7.
26. *Ibid.*
27. Quoted from *Kultura*, 1973, no. 10, Paris, p. 41.
28. *Statistisches Jahrbuch 1980 der BRD*, p. 710.
29. J. Wszelaki, *Communist Economic Strategy*, Washington, 1959, p. 68.

30. These figures are taken from Poland's *Legal Gazette*, no. 40, August 24, 1948, Art. 290, p. 718.

31. Wieslaw Iskra, "RWPG—25 lat," in *Integracja gospodarcza krajów socjalistycznych*, Warsaw, 1974, p. 20.

32. E. Grabowski, *System walutowy wspotczesnego kapitalismu*, Warsaw, 1965, pp. 50 and 53.

33. B. Borisov, *Mezhdunarodnye raschety i valiutno-finansovye protivorechiia stran zapadnoi evropy*, Moscow, 1965, p. 105.

34. E. Triffin, *Europe and the Money Muddle*, London, 1957.

35. L. Frei, *Mezhdunarodnye raschety i finansirovanie vneshnei torgovli sotsialisticheskikh stran*, Moscow, 1960, p. 169.

36. I. Slobin, *Mirovoi sotsialisticheskii rynok*, Moscow, 1963, p. 34.

37. A. Smirnov, *Mezhdunarodnye valiutnye i kreditnye otnosheniia SSSR*, Moscow, 1960, pp. 169 and 175.

38. Adam Zwass, *Pieniadz dwoch rynkow*, Warsaw, 1968, p. 319.

39. A. Bodnar, *Gospodarka europeijskich krajów socjalistycznych*, Warsaw, 1962, p. 42.

40. Wszelaki, *op. cit.*, pp. 68–77.

41. *Neues Deutschland*, June 11, 1953 and E. J. Salter, *Der Permanente Konflikt*, Ullstein Publishers, 1965, p. 137.

42. Quoted from *Adenauer Teegespräche*, 1950–1954, Rhöndorfer Ausgabe, Siedler Publishers, p. 476.

43. Konrad Adenauer, *ibid.*, pp. 476 and 519.

44. *Ibid.*, p. 521.

45. *Ibid.*

46. Salter, *op. cit.*, p. 136.

47. *Berliner Zeitung*, Berlin, August 23, 1953.

48. Adenauer, *op. cit.*, pp. 529 and 765.

49. *Economic Survey of Europe 1964 (Structural trends and prospects in the European economy)*, New York, p. 9.

50. K. Laski, in *Problemy ekonomii politycznej socializmu*, 1956, p. 216.

51. Bruno Kiesenwetter, *Der Ostblok*, Berlin, 1960, p. 32.

52. *Ibid.*, p. 36.

53. G. Adler-Karlsson, *Western Economic Warfare 1947–1967*, Stockholm, 1968, pp. 23, 26, 36 and 46.

54. *Washington Post*, January 18, 1954, *Financial Times*, January 21, 1954, *Handelsblatt*, January 22, 1954.

55. Adenauer, *op. cit.*, p. 767.

56. Jozsef Bognar, *The Socio-political and Institutional Aspects of Integration*, Budapest, 1979, p. 28.

57. *Neues Deutschland*, January 31, 1954.

58. *Frankfurter Rundschau*, December 14, 1953.

59. Quoted from Hansjakob Stehle, *Nachbarn im Osten*, Fischer Publishers, 1971, p. 16.

60. His predecessor, and now Hungary's leading dissident Andràs Hegedüs, calls these three points in Nagy's declaration of intention his "three fatal mistakes." (*Weltwoche*, December 3, 1985).

61. Quoted from Stehle, *op. cit.*, p. 22.

62. Quoted from *Gospodarka Planowa*, Warsaw, 1967/8 and 9.

63. Robert D. Hormats, "On Mr. Gorbachev and Peter the Great," *New York Times*, June 6, 1985.

64. *Pravda*, Moscow, June 11, 1985.

65. *Die Presse*, December 18, 1985.

66. Quoted from Stehle, *op. cit.*, p. 201.

67. *Pravda*, May 25, 1956.

68. *Neues Deutschland*, June 17, 1962.

69. Nikita Khrushchev, "Aktuelle Entwicklungsprobleme des Sozialistischen Weltsystems," in *Probleme des Friedens und Sozialismus*, Prague, 9/1962.

70. *Trybuna Ludu*, December 6, 1962.

71. *Socialist World Market Prices*, A. W. Sijthoff, Leyden, 1969, p. 109.

72. Imre Vincze, *The International Payments and Monetary System in the Integration of the Socialist Countries*, Budapest, 1984, p. 124.

73. Bozyk, *op. cit.*, p. 344.

74. *Pravda*, September 5, 1985.

75. Vladimir G. Treml, *Subsidies in Soviet Agriculture*, Joint Economic Committee, December 31, 1982.

76. *Socialist World Market Prices*, p. 181.

77. From statements by the Romanian representative at the Budapest Conference, G. Siclovan, see *ibid.*, p. 41.

78. *Ibid.*, p. 129.

79. *Ibid.*, p. 62.

80. Karl Marx, *Capital*, Vol. II, Warsaw, 1955, p. 376.

81. V. I. Lenin, *Staat und Revolution*, in *Ausgewählte Werke*, Moscow, 1975, p. 366.

82. *Ibid.*, p. 314.

83. *KPSS v rezolutsiiakh i resheniiakh s"ezdov, konferentsii, plenumov TsK*, Moscow, 1953, part 1, p. 427.

84. J. Kulischer, *Osnovnye voprosy mezhdunarodnoi torgovoi politiki*, Moscow, 1922, p. 68.

85. Z. Atlas, *Ocherki po istorii denezhnogo obrashcheniia v SSSR 1917–25*, Moscow, p. 98.

86. *KPSS . . .*, p. 614.

87. *Ibid.*, p. 691.

88. *Sotsialisticheskoe stroitel'stvo SSSR*, 1936, p. 2.

89. In: *East European Integration and East-West Trade*, edited by Paul Marer and John Montias, Indiana University, 1980, p. 140.

90. Iu. Konstantinov, "Valiutnyi mekhanism sotrudnichestva," in *Ekonomicheskaia Gazeta*, Moscow, 11/1985.

91. *Ibid.*

92. Robert Hirnshaw, "Toward European Convertibility," *Essays in International Finance*, Princeton, N.J., 1958, p. 16.

93. "Pieniadz w wymianie zagranicznej," in *Finanse*, Warsaw, 10/1963.

94. A. Zwass, "Problemy finansowe krajów RWPG," in *Finanse*, Warsaw, 10/1965, translated into English, *JPRS* 29, April 6, 1964.

95. Vincze, *op. cit.*, p. 25.

96. George Garvy, *Money, Banking and Credit in Eastern Europe*, Federal Reserve Bank of New York, 1966, p. 43.

97. In *East European Integration and East-West Trade*, p. 143.

98. A number of organizational changes came into effect on January 1, 1987 without altering the content of the foreign trade and currency monopolies.

99. In the English translation of my book *Monetary Cooperation between East and West*, New York, 1975, p. 19.

100. In: *Integracja ekonomiczna krajów socjalistycznych*, pp. 2–3.

101. Raczkowski, *op. cit.*, pp. 2–3.

102. Konstantinov, *op. cit.*

103. In an interview for the Polish economics journal *Zycie Gospodarcze*, July 26, 1970.

104. Z. Fedorowicz, "Miedzynarodowy Bank Inwestycyjny," in *Bank und Kredit*, Warsaw, 1/1971.

105. Vincze, *op. cit.*, p. 26.

106. Konstantinov, *op. cit.*

107. *Ibid.*

108. Vincze, *op. cit.*, p. 12.

109. In *Vneshniaia Torgovlia*, 1/1970, p. 50.

110. *Dokumente-RGW*, Staatsverlag der DDR, East Berlin, 1971, p. 178.

111. K. Nazarkin, "Zehn Jahre Internationale Bank für Wirtschaftliche Zusammenarbeit," in *Aussenhandel*, 10/1973, Moscow.

112. A. Zwass, *Pieniadz dwóch rynków*, Warsaw, 1968, p. 368.

113. Dr. Axel Lebahn, "Neuentwicklungen der Geschäftstätigkeit und Rechtsgrundlage der internationale Comecon-Banken IBED und IIB," in *RIW/AWD Recht der Internationalen Wirtschaft*, 1979/I, pp. 12 and 13.

114. In *Pravda*, January 21, 1969.

115. P. Glikman, *Rachunek ekonomiczny we wspolpracy krajów RWPG w dziedzinie inwestycji*, Warsaw, 1970, p. 49.

116. J. M. van Brabant, "Long-term Development Credits and Socialist Trade," in *Wirtschaftliches Archiv*, vol. VII, p. 107.

117. L. Rusmich, "Währungsbeziehungen im RGW," in *Aussenhandel der Tschechoslowakei*, 10/1970, p. 3.

118. *Ekonomicheskaia Gazeta*, 1984, no. 21 ("Deiatelnost' MIB in Jahre 1983") and Vincze, *op. cit.*, p. 25.

119. Lebahn, *op. cit.*, p. 13.

120. *Ekonomicheskaia Gazeta*, April 1976.

121. Balance Sheet of the International Investment Bank, published in *Ekonomicheskaia Gazeta*, 21/1984.

122. Konstantinov, *op. cit.*

123. A. Zwass, "Aufgaben und Funktionen der Internationalen Bank für Wirtschaftliche Zusammenarbeit in *Vierteljahresheft 2/1971 des Deutschen Institutes für Wirtschaftsforschung*, p. 14.

124. Vincze, *op. cit.*, p. 10.

125. *Ibid.*

126. Konstantinov, *op. cit.*

127. Ludwig von Mises, *Le Gouvernement Omnipotent*, Paris, 1944, p. 90.

128. H. Kosk, "W poszukiwaniu Kompleksowego rachunku oplacalnosci handlu zagranicznego," in *Gospodarka Planowa*, 1972, no. 9, p. 26.

129. *Wiener Zeitung*, February 3, 1986.

130. *Bulletin der Ungarischen Nationalbank*, June 28, 1985.

131. A. Zwass, "Wechselkurspolitik in der Zentralverwaltungswirtschaft," in *Sammelwerk des Internationalen Währungsfonds und der Oesterreichischen Nationalbank "Geldwertstabilität und Wirtschaftswachstum,"* Göttingen, 1984, p. 134.

132. Source: *Rat für Gegenseitige Wirtschaftshilfe*, Cologne, 1985, Table 8, p. 147.

133. Wesolowski, *op. cit.*

134. K. Zabielski, in *Handel Zagraniczny*, 4/93.

135. Vincze, *op. cit.*, p. 42.

136. *Ibid.*

137. *Rat für Gegenseitige Wirtschaftshilfe*, Table 22.

138. *Ibid.*, Table 24.

139. *Ibid.*, Table 25.

140. *Wochenbericht des Deutschen Institutes für Wirtschaftsforschung* 45–46, 1984, p. 553.

141. *Statistical Yearbook of the CMEA.*

142. Anita Tiraspolsky, "Le désequilibre des échanges agro-alimentaires Est-Ouest," in *Le Monde Diplomatique*, June 1982.

143. Poland's *Statistical Yearbook* for these years.

144. Marie Lavigne, "The Soviet Union inside Comecon," in *Soviet Studies*, vol. XXXV, April 2, 1983, p. 137.

145. *Pravda*, June 13, 1985.

146. Lavigne, *op. cit.*

147. Data of the Vienna Institute for Comparative Economic Studies (Information 1/86).

148. John P. Hardt and Richard F. Kaufman, "Policy Highlights," in *Selected Papers*, submitted to the Joint Economic Committee Congress of the United States, October 28, 1985, p. 8.

149. *Soviet Subsidization of Trade with Eastern Europe. A Soviet Perspective*, Institute of International Studies, California University, I, 1983.

150. "Joint investments and mutual advantages in the CMEA," *Soviet Studies*, no. 2, 1985.

151. "Advantages/Disadvantages in USSR Trade with Eastern Europe," Vienna Institute for Comparative Economic Studies, Bericht 97/VIII 1984.

152. "The Soviet Union Inside Comecon," *Soviet Studies*, no. 4, 1983.

153. "The USSR and Socialist Economic Integration: A Comment," *Soviet Studies*, no. 1, 1984.

154. O. Bogomolov, "Soglasovanie ekonomicheskikh interesov i politiki pri sotsializme," in *Kommunist*, 10/85.

155. Bela Balassa, "Types of Economic Integration" (a talk at the 4th World Congress of the IER, Budapest, VIII, 1974).

156. Lavigne, *op. cit.*, p. 137.

157. Jan Przystupa, "Ceny w handlu zagranicznym, 1980 do 1985," *Polityka*, Warsaw, May 3, 1985.

158. Ibid.

159. Csábá, *op. cit.*, p. 232.

160. Horst Menderhausen, "Terms of trade between the Soviet Union and smaller communist countries," in *Review of Economics and Statistics*, vol. XIIV, 1959.

161. Franklyn Holzman, *Soviet Foreign Trade Pricing*, Washington, 1974.

162. Edward A. Hewett, "The Impact of World Economic Crises on Intra-CMEA Trade," in *The Impact of International Economic Disturbances on the Soviet Union and Eastern Europe*, Pergamon Press, 1980.

163. K. Katushev, "Sotrudnichestvo vo imia velikikh idei sotsializma i kommunizma," in *Ekonomicheskoe sotrudnichestvo stran-chlenov SEV*, 1979, no. 1, p. 7.

164. Vincze, *op. cit.*, p. 181.

165. Lebahn, *op. cit.*, p. 13.

166. J. P. Olejnik, *Integratsionnye protsessy v mirovom sotsialisticheskom khoziaistve*, Moscow, 1981, p. 19.

167. Van Brabant, *op. cit.*, p. 130.

168. J. Motorin, "Metodologicheskie problemy dolgosrochnogo planirovania integratsionnykh protsessov," in *Planovoe Khoziaistvo*, 1975/2.

169. Kálmán Pécsi, *The Future of Socialist Economic Integration*, M. E. Sharpe Inc., 1981, p. 121.

170. K. Barcikowski, "Brüderliches Zusammenwirken—Weg zur Überwindung der

Schwierigkeiten," in *Probleme des Friedens und des Sozialismus*, July 1985, p. 872.

171. Csábá, *op. cit.*, p. 231.

172. John C. Campbell, "Soviet Policy in Eastern Europe: An Overview," in *Soviet Policy in Eastern Europe*, edited by Sarah Terry, Yale University Press, 1984, p. 15.

173. M. Marrese and J. Vanous, *Implicit Subsidies and Non-Market Benefits in Soviet Trade with Eastern Europe*, Berkeley, University of California Press, 1983.

174. Sarah Meiklejohn Terry, "Theories of Socialist Development in Soviet-East European Relations," in *Soviet Policy in Eastern Europe*, p. 233.

175. *New York Times*, January 24, 1982.

176. Michel Tatu, *Power in the Kremlin: From Khrushchev to Kosygin*, New Jersey, Viking, 1970, p. 539.

177. F. Pick, *Currency Yearbook 1973*, p. 24.

178. Campbell, *op. cit.*, p. 23.

179. Zygmunt Zagorski, "The Gorbachev Doctrine—A Mailed Fist," in *New York Times*, July 11, 1986.

180. In *New York Times*, 23/1983, quoted in Terry, *op. cit.*, p. 251.

181. Campbell, *op. cit.*, p. 26.

182. Zbigniew Brzezinski, *The Soviet Bloc*, Harvard University Press, 1960, 1967, p. 285.

183. John P. Hardt, "Soviet Energy Policy in Eastern Europe," in *Soviet Policy in Eastern Europe*, p. 205.

184. Paul Marer, *Soviet Economic Relations with Eastern Europe*; *ibid.*, p. 172; *ibid.*, p. 170.

185. Friedrich von Hayek, "Die Ursprünge und Wirkungen unserer Moral," in *der NZZ*, May 15, 1984.

186. In an interview with the Polish weekly *Polityka*, no. 23, 1986, June 7, 1986.

187. Kurt Mauler, "Die Wirtschaftstätigkeit der RGW-Länder zu Jahresende 1983," in *CA-Quarterly*, 1984, II.

188. John M. Kramer, "Soviet CEMA Energy Ties," *Problems of Communism*, July-August 1985, p. 37.

189. *Ibid.*, p. 42.

190. The declaration was published in *Pravda* on June 16, 1984.

191. Erich Hoorn, "Comecon setzt trotz Tschernobyl auf Kernergie," in *Die Presse*, July 2, 1986.

192. *Herald Tribune*, July 21, 1986.

193. *Polityka*, Warsaw, June 7, 1986.

194. Bogomolov, *op. cit.*

195. *Ibid.*, p. 92.

196. Editorial comment of *Financial Times*, "Soviet leader explains plans for economic reform," June 13, 1986.

197. *Pravda*, April 24, 1985.

198. *Pravda*, June 27, 1985.

199. *Pravda*, June 13, 1985.

200. Dr. V. Kushlin, "Obnovlenie proizvodstva," *Ekonomicheskaia Gazeta*, no. 14, 1985.

201. *Ibid.*

202. Michael McFadden, "The Great Soviet Computer Screw-up," *Fortune*, July 8, 1985.

203. *Pravda*, June 13, 1985.

204. O. Vladimirov, in *Pravda*, June 21, 1985.

205. Gorbachev's speech in *Pravda*, June 24, 1985.

206. "Internationalism v deistvii."

207. Vladimirov, *op. cit.*

208. Matyas Szúrós, "The mutual influence of the national and international in socialist development in Hungary," *Társadalmi Szemle*, 1984, no. 1, Budapest.

209. *Pravda*, June 21, 1985.

210. K. Barcikowski, "Brüderliches Zusammenwirken," in *Probleme des Friedens und des Sozialismus*, 1985, no. 7, p. 872.

211. *Ibid.*

212. Iu. Shiryaev, "An important contribution to deepening fraternal cooperation," in *International Affairs*, 1985, no. 2, p. 49.

213. *Ibid.*

214. Quoted in Christian Schmidt Häuer, "Die Medizin des neuen Mannes," *Die Zeit*, August 16, 1985.

215. A more detailed report is to be found in *Ekonomicheskaia Gazeta*, 1985, no. 27.

216. More detailed treatments in *Pravda*, December 18, 1985, and in *Ekonomicheskaia Gazeta*, 1985, no. 52, and the article by the CMEA Secretary V. Sychev, "Gorizonty nauchno-tekhnicheskogo progressa" in *Ekonomicheskaia Gazeta*, 1986, no. 1.

217. *Der Spiegel*, 1986, no. 2, pp. 211 and 212.

218. *Der Spiegel*, 1986, no. 12 with reference to the theoretical periodical *Kommunist*.

219. *Ibid.*

220. Sychev, *op. cit.*

221. Nikolai Ryzhkov, "Basic Guidelines for Development . . ." (speech).

222. V. Kushlin, "Obnovlenie proizvodstva," in *Ekonomicheskaia Gazeta*, 1985, no. 14.

223. *Narodnoe khoziaistvo SSSR 1922–1982*, Moscow, 1982, p. 225; the data given provide no precise information on the scale of the restructuring, for the kolkhozes were enlarged considerably by mergers.

224. Treml, *op. cit.*, p. 171, and Patrick Cockburn in *Financial Times*, May 16, 1985.

225. Quoted in Patrick Cockburn, "Soviet Party Congress," in *Financial Times*, February 25, 1986.

226. *Pravda*, September 8, 1985.

227. Hans Herbert Götz, "Ein neues Abenteuer für die Planwirtschaft," *Frankfurter Allgemeiner Zeitung*, March 11, 1986.

228. Nicholas Wade, "The Soviet science gap," *New York Times*, July 11, 1986.

229. Quoted in Götz, *op. cit.*

230. Seweryn Bialer and Joan Afferica, "Gorbachev's preference for technocrats," in *New York Times*, February 11, 1986; Alec Nove in a comment on the book by Mikhail Heller and Alexander Nekrich, *Utopia in Power*, in the World Washington Times Corporation, 1986, no. 7 ("Continuity versus Change in the Soviet Union"), p. 421.

231. Nove, *op. cit.*, p. 420.

232. Adam Zwass, *Zwei Weltsysteme*, Euroverlag Publishers, 1985, p. 230 (published in English as *Market, Plan, and State*, M. E. Sharpe, Inc., 1987).

233. *Pravda*, June 19, 1986.

234. On the subject see *Le Monde*, December 15, 1962.

235. *Economic Survey der Ersten Österreichischen Sparkasse-Bank*, Spring 1986, p. 48.

236. Deputy Prime Minister Wladyslaw Gwiazda in an interview with the weekly *Polityka*, June 21, 1986.

237. *Pravda*, September 25, 1980.

238. Zygmunt Szeliga, "Nowe wladze," in *Polityka*, Warsaw, July 12, 1986.

239. *Die Presse*, September 10, 1986.

240. *Handelsblatt*, September 2, 1986.

241. Hardt and Kaufman, *op. cit.*
242. *Economic Survey der Ersten Österreichischen Sparkasse-Bank*, Spring 1986.
243. *Ibid.*, p. 45.
244. Jan Winiecki, "Are Soviet-type Economies Entering an Era of Long-term Decline?" in *Soviet Studies*, July 3, 1986, p. 237.
245. *BfAJ/NfA (11)*, June 12, 1986.
246. Stanislaw Gruzewski, in *Polityka*, Warsaw, August 16, 1986.
247. "Polens Schulden wachsen weiter," *Neue Zürcher Zeitung*, July 15, 1986.
248. Jerzy Kleer, "Ostre rygory," *Polityka*, July 12, 1986.
249. M. Rakowski, "Nie sceptyczni lecz krytyczni," in *Polityka*, July 13, 1986.
250. *Trybuna Ludu*, October 8, 1985.
251. *Polityka*, Warsaw, September 6, 1986.
252. Henryk Rózański, "Budowa Kommunismu w ZSSR i rozwój wspólpracy panstw socjalistycznych," in *Nowe Drogi*, December 1961.
253. *Neue Zeit*, April 2, 1956.
254. *Scinţeia*, August 23, 1963.
255. *Scinţeia*, March 1, 1957 reprinted in *Pravda*, February 6, 1957.
256. M. Horowitz, "Simultaneous Transition of the Socialist Countries to Communism," in *Cercetari Filozofice*, 1959, no. 12.
257. Stehle, *op. cit.*, p. 170.
258. *Ibid.*, p. 171.
259. Quoted in Stehle, *op. cit.*, p. 167.
260. *Wochenbericht des Deutschen Institutes für Wirtschaftsforschung*, nos. 45–46 of November 15, 1984.
261. Marer, *op. cit.*, p. 185.
262. *Wochenbericht der DIW*, no. 45–46 of 1984.
263. *BfAI/NfA (m)*, June 12, 1986.
264. *Ibid.*
265. *Österreichischen Sparkasse-Bank*, p. 51.
266. Quoted in *Polityka*, Warsaw, September 6, 1986.
267. *Österreichischen Sparkasse-Bank*.
268. The mean figures for the five-year period 1985–1990 are from the newspaper *Neuer Weg*, June 29, 1986.
269. "Romäniens abgewerteter Sonderkurs," in *Neue Zürcher Zeitung*, January 21, 1986.
270. *Financial Times*, February 6, 1986: "Hungary fails to live up to five year plan expectations."
271. *Österreichischen Sparkasse-Bank*.
272. *Financial Times*, April 1, 1986: "Oil price fall may herald slacker growth in East-West trade."
273. Ferenc Gerencser, in *Magyar Hirlap*, July 13, 1984.
274. Charles Gati, "Soviet Empire 'Alive But Not Well'," in *Problems of Communism*, March-April 1985, p. 75.
275. *Magyar Hirlap*, August 13, 1983.
276. A more detailed treatment of this subject is to be found in "Hungary, this is Capitalism? Well, no" by Richard Evans, in *Euromoney*, May 1986.
277. Rudolf L. Tökes, "Hungarian Reform Imperatives," in *Problems of Communism*, September-October, 1984, p. 7.
278. Judit Pataki und Katalin Farkas, in *Jel-Kép* (Budapest), 3/1982.
279. Viktor Meier, "Der ungarische Weg ist steinig" in *Frankfurter Allgemeine Zeitung*, June 28, 1986.
280. Evans, *op. cit.*, p. 62.

281. Ferenc Havasi, "Equilibrium through productivity and savings," in *Hungarian Quarterly*, 1983, no. 89, p. 12.
282. Malcolm Rutherford, "Pillow talk in Budapest," in *Financial Times*, November 1, 1985.
283. Tökes, *op. cit.*, p. 12.
284. See Romanov's speech at the 13th Party Congress of the Hungarian Socialist Workers Party in *Pravda*, March 27, 1985.
285. The text of the Kádár interview is from the article by Viktor Meier, "Die Bedingungen in der Sowjetunion sind ganz anders als bei uns," in *Frankfurter Allgemeine Zeitung*, August 7, 1986.
286. *Los Angeles Times*, September 27, 1985.
287. Quoted in *Neue Zürcher Zeitung*, June 5, 1986: "Schwellendes politisches Malais in Ungarn."
288. *Ibid.*
289. Quoted in Tökes, *op. cit.*, p. 9.
290. Hans Dieter Schulz, "Der Griff nach Schlüsseltechnologien," in *Handelsblatt*, December 3, 1985.
291. *Handelsblatt*, April 28, 1986: "DDR/Wieder ein umworbener Kreditnehmer. Banken stehen in Ostberlin Schlange."
292. These data are from Poland's CMEA expert Pawel Bozyk, in Bozyk, *op. cit.*, p. 36.
293. *Handbuch der DDR-Wirtschaft (DIW)*, Reinbek, November 1977, p. 18.
294. Bozyk, *op. cit.*, p. 34.
295. *Economic Survey of Europe in 1969*, Part I, *Structural Trends and Prospects in the European Economy*, New York, p. 9.
296. Estimate by Paul Marer: "Alternative Estimates of the Dollar GNP and Growth Rates of the CMEA Countries," p. 137 in *Selected Papers, Joint Economic Committee, Congress of the United States*.
297. Report No. 2 of the Wharton Economic Forecasting Associates, January 9, 1986.
298. *Neues Deutschland*, October 8, 1985.
299. *Handelsblatt*, April 28, 1986.
300. "Gewinnexplosion bei Industriekombinaten," in *Handelsblatt*, April 10, 1986.
301. *Ibid.*
302. Peter Hoss and Gerhand Schilling, "Neue Anforderungen der intensiv erweiterter Reproduktion an die Leistungsbewertung der Kombinate und Betriebe," in *Wirtschaftswissenschaft*, 1983, no. 3, p. 365.
303. In *Neues Deutschland*, March 11, 1983.
304. *Rude Pravo*, March 23, 1986.
305. *Wochenbericht no. 45/46, 1984 des Deutschen Institutes für Wirtschaftsforschung*; *Handelsblatt*, August 12, 1986: "Stärkerer Warenfluss in Richtung Osten."
306. *Österreichischen Sparkasse-Bank*, p. 65.
307. "RGW-Staaten nahmen mehr Westkredite auf," in *BjAJ (m12)*, June 12, 1986.
308. *Handelsblatt*, August 12, 1986.
309. "Die Tschechoslowakei stellt sich auf Verzögerungen im Kernenergie-Programm ein," in *FAZ*, June 23, 1986.
310. "CSSR-Wirtschaft wächst langsamer," in *Bericht von BfAI/Nfa (2)*, August 22, 1986.
311. "In der Industriemodernisierung hat Prag den Zug verpasst," in *Handelsblatt*, August 26, 1986.
312. *Polityka*, Warsaw, June 5, 1986: "Der XVII. Parteikongress der KPC."
313. *Rude Pravo*, June 19, 1985.
314. *Polityka*, June 8, 1986.

315. *Rude Pravo*, March 18, 1986.
316. In an interview for the Bulgarian periodical *Pogled*, Sofia, July 26, 1985.
317. *Rabotnichesko Delo*, August 20, 1985.
318. Robert D. Kaplan, "Gorbachev Descends on Bulgaria," in *Wall Street Journal*, November 21, 1985.
319. *Österreichischen Sparkasse-Bank*, pp. 25 and 65.
320. A Politburo member of the Bulgarian Communist Party informs Soviet citizens on this in the article "New Horizons," in *Pravda*, Moscow, February 2, 1986.
321. *Pravda*, February 3, 1986.
322. *Ibid.*
323. A. Ross Johnson, "The Warsaw Pact: Soviet Military Policy in Eastern Europe," in *Soviet Policy in Eastern Europe, op. cit.*, p. 254.
324. *Pravda*, November 14, 1954.
325. *Pravda*, March 22, 1955.
326. Quoted in Johnson, *op. cit.*, p. 282.
327. *Ibid.*, p. 261.
328. Johnson, *op. cit.*, p. 262.
329. *Ibid.*, p. 264.
330. *Izvestiia*, Moscow, January 31, 1965.
331. *Pravda*, March 23, 1966.
332. Jeffrey Simon, *Warsaw Pact Forces, Problems of Command and Control*, Boulder: Westview Press, 1984, p. 27.
333. *Ibid.*, p. 45.
334. The former Central Committee Secretary Zdenek Mlynař in *Nachtfrost*, Europäische Verlagsanstalt 1978, pp. 300 and 301 (English translation: *Nightfrost in Prague*).
335. *Izvestiia*, August 25, 1968.
336. *Rude Pravo*, March 19, 1969.
337. *Scînţeia*, April 11, 1969.
338. Douglas A. MacGregor, "Uncertain Allies? East European Forces in the Warsaw Pact," in *Soviet Studies*, 2/10/1986, p. 233.
339. For more on the decisions of the Budapest Conference of the Warsaw Pact see Johnson, *op. cit.*, p. 267.
340. MacGregor, *op. cit.*, p. 235.
341. *Financial Times*, June 1, 1986: "Moscow expected to maintain arms output."
342. *Neue Zürcher Zeitung*, September 15–16, 1985: "Weltweite Steigerung der Militärausgaben, Die Sowjetunion an der Spitze."
343. John P. Hardt and Donna L. Gold, "The Defense Sector," in *Selected Papers*, Joint Economic Committee, Congress of the United States, January 28, 1985, p. 444.
344. *Scînţeia*, May 24, 1985; the cutback announced here was perhaps only a proposal, for on October 20, 1986, Ceausescu announced a referendum on a 5% cutback in defense spending.
345. Quoted in Kusin, *op. cit.*, p. 41.
346. *Polityka*, Warsaw, August 16, 1986.
347. Quoted in Gati, *op. cit.*
348. George Kennan, "Breaking the Spell," *The New Yorker*, October 3, 1983, p. 53.
349. *Moskovskaia Pravda*, 1987, no. 165.
350. *Pravda*, October 15, 1987.
351. *Ibid.*
352. *Pravda*, October 14, 1987.
353. Quoted by Jerzy Kleer in *Polityka*, October 24, 2987.
354. *Pravda*, July 2, 1988.
355. *Ibid.*

Index of Names

Place Name Index

Afghanistan, Council for Mutual Economic Assistance (CMEA), 123; economic sanctions, 125; Soviet invasion, 119

Albania, 4; bilateralism and multilateralism, 20; Council for Mutual Economic Assistance (CMEA), 14; reform movements, 28, 107; Warsaw Pact, 232

Angola, 110; Council for Mutual Economic Assistance (CMEA), 123

Austria, 23–24, 68, 192, 206; economy, 141; and Khrushchev, 22, 136; Paris Agreement, 228; trade relations, 217

Belgium, bilateralism and multilateralism, 19

Brazil, 88

Bulgaria, 4, 205, 258; bilateralism and multilateralism, 20–21; Communist party in, 5, 6; Comprehensive Programs, 82, 83, 85, 226; Council for Mutual Economic Assistance (CMEA), 14, 39, 211, 222–26; currency exchange rates, 75; economy, economic development and policy, 7–8, 10, 11, 91–92, 159, 213, 224; energy policy, 156; International Bank for Economic Cooperation (IBEC), 61, 69; International Investment Bank (IIB), 62; joint CMEA projects, 101, 103, 156; and Khrushchev, 22; leadership in, 185; military spending, 235–37; price regulation, 98; reform

movements, 247; relations with Soviet Union, 16, 232; science and technology, 224–26; Stalinism, 12–13; trade relations, 6, 11, 12, 25, 36, 46, 47, 85, 97, 223; Warsaw Pact, 234

China, 148, 232, 241; military spending, 237; reform movements, 107; science and technology, 36; trade relations, 76; Warsaw Pact, 228, 230, 231

Cuba, 10; Comprehensive Programs, 82, 83, 85, 161, 167; Council for Mutual Economic Assistance (CMEA), 39, 40, 123, 131, 154; International Bank for Economic Cooperation (IBEC), 60, 70; International Investment Bank (IIB), 62; International Monetary Fund (IMF), 17; joint CMEA projects, 150; and Khrushchev, 38; trade relations, 85

Czechoslovakia, 5, 12, 126; bilateralism and multilateralism, 20; Communist party, 6, 13; Comprehensive Programs, 82, 83, 85, 166, 226; Council for Mutual Economic Assistance (CMEA), 14, 39, 41, 211, 216–22, 227; currency exchange rates, 75, 77, 78; economy, economic development and policy, 7–8, 10, 11, 24, 91–93, 159, 175, 212, 213, 221–22; energy policy, 131, 156, 218, 221; International Bank for Economic Cooperation (IBEC), 61; International Investment Bank (IIB), 62, 68; International

About the Author

Dr. Adam Zwass, formerly a senior official in the central banking systems of Poland and the USSR, was Counselor in the CMEA Secretariat in Moscow from 1963 until 1968.

For the last twenty years, Dr. Zwass has been affiliated with Austrian and West German research institutes and has served as an adviser to the Austrian National Bank and major private banks. He is the author of seven books, translated into several languages, and of hundreds of articles published in Europe and the United States. His most recent books in English are *The Eastern European Economies in a Time of Change* (1983) and *Market, Plan, and State: The Two World Economic Systems* (1987).